INTRODUCTION

TO THE

TEXTUAL CRITICISM OF THE GREEK NEW TESTAMENT

BY

EBERHARD NESTLE, PH. AND TH.D.

MAULBRONN

TRANSLATED FROM THE SECOND ED

(*With Corrections and Additions by the Author*)

BY

WILLIAM EDIE, B.D.

KING EDWARD

AND EDITED WITH A PREFACE BY

ALLAN MENZIES, D.D.

PROFESSOR OF DIVINITY AND BIBLICAL CRITICISM IN THE UNIVERSITY OF ST. ANDREWS

Wipf and Stock Publishers

EUGENE, OREGON

Wipf and Stock Publishers
199 West 8th Avenue, Suite 3
Eugene, Oregon 97401

Introduction to the Textual Criticism of the Greek New Testament
By Nestle, Eberhard
ISBN: 1-57910-769-9
Publication date: September, 2001
Previously published by Williams and Norgate, 1901.

EDITOR'S PREFACE.

PROFESSOR EBERHARD NESTLE of Maulbronn is one of the distinguished company of philologists who have in recent years directed their attention to the study of the New Testament. He is by no means a stranger in this country. Readers of the *Expositor* and the *Expository Times* are familiar with his name, and are accustomed to receive from him original and independent discussions of New Testament textual problems. He is consulted by scholars both in this country and on the Continent on questions of Aramaic and Syriac scholarship, and has contributed, in the way of criticism and careful proof reading, to many important publications of English scholars, such as Professor Swete's edition of the Septuagint,[1] the publications of Mrs. Lewis and Mrs. Gibson (*The Sinaitic Palimpsest*, etc.), and the *Gospel of the Twelve Apostles* recently published by Professor Rendel Harris.

The readers of this volume may be glad to know a little more of its author. A native of Württemberg, he was educated at the Gymnasium of Stuttgart and then at the Theological Seminary of Blaubeuren, the latter being one of the four old cloister schools of Württemberg, in which, far from the distractions of large towns, a thorough philological train-

[1] See the Dedication to Dr. Nestle of Professor Swete's *Introduction to the Old Testament in Greek*, just published.

ing is provided for the future clergy of that kingdom. It was as "Praeceptor" of one of these schools that Albrecht Bengel, that great textual critic and unaffectedly pious man, spent the best part of his life, and in his *Marginalien und Materialien* Dr. Nestle gives an interesting account of Bengel as a scholar, and describes the studies of the school over which he presided. Our author studied divinity and oriental languages at the Universities of Tübingen and Leipzig, and considers it one of the happy dispensations of his life that he was permitted to live in England for two years, working in the British Museum and preaching to German congregations in London. He was then Repetent or Tutor at the Theological Seminary of Tübingen, and, after a short period of work as a preacher, was called to the Gymnasium of Ulm to teach Greek, German, Hebrew, and Religion. For two years he filled the vacant professorship of Semitic languages at the University of Tübingen, but, not being appointed to the chair, he returned to Ulm. From there he moved to the Seminary at Maulbronn, which offered better opportunities for combined philological and theological studies.

Dr. Nestle's principal works are:—*Die israelitischen Eigennamen nach ihrer religionsgeschichtlichen Bedeutung* (Proper Names in Israel: their significance for the history of religion), the Prize Essay of the Leiden Tyler Society, 1876. An earlier Prize Essay at Tübingen on the Septuagint and Massorah of Ezekiel was also successful, but was not published.

Psalterium Tetraglottum (*Graece, Syriace, Chaldaice, Latine*), 1879. Sixth and Seventh Editions of Tischendorf's *Septuagint* (with new collation of Codices Vaticanus, Sinaiticus, and Alexandrinus) 1880, 1887.

Septuagintastudien, i.–iii., 1886, 1896, 1898.

Syriac Grammar (Latin, 1881; German, 1888; English, 1889).

Novi Testamenti Graeci Supplementum, 1896 (Collation of Codex Bezae: Apocryphal Gospels).

Philologica Sacra, 1896.

Minor publications collected in *Marginalien und Materialien*, 1893.

Edition of the *Greek New Testament* for the Stuttgart Bible Society, 1898, of which a third edition is now in preparation.

Numerous contributions to theological and literary Journals (*Jahrbücher für deutsche Theologie, Studien und Kritiken, Theologische Literaturzeitung, Literarisches Centralblatt*) and to Herzog-Hauck, *Encyklopädie für Protestantische Theologie.*

The *Introduction* now brought before the English public in Mr. Edie's translation is thus the work of one who is, and has long been, actively engaged in the studies belonging to several parts of the great subject of the text of the New Testament, and who possesses an exact and practised knowledge of the words of the sacred books of Christianity. The present manual accordingly shows the instruments of criticism in actual operation in the hands of a master. It was meant originally for the *Göschen-Sammlung*, a collection of small manuals for the general public, and arose out of the wish of the author to tell his pupils with whom he read the Greek Testament, as well as others, more about the history of the New Testament text than was at the time generally accessible. The handbook was brought out by the theological publishers Vandenhoeck and Ruprecht, literary references being then added to fit it for use by students of theology. It met with a warm welcome from such readers, and the second edition was largely recast so as to meet still further the purposes of students. The long experience of Professor Nestle as a teacher of younger pupils has no doubt enabled him to present the subject so clearly that his book may find favour in the eyes of the general reader, and commend itself to all who care for the New Testament.

The absence of theological bias will not be thought by any wise judge a disadvantage in a work of this character. It will be observed that Professor Nestle does not regard the texts recently formed by great scholars as constituting, either singly or jointly, a *Textus Receptus* in view of which textual enquiry may now desist from its labours, but that he believes that much is still to be learned about the text both of the Gospels and of the other books of the New Testament.

This translation, as the title-page indicates, has been made from the second, enlarged, edition, and the author has kindly furnished various corrections and additions, bringing the book in its English form up to date. Some additional references to English books and periodicals have been inserted by the translator.

A. M.

CONTENTS.

CHAPTER I.

PAGES

History of the Printed Text since 1514, . . . 1–27

Complutensian Polyglot — Aldus — Erasmus — Collections of editions—Literature—First critical edition: Colinaeus—Stephen—Verse division—Beza—Polyglots: Antwerp: Paris: London—Elzevir—*Textus Receptus*—Critical attempts: Caryophilus: Courcelles: Saubert: Simon—Mill—Toinard—Bentley—Gerhard von Maestricht—Bengel—Wettstein—Griesbach—Matthaei—Birch—Moldenhauer—Adler—Scholz—Lachmann—Tischendorf—Tregelles—Westcott and Hort: their types of text—Weymouth—B. Weiss—von Gebhardt—Stuttgart New Testament—Schjøtt—Baljon—Catholic editions: Gratz—van Ess—Gehringer—Patricius—Jaumann—Reithmayer—Hetzenauer—Brandscheid—Apocrypha and Pseudepigrapha.

CHAPTER II.

Materials of the Textual Criticism of the New Testament, ... 28–155

Autographs—Manuscripts—Versions—Quotations—Number of Manuscripts—Uncial and Cursive Script—Age—Material—*Scriptio continua*—Accentuation—Stichometry—Palimpsests — Punctuation — Size — Contents — Lectionaries — Parchment— Ink— Papyrus— Paper— Pen— Manuscripts

PAGES

de luxe—Illustration—Uncials: of the whole New Testament: of the Gospels: of the Acts and Catholic Epistles: of the Pauline Epistles: of the Apocalypse—Minuscules—Ferrar Group—Lectionaries—Versions: Syriac: Peshitto: Curetonian: Lewis: Tatian: Philoxenian: Harklean: Gwynn: Jerusalem: Literature of Syriac Versions—Latin Versions: Old Latin manuscripts: Fathers: The Vulgate: Jerome: Alcuin: Theodulf: Harding: Correctoria Bibliorum: Mazarin Bible: Sixtine and Clementine Vulgate—Egyptian Versions: Bohairic: Sahidic: Middle Egyptian—Gothic—Ethiopic—Armenian—Georgian—Arabic—Patristic Quotations.

CHAPTER III.

Theory and Praxis of the Textual Criticism of the New Testament, ... 156–246

Task and method—Internal criticism—Conjecture—Eclectic method—Genealogical method—External testimony—Lucian: his relation to the Peshitto—Hesychius: Códex B—Eusebius: Pamphilus: Origen: Euthalius: Evagrius: Athos manuscript—Later revisers—Pre-Origenic texts—Heretics: Artemonites, Marcosians, Basilides, Noetus, Valentinians, Gnostics, Marcionites, Arians—Marcion: his relation to the Western text—Tatian: question as to a Greek Harmony: his relation to the Western text—The Western text: theory of Blass: the Lucan writings in Codex Bezae: conclusion of Luke's Gospel: the Apostolic Decree—Rules of Textual criticism: sources of error: illegibility: homoioteleuton: transposition of letters and words: itacism: substitution of synonymous terms: additions: conscious alterations: stylistic, liturgic, and dogmatic changes: critical canons: proper names: textus brevior—Conclusion.

ABBREVIATIONS.

The symbols used to indicate the various manuscripts and versions will be found in the chapter on Materials. The student will compare the Notes in Tischendorf's *Edito octava minor* and the Index in the *Octava maior*, vol. iii. The following contractions are employed in the course of this work:—

GGA. = Göttinger gelehrte Anzeigen.
GK. = Zahn's *Geschichte des neutestamentlichen Kanons.* See p. 196 n. 2.
LCbl. = Literarisches Centralblatt.
PRE. = Protestantische Real-Encyklopädie. See p. 7.
ThLbl. = Theologisches Literaturblatt.
ThLz. = Theologische Literaturzeitung.
ThStKr. = Theologische Studien und Kritiken.
TiGr. = Tischendorf's *N.T. Graece, editio octava maior*, vol. iii. See p. 6.
TU. = Texte und Untersuchungen.
Urt. = Urtext und Uebersetzungen der Bibel. See p. 6f.
W-H. = Westcott and Hort. See p. 21.
W-W. = Wordsworth and White. See pp. 123, 131.
ZdmG. = Zeitschrift der morgenländischen Gesellschaft.
ZfdPhil. = Zeitschrift für deutsche Philologie.
ZfwTh. = Zeitschrift für wissenschaftliche Theologie.

ADDENDA.

Page 6. To the Literature add: Rüegg, *Die neutestamentliche Textkritik seit Lachmann*, Zurich, 1892.

Page 74. Two fragments of N.T. text have been published by Grenfell and Hunt in *The Amherst Papyri, Part I.: The Ascension of Isaiah and other theological fragments* (London, 1900). The first consists of Hebrews i. 1, written, along with Genesis i. 1, in a small uncial hand of the late third, or more probably early fourth, century at the top of a *papyrus* leaf containing a letter from Rome. The verse from the N.T. exhibits the reading τοῖς πατράσιν ἡμῶν, which is not found in any of the manuscripts. The other fragment consists of Acts ii. 11–22 with lacunae, written on vellum and dating apparently from about the fifth or sixth century. It contains a few singular readings such as: (verse 12) πρὸς τ ὸ ν ἄλλον; (13) ἐχλεύαζον λέγοντες, which is practically the reading of D, the only difference being that D has the compound verb διεχλεύαζον; (14) γνωστὸν ὑμῖν, apparently; (17) μετὰ ταῦτα with B instead of ἐν ταῖς ἐσχάταις ἡμέραις, and also, apparently, ἐνύπνια with the *textus receptus*; (20) πρὶν ἢ with the *textus receptus*; (21) ὃς ἂν with the *textus receptus*.

Page 91. Add: J. R. Harris, *Further Researches into the History of the Ferrar Group*, 1900.

Page 106 (5). Add: Hilgenfeld, *Thomas von Heraklea und die Apostelgeschichte*, in the *ZfwTh.*, 1900, 3.

Page 137. Add: Forbes Robinson, *Coptic Apocryphal Gospels*, in *Texts and Studies*, iv. 2, 1896.

Page 139. To Kauffmann's *Beiträge* must now be added: v. *Der codex Brixianus* (*ZfdPhil.* xxxii. pp. 305–335). In this important contribution Kauffmann corroborates the view expressed by Burkitt in the *Journal of Theological Studies*, i. pp. 129–134, that Wordsworth and White were mistaken in regarding the text of codex Brixianus (f) as a recension of the Old Latin closely allied to Jerome's revision. Burkitt holds that the text of Brixianus was corrected from the Vulgate, and afterwards altered in conformity with the Gothic. The only difference between Burkitt and Kauffmann is that the latter believes that the text of Brixianus was derived from an earlier Latin manuscript which had been altered in conformity with the Gothic, and that it was *afterwards* assimilated to the Vulgate. This view must also be noted in connection with the Old Latin codex gue (see p. 118). For an example of the connection between Brixianus and the Gothic see the note to p. 289, below.

Page 162. Add: (9) John, Luke, Matthew, Mark, in cod. min. 90.

Page 289. John vii. 15. For Ἰουδαῖοι f here reads *turbae*, which is interesting as agreeing with the Gothic, which has *manageins*. Compare the view of Burkitt and Kauffmann in the note to p. 139 above. The variant is not mentioned in Tischendorf.

INTRODUCTION

TO THE

TEXTUAL CRITICISM OF THE GREEK NEW TESTAMENT.

CHAPTER I.

HISTORY OF THE PRINTED TEXT SINCE 1514.

IT is not quite creditable to Christian scholarship at the close of the Middle Ages that not a single printed edition of the Greek New Testament appeared during the course of the fifteenth century. The Jews printed their Hebrew Psalter as early as 1477, and the entire Hebrew Bible in 1488.

Editio princeps. Complutensian Polyglot.

1. The honour of producing the first edition belongs to the Spanish Cardinal Francis XIMENES de Cisneros (1437–1517). It was included in the so-called *Complutensian Polyglot*, which takes its name from Complutum (now Alcalà de Henares), where it was printed. The plan of the work was conceived as early as 1502, in celebration of the birth of the future Emperor Charles V. The scholar who had the principal part in it was James Lopez de Stunica. The printing of the New Testament was completed on the 10th January 1514, and of the remaining five volumes, comprising the Old Testament with Grammar and Lexicon, on the 10th July 1517. On the 8th November of the same year the Cardinal died. It was not, however, till

the 22nd March 1520 that Pope Leo X. sanctioned the publication of the work, the two Vatican manuscripts of the Greek Old Testament, which had been borrowed in the first year of Leo's papacy, having been returned on the 9th July 1519.[1] On the 5th December 1521, the presentation copy designed for the Pope, printed on parchment and bound in red velvet, was placed in the Vatican Library. No copies seem to have reached Germany through the trade till the year 1522. Only 600 copies were printed, which were sold at 6½ ducats per copy—about £3 of our present English money. The Cardinal, who enjoyed the income of a king but was content to live like a monk, expended over 50,000 ducats on the undertaking. At the present time, copies of the Complutensian Polyglot, especially those printed on parchment, are counted among the rarest treasures of libraries. The Old Testament is printed in three columns, the Latin text of the Bible used in the Church of the Middle Ages standing between the original Hebrew text of the Synagogue and the Alexandrian Greek version, "like Jesus between the two thieves." The New Testament has only two columns, that on the left containing the Greek text, that on the right the Latin version. For the sake of those learning Greek the corresponding words in each are indicated. The type is modelled on the characters found in good manuscripts. Of accents, the acute alone is used to mark the tone syllable.

LITERATURE.—Scrivener, *Introduction*, ii. c. 7; Hoskier (see below, p. 5); Frz. Delitzsch, *Studien zur Entstehungsgeschichte der Polyglottenbibel des Cardinals Ximenes*, Leipzig, 1871; *Fortgesetzte Studien*, 1886; *Urtext und Uebersetzungen der Bibel*, p. 64. A facsimile of the title-page and colophon will be found in Schaff's *Companion to the Greek Testament and the English Version.* The decree of Pope Leo X. is printed in the Greek and Latin Testament of Van Ess, Tübingen, 1827.

Previous to Ximenes, however, the famous Venetian printer Aldus Manutius had conceived the idea of such a Polyglot.

[1] They were reinserted in the library on the 23rd August.

In the Preface to his undated Greek Psalter (*circa* 1497), a triglot Bible was promised. Of this he was reminded from London by Grocyn on the 6th October 1499. On the 9th July 1501 he wrote about it to the German humanist Conrad Celtes, to whom he sent the first specimen page on the 3rd September of the same year. (Facsimile in Renouard, *L'Imprimerie des Aldes*[2, 3].)

Still earlier, the Magnificat and the Benedictus[1] had been printed among the hymns at the end of the Greek Psalter (Milan, 1481; Venice, 1486). These were the first portions of the Greek New Testament to be printed, while the first printed in Germany appeared at Erfurt in 1501–2. The first edition of the Greek New Testament for sale was Erasmus's edition of 1516.

LITERATURE.—On Aldus, see Nestle, *Septuagintastudien*, i. 2; ii. 11. On Aldus's well-known device, the anchor and dolphin, see Léon Dorez, *Études Aldines*, Revue des bibliothèques, vi. (1896), part 5–6, p. 143 ff.; part 7–9; also J. R. Harris, *The Homeric Centones*, London, 1898, p. 24. The device is emblematic of the favourite motto of Augustus and Titus, ἀεὶ σπεῦδε βραδέως, Semper festina lente.

2. Froben, the printer of Basel, was anxious to forestall the costly edition of the Spanish Cardinal, and with this object appealed on the 15th March 1515 to the famous humanist Desiderius ERASMUS (1467–1536), then in England. His edition appeared as early as the 1st March 1516, and was dedicated on the 1st February to Pope Leo. The printing was begun in the previous September, and was partly superintended by Zwingli's friend, John Oecolampadius of Weinsberg. Erasmus himself confessed afterwards that his New Testament was "præcipitatum verius quam editum," though he boasted that he had employed in its preparation not any sort of manuscripts, but the oldest and most correct copies.[2] As early as 1734, J. A. Bengel recognised that in the Apoca-

Erasmus, 1516.

[1] Mary's Hymn, Luke i. 46–55; and Hymn of Zacharias, Luke i. 68–79.

[2] "Nec eis sane quibuslibet, sed vetustissimis simul et emendatissimis."

lypse Erasmus must have used only one manuscript, and that partly mutilated, so that he was unable to read it correctly and was obliged to supply its lacunæ by means of a retranslation from the Latin into Greek. And this conclusion was confirmed in 1861 by the rediscovery of that very manuscript by Franz Delitzsch in the Oettingen-Wallerstein Library at Mayhingen.[1]

In a parallel column Erasmus gave a translation of the Greek into elegant Latin. The Emperor protected the edition for four years by copyright, but as early as February 1518 it was reprinted by Aldus Manutius in his Greek Bible. It was sanctioned by the Pope on the 10th September 1518. Four successive editions were afterwards prepared by Erasmus: the second in 1519, the third in 1522, the fourth (improved) in 1527, and the fifth in 1535.

In his third edition, Erasmus for the first time incorporated the well-known "comma Johanneum," the passage about the Three Witnesses (1 John v. 7). He did so on the evidence of a manuscript now in Dublin (Montfortianus, 61), in which the

[1] At the present time this text of Erasmus is still disseminated by tens and even hundreds of thousands by the British and Foreign Bible Society of London. To this day the word ἀκαθάρτητος is printed in their editions at Apoc. xvii. 4, though there is no such word in the Greek language as ἀκαθάρτης, meaning uncleanness. In the concluding verses of the New Testament, which were retranslated by Erasmus from his Latin Bible, there stands the lovely future ἀφαιρήσει for ἀφελεῖ. We find also constructions like οὐκ ἔστι, καίπερ ἐστίν, in c. xvii. 8, where, however, the accentuation ἐστίν makes Erasmus responsible for an additional error he did not commit, seeing that he at least printed ἔστιν. Every college lad knows that καίπερ is construed with the participle, though it is not perhaps every one that will see just at once that καὶ πάρεστι is the correct reading. [*Cf.* Mark xv. 6, where the MSS. fluctuate in like manner between ὃν παρῃτοῦντο and ὅνπερ ᾐτοῦντο (ΟΝΠΑΡΗΤΟΥΝΤΟ.)] Other instances where the Textus Receptus has adopted the reading of Erasmus in spite of the fact that it is unsupported by any known MS. are to be found, *e.g.* in 1 Pet. ii. 6 (καὶ περιέχει) and in 2 Cor. i. 6. Luther, who used Erasmus's second edition of 1519, followed him in saying of the Beast, "that is not although it is." This, however, is not so remarkable as that in the year 1883 such things were still allowed to stand in the first impression of the Revised Version of Luther's Bible issued by the Conference of German Evangelical Churches, and only removed in their last Revision of 1892. The error in Apoc. xvii. 8 was copied into the English Authorised Version of 1611 ("is not and yet is") but was corrected by the Revisers of 1884 ("is not and shall come").

passage had probably been inserted from the Vulgate by the English Franciscan monk Roy. From the Vulgate it had already been received, in a slightly different form, into the Complutensian Polyglot. Luther himself purposely omitted it from his version. The first edition of his translation to contain it was that printed at Frankfurt by Feyerabend in 1576. It was not inserted in the Wittenberg editions till 1596. After 1534 no Greek edition appeared without it for the space of 200 years.

LITERATURE.—Scrivener, vol. ii. p. 182 ff.; Frz. Delitzsch, *Handschriftliche Funde*, i., Leipzig, 1861; H. C. Hoskier, *A full Account and Collation of the Greek Cursive Codex Evangelium 604 . . . together with ten Appendices containing* . . . . (B) . . . . *the various readings by the five editions of Erasmus*, 1516, 1519, 1522, 1527, 1535. . . . . (F) *Report of a Visit to the Public Library at Bâle, with facsimile of Erasmus's second MS. Evan.* 2, ... London, 1890. On Erasmus's supplementary matter, the New Version, Annotationes, Paraclesis ad lectorem, Methodus and Apologia, as also on the entire practical and reforming aim of his N.T., see R. Stähelin in the *Protestantische Real-Encyklopädie*, third edition, v. 438. Froude, *Life and Letters of Erasmus*, p. 126 ff.

Collections of editions.

3. The number of editions of the Greek New Testament which have been brought out since the time of Ximenes is about 1000. No library in the world contains them all. In the last century the Danish Pastor Lorck possessed perhaps the largest private collection of Bibles. This was purchased by Duke Charles of Württemberg, and has found a place in the Royal Public Library at Stuttgart. Unfortunately, it is not possible to supplement or enlarge it in the way that it deserves. The largest collection of the present century is that of the late Prof. Ed. Reuss of Strassburg. In his descriptive catalogue he established the genealogy of the separate editions by a collation of the readings in 1000 selected passages. Several editions he was unable to obtain: some he was obliged to regard as of doubtful existence: others, again, mistakenly quoted by previous collectors, he was able to discard once for

all. His labours form the basis of those further researches prosecuted with much ardour chiefly in England and America: in the latter by the German-Swiss scholar Philip Schaff (d. 20th Oct. 1893), and his American friend I. H. Hall (d. 1896), in England by F. H. A. Scrivener (d. 26th Oct. 1891), and in Germany by the American C. R. Gregory. Mention can be made of only a few of these printed editions.

LITERATURE.—Ed. Reuss, *Bibliotheca Novi Testamenti Graeci, cuius editiones ab initio typographiae ad nostram aetatem impressas quotquot reperiri potuerunt collegit digessit illustravit E. R. Argentoratensis*, Brunsvigae, 1872. Tischendorf, *Novum Testamentum Graece ad antiquissimos testes denuo recensuit apparatum criticum apposuit Constantinus de Tischendorf*, Lipsiae (Hinrichs), vol. i. 1869; vol. ii. 1872; vol. iii., *Prolegomena scripsit Caspar Renatus Gregory additis curis Ezrae Abbot*, 1894, 8vo. (vol. iii. cited in the following part of this work under the symbol *TiGr.*). F. H. A. Scrivener, *A Plain Introduction to the Criticism of the New Testament.* Fourth edition, edited by Ed. Miller, 2 vols., London, 1894. P. Schaff, *Companion to the Greek Testament and the English Version.* Fourth edition revised, New York, Harper, 1892. Schaff's *Companion* gives, in an Appendix, Reuss's list of printed editions of the Greek N.T., with additions bringing it down to 1887, by I. H. Hall. It also contains an interesting set of facsimile illustrations of twenty-one standard editions of the Greek N.T., showing in each case the title-page and a page of the print. I. H. Hall, *A Critical Bibliography of the Greek New Testament, as published in America*, Philadelphia, 1883. Also, by the same author, *Some Remarkable Greek New Testaments*, in the Journal of the Society of Biblical Literature and Exegesis, Dec. 1886, 40–63. S. P. Tregelles, *Account of the Printed Text of the Greek New Testament with remarks on its revision and a collation of the critical texts with that in common use*, 1854. Copinger, *The Bible and its Transmission, being an historical and bibliographical view of the Hebrew and Greek Texts, and the Greek, Latin, and other Versions of the Bible (both manuscript and printed) prior to the Reformation. With 28 facsimiles.* London, Sotheran, 1897, large 8vo. H. J. Holtzmann, *Einleitung in das Neue Testament (Allgemeiner Teil, Geschichte des Textes)*, Freiburg, 1886. *Urtext und Uebersetzungen der Bibel in übersichtlicher*

Darstellung, a reprint of the article "Bibeltext und Bibelübersetzungen," in the third edition of the Real-Encyklopädie für protestantische Theologie und Kirche, Leipzig, Hinrichs, 1897, pp. 15–61 (Tischendorf), O. v. Gebhardt, "*Bibeltext des Neuen Testamentes*," PRE, ii. 728–773 (cited hereafter as *Urt.*). C. R. Gregory, *Textkritik des Neuen Testamentes*, vol. i. Leipzig, 1900. Vol. ii. in the press.

4. The first to prepare a really critical edition of the Greek New Testament, *i.e.* one based on a collation of manuscripts, was Simon de Colines (COLINAEUS), the father-in-law of the Parisian printer Robert Stephen (Estienne). In his edition,[1] which appeared in 1534, he adopted for the first time a number of readings that are now generally accepted, though naturally he did not succeed in gaining credit for them. Up till the time of Mill and Bengel the publishers and their more or less uncritical coadjutors simply reprinted the text of Ximenes and Erasmus, mostly the latter, with trifling variations. First critical edition.

Among the innovations introduced by these editors was the choice of a more convenient form. The first editions were all in folio. But in 1521, Anselm, then in Hagenau but previously in Tübingen, reduced the size to quarto; in 1524 Cephaleus in Strassburg still further to octavo; while Valder printed the first miniature edition in Basel in 1536. The smallest edition printed previous to this century is that of Jannon, 1628 (Sedan); the smallest of this century is that of Pickering, 1828 (London).

But a much more important feature was the collation of fresh manuscripts. The credit of being pioneer in this respect rests with the Parisian Typographer-Royal, Robert STEPHEN (1503–1559). He was assisted by his son Henry Stephen (1528–1598), particularly in the preparation of his third edition of 1550, the *Editio Regia*, which takes its name from the inscription on its title-page in honour of Henry II., Βασιλεῖ τ' ἀγαθῷ, κρατερῷ τ' αἰχμητῇ.[1] The first edition, called *O mirificam*, from the opening words of its preface, appeared in 1546. The Editio Regia was the first to contain a critical apparatus Stephen

[1] Facsimile in Schaff's *Companion*.

in which fifteen manuscripts indicated by the Greek letters β—ις were collated with the text of the Complutensian which was designated α. All the manuscripts employed were of late date, with two exceptions, viz., the Codex Bezae, of which we shall have a good deal to say in the sequel, and a Parisian MS. of the eighth century, now known as L.

Verse division. An important innovation of another sort is due to the same Robert Stephen, who printed at Geneva in the following year (1551) a fourth edition containing the Greek text with the Latin version of Erasmus on the outer side and the Vulgate on the inner.[1] With a view to carrying out this arrangement conveniently, he divided the text into separate verses or very small sections, which he numbered on the margin. In this way he introduced into the New Testament not only a convenient verse-enumeration—there are 7959 verses in all—but also the unfortunate practice of printing the text in separate verses. Mill in 1707, and notably Bengel in 1734, were the first to revert to the practice of printing the text in paragraphs divided according to the sense while retaining the enumeration of the verses in the margin. The customary division of the

Chapters. New Testament books into chapters is much earlier, having been first invented in Paris for the Latin Bible by Stephen Langton (died Archbishop of Canterbury in 1228), and at once adopted in the earliest printed editions of the Vulgate. It was employed in the Complutensian Polyglot with a subdivision of the various chapters into A B C etc.

LITERATURE.—*Nov. Test. textus Stephanici* A.D. 1550, *ed.* Scrivener, Camb., 1859, 1871 etc. Hoskier (as above). . . . (B) *A Reprint with corrections of Scrivener's list of differences between the editions of Stephen* 1550 *and Elzevir* 1624, *Beza* 1565 *and the Complutensian, together with fresh evidence* . . . . *by the other editions of Stephen of* 1546, 1549, 1551. . . . Ezra Abbot, *De Versibus*, in *TiGr.* 167–182. I. H. Hall, *Modern Chapters and Verses*, in Schaff's *Religious Encyclopædia*, i. 433. *Journal of the Soc. of Bib. Lit. and Exeg.*, 1883, 60; 1891, 65.

[1] Facsimile in Schaff's *Companion*.

It is frequently stated that copies exist of Stephen's edition of 1551 (the first to contain the verse enumeration) bearing on the title-page the date MDXLI. In the two I examined belonging to the collections of Lorck and Reuss, the two halves of the number MD and LI are far apart. In the case of the Lorck copy it is possible to suppose that a letter has been erased from the middle, but not in the Reuss copy. In his Preface, Stephen says: "Quod autem per quosdam ut vocant versiculos opus distinximus, id, vetustissima Graeca Latinaque ipsius Novi Testamenti exemplaria secuti, fecimus: eo autem libentius ea sumus imitati, quod hac ratione utraque translatio posset omnino eregione Graeco contextui respondere." As Ezra Abbot pointed out, Stephen gave a double number $\frac{19}{20}$ to the verse Τινὲς δὲ . . . . *πρὸς μέ* in Acts xxiv. A similar double enumeration occurs in the previous chapter, where the verse Γ*ράψας* . . . . *χαίρειν* is numbered $\frac{25}{26}$. Accordingly, Abbot's supposition becomes pretty certain, that the verse division was originally made for a Latin copy which, at the passage in Acts xxiv., contained the additional sentence: Et apprehenderunt me clamantes et dicentes, Tolle inimicum nostrum. And in chapter xxiii. several Latin editions show an extra sentence at the place marked with the double number: et ipse postea calumniam sustineret tanquam accepturus pecuniam. But what edition it was from which Stephen took the enumeration into his Greek copy is not yet known. Unfortunately, as Abbot shows (*l.c.* 173–182), later editions frequently deviated from Stephen's enumeration. Even Oscar v. Gebhardt, in his editions of Tischendorf's text, followed in eight instances a different verse division from that recommended by Gregory in his Emendanda (p. 1251 ff.).

Several mistakes in numbering crept into the Stuttgart edition of the N.T., but the division and enumeration have been carefully compared with that of the Reuss copy for the second edition. There are differences in verse-division even in the reprint of Westcott and Hort's Greek Testament (Macmillan fount, 1895), Heb. xii. 22, 23: in Swete's *Gospel of St. Mark* (Mk. ii. 18, 19), and in Cronin's edition of *Codex Purpureus Petropolitanus* (Lk. iii. 23, 24, ix. 7, 8.)

The Textus Receptus is usually indicated by the Greek letter ϛ, the initial of Stephen's name.

Following Stephen, the French theologian Theodore de Bèze (BEZA 1519–1605), the friend and successor of Calvin Beza.

in Geneva, prepared, between 1565 and 1611, four folio and six octavo editions,[1] which are noteworthy as forming, with the last two editions of Stephen, the basis of the English Authorised Version. Beza was the owner of two valuable Greek-Latin manuscripts of the Gospels with the Acts and Pauline Epistles, one of which, the now so famous Codex Bezae, he presented to the University of Cambridge in 1581. He himself, however, made little use of these in his editions, as they deviated too far from the printed texts of the time. Beza seems also, in the preparation of his Geneva edition, to have been the first to collate the oriental versions. For this purpose he employed the Syriac edition of Emmanuel Tremellius (1569), and for Acts and 1 and 2 Corinthians the Arabic version put at his disposal by Franciscus Junius.

LITERATURE.—Scrivener, ii. 188 ff; Hoskier (as above): *the various readings . . . . by the remaining three Bezan editions in folio of* 1582, 1588–9, 1598, *and the 8vo. editions of* 1565, 1567, 1580, 1590, 1604.

Polyglots. 1. Antwerp.

5. The credit of presenting these oriental versions in a convenient combination for the interpretation of the Bible belongs to the so-called *Antwerp Polyglot*, the Biblia Regia, printed in eight folio volumes between 1569 and 1572 by Christopher Plantin, a French printer residing in Antwerp. In this work the Greek New Testament is printed twice, first in vol. v., alongside the Vulgate and the Syriac text with its Latin translation, and again in vol. vi. with the interlinear version of Arias Montanus. Plantin was aided in this enterprise by a grant of 12,000 ducats from King Philip II. It was carried out under the supervision of the Spanish theologian Benedict Arias, called Montanus from his birth-place Frexenal de la Sierra.

"Labore et Constantia" was the motto of this celebrated family of printers, who continued to carry on their trade on the same premises till August 1867. Nine years later the house was sold to the city and converted into the "Musée Plantin."

[1] Facsimiles of Folio 1598 and Octavo 1604 in Schaff's *Companion.*

Of the Antwerp Polyglot 960 ordinary copies were printed, 200 of a better quality, 30 fine, 10 superfine, and 13 on parchment, for which last 16,263 skins were used. One of these Montaigne saw and admired in the Vatican Library; another, the copy dedicated to the Archduke Alba, is in the possession of the British Museum. The undertaking was the glory of Plantin's life, but it was also the beginning of his financial difficulties. Copies were sold to booksellers at 60 gulden each, and to the public at 70 gulden (about £6 and £7). Ordinary copies now fetch from £6 to £7 or £8. At the sale of the Ashburnham Collection in 1897 a parchment copy realised £79. The supplements, including lexical and other matter, are still valuable to a certain extent. But here the collector must note that certain parts have been reprinted.

On the Polyglots, see: *Discours historique sur les principales editions des Bibles Polyglottes. Par l'Auteur de la Bibliothèque Sacrée*, Paris, 1713; especially pp. 301–554, "Pièces justificatives du discours précédent." Also, Ed. Reuss, *Polyglottenbibeln*, PRE², xii. 95–103 (1883). Max Rooses, *Christophe Plantin, Imprimeur Anversois*, Antwerp, 1884. Fol. 100 plates. Also *Correspondance de Plantin*, edited by Rooses. 2 vols. 1886. L. Degeorge, *La Maison Plantin a Anvers.* 3rd ed. Paris, 1886. R. Lorck, *Das Plantin-Haus in Antwerpen.* Vom Fels zum Meer, 1888–9, ix. 328–346. On the double imprint see Rooses, p. 123; A. Rahlfs in Lagarde's Bibliotheca Syriaca, p. 19. On Plantin's connection with the Familists see PRE³, v. 751–755.

A still more extensive undertaking than the Antwerp Polyglot is that brought out in Paris by the advocate Guy Michel LE JAY. This *Parisian Polyglot* extends to ten folio volumes of the largest size, furnished externally in the most sumptuous manner. Le Jay expended his whole fortune on the edition, and was obliged at last to sell it as waste paper, being too proud to accept the offer of Cardinal Richelieu, who wished to purchase the patronage of the enterprise for a large sum and thereby acquire the credit of it. The scholars who gave most assistance in the preparation of the oriental texts were Jean Morin and the Maronite Gabriel Sionita, the latter of whom superintended the Syriac portion. The two volumes of the New Testament, viz. vol. v. 1, comprising the Gospels, **2. Parisian.**

and vol. v. 2, the Acts, Epistles, and Apocalypse, appeared in 1630 and 1633. In addition to the texts printed in the Antwerp Polyglot, the Parisian contained a Syriac version of the so-called Antilegomena, *i.e.* those parts of the New Testament at one time disputed (2 Peter, 2 and 3 John, Jude, and Apocalypse), and it had also an Arabic version, each one being accompanied with a Latin translation.[1]

3. London. Less sumptuous, but more copious, convenient, and critically valuable, is the last, and at the present day still most used of the four great Polyglots—the *London Polyglot* of Brian WALTON (1600–1661). It contains in all nine languages. In the New Testament (vol. v.) there is the Greek text of Stephen with slight alterations, the version of Arias, the Vulgate, Syriac, Ethiopic, Arabic, and (for the Gospels only) Persic versions, each with a literal translation into Latin. The sixth volume also contains Walton's Apparatus, which was re-issued at Leipzig in 1777, and again at Cambridge by F. Wrangham in two volumes in 1828. It is really a kind of Introduction to Biblical Criticism. Finally, in two supplementary parts, there is Edmund Castle's *Lexicon Heptaglotton*, a thesaurus linguae semiticae such as no one since has ventured to undertake.

The London Polyglot first appeared in 1657, under the patronage of Cromwell, but after the Restoration it received a new Preface from the editor, who was raised to the See of Chester by Charles II. In this Preface Cromwell is styled "Magnus Draco ille." Accordingly, bibliophiles draw a sharp line of distinction between republican and loyalist copies. One of the former costs considerably more than the latter, the most recent prices running from £22 to £31. This is said to have been the first work brought out in England by subscription. See Schaff's "*Companion*" for facsimiles of title-page and page of text. Todd: *Life of Brian Walton with the Bishop's Vindication of the London Polyglot Bible.* London, 1821. 2 vols.

For this Polyglot, in addition to the critical works of

[1] Copies of the Parisian Polyglot now cost about £6.

previous scholars, the Codex Alexandrinus of the Greek Bible, sent by Cyril Lucar to Charles I. in 1628, was also employed for the first time. Its readings are set at the foot of the Greek text and indicated by the letter A. This was the origin of the modern custom of indicating manuscripts with Roman letters in the apparatus of critical editions not only of the New Testament but of other books as well, a custom which has generally prevailed since the time of Wettstein. That gift of Cyril Lucar seems really to have awakened for the first time a general desire for critical editions. At the same time it was Walton's edition that made Stephen's text of 1550 the "textus receptus" in England.

6. On the Continent a similar result was attained by the enterprising Dutch printers Bonaventura and Abraham ELZEVIR of Leyden. What scholars had a hand in their edition, if we may speak of scholars at all in this connection, is not known. In 1624 the Elzevirs published, in a handy form and beautifully printed, an edition the text of which was taken mainly from Beza's octavo edition of 1565. In their Preface to a new issue in 1633 they said "textum ergo habes nunc ab omnibus receptum, in quo nihil immutatum aut corruptum damus," while they professed that even the smallest errors—"vel minutissimae mendae"—had been eliminated with judgment and care. By means of this catchword they actually succeeded in making their text the most widely disseminated of all during 200 years. The English Bible Society alone have issued not fewer than 351,495 copies of it in the 90 years of their existence, and at the present time are still printing this text alone. They issued 12,200 copies of it in the year 1894. For several centuries, therefore, thousands of Christian scholars have contented themselves with a text based ultimately on two or three late manuscripts lying at the command of the first editors—Stephen, Erasmus, and Ximenes—a text, moreover, in which the erroneous readings of Erasmus, already referred to, are retained to this day.

Elzevir.

LITERATURE.—Scrivener, ii. 193. Hoskier. . . . (C) *a full and exact comparison of the Elzevir editions of* 1624 *and* 1633, *doubling the number of the real variants hitherto known, and exhibiting the support given in the one case and in the other by the subsequent editions of* 1641, 1656, 1662, 1670, *and* 1678. On the Elzevirs see G. Berghman, *Nouvelles Études sur la Bibliographie Elzevirienne. Supplément a l'ouvrage sur les Elzevier de M. Alphonse Willems*, Stockholm, 1897. Also, A. de Reume, *Recherches historiques, genealogiques et bibliographiques sur les Elzevier*, Brussels. Facsimile of the edition of 1633 in Schaff's *Companion.*

Critical attempts.

7. Even those who were impelled by a greater spirit of research did not yet get back to the oldest attainable sources. In Rome, CARYOPHILUS set about preparing a new edition. With this view, about the year 1625 he collated twenty-two manuscripts with the Antwerp Polyglot—ten for the Gospels, eight for the Acts and Epistles, and four for the Apocalypse. Among these were the most celebrated manuscript of the Vatican Library, the "Codex Vaticanus" *par excellence*, and another of the same collection, dating from the year 949 (Tischendorf's S), one of the oldest manuscripts of the Greek New Testament whose date is known with certainty. The results of this collator's labours were printed at Rome in 1673. But such collations were not then made with that exactitude which is the primary condition of works of this nature at the present day, though even now it is not always observed. In 1658 Stefan de COURCELLES (Curcellaeus, 1586–1659), a native of Geneva, brought out an edition which was printed by the Elzevirs, and which is valuable for its scholarly Introduction, its careful collection of parallel passages, and its fresh collation of manuscripts. In this edition the "Comma Johanneum" was included in brackets. The editor also expressed the opinion that even conjectural readings deserve consideration. Courcelles had further projects in view, but these were interrupted by his death.

In 1672, in Germany, John SAUBERT published a collection of various readings in St. Matthew's Gospel which he had compiled from printed editions, manuscripts, ancient versions, and quotations in the Greek and Latin Fathers.

In 1675 John FELL, afterwards Bishop of Oxford, published anonymously at the Sheldonian Theatre, *i.e.* the Oxford University Press, an edition in the preparation of which more than 100 Greek manuscripts were employed. Among the ancient versions the Gothic of Ulfilas and the Coptic were also made use of.

About the same time (1689) there appeared anonymously at Rotterdam a *Histoire Critique du Texte du Nouveau Testament*, by Richard SIMON, a member of the French Congregation of the Oratory. Simon is the father of the historical method of critical introduction to the New Testament. With his work, what might be called the infancy of New Testament criticism comes to a close. With Mill's New Testament begins the period of its maturity, especially if Simon's works are taken as belonging to it. Such, at least, was the judgment expressed in 1777 by the Göttingen scholar J. D. Michaelis. But we would say rather the period of its youth, for otherwise we should now have reached the time of its old age, and much work still remains to be done.

8. Encouraged by Bishop Fell, John MILL (1645–1707), Mill, 1707.
about 1677, set to work upon an edition which appeared in the year of his death.[1] The value of Mill's New Testament lies in its extended critical apparatus, and particularly in its Prolegomena. An enlarged edition was brought out in 1710 by Ludolf Küster of Westphalia (1670–1716), which, however, had such a small sale that it had to be reissued with a new title-page at Leipzig in 1723, and again at Amsterdam in 1746. In Mill's time the number of various readings in the New Testament was estimated at 30,000: a competent estimate will now make them more than four or five times as many. That is to say, there are almost more variants than words.

Mention must also be made of Nicolaus TOINARD'S Latin-

[1] Facsimile in Schaff's *Companion*.

Greek Harmony of the Gospels, which appeared at Orleans in the same year as Mill's New Testament, and which was the fruit of nearly as many years' labour. Toinard was the first Catholic after Erasmus, and the last previous to Scholz, to undertake a critical edition of the New Testament. He was also the first editor after Beza to estimate properly the critical value of the Vulgate.

Bentley. It was Edward Wells who set the example of greater freedom in the adoption into the text of new readings from the manuscripts. His famous countryman, the great philologist Richard BENTLEY (1662–1742), projected a great critical edition of the New Testament, but unfortunately got no further than the preparation of materials and the publication of his "Proposals" in 1720. He undertook to remove two thousand errors from the Pope's Vulgate, and as many from that of the Protestant Pope (Stephen), without using any manuscript under 900 years old. But as his edition never appeared, his nephew had to refund the 2000 guineas prepaid by the subscribers.

In 1729 MACE published an edition anonymously, in which, perhaps, most courage was shown in departing from the ordinary text. Thereafter, English work in this department was suspended for nearly a century. It was transferred to Germany and the Netherlands by the Swabian scholar Bengel and by Wettstein of Basel.

LITERATURE.—A. A. Ellis, *Bentleii Critica Sacra*, Camb., 1862. R. C. Jebb, *Bentley*, London, 1882. *TiGr.*, 229–240. Wordsworth-White, I. pp. xv–xxviii (see below, p. 123).

Bengel. 9. As early as 1711, G.D.T.M.D., *i.e.* Gerhard de Trajectu Mosae (Maestricht) Doctor, a Syndic of Bremen, published at Amsterdam an edition prefaced by 43 canons or rules of criticism. Thereafter, in 1725, J. A. BENGEL (1687–1752) issued his *Prodromus Novi Testamenti Graeci recte cauteque adornandi*, in which he unfolded a most carefully thought-out scheme for a new edition, undertaking to reduce all Gerhard von Maestricht's 43 canons to one comprehensive rule of four words. That was the principle now commonly expressed in the shorter but less satisfactory form—*lectio difficilior placet.* Bengel himself chose a more careful mode of expression—*proclivi scriptioni praestat ardua.* Six years later he was able to issue his *Notitia Novi Testamenti Graeci recte cauteque adornati.* It was published in 1734 at Tübingen by Cotta in a handsome quarto.[1] In the same year a small octavo edition appeared at Stuttgart in which he urged the duty expressed in the motto,

> Te totum applica ad textum,
> Rem totam applica ad te.

Of the latter, four editions were afterwards brought out. Of the large edition, the Apparatus, pronounced by Haussleiter to be a " memorable work of most solid and productive learning," was reprinted separately after his death. Bengel was too timid. He was unwilling to admit into the text any reading which had not already appeared in some printed edition. But he inserted new readings in the margin and classified them. Out of 149 readings pronounced by Bengel to be genuine, only 20 are not now generally approved. Out of 118 whose genuineness appeared to him probable but not quite certain, 83 are now accepted.

But Bengel's most important contribution to the textual criticism of the Greek New Testament consists in the sound critical principles which he laid down. He recognised that the witnesses must not be counted but weighed, *i.e.* classified, and he was accordingly the first to distinguish two great groups or families of manuscripts. His principles were reaffirmed by the celebrated philologist Lachmann, the first great textual critic of our time, and the advance which the latest English critics have made on Tischendorf is really due to the fact that they have gone back to Bengel.

LITERATURE.—Eb. Nestle, *Bengel als Gelehrter, ein Bild für*

[1] Facsimile in Schaff's *Companion.*

unsere Tage. (In Marginalien und Materialien: also printed separately, Tübingen, 1893.) Scrivener, ii. 204.

Wettstein.

For the time, however, Bengel's rival, John WETTSTEIN (1693–1754), outdid him. His treatise on the Various Readings of the New Testament was published as early as 1713, to be followed by his Prolegomena, which appeared anonymously in 1730, and later by his New Testament,[1] which was issued in two folio volumes in 1751 and 1752. His Apparatus is fuller than that of any previous editor, while he also gives a detailed account of the various manuscripts, versions, and Patristic writers. It was he who introduced the practice, already referred to, of indicating the ancient MSS. by Roman letters and the later MSS. by Arabic numerals. He too, however, still printed the Elzevir text, following Maestricht's edition of 1735. At the foot of the text he placed those readings which he himself held to be correct.

LITERATURE.—Scrivener, *Introduction*, ii. 213; Carl Bertheau, PRE², xvii. 18–24, 1886.

Griesbach.

10. J. J. GRIESBACH (1745–1812) was the first in Germany who ventured to print the text of the New Testament in the form to which his criticism led him. He was the pupil of Salomo Semler, who had combined the principles of Bengel and Wettstein. These principles were adopted and carried out by Griesbach. He enlarged the Apparatus by a more exact use of citations from the Fathers, particularly from Origen, and of various versions, such as the Gothic, the Armenian, and the Philoxenian. In his classification of the witnesses, Griesbach distinguished a Western, an Alexandrian, and a Byzantine Recension. The edition, in four folio volumes, printed by Göschen at Leipzig (1803–1807), is rightly described by Reuss as "editio omnium quae extant speciosissima."[2] His text was more or less faithfully followed by

[1] Facsimile in Schaff's *Companion.*

[2] Facsimile of the second edition, Halle and London, 1796, in Schaff's *Companion.*

many later editors like Schott, Knapp, Tittmann, and also by Theile.

Griesbach's opponent, Christian Friedrich MATTHAEI, a Thüringian (1744–1811), was misled into attributing a too great value to a large number of manuscripts in Moscow of the third, the Byzantine, class. Matthaei.

A considerable amount of critical material was collected at the expense of the King of Denmark by Andreas Birch (afterwards Bishop of Lolland, Falster, and Aarhuus), by D. G. Moldenhauer, and by Adler.

A similar service was rendered, though not with sufficient care, by J. M. Augustin SCHOLZ, Professor of Catholic Theology in Bonn.

LITERATURE.—On Matthaei see O. v. Gebhardt, *Christian Friedrich Matthæi und seine Sammlung griechischer Handschriften*, Leipzig, 1898.

It was Carl LACHMANN (1793–1851) who first broke with the Textus Receptus altogether. He was a master in the domain of textual criticism. He distinguished himself first in the department of classical and Teutonic philology, but came afterwards to render equal service to the textual criticism of the New Testament. His object was to restore the text to the form in which it had been read in the ancient Church about the year 380, going on the ground of the oldest known Greek and Latin manuscripts, *i.e.* the oldest Eastern and Western authorities.[1] He did not claim to go further back than that date with any certainty. But it was still open to question whether that were not possible, and whether the grounds on which Lachmann's work was based might not be still further extended and confirmed. Lachmann.

11. The task which Lachmann set before him was prosecuted with the most brilliant success in and from Germany by Gottlob (Aenotheus) Friedrich Constantin von TISCHENDORF (b. 18th January 1815, d. 7th December 1874). In the course Tischendorf.

[1] Facsimile in Schaff's *Companion*.

of several tours, first in Europe and afterwards in the East, from the year 1841 onwards, he discovered and collated a number of the most important and ancient manuscripts of the Bible. Among these the most notable was the Codex Sinaiticus, found by him on Mount Sinai in 1859, and now in St. Petersburg, the oldest known manuscript of the present day which contains the entire Greek New Testament. On the basis of the material collected by himself and others, Tischendorf prepared eight different editions between 1841 and 1872.[1] His seventh edition, consisting of 3500 copies, appeared in 1859, previous to the discovery of the Sinaiticus. The text of this edition differed from that of 1849 in 1296 instances, of which no fewer than 595 were reversions to the Textus Receptus. The text of the last edition, the octava critica maior, which was issued complete in eleven parts between 1864 and 1872, differed from that of the seventh in 3572 places. The third volume of the editio octava maior, containing the Prolegomena, was completed in three parts, extending to 1428 pages, by Caspar René Gregory between 1884 and 1894, a work which affords the most complete survey of what has been done on the Greek New Testament up to the present time.

LITERATURE.—Scrivener, ii. 235; *TiGr.*, 1–22; *Urt.*, 49–52. Apart from the Editio Octava Maior, the most useful editions will be found to be those of O. v. Gebhardt (see below, p. 23), or the Editio Academica ad editionem oct. maior. conformata, Leipzig, Mendelssohn, 16mo, 1855, twentieth edition, 1899.

Tregelles.

While the editions of Tischendorf were appearing on the Continent, an edition began to be issued in England, which was completed in the course of twenty years. It was the work of a Quaker, Samuel Prideaux TREGELLES (b. 1813, d. 1875), who, while reaping no profit from his undertaking, has left in it a monument to his fidelity. In this edition (1857–1879)[2]

[1] Facsimiles of the edition of 1841, and the octava maior 1872, in Schaff's *Companion.*

[2] Facsimile in Schaff's *Companion.*

those passages in which the editor was unable to pronounce a final judgment from the accessible material are indicated by the form of the type.

Westcott and Hort.

A still more important advance was made by Brooke Foss WESTCOTT (b. 1825), now Bishop of Durham, and Fenton John Anthony HORT (b. 23rd April 1828, d. 30th November 1892). In 1881, these Cambridge scholars, after nearly thirty years of joint labour, published two volumes, the first containing the Text with a brief survey of its history and resulting criticism, the second giving a detailed exposition of their critical principles by Hort himself. They were led by their investigation to distinguish four main types of text:—

(1) A late type, originating in Syria about the year 300, which, issuing from Constantinople, became the prevailing text in later manuscripts, and corresponds essentially with the textus receptus of early printed editions:

(2) A type originating in Alexandria, characterized by linguistic emendations:

(3) A type originating in Syria but reaching the West previous to the year 200, represented essentially by the Old Latin versions on the one hand and by the Syriac on the other, and displaying all sorts of remarkable additions:

(4) The Neutral text, which displays no sort of corruptions.

Westcott and Hort's work is the latest and most thorough attempt yet made at a complete edition of the New Testament.

LITERATURE.—*The New Testament in the original Greek. The text revised by Brooke Foss Westcott, D.D., and Fenton John Anthony Hort, D.D.*, Cambridge and London. Vol. i. Text (Fourth Edition, 1898). Vol. ii., Introduction and Appendix (Third Edition, 1896). A smaller edition of the text, 1885. Text, from new type, in larger form, 1895. For "Some trifling Corrections to W.-H.'s New Testament," see Nestle in the *Expository Times*, viii. 479; ix. 95, 333, 424. See *Life and Letters of F. J. A. Hort*, by his son, A. F. Hort, 2 vols., London, 1896; also article on Hort, by Gregory in the PRE[3], viii. 368. Facsimile of the American Edition with Introduction by Schaff, in Schaff's *Companion*.

Weymouth.

The "Resultant Greek Testament" of R. F. WEYMOUTH affords a convenient comparison of the text of the most important editions.

LITERATURE.—*The Resultant Greek Testament, exhibiting the text in which the majority of modern editors are agreed, and containing the readings of Stephen* (1550), *Lachmann, Tregelles, Tischendorf, Lightfoot, Ellicott, Alford, Weiss, the Bâle edition* (1880), *Westcott and Hort, and the Revision Committee.* By Richard Francis Weymouth. With an Introduction by the Right Rev. the Lord Bishop of Worcester. London, 1886. . . . Cheap Edition, 1892, pp. xix. 644. Besides the editions mentioned in the title, the Complutensian, Elzevir (1633), Scrivener and others are compared in several places.

Weiss.

Quite recently, Bernhard WEISS, of Berlin, began a new and independent revision of the text, which has been published in three large volumes with introduction and explanatory notes.

LITERATURE.—*Das Neue Testament. Textkritische Untersuchungen und Textherstellung von D. Bernhard Weiss. Erster Theil, Apostelgeschichte: Katholische Briefe: Apocalypse.* Leipzig, 1894. *Zweiter Theil, Die paulinischen Briefe einschliesslich des Hebräerbriefs,* 1896. *Dritter Theil, Die vier Evangelien* 1900. Vol. i. is compiled from *Texte und Untersuchungen,* ix. 3, 4; viii. 3; vii. 1. The section in vol. ii. entitled *Textkritik der paulinischen Briefe,* is taken from *TU.* xiv. 3, and the corresponding section in vol. iii. from *TU.* xix. 2 (New Series, iv. 2). See "B. Weiss and the New Testament," by C. R. Gregory in the *American Journal of Theology,* 1897, i. 16–37.

Von Gebhardt.

In Germany, O. von GEBHARDT has done good service by issuing the text of Tischendorf's last edition, with the necessary corrections, and giving in the margin the readings adopted by Tregelles and Westcott-Hort, when these differ from the text. In the "editio stereotypa minor," the differences of Westcott-Hort alone are shown. In his Greek-German New Testament, he also exhibits at the foot of Luther's German text those readings wherein the text of Erasmus's second edition of 1519, used by Luther, differs from that of the last edition of Tischendorf. In this diglot of v. Gebhardt, therefore, one can see at a glance not only how far the Greek text of the present day differs from that printed at the beginning of the sixteenth century, but also the amount of agreement between present-day editors working on such different principles as Tischendorf and Westcott and Hort. In the Adnotatio Critica found in the Appendix to the larger edition, there is a brief digest of the critical Apparatus, but it extends only to those passages where Tischendorf and Westcott-Hort disagree. The editio minor contains 600 pages. One of these, p. 501, shows not a single disagreement between these great editors, while 18 pages exhibit only one variation each, and these, for the most part, mere grammatical trifles.

LITERATURE.—*Novum Testamentum Graece recensionis Tischendorfianae ultimae textum cum Tregellesiano et Westcottio-Hortiano contulit et brevi adnotatione critica additisque locis parallelis illustravit Oscar de Gebhardt.* Editio stereotypa. Lipsiae (Tauchnitz), 1881. Seventh edition, 1896.

N. T. Graece et Germanice. Leipzig, 1881. Fourth edition, 1896. In this edition the Greek is that of Tischendorf's last edition, and the German is the Revised text of Luther (1870). The various readings are shown for both texts, and a selection of parallel passages is also given.

N. T. Graece ex ultima Tischendorfii recensione edidit Oscar de Gebhardt. Editio stereotypa minor. Lipsiae, 16mo., 1887. Fourth edition, 1898.

Stuttgart New Testament.

The text of the Greek and Greek-German New Testaments prepared by me, and issued by the Württemberg Bible Institute, is based on a comparison of the three editions of Tischendorf, Westcott-Hort, and Weymouth. The variations of these editions are shown at the foot of the page, where are given also the readings inserted by Westcott and Hort in their Appendix and omitted by O. v. Gebhardt. From Acts onwards, the readings adopted by Weiss are indicated as well. In a lower margin, a number of important manuscript readings are given. In the Gospels and Acts, these are taken mainly, though not exclusively, from Codex Bezae. In the Greek-German edition, the text (German) is that of the Revised Version of 1892. Below it are given the readings of Luther's last edition (1546), with several of his marginal glosses and earlier renderings.

LITERATURE.—*Novum Testamentum Graece cum apparatu critico ex editionibus et libris manu scriptis collecto.* Stuttgart, 1898. Second corrected edition, 1899. Also issued in two and in ten parts, and interleaved. Third edition in preparation.

Schjøtt.

Fr. SCHJØTT published an edition at Copenhagen in 1897 the text of which was determined by the agreement between the Codex Vaticanus (Claromontanus, from Heb. ix. 14 onwards) and the Sinaiticus. Where they disagreed he called in the next oldest manuscript as umpire. For this purpose he employed for the Gospels the manuscripts A C D E F H I[b] K L P Q T U V X Z Γ Δ, for the Acts and Catholic Epistles A C D E H K L P, for the Pauline Epistles A C D E F G H L P, and for the Apocalypse A C P 1, 18, 38, 49, 92, 95. At the foot of the text his edition gives, in two divisions, a comparison with the Elzevir text and with that of Tischendorf-Gebhardt (1894). From what source Schjøtt derived his knowledge of the Vaticanus and the Sinaiticus is not mentioned. The photograph of the former seems not to have been employed.

LITERATURE.—*Novum Testamentum Graece ad fidem testium vetustissimorum recognovit necnon variantes lectiones ex editionibus Elzeviriana et Tischendorfiana subjunxit Fr. Schjøtt.* Hauniae, 1897, pp. xi. 562.

Baljon.

The edition of J. M. S. BALJON is in the main an abridgment of Tischendorf's octava maior. He avails himself, however, of later discoveries, such as the Sinai-Syriac Palimpsest for the Gospels, and the Syriac version published by Gwynn for the Apocalypse. In Acts, Blass's restoration of the so-called Forma Romana is regularly indicated. No other edition, for one thing, shows more conveniently where recent scholars recognise glosses or other interpolations, or propose transpositions or conjectural emendations and such like. So far, therefore, it may be commended to those who do not possess an edition with a more copious critical apparatus. But even Baljon's New Testament fails to realise the ideal of a practical edition.

LITERATURE.—*Novum Testamentum Graece praesertim in usum studiosorum recognovit J. M. S. Baljon*, Groningae, 1898, pp. xxiii. 731. The first 320 pages are also issued separately as Volumen primum continens Evangelia Matthaei, Marci, Lucae et Ioannis. *Vide* Bousset in the *Theologische Rundschau* for July 1898.

From the Catholic side little has been done in Germany in this department of scholarship for a long time. In 1821 Aloys GRATZ reprinted the Complutensian at Tübingen; while Leander van ESS issued an edition which combined the Complutensian and Erasmus's fifth edition.[1] This also appeared at Tübingen in 1827. Both of these contained the Vulgate, and showed where recent editions gave a different text. Catholic editions.

Reuss mentions two Synopses, one by Joseph GEHRINGER (Tübingen, 1842, 4°), the other by Fr. X. PATRICIUS (Freiburg, 1853, 4°), and two small editions, one of which, by A. JAUMANN (Munich, 1832), was the first to be printed in Bavaria. The other is by Fr. X. REITHMAYER (Munich, 1847), and closely follows the text of Lachmann.

There has also appeared recently at Innsbruck a Greek-Latin edition in two volumes by Michael HETZENAUER, a Capuchin. The first volume contains the Evangelium and the second the Apostolicum. But as the strict Catholic is bound by the decision of the Holy Office, Hetzenauer's edition hardly falls to be considered here. A resolution of

[1] Van Ess's edition was issued with two different title-pages. One of these gives the names of the Protestant editors, Matthaei and Griesbach. But the other omits the names together with the Notanda on the back of the title-page, so that the reader is left in the dark as to the meaning of the symbols Gb, M, etc., in the margin. Most copies omit the Introduction, which contains the Pope's sanction of the editions of Erasmus and Ximenes.

the Holy Office of 13th January 1897 pronounced even the Comma Johanneum (1 John v. 7) to be an integral part of the New Testament. This was confirmed by the Pope on the 15th January, and published in the *Monitore Ecclesiastico* of the 28th February of the same year. An edition in Greek and Latin was issued by BRANDSCHEID at Freiburg in 1893.

It is impossible to enumerate here editions of separate books of the New Testament. Many of these are in the form of Commentaries. In addition to the works of Blass, to which reference will be made later, mention may be made here of a recent and most thorough piece of work—viz., *The Gospel according to St. Mark: The Greek Text, with Introduction and Notes*, by Henry Barclay SWETE, D.D., pp. cx. 412 (London, Macmillan, 1898); also of *The Gospel according to St. Luke after the Westcott-Hort text, edited with parallels, illustrations, various readings, and notes*, by the Rev. Arthur Wright: London, Macmillan, 1900; and of Hilgenfeld's edition of the Acts in Greek and Latin. Berlin, 1899.

Apocrypha and Pseud-epigrapha.

Nor can we enter particularly the field of early Christian Apocrypha and Pseudepigrapha. Those who cannot obtain Hilgenfeld's *Novum Testamentum extra Canonem Receptum*, or Resch's *Agrapha*, or the editions of Tischendorf, Lipsius, and Bonnet, will find a handy and inexpensive selection in my *Supplement* to Gebhardt's editions of Tischendorf.

LITERATURE.—*Novi Testamenti Graeci Supplementum editionibus de Gebhardt-Tischendorfianis adcommodavit Eb. Nestle. Insunt Codicis Cantabrigiensis Collatio, Evangeliorum deperditorum Fragmenta, Dicta Salvatoris Agrapha, Alia.* Lipsiae (Tauchnitz), 1896, pp. 96.

There can be no question that in these last mentioned editions which have been brought out at the end of the nineteenth century, we have a text corresponding far more closely to the original than that contained in the first editions of the Greek New Testament issued at the beginning of the sixteenth century, on which are based the translations into modern languages used in the Christian churches of Europe at the present time. It would be a vast mistake, however, to conclude from the textual agreement displayed in these latest editions, that research in this department of New Testament study has reached its goal. Just as explorers, in excavating the ruined temples of Olympia or Delphi, are able from the fragments they discover to reconstruct the temple, to their mind's eye at least, in its ancient glory—albeit it is actually in ruins—so too, much work remains to be done ere even all the materials are re-collected, and the plan determined which shall permit us to restore the Temple of the New Testament Scriptures to its original form.

CHAPTER II.

MATERIALS OF THE TEXTUAL CRITICISM OF THE NEW TESTAMENT.

EVEN in the age of printing, and with all the security afforded by that invention, it is not always easy or even possible to exhibit or restore the literary productions of a great mind in their original form. One has but to think of the obscurity in which the works of Shakespeare and their early editions are enveloped, or the questions raised over the Weimar edition of Luther's works. And even when the author's original manuscript is still preserved, but the proof-sheets, as is usual, destroyed, we cannot always be certain whether occasional discrepancies between the print and the manuscript are intentional or not. Nay, even when the two agree, there is still the possibility that what the author wrote and allowed to be printed was not what he thought or intended to be read. Did Lessing, *e.g.*, mean us to read in *Nathan* ii. 5, 493, "the great *man* requires always plenty of room," or "the great *tree*" does so? Various writers, in speaking of this or that artist's talents or dexterity, have used the words "haud impigre." To take them at their word, the object of their praise had no such endowment beyond the common. We may be certain that what they meant to convey was the very opposite of what they actually wrote, viz. "haud pigre" or "impigre." As a rule, however, the purchaser of a modern classic may rely upon reading it in the form in which the author intended it to be circulated. It is quite different in the case of those works which were composed at a time when their multiplication was only possible by means of copying, and specially so in the case of those that are older by a thousand years than the invention of printing. For then every fresh copy was a fresh source of errors, even when the copyist was as painfully exact as it was possible for him to be. It is simply astonishing, in view of all the perils to which literary works have been exposed, to find how much has been preserved, and, on the whole, how faithfully.

The matter is, of course, quite a simple one, when by good fortune the author's own manuscript, his **autograph**, is extant. The abstract possibility of this being so in the case of the New Testament writings cannot be denied. Thanks to the dryness of the climate of Egypt and the excellence of ancient writing material, we have documents more than twice the age that the New Testament autographs would be to-day did we possess them. Now and again we find a report circulated in the newspapers that such an original document has been found,—of Peter, *e.g.*, or some other Apostle. About the year 489 it was asserted that the original copy of Matthew had been discovered in the grave of Barnabas in Cyprus. And to the eyes of the devout there are still exhibited not only the Inscription from the Cross, but works from the artist hand of Luke. In reality, however, we have no longer the autograph of a single New Testament book. Their disappearance is readily understood when we consider that the greater portion of the New Testament, viz. the Epistles, are occasional writings never intended for publication, while others were meant to have only a limited circulation. Even in the early ages of the Christian Church, when there must have been frequent occasion to appeal to them, the autographs were no longer in existence. Autographs.

Tertullian (*De Praescriptione Haereticorum*, 36) mentions Thessalonica among the cities in which he believed the letters of the Apostles that were addressed there were still read from autograph copies.[1] "Percurre ecclesias apostolicas, apud quas ipsae adhuc

[1] Zahn, *Geschichte des. N. T. Kanons*, i. 652; *Einleitung*, i. 153.

cathedrae apostolorum suis locis praesident, apud quas ipsae authenticae literae eorum recitantur, sonantes vocem et repraesentantes faciem uniuscuiusque." But when the same author, in his *De Monogamia*, speaks of "Graecum authenticum," he refers not to the autograph, but to the original text as distinguished from a version.

On the copy of Matthew's Gospel found in the grave of Barnabas in Cyprus, *vide* Theodorus Lector (Migne, 86, 189); Severus of Antioch in Assemani, *Bibliotheca Orientalis*, ii. 81; *Vitae omnium* 13 *Apostolorum:* Βαρνάβας ὁ καὶ Ἰωσῆς . . . . οὗτος τὸ κατὰ Ματθαῖον εὐαγγέλιον οἰκειωχείρως γράψας ἐν τῇ τῆς Κύπρου νήσῳ τελειοῦται.[1] In the Imperial Court Chapel the lessons were read from this copy on Holy Thursday of every year. *Vide* Fabricius, *Evv. Apocr.*, 341.

On the supposed autograph of Mark in Venice see Jos. Dobrowsky, *Fragmentum Pragense Ev. S. Marci, vulgo autographi*, Prague, 1778. It is really a fragment of a Latin manuscript of the Vulgate, dating from the seventh century, of which other fragments exist in Prague.

In the *Chronicon Paschale* there is a note on the reading τρίτη for ἕκτη in John xix. 14, to the following effect:—καθὼς τὰ ἀκριβῆ βιβλία περιέχει αὐτό τε τὸ ἰδιόχειρον τοῦ εὐαγγελιστοῦ, ὅπερ μέχρι τοῦ νῦν πεφύλακται χάριτι θεοῦ ἐν τῇ Ἐφεσίων ἁγιωτάτῃ ἐκκλησίᾳ καὶ ὑπὸ τῶν πιστῶν ἐκεῖσε προσκυνεῖται. Bengel himself said on 1 John v. 7:—"Et tamen etiam atque etiam sperare licet, si non autographum Johanneum, at alios vetustissimos codices graecos, qui hanc periocham habeant, in occultis providentiae divinae forulis adhuc latentes, suo tempore productum iri. (N.T. 420, 602, 770.)

In disproof of an alleged autograph of Peter, see Lagarde, *Aus dem deutschen Gelehrtenleben*, Göttingen, 1880, p. 117 f. On legends of this sort among the Polish Jews, on the autograph copy of the Proverbs that Solomon sent to the Queen of Sheba, and now in the possession of the Queen of England, etc., *vide* S. Schechter, *Die Hebraica in der Bibliothek des Britischen Museums*, in the *Jüdisches Literatur-Blatt* for 1888, No. 46.

At the Sixth Ecumenical Council of 680-1, which Harnack (*DG.* ii. 408) says might be called the "Council of Antiquaries and Palaeographers", investigations were instituted in this department with some success.

J. G. Berger, *De Autographis Veterum*, Vitenb., 1723. 4°.

J. R. Harris, *New Testament Autographs* (Supplement to the

[1] From the Cod. Monac. 255 and 551, published by Aug. Thenn in the *Zeitschrift für wissenschaftliche Theologie* 29 (1887), 453.

American Journal of Philology, No. 12), Baltimore, 1882. With three plates.

In this connection reference might be made to the falsifications of Constantine Simonides: *Facsimiles of certain portions of the Gospel of St. Matthew, and of the Epistles of St. James and St. Jude, written on papyrus of the first century.* London, 1862. Fol.

Seeing, then, that the autographs of the New Testament books have all perished, we have to do as in the case of the Greek and Latin classics, viz. apply to later copies of them, the so-called **manuscripts** of which frequent mention has already been made. But while in the case of most literary products of antiquity these manuscript copies are the *only* sources whence we may derive our knowledge of them, we are happily more fortunate in regard to the New Testament. Manuscripts.

The new faith very early and very rapidly spread to distant peoples speaking other languages than that in which the Gospel was first preached. Indeed, even in its native land of Palestine, several languages were in use at the same time. Accordingly, at a very early date, as early as the second, and perhaps, in the case of fragments, even in the first century, there arose in the East, and in the South, and in the West, **versions** of the Christian books very soon after their composition. At first only separate portions would be translated, but as time went on versions of the entire New Testament made their appearance. Manifestly, the value for our purpose of these versions depends on their age and accuracy. It is impossible, without further knowledge, to be certain whether a Greek copyist of later centuries followed his original quite faithfully or not. But a Latin version of the New Testament which dates from the second century, *e.g.*, will represent with tolerable certainty the second century Greek manuscript from which it is derived, even supposing that our present copy of that version is not earlier than the sixth century or even later. But these versions confer yet another advantage. In the case of most, and certainly of the oldest Greek manuscripts, we do not know in what country they originated. Versions.

But it is quite certain that a Latin version could not have originated in Egypt, or a Coptic version in Gaul. In this way we may learn from the versions how the text of the Bible read at a particular time and in a particular region. Lastly, if it should happen that several versions originating in quite isolated regions, in the Latin West, and in the Syrian East, and in the Egyptian South, agree, then we may be certain that what is common to them all must go back to the earliest times and to their common original.

Quotations

In addition to the Greek manuscripts and the versions, we have still a third and by no means unimportant class of material that we can employ in reconstructing our text of the New Testament. We possess an uncommonly rich Christian literature, which gathers volume from the second half, or, at all events, from the last quarter of the first century onwards. Now, what an early Church teacher, or, for that matter, what any early writer quotes from the New Testament will have for us its own very peculiar importance, under certain conditions. Because, as a rule, we know precisely where and when he lived. So that by means of these **patristic quotations** we are enabled to locate our ancient manuscripts of the Bible even more exactly, and trace their history further than we are able to do with the help of the versions. Here, of course, we must make sure that our author has quoted accurately and not loosely from memory, and also that the quotations in his book have been accurately preserved and not accommodated to the current text of their time by later copyists or even by editors of printed editions, as has actually been done even in the nineteenth century. We shall now proceed to describe these three classes of auxiliaries.

LITERATURE.—W. Wattenbach, *Anleitung zur griechischen Palaeographie*, 2nd ed., Leipzig, 1877; V. Gardthausen, *Griechische Palaeographie*, Leipzig, 1879; Fr. Blass, *Palaeographie, Bücherwesen, und Handschriftenkunde*, in I. v. Müller's Handbuch der klassischen Alterthumswissenschaft, 2nd ed., vol. i., Munich, 1892; E. M.

Thompson, *Handbook of Greek and Latin Palaeography*, London, 1891; T. Birt, *Das antike Buchwesen*, Berlin, 1882; W. A. Copinger, *The Bible and its Transmission*; F. G. Kenyon, *Our Bible and the ancient Manuscripts*, London, third edition, 1897; F. H. A. Scrivener, *Six Lectures on the Text of the N.T. and the ancient Manuscripts which contain it*, Cambridge and London, 1875; *A Collation of about 20 Manuscripts of the Holy Gospels*, London, 1853; *Adversaria critica sacra*, Cambridge, 1893; Hoskier; *Urt.*, pp. 16, 54; O. Weise, *Schrift- und Buchwesen in alter und neuer Zeit*, Leipzig (Teubner), 1899 (with Facsimiles: a popular work); F. G. Kenyon, *The Palaeography of Greek Papyri*, Oxford, 1899 (with 20 Facsimiles and a Table of Alphabets, pp. viii., 160); Ulr. Wilcken, *Tafeln zur älteren griechischen Palaeographie, Nach Originalen des Berliner K. Museums*, Berlin and Leipzig, 1891 (with 20 photographs); G. Vitelli e C. Paoli, *Collezione Fiorentina di facsimili paleografici greci e latini*, Firenze, 1884–1897 (with 50 Greek Plates and 50 Latin, Folio); Charles F. Sitterly, *Praxis in Manuscripts of the Greek Testament: the mechanical and literary processes involved in their writing and preservation* (with table of Manuscripts and 13 Facsimile Plates), New York and Cincinnati, 1898, second enlarged edition, 1900; F. Carta, C. Cipolla e C. Frati, *Monumenta Palaeographica sacra: Atlante paleografico-artistico composto sui manuscritti*, Turin, 1899; Karl Dziatzko, *Untersuchungen über ausgewählte Kapitel des antiken Buchwesens. Mit Text, Uebersetzung und Erklärung von Plinii Histor. Nat.*, lib. xiii. § 68, 69, Leipzig, Teubner, 1900.

1. MANUSCRIPTS.

Number of manuscripts.

For no literary production of antiquity is there such a wealth of manuscripts as for the New Testament. Our classical scholars would rejoice were they as fortunate with Homer or Sophocles, Plato or Aristotle, Cicero or Tacitus, as Bible students are with their New Testament. The oldest complete manuscript of Homer that we have dates from the thirteenth century, and only separate papyrus fragments go back to the Alexandrian age. All that is extant of Sophocles we owe to a single manuscript dating from the eighth or ninth century in the Laurentian Library at

Florence. But of the New Testament, 3829 manuscripts have been catalogued up till the present. A systematic search in the libraries of Europe might add still more to the list; a search in those of Asia and Egypt would certainly do so. Gregory believes that there are probably some two or three thousand manuscripts which have not yet been collated, and every year additional manuscripts are brought to light. Most of these are, of course, late, and contain only separate portions, some of them mere fragments, of the New Testament.[1] Not a few, however, go much further back than our manuscripts of the Hebrew Old Testament and most of the Greek and Latin Classics. Only in the case of the Mohammedan sacred books is the condition of things more favourable. These came into existence in the seventh century, and the variations between separate manuscripts are a vanishing quantity, because the text of the Koran was officially fixed at a very early date and regarded as inviolably sacred. Fortunately, one might almost say, it is quite different with the New Testament, which was put together in a totally different way. In its case the very greatest freedom prevailed for at least a century and a half.

The manuscripts of the New Testament being so numerous, it becomes necessary to arrange them. One of the most important considerations hitherto has been that of age, and therefore manuscripts have been divided into **Uncials** (or Majuscules) and **Cursives** (or Minuscules), according to the style of writing in use at earlier or later times.

Uncials.

In early times, as at the present day, inscriptions on monuments and public buildings were engraved in capital letters. This form of writing was also employed for books, especially those containing valuable or sacred writing. The letters were not joined together, but set down side by side.[2] They

[1] The most convenient survey of these is given in Vollert's "Tabellen zur neutestamentlichen Zeitgeschichte: mit einer Uebersicht über die Codices in denen die N.T. Schriften bezeugt sind." Leipzig, 1897. Given in Sitterly (see above, p. 33).

[2] See *e.g.* Plate I.

were called *litterae majusculae, capitales, unciales, i.e.* "inch-high," as Jerome says with ridicule—*uncialibus ut vulgo aiunt litteris onera magis exarata quam codices.* Alongside of this there arose, even previous to the Christian era, a smaller Cursive form (*Minusculae*), for use in common life, in which the letters were joined.[1] This running hand found its way into manuscripts of the Bible in the course of the ninth century. In some cases, in Codex Λ *e.g.*, both styles are found alongside or following each other.[2]

and Cursive script.

The oldest Cursive manuscript of the New Testament, the exact date of which is known, is 481 ^evv.^; it bears the date 835. The great majority of New Testament manuscripts belong to this later date, seeing that out of the 3829 manuscripts there are only 127 Uncials to 3702 Minuscules. Greek copyists not being accustomed to date their manuscripts exactly, it becomes the task of palæography to settle the criteria by which the date and place of a manuscript's origin may be determined. These are the style of writing—whether angular or round, upright or sloping, the punctuation—whether simple or elaborate, and the different material and form of the book. These distinctions, however, are often very misleading. The following table will show the distribution of the manuscripts according to the centuries in which they were written, as given by Vollert, Scrivener, and von Gebhardt[3]:—

	Vollert.	Scrivener.	v. Gebhardt.
IVth Century, . .	5	...	2
Vth ,, . .	4	10	15
VIth ,, . .	18	22	24
VIIth ,, . .	6	9	17
VIIIth ,, . .	8	8	19
IXth ,, . .	23	...	31
Xth ,, . .	4	...	6

[1] See *e.g.* Plate X.

[2] See Scrivener, i. p. 160; Rahlfs, *Göttinger gelehrte Nachrichten*, 1898, i. 98–112.

[3] *TiGr.*, pp. 1233 ff.; Warfield, *Textual Criticism of the N.T.*, p. 47.

Papyrus and parchment.

Manuscripts are distinguished according to the **material** on which they are written, which may be either parchment or paper.

Parchment[a] derives its name from Pergamum, where it was introduced in the reign of King Eumenes (197–159 B.C.). But prior to the use of parchment, and to a certain extent alongside of it, **papyrus**[b] was used, especially in Egypt, down to the time of the Mohammedan Conquest. Papyrus books were originally in the form of rolls (*volumina*). Only a few fragments of the New Testament on papyrus remain. The use of parchment gave rise to the book or Codex form. In the case of parchment codices, a further distinction is drawn between those made of vellum manufactured from the skins of very young calves, and those made of common parchment from the skins of sheep, goats, and antelopes.

Paper.

As early as the eighth century (not the ninth), the so-called **cotton paper** (*charta bombycina*) was introduced from the East. This, however, never consisted of pure cotton, but rather of flax and hemp. It had been in use for a long time in China and the centre of Eastern Asia, but seems to have been unknown in Syria and Egypt till after the fall of Samarcand in 704. From the thirteenth century onwards, paper made of linen was employed.[c]

In the New Testament, both papyrus and parchment are referred to. In 2 Tim. iv. 13, Paul asks that the φελόνης he had left at Troas might be brought to him, and τὰ βιβλία, but specially τὰς μεμβράνας. Here, φελόνης means cloak rather than satchel; τὰ βιβλία are the papyrus books, possibly his Old Testament, while τὰς μεμβράνας are clean sheets of parchment.[d] In 2 John 12 the word χάρτης is used of papyrus. There, and in 3 John 13, τὸ μέλαν is the ink, and the κάλαμος (*lat.* canna) is the reed pen, still used for writing in the East. The quill pen, strange to say, is not mentioned prior to the time of Theodoric the Ostrogoth in the sixth century.[e] The size of a sheet of writing paper may be in-

[a] The references are to the extended notes at the end of this section, pp. 40 ff.

ferred from the passages in 2nd and 3rd John alluded to above.

Scriptio continua.

In order to economize space, the writing was continuous, with no break between the words (**scriptio continua**),[f] breathings and accents being also omitted.[g] This is a frequent source of ambiguity and misunderstanding. In Matt. ix. 18, *e.g.*, ΕΙΣΕΛΘΩΝ may be either *εἶς ἐλθὼν* or *εἰσελθών.* In Mark x. 40, ΑΛΛΟΙΣΗΤΟΙΜΑΣΤΑΙ was rendered "aliis praeparatum," *ἄλλοις* being read instead of *ἀλλ' οἷς.* In Matt. xvi. 23, ΑΛΛΑ may be taken either as *ἀλλὰ* or *ἀλλ' ἃ.* In 1 Cor. xii. 28, again, the Ethiopic translator read *οὖς* instead of *οὓς.* The Palestinian-Syriac Lectionary translates 1 Tim. iii. 16 as though it were *ὁμολογοῦμεν ὡς μέγα ἐστίν.* There is something to be said for this, but Naber's proposed reading of Gal. ii. 11, *ὅτι κατέγνωμεν ὃς ἦν*, cannot be accepted.

Columns.

Most manuscripts show two **columns** to the page. The Sinaitic, however, has four, while the Vatican has three. Columns vary considerably in width. They may be the width of a few letters only, or of an average hexameter line of sixteen to eighteen syllables or about thirty-six letters. Such a line is called a *στίχος*, and as the scribe was paid according to the number of *στίχοι*, we find at the end of several books a note giving the total number of *στίχοι* contained in them. In carefully written manuscripts, every hundredth, sometimes every fiftieth *στίχος* is indicated in the margin. These stichometric additions were afterwards adopted for the entire Bible. Their value in many respects will be obvious.[h]

Lines.

As the church increased in wealth and prestige, New Testament manuscripts acquired a more sumptuous form, either from the luxury of the rich or the pious devotion of kings and churches.[i]

Palimpsests.

Parchment, however, grew more and more expensive, and so the practice arose of using an old manuscript a second time. The original writing was erased by means of a sponge or pumice stone or a knife, and the sheets were then employed to receive other matter, or it might even be the same matter over again. And so we have **Codices Rescripti** or **Palimpsesti** as they were called, a term known to Cicero, who says, though of a wax tablet, "quod in palimpsesto, laudo parsimoniam" (*ad Diversos* vii. 18). Some manuscripts were used as often as three times for distinct works in three different languages *e.g.* Greek, Syriac, and Iberian. Codex I[b] is one of these thrice used manuscripts, being written first in Greek and then twice in Syriac.[k]

Punctuation. Marks of **punctuation** are hardly to be found in the earliest times. It was frequently, therefore, a question with church teachers whether a sentence was to be taken interrogatively or indicatively, or how the sentences were to be divided, as in the case of John i. 3 and 4. In the general absence of punctuation, the appearance of quotation marks in some of the oldest manuscripts, like Codex Vaticanus *e.g.*, to indicate citations from the Old Testament, is remarkable.[1]

Size. The **size** of a manuscript varies from a large folio, which in the case of a parchment codex must have been very expensive, to a small octavo. In regions inhabited by a mixed population we find **bilingual** manuscripts, Greek-Latin, Greek-Coptic, Greek-Armenian, and such like. If the manuscript was designed for use in church, the two languages were written in parallel columns, the Greek frequently occupying the left column or reverse side of the sheet, being the place of honour. In manuscripts intended for use in schools, the translation was written between the lines. Codex Δ is an example of a manuscript with an interlinear version of this sort.

Contents. Of more importance is the distinction of manuscripts according to their **contents**. Of all our recorded Uncials, only one contains the whole of the New Testament complete. That is the Codex Sinaiticus discovered by Tischendorf in 1859. A few others, like Codices Vaticanus, Alexandrinus, Ephraemi, were once complete, but are no longer so. Of the later Minuscules, some twenty-five alone contain the entire New Testament. Of the English Minuscules, five are complete. The fragmentary nature of our manuscripts is intelligible on two grounds. One is that a New Testament codex written in uncial characters is a very bulky and ponderous volume running to about 150 sheets. Comparatively few would be in a position to procure such a costly work all at once. The other reason is that the New Testament itself is not a single book, but a series of different collections, which at first, and even afterwards, were circulated separately. To the same reason is due the great variety in the order of the several parts of the New Testament found in the manuscripts, and still, to a certain extent, in our printed editions.[m] It is not exactly known who it was that first collected and inscribed in one volume the books and the parts that now make up the New Testament. Such a single volume of the entire New Testament was afterwards known as a *πανδέκτης*, and in Latin, *bibliotheca*.[n] The parts into which the New Testament is divided are—

1. The four Gospels.
2. (*a*) The Acts of the Apostles.
   (*b*) The so-called Catholic Epistles, *i.e.* those not addressed to any particular church or individual, viz., James, 1 and 2 Peter, 1, 2, and 3 John, Jude.
3. The thirteen Pauline Epistles, or, including Hebrews, fourteen.
4. The Apocalypse.

Among these incomplete manuscripts of the New Testament may be classed the so-called **lectionaries**—*i.e.* manuscripts containing only those portions read at church services. Following the custom of the Synagogue, in which portions of the Law and the Prophets were read at divine service each Sabbath day, the practice was early adopted in the Christian Church of reading passages from the New Testament books at services. A definite selection of such extracts was formed at an early date from the Gospels and Epistles, and the custom arose of arranging these according to the order of Lectionaries.

Sundays and Holy days, for greater convenience in use. A collection of selected passages from the Gospels was called a Εὐαγγέλιον, and in Latin *Evangeliarium*,[1] in distinction to the books containing the continuous text, which were called Τετραευαγγέλιον, while the selections from the Epistles were known as Ἀπόστολος or Πραξαπόστολος. These lectionaries, though mostly of later origin, are nevertheless important as indicating the official text of the various provinces of the Church. They show, moreover, how sundry slight alterations found their way into the text of the New Testament.

We can easily understand why it is that manuscripts of the Gospels are by far the most numerous, while those of the last book of the New Testament are the fewest. Among the Uncials, 73 contain the Gospels, and only 7 have the Apocalypse. Of these 73 Uncials, again, only 6, viz. א B K M S U, or, if we include Ω, only 7 are quite complete; 9 are almost so; 11 exhibit the greater part of the Gospels, while the remainder contain only fragments. Of the 20 Uncials of the Pauline Epistles, only 1 is entirely complete—viz., א; 2 are nearly complete, D G; 8 have the greater part. It is plain that our resources are not so great, after all, as the number of manuscripts given above would lead us to expect. Here also there are πολλοὶ κλητοί, ὀλίγοι ἐκλεκτοί.

a Parchment.

The manufacture of parchment is perhaps older than that of papyrus. It is said to owe both its name and wide circulation as writing material to the encouragement given to its manufacture by Eumenes II. of Pergamum (197–159 B.C.). Pliny's story,[2] which he gives on the authority of Varro, is that Eumenes wished to found a library which should, as far as possible, excel that of Alexandria. To frustrate this intention Ptolemy Epiphanes prohibited the exportation of papyrus to Asia Minor. (In the list of principal exports of Alexandria, Lumbroso[3] mentions βίβλος and χάρτη in the second

[1] To obviate confusion, it would be well to use the Latin name Evangeliarium. Εὐαγγελιστάριον means a Table of Lections. (See Brightman, in the *Journal of Theological Studies*, 1900, p. 448, and now Gregory, *Textkritik*, i. p. 334 f.)

[2] *Nat. Hist.*, xiii. 11.

[3] *Egitto*, 2nd ed., p. 125.

place after ὕελια, and βιβλία in the seventh.) Eumenes was accordingly obliged to prepare parchment at Pergamum, and hence its name, περγαμηνή. The name first occurs in Diocletian's Price-list,[1] and in Jerome. The word used in earlier times was διφθέραι,[2] or δέρρεις,[3] or μεμβράναι as in 2 Tim. iv. 13, which last was taken from the Latin. At first parchment was less valuable than papyrus, and was used more for domestic and school purposes than for the making of books, as the writing was easier erased from the skin. But it gradually supplanted papyrus, and with its employment came also the change from the roll to the "codex" form of book. If papyrus was the vehicle of Pagan Greek literature, parchment was the means whereby the literature of the new faith became known to mankind, and the remnant of the ancient culture at the same time preserved. Origen's library, which still consisted for the most part of papyrus rolls, was re-written in parchment volumes (σωμάτιον, *corpus*) by two priests shortly before the time of Jerome. Our principal manuscripts of Philo are derived from one of these codices.[4] When Constantine ordered Eusebius to provide a certain number of Bibles for presentation to the churches of his Empire, he sent him, not rolls, but codices, πεντήκοντα σωμάτια ἐν διφθέραις.

Parchment was prepared from the skins of goats, sheep, calves, asses, swine, and antelopes. Our oldest manuscripts of the Bible exhibit the finest and whitest parchment. The Codex Sinaiticus, *e.g.*, displays the very finest prepared antelope skin, and is of such a size that only two sheets could be obtained from one skin. As a rule, four sheets were folded into a quire (quaternio), the separate sheets having been previously ruled on the grain side. They were laid with the flesh side to the flesh side, and the grain side to the grain side, beginning with the flesh side outermost, so that in each quaternio, pages 1, 4, 5, 8, 9, 12, 13, 16 were white and smooth with

[1] *Vide* Th. Mommsen, *Das Diokletianische Edikt über die Warenpreise* (Hermes, xxv. 17–36, 1890); on the fragments recently discovered in Megalopolis, see W. Loring, *Journal of Hellenic Studies*, 1890, 299; also, *Revue Archéologique*, Mars-Avril, 1891, 268.

[2] Herodotus v. 58. On the connection of *litera* and διφθέρα, see M. Bréal, *Rev. des Et. grecques*, iii. 10, 1890, 121 ff., and *Rev. Crit.*, 1892, 13. In Cyprus the schoolmaster was called the διφθεράλοιφος.

[3] *Cf.* Codex D, Mark i. 6.

[4] *Cf.* Victor Schultze, *Rolle und Codex*, in the Greifswalder Studien, Gütersloh, 1895, p. 149 ff.

the lines showing in relief, while the others, 2, 3, 6, 7, 10, 11, 14, 15 were darker and rough, with indented lines.[1]

Ink. For writing on papyrus, ink made of soot was employed. Three parts of lamp-black were mixed with one part of gum and diluted with water. This ink, however, was easily washed off, and did not stick well to parchment, and therefore recourse was had to ink made of gall nuts. Sulphate of iron was afterwards added to it, with the result that the writing material is frequently corroded with the ink. From its having been boiled the mixture was also called ἔγκαυστον, hence our word "ink" (encre). Many old recipes for making ink are still preserved.[2] Even in early Egyptian writing, coloured inks, specially red, were used. One of the most beautiful manuscripts extant is a Syriac Codex in the British Museum, of date 411, in which the red, blue, green, and yellow inks are still quite fresh. Eusebius used cinnabar for numbering the paragraphs, and Jerome makes mention of minium or vermilion. In times of great wealth parchments were dyed purple and inscribed with gold and silver letters.

b Papyrus. Among ancient writers, Pliny gives the fullest description of the preparation of papyrus, in his *Historia Naturalis*, xiii. 11.[3] The sheets were prepared, not from the bark, but from the pith of the plant. This was cut into strips (σχίδας) as thin and broad, and,

[1] *Vide* C. R. Gregory, *Sur les cahiers des manuscrits grecs*, Académie des Inscriptions, Aug. 1885; Berliner Phil. Wochenschrift, 1886, v. 159 ff.

[2] *E.g.* in Cod. Barocc. 1 in the Bodleian, and in several Syriac manuscripts.

[3] *Vide* G. Ebers, *Kaiser Hadrian*: also *The Writing Material of Antiquity*, by Ebers, in the Cosmopolitan Magazine, New York, Nov. 1893; and especially Dziatzko (see above, p. 33). On the papyrus plant (Cyperus papyrus L., Papyrus Antiquorum Willd.), see Bernard de Montfaucon, *Dissertation sur la plante appelée Papyrus, sur le papier d'Égypte*, etc. Memoires de l'Académie Royale des Inscriptions et Belles Lettres, T. vi. Paris, 1729, 4to., pp. 592–608; Franz Woenig, *Die Pflanzen im alten Aegypten, ihre Heimat, Geschichte, Kultur*, Leipzig, 1886, pp. 74–129. J. Hoskyns-Abrahall pointed out that it is found in Europe, not only in the neighbourhood of Syracuse in Sicily, but also on the shores of Lake Trasimene: see *The Papyrus in Europe*, in the Academy, 19th Mar. 1887. Lagarde raised a question as to the etymology of the word papyrus (which has not yet been explained), whether it might not be derived from Bura on Lake Menzaleh, where it was first manufactured, *pa* being the article in Egyptian; see his *Mitteilungen*, ii. 260. If this is so, there is the more reason for pronouncing the *y* long, as ancient writers did, and not short as the modern fashion is—papýrus, not pápyrus. *Cf.* Juvenal, iv. 24; vii. 101; Mart. iii. 2; viii. 44; x. 97. Catull. xxxv. 2. Ovid, *Met.* xv. 753; *Trist.* iii. 10, 27.

according to some, as long as possible. These were laid side by side as firmly as might be, to form the first layer (σχέδα). On this a second layer was laid crosswise and fastened to the lower with moisture or gum. The two layers were then compressed to form the writing sheet (σελίς), which was carefully dried and polished with ivory or a smooth shell. The roll (τόμος, κύλινδρος) consisted of a number of σελίδες joined together to make one long strip—sometimes as much as 20 or 40 feet long, or even longer. The upper side, the side used for writing on, was the one in which the fibres ran in a horizontal direction parallel to the edge of the roll.[1] The under or outer side was only used in cases of necessity.[2] The first sheet (πρωτόκολλον) was made stronger than the rest, and its inner edge was glued to a wooden roller (ὄμφαλος), with a knob at the end (κέρας). The margin of the roll, what corresponds to the edge of our books, was frequently glazed and coloured, while the back was protected against worms and moths by being rubbed with cedar oil. The title was inscribed on a separate label of parchment (σίττυβος or σίλλυβος). The separate rolls were enclosed in a leather case (διφθέρα or φαινόλης, see 2 Tim. iv. 13), and a number of them kept in a chest (κιβωτός or κίστη).

On the literature cf. also Paul Krüger, *Ueber die Verwendung von Papyrus und Pergament für die juristische Litteratur der Römer*, Zeitschrift der Savigny-Stiftung für Rechtsgeschichte. Roman section, viii. pp. 76–85 (1887). Wilcken, *Archiv für Papyrus-Forschung und verwandte Gebiete*, Leipzig, Teubner. F. G. Kenyon, *Palaeography of Greek Papyri*. C. Haeberlin, *Griechische Papyri*, Leipzig, 1897: "Nearly 150 years have fled since 432 complete Rolls and 1806 Papyrus Fragments were discovered in the year 1752 at Herculaneum, in the Villa of L. Calpurnius Piso Caesoninus, the pupil and friend of the Epicurean philosopher Philodemus. Then twenty-five years later the soil of Egypt, that home and nursery of literature, opened for the first time to vouchsafe to us a Greek Papyrus Roll, destined to be the forerunner of a series of discoveries often interrupted but never ceasing altogether. It was, perchance, not the only one of its kind; but out of the fifty rolls accidentally

[1] See U. Wilcken, *Recto oder Verso*, Hermes, 1887, 487–492.

[2] Apoc. v. 1 can no longer be cited in support of this practice, seeing we must take καὶ ὄπισθεν with κατεσφραγισμένον, according to Grotius and Zahn. On ὀπισθόγραφον, *cf.* Lucian, *Vitarum Auctio*, 9; Pliny, 3, 5; *a tergo* Juvenal, 1, 6; *in aversa charta*, Martial, 8, 22.

discovered in the year 1778 by Arabian peasants in the neighbourhood of Memphis, it alone had the fortune to come into the possession of Cardinal Stefano Borgia. The rest were burned by their unsuspecting discoverers, who found a peculiar pleasure in the resinous odour that arose from their smoking pyre."

c Paper. The collection of manuscripts brought from the East by the Archduke Rainer gave a stimulus to the study of the early history of paper-making, and at the same time supplied the materials for a more exact investigation of the subject than had previously been possible. Earlier works, therefore, like that of G. Meerman, *De Chartae vulgaris seu lineae Origine*, ed. J. v. Vaassen, Hagae Comitum, 1767, have been superseded. The manufacture of paper seems to have been introduced into Europe by the Moors in Spain, where it went by the name of *pergameno de panno* to distinguish it from the *pergameño de cuero*. In the Byzantine Empire it was called ξυλοχάρτιον or ξυλότευκτον, as being a vegetable product. It came afterwards to be known as χάρτης Δαμασκηνός, from its chief place of manufacture. The Arabs introduced it into Sicily, whence it passed into Italy. After 1235, we find paper mentioned as one of the exports of Genoa. European paper is distinguished from that of Eastern manufacture chiefly by the use of water marks, such as ox-heads, *e.g.*, which were unknown in the East. Older sorts of paper bear a great resemblance to parchment. The Benedictine monks, who owned the fragments of Mark's Gospel preserved in Venice, asserted that they were written on bark. Montfaucon declared the material to be papyrus. Massei said it was cotton paper. But the microscope shows it to be parchment. In many manuscripts a mixture of parchment and paper is found. This is so in the Leicester Codex, in which the leaves are regularly arranged in such a way that the outer and inner sheets of a quire are of parchment, while the three intermediate sheets are of paper. See J. R. Harris, *The origin of the Leicester Codex of the New Testament*, 1887, p. 14 ff.

Lead. Lead was also employed in early times for writing on. Budde sees a reference to this practice in the well-known passage, Job xix. 24. He holds that the lead there mentioned is not to be supposed as run into letters cut out in the rock, which would be a very unlikely thing to do, and a practice for which there is no evidence. He would therefore correct the text so as to read "with an iron pen on lead." Hesiod's Ἔργα, *e.g.*, was preserved on lead in the temple of the Muses on Helicon.[1] A leaden tablet from Hadrumet contains an incantation showing strong traces of O.T. influence.[2] At Rhodes there was recently discovered a roll of lead inscribed with the 80th Psalm, which was used as a charm to protect a vineyard.[3]

Clay and brick were also used as writing material, a fact which Strack has omitted to mention in his article on Writing in the *Realencyklopädie* (see Ezek. iv. 1). So far, however, no traces of N.T. writing have been discovered in the Ostraca literature of which we have now a considerable quantity. We have tiles of this sort dating from a period of over a thousand years from the time of Ptolemy Philadelphus onwards, inscribed with ink and a reed pen. Several of these contain portions of literary works such as those of Euripides.[4] Clay.

Linen was also written on.[5] It was used, *e.g.*, for the Sibylline Oracles (lintea texta, carbasus: *Orac. Sib.* ed. Alexandre, ii., 159, 178, 189). But up to the present no N.T. writing has been found on linen. Linen.

On Paul's "books and parchments," see Zahn, *Kanon* ii., 938 ff. I am not aware if J. Joseph takes up this point or not in his La Bibliothèque de l'Apôtre Paul (Chrétien Évang., 1897, v. 224–227). In the *Theol. Tijdschrift*, 1898, p. 217, the view that the μεμβράναι Paul sent for were blank sheets of parchment is called in question. The most natural explanation, certainly, is that they were. d Paul's "books."

The N.T. makes no mention of the metal, wood, or bone stilus. By "the wild beast of the reeds" (Ps. lxviii. 31) the Rabbis understood the reed pen, which in Syriac also is commonly denoted by קנה, and they took it as referring to Rome and the Emperor, who decided the fate of nations with a single stroke of his pen.[6] Luther, moreover, was not without precedent in speaking of "governors with the pen" in Jud. v. 14, as the Syriac version renders it in the same way. In Ps. xlv. 2, the Hebrew עֵט is rendered κάλαμος (LXX), σχοῖνος (Aquila), and γραφεῖον (Symmachus). It is also rendered e Pen.

[1] Pausanias, ix. 31, 4.

[2] Deissmann, *Bibelstudien*, 26–54.

[3] Hiller von Gaertringen, *Berl. Sitz.-Ber.*, 21st July 1898.

[4] See Wilcken, *Verein von Alterstumsfreunden im Rheinland.* Heft lxxxvi. p. 234; also the *Berl. Phil. Wochenschrift*, 1889, 26.

[5] *Cf.* Livy, B. iv. c. 7; Pliny, xiii. 11, "postea publica monumenta plumbeis voluminibus mox et privata linteis confici coepta sunt."

[6] *Jüdisches Literaturblatt*, 1889, 10.

σχοῖνος by the translator of Jeremiah viii. 8, where Aquila has γραφεῖον. Σχοῖνος must therefore be added to the Bible names for pen. Γραφίς for γραφεῖον, mentioned alongside of ὄνυξ ἀδαμάντινος in Jer. xvii. 1, seems to belong to the Spanish-Greek of the Complutensian, but is really classic, as also its diminutive γραφίδιον. According to the Rabbis, pens were among the things God made in the evening of the last day of the creation. They were also venerated by the Egyptians and the Greeks as an invention of the Deity.[1] According to Antisthenes[2] or Democritus,[3] a young man, in order to enter the school of wisdom, requires to have a βιβλιαρίου καινου (= καὶ νοῦ) καὶ γραφείου καινου καὶ πινακιδίου καινου. In Cyprus, the stilus is called ἀλειπτήριον, and the γραμματοδιδάσκαλος in like manner διφθεράλοιφος.[4] In the recently discovered fragments of Diocletian's *List of Wares*, the section περὶ πλούμου (goose, swan, and peacock feathers) is followed by that περὶ καλάμων καὶ μελανίου, and then by that περὶ ἐσθῆτος. Ink costs 12 drachmae the quart; Paphian and Alexandrian κάλαμοι[5] cost 4 drachmae; and κάλαμοι δευτ[έρας] φώρ[μης] the same. Baruch, the ἀναγνωστής, purchased ink and a pen in the market of the Gentiles, in order to write his letter to Jeremiah (ἀποστείλας εἰς τὴν ἀγορὰν [v. l. διασπορᾶς] τῶν ἐθνῶν ἤνεγκε χάρτην καὶ μέλανα [v. l. μελαν]).[6] Demosthenes was not the only possessor of a silver stilus. Boniface, *e.g.*, had one of that sort sent him from England.

Reading and writing.

The following is a list of expressions relating to reading and writing taken from the Greek Versions of the O.T. It makes no claim to be complete. The passages will be found in Hatch and Redpath's *Concordance to the Septuagint*.

ἀκριβόω, ἀναγιγνώσκω, ἀνάγνωσις, ἀναγνωστής, ἀντίγραφον, ἀποκαλύπτειν; βιβλιαφόρος (βιβλιο-), βίβλινος, βιβλιογράφος (Est. iii. 13, Complut.), βιβλιοθήκη, βιβλίον (βυ-), βιβλιοφυλάκιον, βίβλος (βυ-);

[1] *Cf.* the verses inscribed on a marble tablet discovered in Andros by Ross in 1844:—

ἐγὼ χρυσόθρονος Ἶσις . . . .
ἀφαλέων Ἕρμανος ἀπόκρυφα σύμβολα δέλτων
εὑρόμενα γραφίδεσσιν ἅ τ' ἔξυσε πᾶσι χαράξας
φρικαλέον μύσταις ἱερὸν λόγον . . . .

[2] See Nestle, *Bengel*, p. 105.

[3] *Zeitschrift für das Humanistische Gymnasium*, 1896, p. 27.

[4] O. Hoffmann, *Griechische Dialekte*, i. 107.

[5] Probably pens of the first quality—μονογόνατοι.

[6] Harris, *Last Words of Baruch*, vi. 17, p. 56.

γαζά, γράμμα, γραμματεία, γραμματεύειν, γραμματεύς, γραμματικός, γραμματοεισαγωγεύς, γραπτόν, γράφειν (*ἀνα-, ἀπο-, ἐπι-, κατα-, συν-*), *γραφεῖον* (*σιδηροῦν*), *γραφεὺς* (*ταχινός*), *γραφή* (*ἀνα-, ἀπο-, συν-*), *γραφικός, γραφίς*; *διφθέρωμα, διώκειν*; *εἴλημα, εἰς-* or *ἐνχαράττειν, ἐπιστολή, ἑρμηνεύω, ἐπιστάμενος γράμματα*; *θησαυροφύλαξ*; *κάλαμος* (*καλαμάριον, vide* Field's *Hexapla* on Ezek. ix. 2) *κάστυ, κεφαλίς*; *μαχθάμ, μέλαν, μελανοδοχεῖον, μίλτος, μνημόσυνον, μολίβος, μολίβδινος*; *ξυρός*; *ὄνυξ ἀδαμάντινος, ὀξυγράφος*; *πινακίς, πινακίδιον, πτύξ, πτυχή, πυξίον*; *σελίς, σμίλη, στηλογραφία, σφραγίζειν, σφραγίς, σχοῖνος*; *τόμος* (*χαρτοῦ καινοῦ μεγάλου*, Isa. viii. 1; also 1 Esdras vi. 23 for *τόπος*), *τεῦχος, τύπος*; *χάρτης, χαρτίον, χαρτηρία.*

f Diastole and hyphen.

Ancient Homeric grammarians used to debate whether contiguous letters were to be read as one word or not. To obviate misunderstanding, they employed the *ὑποδιαστολή* as the mark of division (*ὅ, τι, e.g.*), and the *ὑφ' ἕν* as the mark of combination (*Διόσκουροι*, not *Διὸς κοῦροι*). Such marks are also found in manuscripts of the Bible, in the Septuagint, *e.g.*, in the case of proper names. It goes without saying that the scriptio continua made the reading as well as the copying of manuscripts a matter of some difficulty. Hermas (Visio ii. 1) says of the book given him to copy *μετεγραψάμην πάντα πρὸς γράμμα· οὐχ ηὕρισκον γὰρ τὰς συλλαβάς.*[1] For two instructive mistakes in the Latin interlinear version of Codex Boernerianus see p. 77.

g Breathings and accents.

Breathings and accents were found in various manuscripts of the Bible as early as the time of Epiphanius and Augustine. In our oldest manuscripts they seldom occur before the seventh century. They were inserted by the first hand of the Ambrosian Hexateuch (Swete's F), which is ascribed to the first half of the fifth century by Ceriani. They seem to have been added to the Codex Vaticanus by the third hand, probably in the twelfth century, and do not always conform to our rules. Augustine, commenting on the rival readings *filiis* and *porcina*, in Psalm xvi. 14, says: "quod (porcina) alii codices habent et verius habere perhibentur, quia diligentiora exemplaria per accentus notam eiusdem verbi graeci ambiguitatem graeco scribendi more dissolvunt, obscurius est" (ii. 504–5, in Lagarde's *Probe einer neuen Ausgabe*, p. 40). Similarly, speaking of the difference between *ῥάβδου αὐτοῦ* and *ῥάβδου αὑτοῦ*, Gen. xlvii. 31, he says:—"fallit enim eos verbum graecum, quod eisdem literis scribitur sive *eius* sive *suae*;

[1] *Vide* Harnack, *T. und U.*, ii. 5, p. 68.

sed accentus [=spiritus] dispares sunt et ab eis qui ista noverunt, in codicibus non contemnuntur" (iv. 53 ed. Lugd. 1586, cited by Scrivener, i. p. 47).

Abbreviation. The practice of abbreviating words of frequent occurrence like $\overline{\Theta\Sigma}$, $\overline{X\Sigma}$, $\overline{AN\text{O}\Sigma}$ goes back to very early times. So, too, does the use of letters as numerals, I for 10, etc.

Divisions. In dividing syllables the Greek copyists in general observed the rule of beginning each new line with a consonant. A good many exceptions occur however, especially in the Vaticanus, most of which have been corrected by a later hand. These are indicated in the third volume of Swete's edition of the LXX. A good instance of this is seen in Jer. xiv. 12, where the Vaticanus and Marchalianus both originally had προσ ενεγκωσιν, which in the former is corrected to προ σενεγκωσιν, and in the latter to προσε νεγκωσιν. For examples from the O.T. portion of the Codex Vaticanus see Nestle's *Septuagintastudien*, ii. 20.

h Stichometry. Carefully written manuscripts of the Old and New Testaments are provided with a system of stichometry just as occurs in the better manuscripts of the classics, as *e.g.* Herodotus and Demosthenes. In the N.T. it is found specially in those Pauline Epistles that go back to the recension of Euthalius. One of the writers of the Codex Vaticanus has copied, in several of the books of the O.T., the stichometric enumeration which he found in his original, and the numbers show that the manuscript he copied contained almost twice as much matter in a line as the one he himself wrote. See Nestle, *Septuagintastudien*, ii. 20 f.; Lagarde, *Die Stichometrie der syrisch-hexaplarischen Uebersetzung des alten Testaments* (*Mitteilungen*, iv. 205–208). On the stichometric list in the Codex Claromontanus of the Pauline Epistles (D_2), see p. 76.

American scholars have counted the number of words in the Greek N.T. In Matthew the number is 18,222, in Mark 11,158, in Luke 19,209. Unfortunately, I am unable to give the total number in the N.T. See Schaff's *Companion*, pp. 57, 176.

Graux (*Revue de Philologie*, ii.) has counted not only the words but the letters in the various books. The numbers are given in Zahn's *Geschichte des N.T. Kanons*, i. 76. They are as follows:—

	Letters.	Stichoi.
Matthew, ...	89,295	2480
Mark, ...	55,550	1543

	Letters.	Stichoi.
Luke, ...	97,714	2714
John, ...	70,210	1950
Acts, ...	94,000	2610
3 John, ...	1,100	31
Apocalypse, ...	46,500	1292
For Philemon, Zahn gives .	1,567	44

In this last epistle I find that my edition has 1538 letters, or including the title 1550. The lines in my edition happen to coincide as near as may be with the ancient stichoi. 41 stichoi at 36 letters to the stichos would give a total of 1476. Now in the 41 complete lines which my edition gives to Philemon I find 1469 letters, that is, only 7 fewer. In Jude, again, Graux enumerates 71 stichoi, while my edition shows exactly 70 lines or 71 with the title. For stichometric calculations, therefore, this edition will prove very convenient.

For a "Table of Ancient and Modern Divisions of the New Testament," see Scrivener, i. 68; also Westcott, *Canon*, Appendix D, xix., xx.; *Bible in the Church*, Appendix B, 4.

Cola and commata.

The Cola and Commata were quite different from the stichoi. The length of the latter was regulated according to the space (space-lines), that of the former by the sense and structure of the sentence (sense-lines). On cola and commata see Wordsworth and White, *De colis et commatibus codicis Amiatini et editionis nostrae*, in the *Epilogus* to their edition of the Vulgate, i. pp. 733–736. On the stichometry proper see *Ibid.*, p. 736, *De stichorum numeris in euangeliis*.

Manuscripts de luxe.

Solomon perfumed with musk the letter he sent to Bilqis, Queen of Sheba, who herself could both read and write.[1] Mani inscribed characters on white satin in such a way that if a single thread was drawn out the writing became invisible.[2] On gold and silver writing among the Syrians see Zahn, *Tatian*, *Forschungen*, 108, n. 1; also R. Wessely, *Iconographie* (*Wiener Studien*, xii. 2, 259–279). The earliest mention of this kind of writing that I know is in the Epistle of Aristeas,[3] σὺν . . . ταῖς διαφόροις διφθέραις, ἐν αἷς [ἦν] ἡ νομοθεσία γεγραμμένη χρυσογραφίᾳ τοῖς Ἰουδαϊκοῖς γράμμασι, θαυμασίως εἰργασμένου

[1] Socin, *Arabic Grammar*, 2nd ed., p. 55, line 14; p. 56, line 12.

[2] *ZdmG.*, xliii. 547.

[3] Konstantin Oikonomos, περὶ τῶν ό ἑρμηνευτῶν, Bk. iv. p. 975.

τοῦ ὑμένος καὶ τῆς πρὸς ἄλληλλα συμβολῆς ἀνεπαισθήτου κατεσκευασμένης. In Alexander's copy of the Pentateuch the name of God was written in gold letters.[1]

On the fineness of the parchment and the beauty of the writing see Chrysostom, *Hom.* 32 *in Joannem*: σπουδῆς περὶ τὴν τῶν ὑμένων λεπτότητα καὶ τὸ τῶν γραμμάτων κάλλος. Ephraem Syrus commended this Christian munificence, as is pointed out in the *Histor. Polit. Blätter*, 84, 2, 104. Gold writing is also mentioned in the Targum on Ps. xlv. 10.

The passage in the Epistle of Theonas to Lucian referring to the use of purple-dyed parchment is thought by Batiffol to be derived from that in Jerome's Commentary on Job, and he founds on this an argument against the genuineness of the Epistle.[2] In the Martyrium of Qardagh the Persian, particular mention is made of the remarkable beauty and whiteness of the parchment (σωμάτιον) on which he wrote his epistles.[3]

For the preparation of his Bible, Origen procured the services not only of rapid writers (ταχυγράφοι) but also of girls who could write beautifully (καλλιγράφοι). Cassiodorus pleads—qui emendare praesumitis, ut superadjectas literas ita pulcherrimas facere studeatis, ut potius ab *Antiquariis* scriptae fuisse judicentur.[4] We also find him making proposals for expensive bindings in the *De Inst.*, c. 30, a passage which, according to Springer,[5] has been overlooked in the literature on illustrated bindings in modern histories of art.

On various decorated manuscripts see W. Wattenbach, *Ueber die mit Gold auf Purpur geschriebene Evangelien-handschrift der Hamiltonschen Bibliothek*, in the *Berliner Sitz.-Ber.*, 7th March 1889, xiii. 143–156. Cf. *Berl. Phil. Wochenschrift*, 1889, 33, 34. This manuscript purported to be a gift to Henry VIII. from Pope Leo X., but was rather from Wolsey. Bishop Wilfrid of Ripon (670–688) had the four Gospels written with the finest gold. Boniface requested his English friends to send him the Epistles of Paul written with gold in order therewith to impress the simple-minded Germans (Ep. 32, p. 99), a fact of which Gustav Freitag makes use in his *Ingo und Ingraban*, p. 476. (See *Die Christliche Welt*, 1888, 22.) *Cf.* also the manuscripts of Theodulf in Paris and Puy (see below,

[1] Hody, 1684, p. 254 ff.

[2] *Vide* Harnack in the *ThLz.*, 1885, cols. 321, 324, n. 5.

[3] Ed. Feige, p. 53.

[4] *Divin. Lect.*, c. xv.

[5] *Sächs. Sitz.-Ber.* (1889), xi. 4, 369.

p. 125). The Cistercians forbade the use of gold and silver bindings or clasps (firmacula) and also of different colours.

Illustration.

Illustrations must have made their appearance in Greek manuscripts a whole century earlier than has hitherto been supposed if H. Kothe is right in his interpretation of the passage in Diogenes Laertius, ii. 3, 8 (= Clem., *Strom.*, i. 78, p. 364, Potter): *πρῶτος δὲ Ἀναξαγόρας καὶ βιβλίον ἐξέδωκε σὺν γραφῇ* ("with a picture": formerly read as *συγγραφῆς*). In addition to the works of Aristotle and the obscene poems of Philainis, illustrated manuscripts were known to exist of the works of the astronomers Eudoxus and Aratus, of the botanist Dioscorides, of the tactician Euangelos, and of the geographer Ptolemy. A description of the earliest illustrated Bibles is given by Victor Schultze in the *Daheim*, 1898, No. 28, 449 ff., with good facsimiles. On the horses in the chariot of Elijah in a Greek manuscript of the ninth century in the Vatican Library, and on the pictures of the horsemen in the codex of Joshua also contained there, see F. aus'm Weerth in the *Jahrbuch des Vereins von Altertums-Freunden im Rheinland*, Heft 78 (1884), Plate VI.

Cassiodorus had a Pandectes Latinus—*i.e.* a manuscript of the Old Latin Bible of large size—which contained pictures of the Tabernacle and the Temple. There is an old work on this subject by P. Zornius entitled *Historia Bibliorum pictorum ex antiquitatibus Ebraeorum et Christianorum illustrata cum figuris*, Lipsiae, 1743, 4to; and by the same author, *Von den Handbibeln der ersten Christen*, Lips. 1738, also *Historia Bibliorum ex Ebraeorum diebus festis et jejuneis illustrata*, Lips., 1741. See also Georg Thiele, *De antiquorum libris pictis capita quattuor*, *Marburg*, 1897.

Palimpsests.

Palimpsests of Bible manuscripts came to be prohibited by the Church. The Sixth Ecumenical Council (Trullan, Concilium quinisextum, 680–681), in its 68th canon, *Περὶ τοῦ μὴ ἐξεῖναί τινι τῶν ἁπάντων βιβλία τῆς παλαιᾶς καὶ νέας διαθήκης διαφθείρειν*, forbids the sale of old manuscripts of the Bible to the *βιβλιοκάπηλοι* or the *μυρεψοί*, or to any persons whatever.[1] There was naturally a special aversion to letting such manuscripts fall into the hands of Jews; but yet there were discovered, in the lumber room of the Synagogue of Old Cairo, fragments of a Greek MS. of the Gospels, which had

[1] Balsamon, the Canonist (c. 1200), complains that *τινὲς δι' αἰσχροκέρδειαν βιβλίων τῶν θείων γραφῶν ἐμπορευόμενοι ἀπήλειφον*, and he requests *σημειῶσαι ταῦτα διὰ τοὺς βιβλιοκαπήλους τοὺς ἀπαλείφοντας τῶν θείων γραφῶν*.

been afterwards employed to receive Jewish writing. Parchments of this sort were at first used only for rough drafts and such like, instead of wax tablets from which the writing could be erased again.

l Punctuation. A good example of the importance of punctuation will be found in Lk. i. 35, on which see p. 201. Compare also Lk. xxi. 8, 1 Tim. ii. 5, where Lachmann punctuates *καὶ ἀνθρώπων ἄνθρωπος,*. By a different punctuation in Heb. i. 9, Tischendorf and Westcott-Hort make ὁ Θεός vocative and nominative respectively. In the former case the Messiah is God, in the other God is the one who anoints him. This difference was not observed at first by O. v. Gebhardt. Similarly there is a difference between the text and the margin of Westcott and Hort in verse 8, where by the insertion or omission of the two commas before and after ὁ Θεός the meaning is either that Messiah is God or that God is Messiah's throne. Considering the importance of such marks of division, the rule laid down by Ephraem Syrus in the year 350, and again emphasized by Bengel and Lagarde, should be carefully attended to in the New Testament: *εἰ κέκτησαι βιβλίον, εὔστιχές κτῆσαι αὐτό· μήποτε εὑρεθῇ ἐν αὐτῷ πρόσκομμα τῷ ἀναγινώσκοντι ἢ μεταγράφοντι* (see Nestle, *Bengel als Gelehrter*, p. 24). Compare also what Chrysostom says regarding punctuation on Mt. viii. 9: *τινὲς δὲ καὶ οὕτως ἀναγινώσκουσι τουτὶ τὸ χωρίον· εἰ γὰρ ἐγὼ ἄνθρωπος ὤν, καὶ μεταξὺ στίξαντες ἐπάγουσιν· ὑπὸ ἐξουσίαν ἔχων ὑπ' ἐμαυτοῦ στρατιώτας.* See also Victor (or whoever it is) on Mk. xvi. 9. On the change of the sense by means of false emphasis or punctuation see below, pp. 204(7), 276. J. A. Robinson thinks it probable that ὁ Ἀγαπητός is a separate title of the Messiah, and would point ὁ υἱός μου, ὁ Ἀγαπητός in Mk. i. 11, ix. 7 on the authority of the *Ascensio Esaiae* and the Old Syriac (see Hastings' *Bible Dictionary*, ii. 501).

m Contents. On the contents of Bible manuscripts see Zahn, *GK.* i. 62 f. According to him Jerome's Old Testament was in 14 volumes. In addition to some entire Bibles Cassiodorus had the Scriptures written out in 9 codices. Of these vol. VII. comprised the Gospels, VIII. the Epistles, and IX. the Acts and Apocalypse. Leontius speaks of 6 books of the New Testament, of which probably I. was Mt. and Mk., II. Lk. and Jn., III. Acts, IV. Catholic Epistles, V. Pauline Epistles, VI. Apocalypse. As a rule the Gospels and the Pauline Epistles made two codices.

In cod. ℵ we find that the different parts of the New Testament display a different type of text, from which we may conclude that the codex was copied, not from a single manuscript but from several.

Similarly, the singular type of text exhibited by cod. Δ in Mark would show that this codex, or that from which it was copied, was transcribed from different rolls or codices, each containing one Gospel. See Zahn, *GK.* i. 63.

On the designation *Bibliotheca* and *Pandectes* for Bible manuscripts, see Zahn, *GK.* i. 65. On τεῦχος, *ibid.* 67. He informs us that the earliest mention of a Christian *bibliotheca* and its *armaria* is in the heathen protocol of the year 304, in the *Gesta apud Zenophilum* given in Dupin after Optatus, p. 262. The next earliest notice is in Augustine. The custodians of the bibliothecae were probably the Readers. In Ruinart's *Acta Saturnini* a certain Ampelius is mentioned as "custos legis, scripturarumque divinarum fidelissimus conservator." From Irenaeus, iv. 33, 2 Lessing concluded that at that time the few existing copies of the Scriptures were in the custody of the clergy, and were only to be perused in their presence. (*Zusätze zu einer nötigen Antwort.* Works, ed. Maltzahn, xi. 2, 179.) On this point see Zahn, *GK.* i. 140. n Bibliotheca.

(*a.*) UNCIAL MANUSCRIPTS.

א CODEX SINAITICUS, now in St. Petersburg, contains the entire New Testament written in the fourth or more probably at the beginning of the fifth century. The story of its discovery and acquisition is quite romantic. When Tischendorf, under the patronage of his sovereign King Frederick Augustus of Saxony, came to the Convent of St. Catherine on Mount Sinai for the first time in 1844, he rescued from a basket there forty-three old sheets of parchment which, with other rubbish, were destined for the fire. In this way he obtained possession of portions of one of the oldest MSS. of the Old Testament, which he published as the Codex Frederico-Augustanus (F-A) in 1846. At the same time he learned that other portions of the same Codex existed in the Monastery. He could find no trace of these, however, on his second visit in 1853. But on his third visit, undertaken with the patronage of the Emperor of Russia, the steward of the monastery brought him, shortly before his departure on the 4th February 1859, what א

surpassed all his expectations, the entire remaining portions of the Codex comprising a great part of the Old Testament and the whole of the New, wrapped up in a red cloth. Not only was the New Testament perfect, but in addition to the twenty-seven books, the MS. contained the Epistle of Barnabas and part of the so-called Shepherd of Hermas, two books of the greatest repute in early Christian times, the Greek text of which was only partially extant in Europe. Tischendorf managed to secure the MS. for the Emperor of Russia, at whose expense it was published in four folio volumes in the year 1862 on the thousandth anniversary of the founding of the Russian Empire. In return for the MS. the monastery received a silver shrine for St. Catherine, a gift of 7000 roubles for the library and 2000 for the monastery on Mount Tabor, while several Russian decorations were distributed among the Fathers.

Unfortunately the art of photography was not so far advanced thirty-eight years ago as to permit a perfect facsimile to be made of the MS., and Tischendorf had to be content with a printed copy executed as faithfully as the utmost care and superintendence would admit.

To what date does the manuscript belong? There is still extant a letter of the first Christian Emperor Constantine dating from the year 331, in which he asks Eusebius, Bishop of Caesarea in Palestine, to provide him with fifty copies of the Old and New Testament for use in the principal churches of his empire (*πεντήκοντα σωμάτια ἐν διφθέραις ἐγκατασκεύοις*) and puts two public carriages at the bishop's disposal for their safe transport. We have also the letter that Eusebius sent along with these Bibles, in which he consigns them *ἐν πολυτελῶς ἠσκημένοις τεύχεσι τρισσὰ καὶ τετρασσὰ*—*i.e.* "in expensively prepared volumes of three and four." With former scholars Tischendorf understood the expression *τρισσὰ καὶ τετρασσὰ* of the number of sheets in the quires of the manuscripts, as though they had been composed of ternions and quaternions of twelve and sixteen pages respectively. Others took it as referring to the number of columns on the pages,

Codex Sinaiticus, which Tischendorf believed to be one of these fifty Bibles, being unique in showing four columns to the page. The most probable explanation of the phrase is, however, that it indicates the number of volumes each Bible comprised, and means that each Bible of three or four parts, as the case might be, was packed in a separate box.[1] Tischendorf, as has been said, saw in Codex Sinaiticus one of these fifty Bibles. He also thought that א was the work of four different scribes, and was confident that one of these, the one who had written only six leaves of the New Testament, was the scribe of Codex Vaticanus. But other authorities bring א down to the beginning of the fifth century.

One can understand how it was that Tischendorf was led to overrate the value of this manuscript at first, and to call it by the first letter of the Hebrew alphabet to signify its pre-eminence over all other manuscripts. The claim is so far justified that it is at least one of the oldest manuscripts, and of the oldest the only one that contains the entire New Testament. The order is that of the Gospels, Pauline Epistles (among which Hebrews is found after 2 Thess.), Acts, Catholic Epistles, Apocalypse, after which come Barnabas and Hermas.[2] This same order is observed in the Old Syriac Bible, and in the first printed Greek New Testament, the Complutensian Polyglot. The fact that Barnabas is still tacitly included in the books of the New Testament

[1] On Constantine's Bibles, see Westcott, *Canon*, c. ii. p. 426; *Bible in the Church*, c. vi. p. 155 ff.; Zahn, *Geschichte des N. T. Kanons*, i. 64. Zahn combats the supposition that the entire Bible was contained in each Codex, pointing out quite rightly that in that case the latter could not have been εὐμετακόμιστα, and moreover that Constantine speaks of σωμάτια, which does not mean codices but something much more indefinite. Nor does he believe that Eusebius intended to specify the number of sheets in each quire of the Codex or of the columns in which it was written. "The fifty Bibles might and would be distributed in 200 to 400 volumes." According to the view taken above there would be from 150 to 200 of these. *Cf.* Scrivener, i. p. 118, n. 2.

[2] For the order of the books in א, see Westcott, *Bible in the Church*, Appendix B, "Contents of the most ancient MSS. of the Bible (A, B, א, D, Amiat.)"; *Hist. of the Canon*, Appendix D, "Catalogues of Books of the Bible during the first eight Centuries."

may be taken equally as indicating the age of א itself or that of the exemplar from which it was copied.[1] Jerome's recension of Origen's Lexicon of Proper Names in the Greek New Testament is still extant, and in it Barnabas is cited like the other books. In the Catalogus Claromontanus, which is a very old list of the books of the New Testament, Barnabas is even found before the Apocalypse, an arrangement which is not found again in the succeeding centuries.

Canons. א is also the oldest MS. that has the so-called **Ammonian Sections** and **Eusebian Canons.** In order to facilitate the study of the Gospels, Ammonius of Alexandria arranged, alongside of Matthew's Gospel, the parallel passages in Mark, Luke, and John. For this purpose he was obliged of course to dislocate these last.[2] Eusebius, however, simply divided the four Gospels into 1162 sections—viz., 355 in Matthew, 233 in Mark, 342 in Luke, and 232 in John. These he numbered consecutively in each Gospel, and then arranged the numbers in ten Canons or Tables. The first contained those passages which are found in all the four Gospels; the second, third, and fourth those common to any particular combination of three; the fifth to the ninth comprised the passages common to any two, and the tenth those peculiar to each one. The number of its Canon was then set under that of the section in the margin, and the Table inserted at the beginning or end of the manuscript. By this means it was possible to know in the case of each section whether a parallel was to be found in the other Gospels, and where. In the margin opposite John xv. 20, *e.g.*, we find the numbers $\frac{\rho\lambda\theta}{\gamma}$, *i.e.* $\frac{139}{3}$. This tells us that this 139th section of John is also found in Matthew and Luke. For on referring to Canon 3 we find that it contains the passages common to John,

[1] Six leaves are now wanting between Barnabas and Hermas. What did these contain, shall we suppose? Perhaps the Didache. Schmiedel makes a different conjecture in the *Literarisches Centralblatt*, 1897, n. 49.

[2] *Vide* Wordsworth and White, *Epilogus*, p. 737, *De Sectionibus Ammonianis in Evangeliis*.

Matthew, and Luke, and that this section numbered 139 in John, is 90 in Matthew and 58 in Luke. And the sections being numbered consecutively in each Gospel, we easily ascertain that the former is Matthew x. 24, and the latter Luke vi. 40. These, or similar numbers, were afterwards inserted in the lower margin of manuscripts, as, *e.g.*, in Codex Argenteus of the Version of Ulfilas. They are still printed alongside the text in our larger editions, though, of course, owing to the introduction of our system of chapter and verse division they have lost their main significance.

Now, a Codex like א represents to us not one manuscript only, but several at once. It embodies first of all the manuscript from which its text was immediately derived, and then also that or those by which it was revised. That is to say, after the manuscript was written by the scribe, either to dictation or by copying, it was, particularly in the case of a costly manuscript, handed over to a person called the διορθωτής and revised. This might be done several times over; it might be done by a later owner if he were a scholar. But it might happen, as in the case of א *e.g.*, that the exemplar by which the manuscript was revised was not the identical one from which it had been copied but a different one, perhaps older, perhaps exhibiting another form of text altogether. Tischendorf distinguished no fewer than seven correctors in א. One of these, belonging, it may be, to the seventh century, adds a note at the end of the book of Ezra to the following effect,—"This codex was compared with a very ancient exemplar which had been corrected by the hand of the holy martyr Pamphilus; which exemplar contained at the end the subscription in his own hand: 'Taken and corrected according to the Hexapla of Origen: Antonius compared it: I, Pamphilus, corrected it.'"[1] A similar note is found appended to the Revisions.

[1] Ἀντεβλήθη πρὸς παλαιότατον λίαν ἀντίγραφον δεδιορθωμένον χειρὶ τοῦ ἁγίου μάρτυρος Παμφίλου· ὅπερ ἀντίγραφον πρὸς τῷ τέλει ὑποσημείωσίς τις ἰδιόχειρος αὐτοῦ ὑπέκειτο ἔχουσα οὕτως· μετελήμφθη καὶ διορθώθη πρὸς τὰ ἑξαπλᾶ Ὠριγένους· Ἀντωνῖνος ἀντέβαλεν· Πάμφιλος διόρθωσα.

Book of Esther, where it is also pointed out that variants occurred in the case of proper names. Traces are still discoverable in the Psalms which go to prove that the corrector's Bible agreed with that of Eusebius, while the manuscript itself had been copied from one that was very different.

A considerable number of scholars are of opinion that ℵ was written in the West, perhaps in Rome. (*See Plate I.*)

Tischendorf: (1) *Notitia editionis*, 1860; (2) *Bibliorum Codex Sinaiticus Petropolitanus*, Petropoli, 1862, fol. Vol. I., Prolegomena et Commentaria; Vol. IV., Novum Testamentum. (3) *N. T. Sinaiticum*, Lips. 1863. (*Die Anfechtungen der Sinaibibel*, Lips. 1863; *Waffen der Finsterniss wider die Sinaibibel*, Lips. 1863.) (4) *N. T. Graece ex Sinaitico Codice omnium antiquissimo*, Lips. 1865. *Collatio textus graeci editionis polyglottae cum Novo Testamento Sinaitico. Appendix editionis Novi Testamenti polyglottae*, Bielefeldiae. Sumptibus Velhagen et Klasing, 1894, large 8vo, pp. iv. 96. (Preface only by Tischendorf.) On Kenyon's showing, the recent papyrus discoveries give no occasion for abandoning the conclusions formerly come to regarding the age of these parchment manuscripts (*Palaeography*, p. 120). Scrivener, *A full Collation of the Codex Sinaiticus with the Received Text of the N. Testament*, 2nd edition, 1867. Ezra Abbot, "On the comparative antiquity of the Sinaitic and Vatican Manuscripts of the Greek Bible," *Journal of the American Oriental Society*, vol. x., i. 1872, pp. 189 ff.

A. A. CODEX ALEXANDRINUS: middle or end of the fifth century: written probably at Alexandria: contains a note in Arabic stating that it was presented to the library of the Patriarch of Alexandria in the year 1098. The Codex was sent by Cyril Lucar, Patriarch of Constantinople, to Charles I. of England in 1628, and was deposited in the library of the British Museum on its foundation in 1753, where it has been ever since. It has been employed in the textual criticism of the New Testament since the time of Walton. It was printed in 1786 by Woide in facsimile from wooden type. The Old Testament portion of it was also published in 1816–1828 by Baber. The entire manuscript was issued in autotype facsimile in 1879 and 1880.

The Codex is defective at the beginning of the New Testament, the first twenty-six leaves down to Matthew xxv. 6 being absent, as also two containing John vi. 50–viii. 52, and three containing 2 Cor. iv. 13–xii. 6. It also contains after the Apocalypse the (first) Epistle of Clement of Rome and a small fragment of the so-called second Epistle, which is really an early sermon. In the Codex these are recognised as parts of the New Testament, inasmuch as in the table of contents prefixed to the entire work they are included with the other books under the title *ἡ καινη διαθηκη*.[1] After them is given the number of books *ὁμου βιβλια*, only the figures are now, unfortunately, torn away. The contents indicate that the Psalms of Solomon should have followed, but these have been lost with the rest of the manuscript.

A is distinguished among the oldest manuscripts by the use of capital letters to indicate new sections. But in order to economize room and to obviate spacing the lines, the first letter of the section, if it occurs in the middle of a line, is not written larger, but the one that occurs at the beginning of the next whole line is enlarged and projects into the margin. (*See Plate I.* 2.) Later scribes have copied this so slavishly that they have written these letters in capitals even when they occur in the middle of the line in their manuscripts. The Egyptian origin of this Codex is shown by its use of Coptic forms for A and M. In several books A displays a remarkable affinity with Jerome in those very passages where he deviates from the older Latin version.

The books in A follow the order—Gospels, Acts, Catholic Epistles, Pauline Epistles, Apocalypse. (Westcott, *Canon*, Appendix D. xii.; *Bible in the Church*, Appendix B.)

Woide, 1786; eiusdem, *Notitia codicis Alexandrini*, *Recud. cur. notasque adjecit* G. L. Spohn, Lipsiae, 1788; Cowper, 1860; Hansell, 1864; Photographic facsimile by Thompson, 1879; and in the Facsimiles of the Palæograpical Society, Pl. 106.

[1] This agrees with the last of the so-called Apostolic Canons (85), which includes Κλήμεντος Ἐπιστολαὶ δύο among the Books of the New Testament after the Epistles of James and Jude. See Westcott, *Canon*, Appendix D. iii. a.

The mixed character of the text of A was early observed; see Lagarde, *Gesammelte Abhandlungen*, p. 94.

C. F. Hoole ascribes the Codex Alexandrinus to the middle of the fourth century (Oxford, Clarendon Press, 1891; see *Academy*, July 25, 1891, 73).

B. B. CODEX VATICANUS *par excellence*, No. 1209 in the Vatican Library at Rome, inserted there shortly after its foundation by Pope Nicolas V., and one of its greatest treasures. Like A it once contained the whole of the Old Testament with the exception of the Books of Maccabees. The first 31 leaves, containing Gen. i. 1–xlvi. 28, are now wanting, as well as 20 from the Psalms containing Ps. cv. (cvi.) 27–cxxxvii. (cxxxviii.) 6. The New Testament is complete down to Heb. ix. 14, where it breaks off at καθα[ριει]. 1 and 2 Tim., Titus, Philemon, and the Apocalypse are, therefore, also wanting. Rahlfs supposes that the manuscript may have originally contained the Didache and the Shepherd of Hermas as well. Erasmus obtained some account of this manuscript, and Pope Sixtus V. made it the basis of an edition of the Greek Old Testament, which was published in 1586, thereby determining the *textus receptus* of that portion of the Bible.—Would he had done the same for the New Testament! This task was undertaken afterwards, specially by Bentley and Birch. Professor Hug of Freiburg recognised the value of the Codex when it was removed from Rome to Paris by Napoleon in 1809. Cardinal Angelo Mai printed an edition of it between 1828 and 1838, which, however, did not appear till 1857, three years after his death, and which was most unsatisfactory. After Tischendorf had led the way with the Codex Sinaiticus, Pope Pio Nono gave orders for an edition, which was printed between 1868 and 1872 in five folio volumes. Not till 1881, however, did the last volume of this edition appear containing the indispensable commentary prepared under the supervision of Vercellone, J. Cozza, C. Sergio, and H. Fabiani, with the assistance of U. Ubaldi and A. Rocchi. Then at last the manuscript was photographed, the New Testament in 1889, and the Old Testament, in three volumes, in 1890—a veritable *ἡλίου ἀνάθημα*. No facsimile now can give any idea of its original beauty, because a hand of the tenth or eleventh century—or as the Roman editors say, a monk called Clement in the fifteenth century—went over the whole manuscript, letter by letter, with fresh ink, restoring the faded characters and at the same time adding accents and breathings in accordance with the pronunciation of his time (*ἅμαξα*, for example, and *ἀλώπηξ, δὲ*). The Old Testament is the work of at least two scribes, one of whom wrote down to 1 Sam. ix. 11, and the other to the end of 2 Esdras. Tischendorf's opinion with regard to the writer of the New Testament has been already noticed. There can be no question that B is more carefully written than ℵ. In the Gospels the Vatican exhibits a peculiar division into 170, 62, 152, and 80 sections respectively, which is found also in Ξ; in the Acts there is a double division into 36 and 69.[1] The enumeration affixed to the Pauline Epistles shows that these were copied from a manuscript in which Hebrews came after Galatians, though in B its position has been changed so as to follow 2 Thessalonians. The copyist has also retained in part of the Old Testament the enumeration of the stichoi which he found in his original. In the New Testament the order of the books is Gospels, Acts, Catholic Epistles, Pauline Epistles. An increased interest would be lent to this manuscript if, as has been supposed, it represents the recension of the Egyptian Bishop and Martyr Hesychius, of which Jerome makes mention in two places. (Bousset, *Textkritische Studien zum Neuen Testament*, pp. 74–110, see especially p. 96.) On the Egyptian character of B, see also Burkitt in *Texts and Studies*, v. p. viii. f., and compare below, p. 183 f. (*See Plate IV.*)

Hug, *Commentatio de antiquitate codicis Vaticani*, 1810. Vercellone, *Dell' antichissimo codice Vaticano della Bibbia Greca*, 1859; reprinted

[1] On the Alexandrian division of the Gospels into 68, 48, 83, and 18 sections respectively, see Kenyon in the *Journal of Theological Studies*, i. 149.

in his *Dissertazioni accademiche*, Roma, 1864, 115 ff. First facsimile reproduction, *Bibliorum sacrorum Graecus Codex Vaticanus .... collatis studiis Caroli Vercellone et Josephi Cozza editus*, vol. v., Rome, 1868; vol. vi. (Proleg. Comment. Tab. ed. Henr. Fabiani et Jos. Cozza), 1881; *cf. ThLz.*, 1882, vi. 9. A. Giovanni, *Della Illustrazione dell' edizione Romana del Codice Vaticano*, Rome, 1869. Photographic edition, *Novum Testamentum e Codice Vaticano* 1209 .... *phototypice repraesentatum* .... *curante Jos. Cozza-Luzi*, Rome, 1889, fol.; see H. C. Hoskier, *The Expositor*, 1889, vol. x. 457 ff.; O. v. Gebhardt, *ThLz.*, 1890, 16; Nestle, *Sep.-St.*, ii. 16 ff. Alf. Rahlfs, *Alter und Heimat der Vatikanischen Bibelhandschrift* (Nachrichten der Gesell. der Wiss. zu Göttingen, Philologisch-historische Klasse, 1889, Heft i. pp. 72–79). In this article Rahlfs seeks to prove that the number and order of the books in the Old and New Testaments contained in B correspond exactly to the Canon of the Scriptures given by Athanasius in his thirty-ninth Festal Letter of the year 367. In it, Athanasius, after mentioning all the canonical books of the Bible, including those of the N. T., cites the extra-canonical books of the O. T. which are allowed to be read, putting them after the second group, βίβλοι στιχήρεις, because two of these books, Wisdom and Sirach, were to be written στιχηδόν. In the N. T. the Greek and Syriac forms of the Festal Letter put Hebrews expressly between the Epistles to the Churches and the Pastoral Epistles. In the Sahidic version of the Letter, however, Hebrews stands before Galatians. This latter arrangement is evidently the survival of a pre-Athanasian order which has been longer preserved in the Sahidic translation.[1] But if B is the work of Athanasius, it follows that it cannot be one of the Bibles ordered by Constantine. In this case it would rather be written in Egypt, and we should have in it the Recension of Hesychius, as Grabe supposed was the case in the O. T., while Hug held the same view in regard to the N. T. text of this manuscript (see below, c. III.). Against the theory of Rahlfs, see O. v. Gebhardt in the *Theologische Litteraturzeitung*, 1899, n. 20.

[1] For the Festal Letter, see Westcott, *Canon*, App. D. xiv., p. 554; *Bible in the Church*, p. 159 ff.; Preuschen's *Analecta*, pp. 144 ff.; Burgess, *Festal Letters of Athanasius translated from the Syriac*, p. 137. Sahidic published by C. Schmidt in the *Nachrichten* mentioned above, 1898, p. 167 ff. He holds it to be the original form of the Letter.

C. CODEX EPHRAEMI RESCRIPTUS, No. 9 in the National Library at Paris, the most important of the palimpsests. This manuscript receives its name from the fact that in the twelfth century thirty-eight treatises of Ephraem, the Syrian Father (d. 373), were written over the original text. After various attempts had been made at its decipherment by Wettstein and others, Tischendorf in 1843 and 1845 published as much of the New and Old Testaments as he was able to make out after eighteen months' labour, thereby establishing his reputation as a textual critic. C.

The manuscript once contained the entire Bible, but the whole of 1 and 2 Thessalonians has been lost, as also some 37 chapters from the Gospels, 10 from the Acts, 42 from the Epistles, and 8 from the Apocalypse. There is no trace of a chapter division in Acts, Epistles, or Apocalypse. This last seems to have been copied from an exemplar consisting of about 120 small leaves, one of which had been displaced by some mistake. The Codex dates from the fifth century, and may possibly have been written in Egypt. Its earliest corrections are important, and were inserted in the sixth century.

A detailed list of the contents of C is given by Scrivener, vol. i. 121. Facsimile, *ibid.*, Plate X. p. 121.

Tischendorf, *Th. St. und Kr.*, 1841, 126 ff; N.T. edited 1843, O. T. 1845. Lagarde, *Ges. Abhandlungen*, p. 94. The page of the O. T. which Tischendorf issued in facsimile has most unfortunately disappeared, as Martin points out in his *Description technique des manuscrits grecs relatifs au N. T., etc.*, Paris, 1884, p. 4. A. Jacob, *Notes sur les MSS. grecs palimpsestes de la Bibliothèque Nationale, in Melanges Julien Havet*, 759–770.

The foregoing is what remains of the four great manuscripts which once contained the whole Bible. It will be observed that at the present time they are distributed among the Capitals of the great branches of the Christian Church—viz., St. Petersburg (Greek), Rome and Paris (Roman), and London (Anglican). German scholars have taken a foremost place in the work of their investigation.

D. D. CODEX BEZAE CANTABRIGIENSIS, inferior to the foregoing in age, compass, and repute, but perhaps surpassing all of them in importance, by reason of its unique character. The manuscript was presented to the University of Cambridge in 1581 by Calvin's friend Theodore Beza, "ut inter vere christianas antiquissimae plurimisque nominibus celeberrimae." It is not earlier than the beginning of the sixth century, but is of peculiar importance as the oldest of the Greek-Latin manuscripts of the Bible. It now contains, with certain lacunæ, the Gospels (in the order Matthew, John, Luke, Mark), the concluding verses of the Latin text of 3 John, followed immediately by the Acts, showing that in this manuscript the Epistle of Jude either stood somewhere else or was absent altogether. At least nine later hands can be distinguished in it. The first scribe was more familiar with Latin than Greek, and therefore inserts a Roman letter here and there in the middle of a Greek word, and has frequently to use the sponge to wash out the mistakes he makes in writing his manuscript.[1] Innumerable passages occur, particularly in Luke and Acts, where the text of D differs in the most remarkable manner from that of all the Greek manuscripts we are acquainted with. It alone, *e.g.*, contains after Luke vi. 4 the incident of the man working in the field on the Sabbath day, to whom Jesus said, "O Man, if thou knowest what thou doest, blessed art thou, but if thou knowest not, thou art cursed and a transgressor of the Law." It is the only one also that has the words in Luke xi. 2, "when ye pray, use not vain repetitions as the λοιποί." In Luke xxiii. 53, it says that the stone before the grave of Jesus was of such a size ὃν μόγις εἴκοσι ἐκύλιον, an addition in which it has the support of only one Latin MS. and the Sahidic Version. Again in Acts xii. 10, it is alone in recording that there were seven steps down from the prison in Jerusalem (κατέβησαν τοὺς ἑπτὰ βαθμούς). Other examples might be given of similar peculiar interpolations for the explanation of which reference must be made to c. III. below.

[1] *E.g.* ΑΠΕCΤΑLΚΕΝ, 122*b*, 4.

Its companion Latin text d is not translated directly from its own Greek but from the Greek of the parent manuscript. Seeing that the manuscript was discovered in the Monastery of Irenæus at Lyons, and that its text agrees with the Scripture quotations found in that Father even in the matter of clerical mistakes, it is possible that the Greek text is derived from his copy. The Greek occupies the left-hand page of the open volume, which is the place of honour. (*See Plates II and III.*)

Kipling, Facsimile edition, *Codex Th. Bezae Cantabrigiensis*, 1793, 2 vols.; Scrivener, *Bezae Codex Cantabrigiensis. An exact copy in ordinary type . . . with critical introduction, annotations, and facsimiles.* 4to, pp. lxiv + 453, 1864. Collation of the same by Nestle, *Supplementum*, 1896 (see p. 26). Cambridge University Press, *Photographic facsimile. Codex Bezae Cantabrigiensis Quattuor Evangelia et Actus Apostolorum continens Graece et Latine.* 2 vols., pp. 830, 1899. 12 guineas. (See *Literature*, 29th April 1899, p. 451 ff.); Dav. Schulz, *Disputatio de Codice D.*, 1827; K. A. Credner, *Beiträge zur Einleitung*, vol. i., 1832, pp. 452–518; J. R. Harris, *Codex Bezae. A study of the so-called Western Text of the N. T.* (*Texts and Studies*, vol. ii.) Cambridge, 1891; also *Credner and the Codex Bezae. A Lecture delivered in the Divinity School, Cambridge, 19th Nov.* 1892. (*The Classical Review*, vol. vii. 6, *June* 1893, pp. 237–243); Chase, *The Old Syriac Element in the text of Codex Bezae*, London, 1893; also *The Syro-Latin Text of the Gospels*, London, 1895; Nestle, *Some Observations on the Codex Bezae* in the *Expositor*, v. 2, 1895, p. 235; H. Trabaud, *Un curieux manuscrit du N. T.* in the *Revue de théologie et de philosophie*, Lausanne, 1896, p. 378; Fr. Blass: 1. *Die zwiefache Textüberlieferung in der Apostelgeschichte* (*Th. St. Kr.*, 1894, p. 86 ff.); 2. *Acta Apostolorum sive Lucae ad Theophilum Liber alter. Editio philologica*, Göttingen, 1895; 3. *Acta Apostolorum . . . secundum formam quae videtur Romanam*, Leipzig, 1896; 4. *Ueber die verschiedenen Textformen in den Schriften des Lukas* (*Neue Kirchliche Zeitschrift*, 1895, p. 712); 5. *De duplici forma Actorum Lucae* (*Hermathena*, Dublin, 1895, p. 121); 6. *De variis formis Evangelii Lucani* (*Ibid.*, Dublin, 1896, p. 291); 7. *Neue Texteszeugen für die Apostelgeschichte* (*Th. St. Kr.*, 1896, p. 436); 8. *Evangelium secundum Lucam sive Lucae ad Theophilum Liber prior. Secundum formam quae videtur Romanam*, Leipzig, 1897; B. Weiss, *Der Codex D in der Apostelgeschichte. Textkritische*

Untersuchung, Leipzig, 1897, (=Texte und Untersuchungen. N. F. Zweiter Band, Heft 1); F. Graefe, *Der Codex Bezae und das Lucas-evangelium, Th. St. Kr.*, 1898, i. 116–140; compare especially, *On the Italian Origin of Codex Bezae.* 1. *Codex Bezae and cod.* 1071, by the Rev. K. Lake; 2. *The Marginal Notes of Lections*, by the Rev. F. E. Brightman in the *Journal of Theological Studies*, i. 3 (April 1900) pp. 441–454. Codex 1071 is a minuscule on Mt. Athos, in which the text of the Pericope Adulterae (John viii.) is essentially the same as the singular text exhibited by D. It seems to have come from Calabria. The lectionary indicated in the margin of D points to a mixed Greek and Latin population such as that in the South of Italy.

In what follows the manuscripts are grouped according to their contents as copies of the Gospels, Acts and Catholic Epistles, Pauline Epistles, or of the Apocalypse.

Gospels.

E. CODEX BASILIENSIS, by some ascribed to the seventh century, but belonging more probably to the eighth: brought to Europe by Cardinal John de Ragusio, who was sent on a mission to the Greeks by the Council of Basel (1431): used by Mill, Bengel, and Wettstein: Luke iii. 4–15 and xxiv. 47–53 wanting: has been in the University Library at Basel since 1559. (Scrivener, i. p. 131, Plate XI. 27.)

F. BOREELIANUS, written in the ninth century: so called as belonging at one time to a Dutchman named John Boreel: now in Utrecht: has many lacunæ, some of which have arisen since Wettstein collated the manuscript in 1730. (Scrivener, i. 131, Plate XI. 28.)

F^a. COISLINIANUS, of the seventh century, though some say the sixth and others the eighth: consists of only 26 verses from Matthew, Luke, John, Acts, 1 and 2 Cor., Gal., Col., and Heb., written on the margin of a famous Parisian manuscript of the Octoteuch in Greek containing Gen.–Deut., Josh., Jud., and Ruth. List of contents of F^a in Scrivener, i. 134.

G. SEIDELIANUS, of the tenth century: part of it in the British Museum in London and part in Trinity College, Cambridge: brought from the East by Seidel and presented in 1718 by the Berlin Librarian La Croze to J. Chr. Wolf, a clergyman in Hamburg who cut out half a page to send to Bentley in 1721. (Scrivener, i. 131, Plate XI. 29.)

H. SEIDELIANUS II., of the ninth century, in Hamburg: bequeathed with his library to his native city by Wolf, and rediscovered there in 1838. (Scrivener, i. 134, Plate XII. 31.)

I. TISCHENDORFIANUS II., fragments of seven manuscripts in St. Petersburg found by Tischendorf in the Monastery of Mar Saba, near the Dead Sea: consists of 28 palimpsest leaves with Greek writing of the tenth century containing only 255 verses of the New Testament, of which 190 are from the Gospels: the three oldest leaves are of the fifth century; some of them are perhaps parts of a once complete Bible: detailed list of contents in Scrivener, i. 134 f.

I^b. So indicated by Tischendorf in his eighth edition, formerly known as N^b, of the fourth or more probably the fifth century: a threefold palimpsest written first in Greek and afterwards twice in Syriac: contains 17 verses from John's Gospel: now in the British Museum: list of verses in Scrivener, i. 141.

K. CYPRIUS, No. 63 in the National Library at Paris: middle of the ninth century: purchased in Cyprus for Colbert in 1673: one of the six, or including Ω seven, complete uncial manuscripts of the Gospels, the others being א BMSU (Ω). Facsimile in Scrivener, i., Plate VII. p. 153.

L. REGIUS, No. 62 in the National Library at Paris: of the eighth century: contains the four Gospels complete with the exception of five lacunæ in Matthew iv. v. and xxviii., Mark x. and xv., and in John xxi.: important as showing the double conclusion of Mark's Gospel which is exhibited as yet, except in versions, in only three other uncials (ך, ק, and Ψ) and one minuscule (see Plate X.). Facsimile of L, Mark xvi. 8, 9, in Scrivener, i., Plate IX. 21, p. 137. The conclusions, as found in L, ך, ק, and Ψ, are printed and discussed in Swete's *Gospel according to St. Mark*, pp. xcviii, xcix. See also Westcott and Hort's Introduction, Appendix, p. 28 ff.; Scrivener, ii. 337; Hastings' *Dictionary of the Bible*, iii. p. 13.

M. CAMPIANUS, 48 in the National Library, Paris: of the ninth century: presented to Louis XIV. by the Abbé François de Camps, 1st January 1706: contains the four Gospels complete: one of the oldest manuscripts, with the exception of D, that exhibit the pericope of the adulteress, John vii. 53 ff. Facsimile in Scrivener, i., Plate XII. p. 134.

N. PURPUREUS, belonging to the end of the sixth century: one of the most lovely manuscripts, consisting of 45 leaves, of which 6 are in the Vatican Library at Rome, 4 in the British Museum, 2 in Vienna, and the remaining 33 in the Monastery of St. John in Patmos, from which, in all probability, the others were carried off. The manuscript is written with silver letters on a purple ground, only the letters are not printed on it with movable type as was formerly supposed in the case of the similar Codex Argenteus of Ulfilas. The contents are given in Scrivener, i. 139 f., and a facsimile at p. 98, Plate V. 182 other leaves belonging to this manuscript were recently acquired in Cappadocia for Russia.

The Vienna fragment is most beautifully printed in facsimile in that superb work, *Die Wiener Genesis*, edited by Wilh. Ritter von Hartel and Franz Wickhoff: Supplement to vols. xv. and xvi. of the *Jahrbuch der kunsthistorischen Sammlungen des Allerhöchsten Kaiserhauses*. Vienna, 1895. Hartel (p. 142) sees no reason why the manuscript should not be ascribed to the fifth century.

The text of Codex N, including the new Russian fragments, has been published with Introduction and Appendix by the Rev. H. S. Cronin in *Texts and Studies*, v. 4, 1899. The Appendix contains a collation of the Gospel of Mark in the Codex Imperatricis Theodorae (Scriv. 473: Hort 81: Tisch. 2^{pe}: Greg. 565; see note on p. 151). See Nestle in the *Zeitschrift für wiss. Theologie*, 42 (1899), pp. 621–623.

Some leaves of another purple manuscript have been acquired in Paris. See H. Omont, *Acad. des Inscr.*, Mars–Avril 1900.

O. In Moscow, consists of a few leaves taken from the binding of a book: contains 15 verses from John's Gospel i. and xx.: written in the ninth century.

O^{a-h}. Psalters, in which are found, after the Psalms among the poetic selections from the Bible, the Magnificat, the Benedictus, and the Nunc Dimittis from the first and second chapters of Luke's Gospel. O^c is a Greek Psalter of the sixth century written in Latin characters and is at Verona. O^d is a purple Psalter of the seventh century at Zurich. O^e at St. Gall is a Psalter of the ninth century, written partly in Latin and partly in Greek.

P and Q. Two palimpsests at Wolfenbüttel, the former belonging to the sixth and the latter to the fifth century. P, it appears, came from Bobbio and was afterwards at Weissenburg, Mayence, and Prague. Q, together with a portion of Ulfilas's Gothic Bible, has been employed to receive the works of Isidore of Seville. The codices were edited with great care by Tischendorf in 1869.

R. NITRIENSIS, of the sixth century: in the British Museum: consists of 48 leaves containing some 516 verses from Luke's Gospel, over which and a manuscript of 4000 verses of the Iliad, the Syriac works of Severus of Antioch were written in the ninth century. The palimpsest was brought from the Nitrian Desert in 1847, and deposited in the British Museum. (Scrivener, i. 145, Plate VI, 17.)

S. VATICANUS 354: one of the earliest manuscripts of the Greek New Testament that bears an exact date. At the end is written, *ἐγράφη ἡ τιμία δέλτος αὕτη διὰ χειρὸς ἐμοῦ Μιχαὴλ μοναχοῦ ἁμαρτωλοῦ μηνὶ Μαρτίῳ ά, ἡμέρᾳ έ, ὥρᾳ ς́, ἔτους ϛυνζ′, ἰνδικτίωνος ζ′*, *i.e.* at six o'clock on Thursday, 1st March 6457 in the 7th Indiction[1] or 949 A.D.

T^a. Of the fifth century: in the Museum Borgianum at Rome: written probably by a Coptic monk: unfortunately a mere fragment containing only 17 leaves from Luke and John: is written in two columns, that on the left containing a Sahidic version. T^b, similar small fragments of John in St. Petersburg of the sixth century. T^c, also of

[1] An Indiction is a cycle of fifteen years, computed by the Greeks from 1st September 312 A.D. Its introduction was ascribed to Constantine the Great. See Scrivener, i., App. C, p. 380.

the sixth century, a fragment of Matthew, formerly in the possession of Bishop Porfiri Uspenski of Kiev, and now at St. Petersburg. T^d, of the seventh century, in Rome, part of a Sahidic-Greek Evangeliarium, containing a few verses from Matthew, Mark, and John. T^e, of the sixth century (?), at Cambridge, consists of four verses, Matthew iii. 13–16. T^h (T^k in *TiGr.* p. 450), three leaves from Matthew xx. and xxii. T^{i-r}, fragments of six Greek-Coptic and three Greek Gospels of the ninth and tenth centuries, but possibly the seventh and eighth, published by Amélineau in vol. xxxiv. of the *Notices et Extraits de la Bibliothèque Nationale*, 1895, 363 ff.; *cf.* v. Dobschütz in the *Lit. Cent.-Blatt.*, 1895, 42, 1857. T^l contains the double conclusion of Mark's Gospel. T^{woi}, similar leaves at Oxford which once belonged to Woide, but by a different hand from T^a.

To these Græco-Coptic fragments there is now to be added two chapters of John's Gospel (iii. 5–iv. 49), in Greek and Middle Egyptian, written in the sixth century. They are published by W. E. Crum and F. G. Kenyon in the *Journal of Theological Studies*, i. 3 (April 1900), pp. 415–433. The find contains no remarkable readings. The editors call its text neutral, and think it helps to show that Egypt was the home of such correct and upright texts. (T^w Greg.)

U. NANIANUS, so called from a former possessor: of the end of the ninth or beginning of the tenth century: in Venice: a very beautiful and complete manuscript of the Gospels, with ornamentations in gold. (Scrivener, i. 137, Plate IX. 22.)

V. Formerly at Mount Athos, now in Moscow: of the ninth century: first employed by Bengel and Wettstein through the medium of G. B. Bilfinger.

W. Various small fragments: W^a of the eighth century in Paris: a fragment of Luke. W^b of the eighth century (or the ninth) in Naples: a palimpsest with parts of Matthew, Mark, and Luke. W^c of the ninth century at St. Gall: a palimpsest, containing fragments of Mark and Luke, perhaps once bilingual, Greek-Latin. W^d of the ninth century in Cambridge. W^e of the ninth century: part of John, at Mount Athos, Oxford, and Athens. W^f of the ninth century: in Oxford: fragment of Mark. W^g of the ninth century: consisting of 36 palimpsest leaves with 497 verses from Matthew, Mark, Luke, and John, in the British Museum. W^h of the ninth century: in Oxford: part of Mark. W^{i-m} in Paris, of the seventh to the eighth or ninth century: fragments of Mark and Luke, of which W^i and W^k are printed in Omont's *Catalogue des Manuscrits Grecs, Latins, Français, et Éspagnols et des Portulans, recueillis par feu Emmanuel Miller*, Paris, 1897. W^n of the seventh century, in Vienna: fragments of John. W^o of the ninth century, in Milan: 16 mutilated palimpsest leaves, containing portions of Matthew, Mark, and Luke.

X. MONACENSIS, written at the end of the ninth or beginning of the tenth century, now in Munich, contains the Gospels, with lacunæ, and a commentary, in the order Matthew, John, Luke, Mark. Scrivener, i. 343, Plate XIII. 38; for contents see *ibid.*, p. 152.

X^b. Fragment containing Luke i. 1–ii. 40, hitherto reckoned among the minuscules and numbered 429; also in Munich.

Y. Belonging to the eighth century, in the Barberini Library at Rome: 6 leaves containing John xvi. 3–xix. 41.

Z. A palimpsest in Dublin of the fifth or sixth century, containing 295 verses of Matthew's Gospel. Scrivener, i. 153; Plate VII. 18.

The Roman alphabet not being sufficient for the number of uncial manuscripts, recourse was taken to those letters of the Greek and Hebrew which have a distinct form from those already employed. It was proposed by others to reserve the Greek letters for those manuscripts no longer extant, whose text can be reconstructed from a number of kindred manuscripts as their common archetype.

Γ. Of the ninth or tenth century: part in Oxford and part in St. Petersburg, the former having been obtained from Tischendorf in 1855 and the latter in 1859: contains the whole of Luke and John, but Mark is defective from iii. 34 to vi. 20, while Matthew is still more defective. The writing of the manuscript was finished on a certain Thursday, the 27th November, in the eighth year of an indiction. Tischendorf accordingly fixed its date as 844. It was previously assigned by Gardthausen to the year 979. Scrivener, i. 134, Plate XII. 35.

Δ. SANGALLENSIS, written at the end of the ninth or beginning of the tenth century: now at St. Gall, where it was probably transcribed by an Irish monk: has an interlinear Latin version, and was not, therefore, like D, intended for church but for school purposes. The Codex has the four Gospels complete with the exception of John xix. 17–35. In Mark the text shows a closer agreement with CL than in the other Gospels. The manuscript has been copied from one written *scriptione continua*, and in consequence the words are often wrongly divided. See G_3 below, p. 77.

Θ^{a-d}. Small fragments brought from the East by Tischendorf, of which Θ^{a} belongs to the seventh century, and Θ^{bcd} to the seventh, sixth, and seventh or eighth century respectively. The first is in Leipzig, the others in St. Petersburg. Θ^{e-h} were formerly in the possession of Bishop Porfiri of Kiev.

Λ. Of the ninth century: contains the Gospels of Luke and John entire: evidently the second part of a minuscule brought to St. Petersburg by Tischendorf, No. 566 ^{evv} (Greg.)[1]: marginal scholia are affixed to four passages in Matthew—viz. iv. 5, xvi. 17, xviii. 22, xxvi. 74, giving the readings of *τὸ Ἰουδαϊκόν*, *i.e.* the lost Gospel according to the Hebrews, and its subscription runs, *ἐγράφη καὶ ἀντεβλήθη ἐκ τῶν Ἱεροσολύμοις παλαιῶν ἀντιγράφων τῶν ἐν τῷ ὄρει ἁγίῳ ἀποκειμένων· ἐν στίχοις βφιδʹ* (2514) *κεφαλαῖς τνέ* (345). The manuscript is in the Bodleian Library at Oxford. Scrivener, i. 131, Plate XI. 30.

Cf. von Dobschütz, *Zwei Bibelhandschriften mit doppelter Schriftart* (*Th. Lz.*, 1889, iii. 74 f.).

[1] See Scrivener, i. p. 160, under Λ. This minuscule seems to be omitted from Scrivener's list. See below, p. 185.

Ξ. ZACYNTHIUS, a palimpsest of the eighth century from Zante, now in the Library of the British and Foreign Bible Society in London: the earliest manuscript with a commentary: has the same system of chapter division as B, and is oftener found supporting B against A than *vice versa.*

Π. Of the ninth century: contains the Gospels almost complete: once the property of a Greek of Smyrna called Parodos: procured by Tischendorf for the Emperor of Russia.

Σ. Of the sixth century: written on purple with gold and silver lettering and 17 miniatures, being the earliest manuscript to contain such: rescued from obscurity in 1879 by Oscar v. Gebhardt and A. Harnack, who discovered it at Rossano in Calabria: hence designated as Codex Rossanensis: is nearly related to N. Scrivener, i. 124, Plate XIV. 43.

O. v. Gebhardt, *Die Evangelien des Matthäus und des Marcus aus dem Codex Purpureus Rossanensis herausgegeben* (T. und U., i. 4, 1883). A. Haseloff, *Cod. Pur. Rossanensis. Die Miniaturen der griechischen Evangelien-Handschrift in Rossano. Nach photographischen Aufnahmen herausgegeben.* Leipzig, 1898 (contains 14 facsimiles of the text and 15 photographic plates). *Vide* S. Berger in *Bull. Crit.*, 1899, 6: also F. X. v. Funk, *Die Zeit. des Cod. Rossanensis* in the *Hist. Jahrbuch der Görresgeschellschaft*, xvii. 2, 1896, 331–344.

Φ. CODEX BERATINUS, of the sixth century: at Berat in Albania: like the last a purple Codex with silver writing: contains portions of Matthew and Mark: seen and published by Batiffol. Scrivener, i. 166, Plate XV.

Ψ. Fragments of the eighth or ninth century at Athos: contains Mark ix. 5 to the end, Luke, John, Acts, seven Catholic Epistles, Romans to Philemon, and Hebrews: exhibits after Mark xvi. 8 the same double conclusion as is found in L and one Sinai manuscript. On some readings of Ψ, see Lake in the *Journal of Theological Studies*, No. i. p, 88; ii. pp. 290–292.

Ω. Of the eighth or ninth century: in the Monastery of Dionysius at Athos: contains the Gospels entire.

The last-mentioned codices have not yet been thoroughly collated, some of them having been only recently discovered.

The following are indicated by Hebrew letters.

ב. Of the ninth or tenth century: in the Monastery of St. Andrew at Athos: contains the Gospels with lacunæ.

ג. GREGORIANUS, a purple manuscript from Cappadocia now admitted to be part of N.

$ד^{6-13}$. Several leaves dating from the fifth to the ninth century, discovered at Sinai by J. R. Harris and published by him (*Biblical fragments from Mount Sinai*, 1890): $ד^{12}$ contains the double conclusion of Mark: $ד^{13}$ is a purple fragment of the seventh century containing a few verses from the first chapter of Luke, perhaps only a quotation.

ק. Swete indicates with this letter the fragment cited above as T^1, which exhibits the double conclusion of Mark's Gospel. See his *Gospel according to St. Mark*, pp. xcii., xcix.

ר. An Oxyrhynchus fragment of the fifth or sixth century, published by Grenfell and Hunt, *The Oxyrhynchus Papyri*, Part I. with eight Plates, London, 1898: contains only Mark x. 50 f. and xi. 10 f.: cited by Swete. (T^g Greg.)

Part II. of *The Oxyrhynchus Papyri* (1899, pp. 1–8) contains a fragment of John's Gospel (cc. i. and xx.) from a sheet of a papyrus codex written between 200 and 300 A.D. This is one of the earliest fragments that have been discovered of a papyrus *book* (not a *roll*). It exhibits already the abbreviations usually found in theological manuscripts, such as $\overline{\Theta\Sigma}$, $\overline{\mathrm{IH}\Sigma}$, $\overline{\mathrm{X}\Sigma}$, $\overline{\Pi\mathrm{NA}}$. The Codex agrees with א in several readings not found elsewhere. (T^x Greg.) See *Addenda*, p. xv.

Acts and Catholic Epistles.

The second group is composed of manuscripts of the Acts and Catholic Epistles which are distinguished from those in the first by affixing the exponent $_2$ at the bottom of the symbol.

א A B exhibit the Acts and Catholic Epistles complete:

E_2 D have the Acts all but entire:

K L have the Catholic Epistles complete:

C P have the greater part of them.

For ℵ A B C D F^a (a few verses of the Acts), see above.

E_2. LAUDIANUS 35, in Oxford, written at the end of the sixth century: bilingual, Latin-Greek, the Latin occupying the place of honour on the left: breaks off at Acts xxvi. 29: the text very peculiar and somewhat like that of D. The manuscript was formerly in Sardinia, and was probably brought to England by Theodore of Tarsus in 668. It was employed by the Venerable Bede (d. 735) in his *Expositio* of the Acts and afterwards in his *Expositio Retractata*. Archbishop Laud presented the manuscript with many others to the University of Oxford. Fell and Mill made use of it. Scrivener, i. 121, Plate X. 25.

G_2. Of the seventh century, a single leaf in St. Petersburg containing Acts ii. 45–iii. 8, torn from the cover of a Syriac manuscript.

G^b. Of the ninth century, a palimpsest of six leaves in Rome containing portions of Acts xvi. 32–xviii. 20. (Vat. Gr. 2302.)

H_2. Ninth century, in Modena, has the Acts with some lacunæ.

I_2. Fragments in St. Petersburg of the fifth and seventh centuries: four leaves from three different manuscripts of the Acts.

K_2. Of the ninth century: brought to Moscow from Athos: contains the Catholic and Pauline Epistles.

L_2. Written at the end of the ninth century: in the Angelica Library at Rome: contains the Acts from c. viii. onwards, the Catholic Epistles, and the Pauline down to Hebrews xiii.

P_2. Of the ninth century: formerly in the possession of Bishop Porfiri of Kiev and now at St. Petersburg: published by Tischendorf: contains Acts, Catholic and Pauline Epistles, and Apocalypse, with several lacunæ.

S_2. Of the eighth or ninth century: at Athos: contains Acts, Catholic Epistles, Romans, portions of 1 and 2 Corinthians, and Ephesians.

$ב_2$. A palimpsest of the fifth century: in Rome: rediscovered by Batiffol: consists of fragments of Acts, James, 1 and 2 Peter, 1, 2, and 3 John, Romans, 1 and 2 Corinthians,

Ephesians, Philippians, Colossians, 1 Thessalonians, 1 and 2 Timothy, Titus, Philemon, and Hebrews.

Pauline Epistles.

The third group is composed of manuscripts of the Pauline Epistles. Of these there is a comparatively large number, which may be taken as indicating the important position ascribed to Paul even in early times. א, however, is the only Codex that contains his Epistles complete; in D L they are almost complete, and A B C E F G K exhibit the greater part of them.

For א A B C, see above.

A is defective in 2 Cor. iv. 13–xii. 6 inclusive.

B breaks off at Hebrews ix. 14, consequently 1 and 2 Timothy, Titus, and Philemon are wanting.

D_2. CODEX CLAROMONTANUS: takes its name from Clermont near Beauvais. The manuscript was written in the sixth century, and is bilingual in Greek and Latin, having the Greek on the left-hand page. The Greek is wanting in Rom. i. 1–7, 27–30, and in 1 Cor. xiv. 13–22. In Gal. v. 9 D_2 reads δολοῖ, and in verse 14 ἐν ὑμῖν, in both places agreeing with Marcion. At least nine hands are distinguishable in the manuscript, one of whom corrected the text in over 2000 places in the ninth or tenth century. Two leaves are palimpsest, their text being written over part of a play of Euripides. Hebrews has evidently been copied into the Codex from a different manuscript by a later scribe. Before it is a list of "versus scribtuarum sanctarum," one of the oldest stichometric catalogues of the books of the Old and New Testaments, which is derived from an early Greek original. This Catalogus Claromontanus is given in Westcott's *History of the Canon*, App. D, xx. p. 563, and in his *Bible in the Church*, App. B, p. 309. See also Zahn, *Geschichte des N. T. Kanons*, II. 157–172, 1012; Jülicher, *Einleitung*, § 40. Thirty-five leaves of Codex D_2 were stolen by John Aymont in 1707, but afterwards restored by their purchasers, some of them in 1720, and the others in 1729. (*See Plates II. and III.*)

E_3. SANGERMANENSIS, of the ninth century: also Greek-Latin: brought from St. Germain de Près to St. Petersburg during the Revolution: in the Greek merely an incorrect transcript of D_2, and may therefore be dismissed. See p. 179 n. 1.

F_2. AUGIENSIS, of the ninth century: another Greek-Latin manuscript: defective in Rom. i. 1–iii. 19; 1 Cor. iii. 8–16; vi. 7–14; Col. ii. 1–8; Philemon 21–25: Hebrews from the first only in the Latin. The manuscript was formerly at Reichenau (Augia Dives, hence its name). It was purchased by Bentley in 1718 for 250 Dutch florins, and is now at Cambridge. An edition of it was published by Scrivener in 1859. For F^a, see above, p. 66.

Scrivener, *An exact transcript of the Codex Augiensis . . . to which is added a full collation of fifty manuscripts containing various portions of the Greek N. T.*, 1859. F. Zimmer, *Der Codex Augiensis eine Abschrift des Boernerianus* (*ZfwTh.*, 1887, i. 76–91).

G_3. BOERNERIANUS, of the ninth century, so called from Professor C. F. Boerner of Leipzig, who purchased it in 1705: now in Dresden. It is a Greek-Latin manuscript, the Latin being interlinear. It is manifestly the second part of Δ, and has a close affinity with F_2, though the Greek of F was not copied from G, as Zimmer and Hort assert. The fact is rather that both are derived from one and the same original, in which *e.g.* ως γαγγρα ινα νομην εξει, sicut cancer ut serpat, was found in 2 Tim. ii. 17, and ημεθα δε δουλωμενοι, eramus autem servientes, in Gal. iv. 3. This manuscript contains some interesting Irish verses.[1] At the end of Philemon there stands the title προς Λαουδακησας, ad laudicenses, but the Epistle that should have followed has been lost.

P. Corssen, *Epistularum Paulinarum codices graece et latine scriptos Augiensem, Boernerianum, Claromontanum examinavit, inter se*

[1] "To Rome to come, to Rome to come,
Much of trouble, little of profit,
The thing thou seekest here,
If thou bring not with thee, thou findest not"; etc., etc.
See Scrivener, i. 180.

comparavit, ad communem originem revocavit. Specimen primum, 1887. *Alterum,* 1889.

H_3. Written in the sixth century, one of the most valuable manuscripts, but unfortunately incomplete. Its leaves were used in 975 and 1218 to cover some manuscripts at Mount Athos. Forty-one of these have been rescued, of which 22 are now in Paris, 8 at Mount Athos, 3 in St. Petersburg, 3 in Moscow, 2 in Turin, and 3 in Kiev. They contain portions of 1 and 2 Corinthians, Galatians, Colossians, 1 Thessalonians, 1 and 2 Timothy, Titus, and Hebrews. The value of the manuscript is indicated in the subscription, which runs, "I, Euthalius,[1] wrote this volume of the Apostle Paul as carefully as possible in stichoi, so that it might be read with intelligence: the book was compared with the copy in the library at Cæsarea, written by the hand of Pamphilus the saint."[2] The subscription may of course have stood in the original of H, and simply been copied into it along with the text, as in the case of the minuscules 15, 83, and 173 of the Acts. But no matter, it serves to locate the text of this manuscript, and it is one of our main witnesses for the so-called **Euthalian Recension** of the Acts and Catholic Epistles.

Euthalian Recension.

In or previous to the year 396, a deacon called Euthalius, afterwards known as Bishop of Sulce,[3] published an edition of the Acts and Catholic and Pauline Epistles, in which, following the rules laid down by the Greek schools of oratory, the text was carefully broken up into lines, the length of which depended on the sense (*sense-clauses*), and divided into paragraphs or chapters. Euthalius also provided a system of Church lections, added a summary of contents to the various chapters, and catalogued the quota-

[1] Or Evagrius. The name is difficult to decipher. See below, pp. 188 ff.

[2] Ἔγραψα καὶ ἐξεθέμην κατὰ δύναμιν στειχηρὸν τόδε τὸ τεῦχος Παύλου τοῦ ἀποστόλου πρὸς ἐγγραμμὸν καὶ εὐκατάλημπτον ἀνάγνωσιν . . . ἀντεβλήθη δὲ ἡ βίβλος πρὸς τὸ ἐν Καισαρίᾳ ἀντίγραφον τῆς βιβλιοθήκης τοῦ ἁγίου Παμφίλου χειρὶ γεγραμμένον αὐταῦ.

[3] Perhaps in Sardinia, see below. Cf. Scrivener, i. p. 63 n. 1.

tions from the Old Testament and elsewhere in the separate Epistles and in the entire group. This edition became a sort of model for later times, and seems to have been made use of for the Armenian version among the rest. The comparison of the manuscript with those of Pamphilus, as well as other additions, would seem then to have been made on the occasion of a later revision. Ehrhard, however, thinks that we have the autograph edition of this system in Codex H, but that Evagrius is to be read instead of Euthalius in the place where the name has been erased. This view is combated by Dobschütz, and in part rightly. Working independently of both, Conybeare, from Armenian sources, establishes the year 396 as the date of Euthalius. But in a parchment manuscript of the eleventh century in the library of the Laura at Mount Athos, Wobbermin found a fragment of a dogmatic treatise with the inscription, Εὐθαλίου ἐπισκόπου Σούλκης ὁμολογία περὶ τῆς ὀρθοδόξου πίστεως, from which he makes out that Euthalius lived in the second half of the seventh century and that Sulce was in Sardinia. See G. Krüger in the *Lit. Cent. Blatt* 1899, No. 14.

Omont, *Notice sur un très ancien manuscrit grec en onciales des épîtres de S. Paul*, Paris, 1889. J. A. Robinson, *Euthaliana*, Texts and Studies, iii. 3, 1895. (See S. Berger, *Bull. Crit.*, 96, 8.) Th. Zahn, *Euthaliana*, *Theol. Lit. Blatt.*, 1895, 593, 601. Ehrhard, *Der codex H ad Epistolas Pauli und Euthalius diaconus*, *Eine palaeographisch-patrologische Untersuchung* in the *Centralblatt für Bibliothekswesen*, 1891, pp. 385–411. E. v. Dobschütz, *Ein Beitrag zur Euthaliusfrage*, in the same magazine, 1893, pp. 49–70; *Euthaliusstudien* in the ZKG. xix. pp. 107–154 (1898): also, *Euthalius*, in the PRE^3, v. pp. 631–633 (1898). Islinger, *Die Verdienste des Euthalius um den neutestamentlichen Bibeltext*, Hof. 1867 (Prog.). Conybeare, *On the Codex Pamphili and date of Euthalius*, in the *Cambridge Journal of Philology*, xxiii. 241 (1895). R. L. Bensly, *The Harklean Version etc.*, pp. 9, 27 (1889). See also J. A. Robinson, *Texts and Studies*, vi. 1; C. Butler, *The Lausiac History of Palladius*, p. 104 ff., and note 2, p. 188 below.

I_2, K_2, L_2, P_2 } See above, p. 75.

M_2. CODEX RUBER, of the ninth century: four leaves written in bright red ink or other colouring matter, two of them in London and the other two in Hamburg.

N_2. Of the ninth century, consisting of two leaves with portions of Galatians and Hebrews: in St. Petersburg.

O_2. Of the ninth century, two leaves in the same library containing portions of 2 Corinthians.

O^b. Of the sixth century, one leaf with part of Ephesians: in Moscow.

Q_2. Of the fifth century, five *papyrus* leaves with fragments of 1 Corinthians: in St. Petersburg.

R_2. Of the seventh century, a single leaf with part of 2 Corinthians: in Grotteferrata.

S_2. See above, p. 75.

T^g. A few sentences from 1 Timothy. See *TiGr.*, p. 441.

T^s. Two leaves containing 1 Corinthians i. 22–29, written in the ninth or tenth century, and published simultaneously with T^{i-r}. Gregory now designates T^g as $T^{a\ Paul}$, and T^s as $T^{b\ Paul}$.

$ב_2$. See above, p. 75.

$ד^{14}$. A fragment of papyrus containing part of 1 Corinthians, cc. i., ii., iii., written in the fifth century.

The first seven verses of the first chapter of Romans have been published in *The Oxyrhynchus Papyri*, Part II. (pp. 8 f., Plate II.). The fragment is probably a schoolboy's exercise. It is written in a large rude uncial hand, and dates from the first half of the fourth century. In verse 7 it reads $\overline{\text{ΚΥ}}$ $\overline{\text{ΧΡΥ}}$ $\overline{\text{ΙΗΥ}}$.

Apocalypse. There are fewest manuscripts of the Apocalypse. It is found entire only in א A B, while C and P exhibit portions of it. In the Apocalypse, however, it is to be observed that Codex B is not the famous Codex Vaticanus 1209, but a much later manuscript 2066, dating from the end of the eighth century. It would be better, therefore, with some editors, to call it Q or B_2.

Altogether the number of Greek manuscripts is as follows[1]:—

UNCIALS:		
Gospels,		73
Acts and Catholic Epistles,		19
Pauline Epistles,		28
Apocalypse,		7
	Total,	127
CURSIVES,		3702

Book-hand and hand of common life.

In closing our survey of the extant uncials, it is to be borne in mind that we are not at liberty to regard even the oldest of them as presenting the very form of the New Testament autographs. The books of the New Testament, at all events the majority of them, were not originally intended for publication at all, while the others were meant for only a limited circle of readers. Now these recent papyrus discoveries have shown conclusively what a vast difference existed even in those days between the **book-hand** and what we may call the **hand of common life** and business. A glance at Kenyon's *Palæography of Greek Papyri* will show how fundamental is the distinction between literary and non-literary papyri. That writer states that in many cases the difference is just as marked as between handwriting and print at the present day, and he instances also the distinction between the book-hand and the charter-hand of the Middle Ages. Of course documents of this or the other class may occasionally be found written in the hand that is not the usual one, a prescription, *e.g.*, in book-hand, or conversely a literary text in the hand of common life. The greater part of Aristotle's work on the *Polity of the Athenians*, for instance, has been preserved in the common hand. This papyrus, which is

[1] See Scrivener (Miller), i. p. 397*.

F

attributed to the first century of the Christian era, is the work of four scribes. But only one of these writes in a style approximating to the book-hand; the other parts are written in a very cursive style on the back of an old account, probably by one who had borrowed a copy of the work for a short time and transcribed it with the help of two or three friends or slaves. Kenyon quite properly instances this as an illustration of the manner of the origin and propagation of the New Testament books, and suggests that this mode of propagation has to be considered in connection with times of persecution. Our very oldest manuscripts are superb codices, editions de luxe, such as could be prepared only in an age when the Church had attained a position of affluence and power. The distinction referred to above is one that has had but little attention paid to it hitherto, as is shown by the illustration given in Harris's excellent work on the New Testament autographs. It is manifest at the same time that this consideration is of great importance in trying to understand the origin and dissemination of the various readings that occur in our manuscripts. It is just a pity that Kenyon has not given a sample of this manuscript of Aristotle in his book, seeing that the latter is more accessible to the ordinary student than the complete facsimile edited in 1891 by the Trustees of the British Museum, or the Plate published in the second volume of the work of the Palæographical Society.

Uncial and minuscule script.

A further consideration is emphasised by means of these papyrus discoveries—viz. that **no distinction of time** can be drawn between the uncial and cursive hands found in the manuscripts. Even in the very earliest documents the hand of common life displays a very cursive character, and a fairly cursive uncial hand with ligatures is not necessarily later than an uncial hand without ligatures. It is somewhat different in the case of writing on parchment: here the old distinction of uncial and minuscule manuscripts is rightly maintained, only we must guard against supposing that the minuscule hand and the cursive are quite the same thing ; nor must we forget that for a considerable time the older uncial and the later minuscule scripts were in use together.[1] The sharp line of demarcation, therefore, which has hitherto been drawn in the textual criticism of the New Testament between these two classes of manuscripts has no real justification in fact. The present account, however, is intended merely as a survey of the position of things up to the present, and the following description of the minuscules is subject to that limitation.

(*b.*) SOME OF THE MORE IMPORTANT MINUSCULES.

When the Greek New Testament began to be printed, the editors had necessarily to be content with indifferent and late minuscules, and even those who followed them, like Bentley and Lachmann, thought they were at liberty to disregard these altogether and to found their text exclusively on the oldest uncials. They forgot that the text of a late manuscript may be derived from a very early and good source through comparatively few intermediaries, and that it is possible to reconstruct a lost original by means of a comparison of several witnesses. Accordingly, in more recent times, English editors like Tregelles, Burgon, Ferrar, Hoskier, and Scrivener have rendered great service in the way of collating manuscripts, and the last-mentioned as well as Gregory in Germany has also catalogued them. At the present moment a systematic investigation in this department is being carried on in Berlin. Most of the minuscules are still written on parchment which began to be mixed with paper in the ninth century, and was ultimately superseded by it. Various minuscules contain commentaries and other additional matter, such as the List of the Seventy Apostles, short Biographies of the Apostles, Summaries of the journeys of St. Paul, or notes as to the date and place of the composition of the different books. When dates are given in the manuscripts, Minuscules.

[1] Compare the remarks of Grenfell-Hunt on the papyrus (and vellum) books and their respective handwritings in Part II. of the *Oxyrhynchus Papyri*, p. 2 f.

they are still as a rule computed in the Byzantine manner, reckoning from the Creation of the world (5508 B.C.). In only a few cursives is the date reckoned from the Birth of Christ.

Since the time of Wettstein the minuscule manuscripts have been indicated by Arabic numerals, the numbers in each of the four groups beginning with 1, so that one and the same manuscript may have three or four numbers—$18^{\text{evv.}}$ *e.g.* being $113^{\text{Acts,}}$ $132^{\text{Paul,}}$ and $51^{\text{Apoc.}}$, while 209^{evv} is the same as $95^{\text{Acts,}}$ $108^{\text{Paul,}}$ and $46^{\text{Apoc.}}$ It is still more awkward that in the two principal works on the minuscules, that of Scrivener and of Gregory, the recently discovered manuscripts are numbered differently. Our enumeration will follow that of Scrivener.

Minuscules of the Gospels.

1 (Acts 1, Paul 1). Of the tenth century, but according to others of the twelfth or the thirteenth, in Basel, with beautiful miniatures which were stolen prior to 1860. The manuscript was borrowed by Reuchlin and used by Erasmus for his second edition. (Scrivener, i. 137, Plate IX. 23.)

2. Of the twelfth century, though some strangely suppose the fifteenth: also in Basel: formerly purchased for two Rhenish florins: printed by Erasmus.

3. Of the twelfth century, in Vienna, lent to Erasmus for his second edition.

4–41 are all in the National Library at Paris. 4–9 and 38 were used by Stephen. The most notable among them is 13, together with 69, 124, 211, 346, 348, 556, 561 (788), 624, and 626, which are remarkable for their very peculiar form of text and their additions.[1] Luke xxii. 43, 44 is found after Matthew xxvi. 39, and John vii. 53–viii. 11 after Luke xxi. 38. The subscriptions, moreover, state that Matthew was written in Hebrew eight years after our Lord's Ascension, and contained 2522 ρηματα and 2560 stichoi, Mark ρωμαιστι ten years

Ferrar Group.

[1] Facsimiles of 13, 69, 124, 346 are given in Abbott's *Collation of Four Important Manuscripts* (Dublin, 1877); see Scrivener, i. 343, Plate XIII, 40.

after the Ascension with 1675 ρηματα and 1604 stichoi, Luke ελληνιστι fifteen years after with 3803 (*lege* 3083) ρηματα and 2750 stichoi, and John thirty-two years after with 1938 ρηματα. These manuscripts were referred to a common archetype by the Irish scholar Ferrar, and were accordingly denominated the Ferrar Group, and indicated by the letter Φ before that symbol was appropriated to the Codex Beratinus. Most of them came from Calabria, and another has lately been added to the number. Their additions, however, as Rendel Harris shows, are rather of Syrian origin. In the first edition I ventured to suggest that these manuscripts might go back to Lucian the Martyr (d. 312) of whom Jerome makes mention, saying that he knew of codices quos a Luciano (et Hesychio) nuncupatos paucorum hominum adserit perversa contentio, quibus . . . . nec in novo testamento profuit emendasse, cum multarum gentium linguis scriptura ante translata doceat falsa esse quae addita (cod. E *edita*) sunt. That, however, is not possible in the event of the so-called Syrian recension being the work of Lucian, which Hort indicates as possible. In any case, these minuscules have preserved to us a very early attempt to restore the text.

16 is noteworthy as being written in four different colours according to the contents. The continuous narrative is written in green, the words of Jesus and the Angels are in red and occasionally in gold, the words of His followers are in blue, while those of the Pharisees, the multitude, and of the devil, are written in black.

28. Contains relics of a very ancient text and bears some resemblance to D.

33. Written about the tenth century: the "queen of the cursives": its text bears a greater resemblance to that of B, D, L than does that of any other cursive. The manuscript is much damaged, but 34, which is equally old, is still in splendid condition, as though it were fresh from the hand of the artist. (Scrivener, i. 343, Plate XIII. 39.)

38. Sent by the Emperor Michael Palæologus to St. Louis (d. 1270).

51. At Oxford: text resembles that of the Complutensian.

59. At Cambridge: has many points of connection with D.

61. Of the fourteenth or fifteenth century. This is the notorious Codex Montfortianus, now in Dublin, which derives its name from one of its later possessors. It was this manuscript, "codex apud Anglos repertus," that decided Erasmus to insert in his third edition of 1522 the passage of the Three Heavenly Witnesses, 1 John v. 7, 8. It was probably written by a Franciscan monk of the name of Froy or Roy. Its twin brother, the parchment codex Ravianus (Rau), formerly numbered 110, and now in Berlin, which also contains the passage, proves to be nothing more than a transcript of the text of the Complutensian. Manuscripts, it may be observed, continued to be prepared long after the invention of printing. Melanchthon, *e.g.*, wrote out the Epistle to the Romans three times in Greek; and the manuscript in the Zurich Library hitherto cited as 56 Paul is nothing else than a copy of Erasmus's printed edition of 1516 made by Zwingli in the following year.

69. *Cf.* 13 above, and see J. R. Harris, *Origin of the Leicester Codex of the New Testament*, 1887. (Scrivener, i. 343, Plate XIII. 40.)

77 and 78. Formerly in the fine library of Matthias Corvinus, King of Hungary (d. 1490).

90. In this manuscript the Gospels are in the order John, Luke, Matthew, Mark.

106. Would be important, but has been lost sight of since the time of Wettstein.

140. Presented to Pope Innocent VII. by the Queen of Cyprus. This manuscript reads διηρθρώθη in Luke i. 64, therein agreeing with the Complutensian.

146–153. In Rome, came from Heidelberg.

154–156. Once the property of Christina, Queen of Sweden.

157. In Rome: its text is said to bear a considerable resemblance to the quotations found in the early Christian writer Marcion. See below, p. 211.

164. The subscription of this manuscript states that it was compared with certain ancient manuscripts in Jerusalem.

205–215 and 217 are in Venice, being part of the donation of Cardinal Bessarion. 209 contains the whole of the New Testament, and was the Cardinal's own copy which he had with him at the Council of Florence in 1439.

218–225 are in Vienna.

226–233 are in the Escorial.

237–259 are at Moscow, with the exception of four at Dresden.

263–320 are in Paris, with the exception of 272, which was removed thence to the British Museum.

274 exhibits the shorter conclusion of Mark's Gospel in the lower margin. (See Plate X.)

405–418 are now in Venice, and, like U, once belonged to the Nani family.

422–430. In Munich.

431. This manuscript is sometimes stated to have perished at Strassburg, in the war of 1870, like 180 Acts. This, however, is incorrect.

452. In Parma, one of the most superb codices.

473. Of the ninth and tenth centuries, a purple manuscript with gold lettering, said to have been written by the Empress Theodora. See under N. above, and note, p. 151.

481, dated 7th May 835, is the earliest manuscript of the Greek New Testament bearing an exact date.

531. Written in a microscopic hand.

604. Written in the twelfth century, now in the British Museum, exhibits 2724 variations from the Textus Receptus, and has besides 270 readings peculiar to itself. It is the only witness we know that supports that peculiar form of the second petition of the Lord's Prayer found in Marcion in the second century, and in Gregory of Nyssa in the fourth, ἐλθέτω τὸ ἅγιον πνεῦμά σου ἐφ' ἡμᾶς καὶ καθαρισάτω ἡμᾶς (Luke xi. 2).[1]

[1] See Blass's *Praefatio* to his edition of Luke, pp. lxix f. (1897), and compare Hastings' *Dictionary of the Bible*, iii. p. 144; Hoskier, above, p. 5; below, p. 211.

743 has the double conclusion in Mark.

1071. See under D, p. 66.

In his *Gospel according to St. Mark*, Swete cites frequently, in addition to those just mentioned and those of the Ferrar Group, 1, 28, 33, 66, 109, 118, 131, 157, 209, 238, 242, 299, 435, 473, 475, 556, 570, 736.

ACTS.

2 and 4. Used by Erasmus.

7–10. Used by Stephen.

15, 83, 173. These, like ℵ in the Old Testament and H_3, were compared with the Codex of Pamphilus—*i.e.* were faithfully copied from such an exemplar.

33. The parent manuscript of Montfortianus. See above, p. 86.

42. Closely related to the Complutensian.

52. Once in the possession of Stunica, the chief editor of the Complutensian. It has now disappeared.

61 has been designated the most important minuscule of the Acts. This, however, is an exaggeration.

137 supplements D E where these are defective.

158. Used by Cardinal Mai to supply the defects of Codex B in the Pauline Epistles.

162. Of the fourteenth or fifteenth century, now in Rome: a bilingual in Latin and Greek: contains the passage 1 John v. 7.

182. Numbered 110 by Hort, who calls it one of the best of the cursives.

220. One of the finest manuscripts of the latter part of the New Testament.

232. An equally superb copy, on which a monk called Andreas bestowed three years' labour.

246. Written in gold letters for Charlotte, Queen of Cyprus (d. 1487).

419. Written in 800 by the Empress Maria, after being divorced by Constantine VI.

PAULINE EPISTLES.

7. Used by Erasmus.

56 and 66 are quite worthless, being simply copies of Erasmus's printed text. (See above under 61[evv]).

67. A valuable manuscript on account of its corrector having evidently made use of an exemplar with a text very closely akin to that of B M.

80 bears a close resemblance to 69[evv].

APOCALYPSE.

1. This was the only manuscript at Erasmus's command for this part of the New Testament. It is defective in the last chapter from verse 16 to the end. For the rest it exhibits a fairly good text. (See p. 3 f.)

36. A text akin to א.

38 has a text resembling that of A C.

68. Resembles A.

95 does so still more. This last has the reputation of being one of the best minuscules of the Apocalypse.

The number of minuscules under each class is, according to Scrivener (Miller), as follows :—

Gospels,	1326
Acts and Catholic Epistles,	422
Pauline Epistles,	497
Apocalypse,	184
	2429

A great many New Testament manuscripts are in England. Some are in the possession of private individuals, like those at Parham Park in Sussex belonging to Lord de la Zouche. In 1870–72 the Baroness Burdett Coutts brought with her from Janina in Epirus over one hundred manuscripts, of which sixteen were of the Gospels, one of them belonging to the Ferrar Group, and as many were Evangeliaria. There are

136 manuscripts of the New Testament in the British Museum.

The number in Great Britain is	438
In the National Library of Paris, . . .	298
In Germany, ...	140
In Italy, ...	644

For the total number of Greek manuscripts arranged according to countries, see Scrivener, i., Indices I., II., pp. 392 ff.

What a vast number of manuscripts are still waiting to be examined is shown by the account given by Dr. von der Goltz. Accompanied by Dr. G. Wobbermin, he made a journey to Athos in the winter of 1897–98, and there in that ancient Monastery, the Laura of St. Athanasius, he found, among about 1800 manuscripts altogether, including Lectionaries, some 250 codices of the New Testament, of which only a very few have been noted by Gregory. And these manuscripts may be of the very utmost importance, as witness the further statement of the same explorer. He was looking through the manuscripts of the Apostolos, to which he and his companion had to give most of their attention, when his eye fell on one written in the tenth or eleventh century, containing the following note before the Pauline Epistles: *γεγράφθαι ἀπὸ ἀντιγράφου παλαιοτάτου, οὗ πεῖραν ἐλάβομεν ὡς ἐπιτετευγμένου ἐκ τῶν εἰς ἡμᾶς ἐλθόντων Ὠριγένους τόμων ἢ ὁμιλιῶν εἰς τὸν ἀπόστολον . . . . ἐν οἷς οὖν παραλλάττει ῥητοῖς πρὸς τὰ νῦν ἀποστολικά, διπλῆν τὴν λεγομένην παρεθήκαμεν ἔξωθεν, ἵνα μὴ νομισθῇ κατὰ προσθήκην ἢ λεῖψιν ἡμαρτῆσθαι τουτὶ τὸ ἀποστολικόν.* And from the subscription at the end of the Pauline Epistles we learn that the manuscript, or, as von der Goltz believes, the exemplar from which it was copied, was written by a monk called Ephraim. See further in von der Goltz, *Eine textkritische Arbeit des zehnten bezw. sechsten Jahrhunderts herausgegeben nach einem Kodex des Athosklosters Lawra. Mit einer Doppeltafel in Lichtdruck.* Leipzig, 1899. (Texte und Untersuchungen, Neue Folge, ii. 4); and compare below, p. 190.

LITERATURE.—On 2^{evv}, see Hoskier, above, p. 5.

On 13, see W. H. Ferrar, *Collation of four important Manuscripts of the Gospels*, edited by T. K. Abbott, Dublin, 1877. J. P. P. Martin, *Quatre manuscrits du N. T., auxquels on peut ajouter un cinquième*, Amiens, 1886. J. R. Harris, *On the Origin of the Ferrar Group*, London, 1894. K. Lake, "Some new members of the Ferrar Group of MSS. of the Gospels," in the *Journal of Theological Studies*, I. i. pp. 117–120. The well-known manuscript of the pre-Lutheran German Bible, the Codex Teplensis, has the words from John viii. 2, "in the morning he came again into the temple," after Luke xxi. 38, an arrangement similar to that which is characteristic of the Ferrar Group, in which John vii. 53–viii. 11 is found after Luke xxi. 38. See S. Berger, *Bull. Crit.*, 1894, p. 390. See *Addenda*, p. xv.

On 561, Codex Algerinae Peckover, see J. R. Harris in the *Journal of the Exegetical Society*, 1886, 79–96.

On 892^{evv}, see Harris, "An Important Manuscript of the N. T." in the *Journal of Biblical Literature*, ix., 1890, 31 ff.

On Minuscules of the Apocalypse, see Bousset, *Textkritische Studien* in *T. und U.*, xi. 4.

C. R. Gregory, "Die Kleinhandschriften des N. Testaments" (*Theologische Studien für B. Weiss.*, Göttingen, 1897, 274–283).

E. J. Goodspeed, "A Twelfth Century Gospel Manuscript" (*Biblical World*, x. 4).

(*c.*) LECTIONARIES.

Till quite recently the Lectionaries, or Books of Church Pericopae, were even more neglected than the minuscules. And yet they are reliable witnesses to the text of the Bible in the provinces to which they belong, on account of their official character and because their locality can be readily distinguished. The slight alterations of the text occurring at the beginning of the pericopae, and consisting usually in the insertion of the subject of the sentence or of an introductory clause, are easily recognisable as such, and deceive no one. It is not always easy to determine the date of such books, because the uncial hand was employed in this sort of manuscript much longer than in the others. Among the oldest, perhaps, **Lectionaries.**

is 135, a palimpsest (of which there is a considerable number among the Lectionaries), assigned by Tischendorf to the seventh century, and 968, written on papyrus and ascribed to the sixth century, which was found in Egypt in the year 1890. When these Lectionaries originated has not yet been clearly made out.[1] Up till the present 980 Evangeliaria—*i.e.* Lessons from the Gospels—have been catalogued, and 268 Apostoli or Praxapostoli—*i.e.* Lessons from the Acts and Epistles. Some of them are magnificently executed; some, alas, have been sadly mutilated. 117, in Florence, is a very beautiful codex; and 162, in Siena, is perhaps "one of the most splendid Service-books in the world." 235 may have been written in part by the Emperor Alexius Comnenus (1081–1118). 286 is the Golden Evangeliarium on Mount Sinai, dating from the ninth to the eleventh century, though the tradition of the monks says that it was written by no less a personage than the Emperor Theodosius (d. 395). Tischendorf's 352–360 are now in the National Library at Paris. 355 is printed in Omont's *Catalogue* (see above, p. 71). 45^evl is a fragment of black parchment inscribed with gold letters preserved at Vienna.[2] 40 is kept in the Escorial along with the reliques of St. Chrysostom, and regarded as his autograph.[3] Bilingual Lectionaries are also found, in Greek and Arabic for example. The arrangement of these Service-books varies with the time and region in which they were composed. Several fragments which were formerly regarded as parts of manuscripts of the

[1] Zahn asserts that traces of a system of Lections are to be found as early as in Irenaeus, and likewise in Codex D. *Einleitung*, ii. 355, on Luke i. 26.

[2] On Luke viii. 15 Tischendorf observes that in 49^evl (a Lectionary of the tenth or eleventh century, now in Moscow, presented to the Monastery of the Mother of God τοῦ βροντοχίου by Nicephorus, Metropolitan of Crete, and Antistes of Lacedæmon, in 1312) the lection εἰς τὰς ἔξω ἐκκλησίας ended with this verse (15) and the words attached to it, "And so saying He cried, He that hath ears to hear, let him hear," and that the additional verses were not read εἰς τὴν μεγάλην ἐκκλησίαν, but vv. 20, 21–25 followed immediately after the words ἐν ὑπομονῇ (v. 15).

[3] On the "Livre d'Évangiles reputé avoir appartenu à S. Jean Chrysostome," *cf.* Ch. Graux, in the *Revue de Philologie*, Avril 1887.

Gospels should perhaps be classed among the Evangeliaria—*e.g.* the solitary leaf of a Bible manuscript Würtemberg is known to possess, and the Tübingen Fragment, formerly classed among the uncials as R of the Gospels, but now enumerated as 481[evl]. An important Syriac Lectionary will fall to be considered under the head of the Versions.

For further details, reference must be made to Scrivener, to *TiGr.*, and now especially to Gregory, *Textkritik*, i. pp. 327–478.

2. VERSIONS.

Our second source of material for the reconstruction of the text of the New Testament is the early Versions. The value of their testimony depends on their age and fidelity. When did the first versions originate? This question reminds us of the Inscription on the Cross, a portion of which is still exhibited in Rome. It was written in Hebrew, Greek, and Latin. But we may get further back still. Palestine at the time of Christ was a country where the most diverse languages and dialects came into contact with each other. In the last century B.C. a transformation had occurred, which might be regarded as a counterpart to the supplanting of Norman French by English, or of Low by High German. Aramaic had already taken the place of the old Hebrew, and after the time of Alexander came the intrusion of Greek, and later still of Latin. Some of the disciples of Jesus bore old Hebrew names, like James (Ἰάκωβος) and John (Ἰωάννης); others had names wholly or partly Aramaic, as Cephas (= Peter), the cognomen of Simon, and Bartholomew; while others, again, had Greek names, as Philip (Φίλιππος) and Andrew (Ἀνδρέας). To the question what language Jesus Himself spoke, the most probable answer is that it was Aramaic with a Galilean colouring. "Thou art a Galilean, thy speech bewrayeth thee," said the Jerusalem girl to Peter. The Galileans, like the Babylonians and the Samaritans, were recognisable by their not distinguishing the gutturals so sharply as the pure Jews did. At the same time, Jesus

Versions.

certainly understood the Hebrew of the Old Testament. But those words of His that have been preserved are Aramaic—*talitha, abba*, and so is *sabaqtani* in Matthew xxvii. 46, and Mark xv. 34, if that is the original form of the text, and not *asabthani*, as a number of manuscripts show.

In what language, however, the first record of the preaching of the Gospel was made, whether it was in the classic Hebrew of the Old Testament or in the Aramaic of the time, is still subject of dispute.[1] But as this question is of moment only for the original sources, and even then for only a certain part of the New Testament—viz. the Gospels—it does not fall to be considered here. We have to do only with those versions that are derived from the Greek, and again with those of them only that are important for the criticism of the text, which are the oldest.

The versions which are of consequence here may be placed under three or four heads.

East. In the East, Antioch, with its semi-Greek, semi-Syrian population, very early became the centre of the new faith, which, indeed, obtained its name there, and must very soon have established itself in Damascus and Mesopotamia. In that region the form of Aramaic now commonly known as Syriac was spoken.

West. In the West, Greek was mostly spoken and understood, even in Rome. Paul consequently, and others as well as he, wrote to Rome in Greek. At the same time, the need must have existed, even in the second century, of having the Gospel in the Latin language in parts of Africa, in the north of

South. Italy, and in the South of Gaul. Quite as early, perhaps, the new faith spread to Egypt, which at that time was a kind of centre of religious culture, and so we find in Egypt not one but several versions in various dialects.

The Gothic version of Ulfilas deserves special mention as being the oldest monument of Christianity among the

[1] *Cf.* Eusebius, *Demons. Evan.*, iii. 7, 15, βάρβαροι καὶ Ἕλληνες τὰς περὶ τοῦ Ἰησοῦ γραφὰς πατρίοις χαρακτῆρσιν καὶ πατρίῳ φωνῇ μετελάμβανον. Zahn, GK. i. 33; Theoph., v. 64; Laud. Const., xvii. 9.

Germanic people, and valuable too in the criticism of the text.

L. J. M. Bebb, *Evidence of the Early Versions and Patristic Quotations*, etc., in *Studia Biblica*, ii., Oxford, 1890. Lagarde, *De Novo Testamento ad Versionum Orientalium fidem edendo.* Berlin (1857); with slight alterations in his *Ges. Abhandlungen*, 1886, pp. 84–119. Reprinted 1896. *Urtext* (see p. 7). Copinger (see p. 6). An earlier bibliographical work is the *Bibliotheca Sacra post . . . . Jacobi Le Long et C. F. Boerneri iteratas curas ordine disposita, emendata, suppleta, continuata ab A. G. Masch.* Halle, 1778–90, 4to. *Pars I., De editionibus textus originalis. Pars II., De versionibus librorum sacrorum* (3 Vols.). R. Simon, *Histoire critique des versions du N. T.*, 1690. *Nouvelles observations sur le texte et les versions du N. T.*, 1695.

(*a*.) SYRIAC VERSIONS.

The Bible used in the Syrian Church has long and deservedly borne the honourable appellation of "the Queen of the Versions." It was first published in 1555 at the expense of the Emperor Ferdinand I. by J. Albert Widmanstadt with the assistance of a Syrian Jacobite called Moses, who came from Mardin as legate to Pope Julius III. The type for this edition was beautifully cut by Caspar Kraft of Ellwangen. All the branches into which the Syrian church was divided in the fifth century have used the same translation of the Scriptures. To this day the Syriac New Testament wants the five so-called Antilegomena—viz. 2 Peter, 2 and 3 John, Jude, and the Apocalypse—a sufficient proof that it goes back to a time and a region in which these books were not yet reckoned in the Canon of the New Testament. In place of these it contained in early times an alleged Third Epistle of Paul to the Corinthians, and an Epistle of the Corinthians to Paul (*cf.* below, p. 142). To distinguish it from other Syriac translations, this Version has been called by Syriac scholars, since the tenth century, the Peshiṭto—*i.e.* the "Simple" or

Peshitto.

perhaps the "Common," which is sometimes pronounced Peshiṭtâ (פְּשִׁיטְתָא) and spelt simply **Peshitto**.

When and where was this translation made? An ancient Syrian tradition asserts that it was done by the Apostle Thaddaeus, who came on a mission to Abgar Uchama—*i.e.* Abgar the Black—King of Edessa, after the death of Jesus, which mission, they say, arose out of a correspondence that Abgar had previously had with Jesus. Another tradition ascribes it to Aggaeus (Aggai), the disciple of Thaddaeus, and it is even attributed to Mark the Evangelist. It is also said that Luke was by birth a Syrian of Antioch, a tradition which may preserve an element of truth.

The earliest notice of a Syriac Gospel is found in Eusebius's *Ecclesiastical History*, iv. 22. That historian mentions that Hegesippus (c. 160–180) quotes certain things from the Gospel of the Hebrews—*i.e.* of the Palestinian (?) Jewish Christians, and from the Syriac (*sc.* Gospel), and particularly from the Hebrew dialect, showing that he himself was a convert from the Hebrews (*ἔκ τε τοῦ καθ' Ἑβραίους εὐαγγελίου καὶ τοῦ Συριακοῦ καὶ ἰδίως ἐκ τῆς Ἑβραΐδος διαλέκτου τινὰ τίθησιν, ἐμφαίνων ἐξ Ἑβραίων ἑαυτὸν πεπιστευκέναι*). This can hardly be understood otherwise than as implying that a Syriac version was already in existence. Whether it contained all the four Gospels or only one of them, or Tatian's Harmony of the Gospels, as Michaelis supposed and as Zahn has recently shown some ground for believing, or whether it contained a primitive Gospel, now perished, cannot be established with certainty.

From the middle of the present century manuscripts of this version have found their way into European libraries in great numbers. Some of these are inestimable. At least ten date from the fifth, and thirty from the sixth century. This is somewhat remarkable when we remember how small a remnant of the Greek manuscripts has been preserved. G. H. Gwilliam is at present engaged on an edition of the Syriac Tetraevangelium for the University of Oxford on the basis of forty manuscripts. The task might seem to be an easy one, considering that these Syriac manuscripts display a far greater unanimity in their text than is found in any written in Greek. The difficulty in their case lies in another direction.

Curetonian. In the year 1842 a Syriac manuscript containing considerable portions of the Gospels was brought from Egypt and deposited in the British Museum. It was afterwards published by Dr. Cureton in 1858 with the title "Remains of a very antient recension of the four Gospels in Syriac hitherto unknown in Europe." Cureton himself thought he had discovered the original of St. Matthew's Gospel in this version. While this was easily shown to be a mistake, the question as to the relationship between the Curetonian Syriac and the Peshitto, whether the two texts are independent of each other, or if not, which is the earlier and which the recension, is not yet decided.

Lewis. It seemed as if the solution of the problem was in sight when fragments of a Syriac palimpsest were discovered on Mount Sinai in February 1892 by Mrs. Lewis and her sister, Mrs. Gibson. These they perceived to be part of a very old manuscript of the Gospels, and Professor Bensly of Cambridge recognised that their text was closely related to that of the Curetonian. (*See Plate V.*) A second expedition was made to Sinai in the spring of 1893, when the fragments were transcribed by Professor Bensly, F. C. Burkitt, and J. R. Harris. As Bensly died three days after their return, the manuscript was published by the others in 1894, with an introduction by Mrs. Lewis. On a third visit to Sinai this lady completed the work of the triumvirate, and also published an English translation of the whole. How, then, is this Sinai-Syriac or Lewis-Syriac, as it is called, related to the Curetonian and to the Peshitto? The problem becomes more complicated still by the introduction of a fourth factor, the most important of them all.

Tatian. From early sources it was known that Tatian,[1] a Syrian and

[1] The date of Tatian's birth is uncertain. Zahn decides for the year 110. He was in the prime of manhood by the year 160. See Hastings, *Bible Dictionary*, ii. p. 697.

a pupil of Justin Martyr, composed a harmony of the Gospels called the **Diatessaron**—*i.e.* τὸ διὰ τεσσάρων εὐαγγέλιον, an expression which may be taken either as referring to the four Gospels or as a musical term equivalent to *harmony* or *chord*. This Harmony was in use among the Syrians till the fifth century. Theodoret, Bishop of Cyrus, informs us that he destroyed 200 copies of it in his semi-Syriac, semi-Greek diocese.[1] About the same time Bishop Rabbulas of Edessa (407–435) instructed his presbyters and deacons to see that all the churches possessed and read a copy of the Distinct Gospel—*i.e.* not mixed or harmonised. The Lewis-Syriac bears this very title, *Gospel of the Distinct* or *Divided*, which is found also as the title of Matthew's Gospel in the Curetonian version. Tatian's Harmony has not yet been discovered in Syriac, but a Latin Harmony of the Gospels derived from it has long been known, and in 1883 a Harmony in Arabic was published by Ciasca which proves to be a translation from the Syriac made by Ibn et-Tabib (d. 1043) or a recension of it. Again, in 1836 the Armenian version of a Syriac Commentary by Ephraem of Edessa (d. 373) was printed, and translated into Latin in 1876. [*Evangelii concordantis expositio facta a S. Ephraemo doctore Syro. In Latinum translata a J. B. Aucher, ed. G. Moesinger.* Venetiis.] Finally Theodor Zahn discovered in the works of the Syriac writer Aphraates, who wrote between 337 and 345, quotations which must be derived from this Harmony of Tatian; and isolated quotations from Tatian are also found in later Syriac authors. And so the materials are provided for deciding the question whether or not Tatian made use of an earlier Syriac version in the preparation of his Harmony, and how T(atian), $Syr^{cu(reton)}$, Syr^{sin} and $Syr^{sch(aaf)}$ [2] are related to each other. The most probable view perhaps is that T is the earliest form in which the Gospel came to Syria, that in Syr^{cu} and Syr^{sin} we have two attempts to exhibit T in the form of a version of the separate Gospels which

[1] See below, p. 213, n. 3.

[2] The Peshitto, so indicated from the principal edition by Schaaf, 1708–9.

were not generally accepted, while Syr^{sch} actually succeeded and passed into general use.

The interest attaching to this question may be learned from the form in which the text of Matthew i. 16 is given in these witnesses. Syr^{sch} agrees exactly with our present Greek text, but Syr^{cu} presents a form which, when translated into Latin, reads, *Joseph cui desponsata virgo Maria genuit Jesum Christum.* Now, the only Greek manuscripts that present a form corresponding to this are four minuscules, 346, 556, 624 and 626, which differ in this respect even from the other members of the Ferrar Group to which they belong. In these four manuscripts the verse reads, Ἰωσὴφ ᾧ μνηστευθῆσα (*sic*) παρθένος Μαριὰμ ἐγέννησεν Ἰησοῦν τὸν λεγόμενον Χριστόν. In the Latin, however, this text is represented by a number of the oldest manuscripts, seven at least, one of which omits the word *virgo*, while two have *peperit* instead of *genuit*, and τὸν λεγόμενον is omitted. But in Syr^{sin} we find: *Joseph: Joseph autem cui desponsata* (*erat*) *virgo Maria genuit Jesum Christum.* The passage is similarly cited in the recently published *Dialogue of Timotheus and Aquila*,[1] along with two other forms, thus:— Ἰακὼβ ἐγέννησεν τὸν Ἰωσὴφ τὸν ἄνδρα Μαρίας, ἐξ ἧς ἐγεννήθη Ἰησοῦς ὁ λεγόμενος Χριστὸς, καὶ Ἰωσὴφ ἐγέννησεν τὸν Ἰησοῦν τὸν λεγόμενον Χριστόν.

The exact wording of Tatian can no longer be determined, but it is evident that of these three forms in which the verse is found, only one or none can be the original. If we had no more than our oldest uncials or the great body of our minuscules to go by, no one could have the slightest suspicion that in our Greek text all is not in perfect order. But here, in an old Syriac fragment from the far East, there suddenly appears a reading which is also found in Latin witnesses from the far West, and which is confirmed by four

[1] *The Dialogues of Athanasius and Zacchaeus, and of Timothy and Aquila.* Edited with Prolegomena and Facsimiles by F. C. Conybeare (Oxford, 1898; *Anecdota Oxoniensia, Classical Series, Part VIII.*). See Notice in the *Lit. Cbl.*, 1899, No. 5, col. 154 f.

solitary Greek manuscripts, written probably in Calabria at the close of the Middle Ages. How are these facts connected, and how do they stand to the other two readings, that of the common Greek text, and that of the Lewis-Syriac? The history of the text of the New Testament presents many such problems.

Philoxenus-Polycarp.

But Syrian scholars were not satisfied with those forms of the New Testament already mentioned. In the year of Alexander 819 (A.D. 508),[1] a new and much more literal version was made from the Greek at the desire of Xenaia (Philoxenus), Bishop of Mabug[2] (488–518), by his rural Bishop Polycarp. Part of this version was published in England by Pococke in 1630—viz. the four Epistles in the Antilegomena not included in the Peshitto, 2 Peter, 2 and 3 John, and Jude. Unfortunately this edition was prepared from a somewhat inaccurate manuscript, which is now in the Bodleian Library. The later European editions of the Syriac New Testament took the text of these Epistles from Pococke's edition, which was also the one used for critical editions of the Greek text. In 1886 Isaac H. Hall published a phototype edition of another manuscript of this version (the Williams MS.), the property of a private gentleman in America, and corrected from it the text of the Syriac New Testament issued by the American Bible Society. The other parts of this version have not yet been found, but the same American scholar thought he discovered the Gospels in a ninth century manuscript belonging to the Syrian Protestant College in Beirut, and deposited in the Library of the Union Theological Seminary in New York.[3] Bernstein thought he made the same discovery in 1853 in a manuscript belonging to the Angelica Library in Florence.

Thomas of Heraclea.

On the basis of four manuscripts sent from Diarbeker in 1736 to Dr. Gloucester Ridley, Joseph White published,

[1] Dates are still reckoned in Syria according to the Greek era, counting from the year 312 B.C.

[2] Hierapolis, now Membidsch on the Euphrates.

[3] I. H. Hall, *Syriac Manuscript Gospels of a Pre-Harklensian Version*, 1883.

between 1778 and 1803,[1] a version which he designated by the name of *Versio Philoxenia*, and which still passes under this title. But this so-called Philoxenian version is not the identical version made for Philoxenus by Polycarp, but a revision undertaken by Thomas of Heraclea (Charkel), in the year 616–7. This revision was made at Alexandria with the object of making the Syriac text represent the Greek as closely as possible, even to the order of the words and the insertion of the article. The critical symbols used by Homeric commentators, the asterisk and the obelus, as well as numerous marginal notes, were employed to indicate the various readings found in the manuscripts. And it is very remarkable to observe that there were manuscripts in Alexandria at the beginning of the seventh century which were regarded by Thomas of Harkel as particularly well authenticated, but which deviate in a marked degree from the bulk of our present manuscripts, and which, especially in the Acts, agree almost entirely with Codex D, which occupies so singular a position among Greek manuscripts. A new edition of the Syriac text is necessary before any further use can be made of it in the criticism of the New Testament. Mr. Deane set himself to this task, going on the basis of sixteen manuscripts in England alone, but unfortunately he was unable to bring it to a conclusion.

The Apocalypse was first edited in 1627 by de Dieu at Leyden, from a manuscript that had been in the possession of Scaliger. It is found in a few other manuscripts, in one, *e.g.*, that was transcribed about this same time for Archbishop Ussher from a Maronite manuscript at Kenobin on Mount Lebanon. It is not found in the Syriac New Testament, but the later editions insert it from de Dieu. In Apoc. viii. 13, instead of "an eagle in the midst of heaven" (ἐν μεσουρανήματι), the Syriac translator took it as "in the

Apocalypse.

[1] The Gospels appeared in 1778, the Acts and Catholic Epistles in 1799, and the Pauline Epistles in 1803.

midst with a bloody tail" (μεσος, ουρα, αιμα). Another Syriac version, in which this error is avoided, was discovered in 1892 by J. Gwynn in a Codex belonging to Lord Crawford, and published by him as the first book printed in Syriac at the Dublin University Press. Still more interesting is it to know that in a manuscript, once the property of Julius Mohl, and now in Cambridge, both the so-called Epistles of Clement are found after the Catholic Epistles. This manuscript, part of which was published by Bensly in 1889 (see above, p. 79), contains a note at the end to the effect that it was derived, so far as the Pauline Epistles are concerned, from the copy of Pamphilus.[1]

About the same time and in the same region, Paul of Tella translated one of the best Greek manuscripts of the Old Testament into Syriac almost as literally as Thomas of Harkel, thereby doing immense service in the construction of the Syriac Hexapla, a work of inestimable value for the textual criticism of the Old Testament.

Evangeliarium Hierosolymitanum.

Mention may be made here of another Syriac version of the New Testament, the so-called *Jerusalem* or *Palestinian Syriac* (Syr^{hr} or Syr^{hier}). This version, hitherto known almost solely from an Evangeliarium in the Vatican of the year 1030, was edited by Count Miniscalchi Erizzo at Verona in 1861–4, and an excellent edition was published in 1892 in *Bibliothecae Syriacae a Paulo de Lagarde collectae quae ad philologiam sacram pertinent.* And now not only have two fresh manuscripts of this Evangeliarium been discovered on Mount Sinai by J. R. Harris and Mrs. Lewis, and edited by Mrs. Lewis and Mrs. Gibson, but fragments of the Acts and

[1] In Tischendorf's critical apparatus these fragments are indicated as Syr$^{\text{p(osterior)}}$ or as Syr$^{\text{whit(e)}}$. It would be better to use the symbol Syr$^{\text{po(lycarp)}}$ for the first version of 508 made by Polycarp for Philoxenus, and Syr$^{\text{tho(mas)}}$ for Thomas of Harkel's recension of 616. Gebhardt's notation is as follows :—Syr^{a} is the Curetonian; Syr^{b} is the Peshitto; Syr^{c} is the Harklean, of which again Syr^{ct} is the text, Syr^{cm} the margin, Syr$^{\text{c*}}$ sub asterisco; Syr^{d} is the Jerusalem Syriac; while Syr^{bodl} is the text of 2 Peter, 2 and 3 John, and Jude. Zahn proposes to indicate the Philoxenian (Tischendorf's Syr^{bodl}) by Syr^{2}, and the Harklean by Syr^{3}; for the Gospels he would employ Syr^{c}, Syr^{s}, Syr^{h}; Syr^{1}, therefore, is the Peshitto.

Pauline Epistles have also been found and published, as well as portions of the Old Testament and other Church literature.[1] The dialect in which these fragments are written is quite different from ordinary Syriac, and may, perhaps, bear a close resemblance to that in which Jesus spoke to His disciples. At what time and in what region this entire literature took its rise is not yet determined with certainty. The Greek text on which the Evangeliarium is based has many peculiarities. In Matthew xxvii. 17, *e.g.*, the robber is called Jesus Barabbas, or, rather, Jesus Barrabbas, a fact known to Origen, but now recorded only in a few Greek minuscules by the first or second hand.

What used to be called the Versio Karkaphensis or Montana is not really a version, but merely the Massoretic work of a monastery school intended to preserve the proper spelling and pronunciation of the text of the Bible.

No other branch of the Church has taken such pains as the Syrian, faithfully to transmit and to circulate the Gospel. From the mountains of Lebanon and Kurdistan, from the plains of Mesopotamia and the coast of Malabar, and even from distant China there have come into the libraries of Europe Syriac manuscripts of the utmost value for the textual criticism of the New Testament.

LITERATURE on the Syriac Versions:—

J. G. Christian Adler, *Novi Testamenti Versiones Syriacae, Simplex, Philoxeniana, et Hierosolymitana. Denuo examinatae et ad fidem codicum manu scriptorum . . . . novis observationibus atque tabulis aere incisis illustratae.* Hafniae, pp. viii. 206. *With eight Plates.* 1789, 4to. For the complete list of editions up to 1888, see my *Litteratura Syriaca* (Syr. Gr., 2nd edition, pp. 20 ff.). Appendix thereto in *Urt.*, 227 ff.; R. Duval, *La Littérature Syriaque.* Paris, 1899, pp. 42–67; *TiGr.*, 813–822; Scrivener, fourth edition, ii. 6–40, with the help of Gwilliam and Deane; *The Printed Editions of the Syriac New Testament*, in the *Church Quarterly Review*, 1888,

[1] Land, in the *Anecdota Syriaca*, iv., 1875; Harris, *Biblical Fragments from Mount Sinai*, 1890; Gwilliam, in the *Anecdota Oxoniensia*, Semitic Series, i. 5, 1893; ix. 1896; Lewis-Nestle-Gibson, *Studia Sinaitica*, vi.

July, 257–297; G. H. Gwilliam, in the *Studia Biblica et Ecclesiastica* (Oxford), ii. 1890, iii. 1891; F. C. Conybeare, *The growth of the Peshitta Version of the New Testament*, in the *American Journal of Theology*, 1897, iv. 883–912; Burkitt, in the *Journal of Theological Studies*, i. (July 1900), 569 ff., referring to his forthcoming edition of the Evangelion da-Mepharreshe, says that he has had to go over the Gospel quotations of St. Ephraem, and closes by saying, "I confess that I am unconvinced that what we call the New Testament Peshitta was in existence in St. Ephraem's day, and I believe that we owe both its production and victorious reception to the organizing energy of the Great Rabbula, Bishop of Edessa from 411 to 435 A.D."

1. Till Gwilliam's edition of the Gospels appears, which has been promised since 1891, the best edition will be the Editio Princeps of Widmanstadt, 1555; then that of Leusden and Schaaf, *Novum Domini nostri Jesu Christi Testamentum Syriacum cum versione latina cura et studio J. Leusden et C. Schaaf editum. Ad omnes editiones diligenter recensitum et variis lectionibus magno labore collectis adornatum.* Lugd. Bat., 1709, 4to. *Acc. Schaaf, Lexicon Syriacum concordantiale.* The text reprinted by Jones at Oxford, 1805; the editions of the London Bible Society, 1816 and 1826, and better still, the Syriac and New-Syriac editions of the American Mission in Urmia, 1846, and of the American Bible Society of New York, 1868, 1874, and frequently (with the Nestorian vocalisation). An edition is promised from the Jesuit Press at Beyruth, *Nouveau Testament Syriaque en petits caractères, d'après plusieurs manuscrits anciens, éd. par le P. L. Cheikho.*

The New Testament part of the Peshitto has been very much neglected in the present century. On the O.T., investigations, chiefly in the form of dissertations on most of the books, have been published, establishing the relation of the Syriac to the Massoretic text, the Septuagint, and the Targum. But almost nothing of this sort has been done for the N.T., at least in Germany, since the time of Michaelis and Löhlein. The question has never once been taken up how many translators' hands can be distinguished in the N.T.

J. D. Michaelis, *Curae in Versionem Syriacam Act. Apost. cum consectariis criticis de indole, cognationibus et usu versionis Syriacae tabularum Novi Foederis.* Göttingen, 1755. C. L. E. Löhlein, *Syrus Epistolae ad Ephesios interpres in causa critica denuo examinatus*, Erlangen, 1835.

2. Cureton's *Remains* (1858) is now out of print. Till Burkitt's

new edition appears its place will be taken by Baethgen's Retranslation into Greek (*Evangelienfragmente. Der griechische Text des Curetonschen Syrers wiederhergestellt*, Leipzig, 1885); and more especially by Albert Bonus's *Collatio codicis Lewisiani rescripti evangeliorum Syriacorum cum codice Curetoniano*, Oxford, 1896; and by Carl Holzhey's *Der neuentdeckte Codex Sinaiticus untersucht. Mit einem vollständigen Verzeichnis der Varianten des Codex Sinaiticus und Codex Curetonianus*, Munich, 1896. See A. Bonus, *The Sinaitic Palimpsest and the Curetonian Syriac*, in the *Expository Times*, May 1895, p. 380 ff. The publications of T. R. Crowfoot, *Fragmenta Evangelica, Pars I., II.*, 1870, 1872, and *Observations on the Collations in Greek of Cureton's Syriac Fragments*, 1872, contain useful material, but there are a good many mistakes.

3. The Editio Princeps of the Lewis text is, of course, that of Bensly, Harris, and Burkitt, *The Four Gospels in Syriac, transcribed from the Sinaitic Palimpsest. . . . .* Cambridge, 1894. To this must be added its complement by Mrs. Lewis, *Some Pages of the Four Gospels retranscribed* (with or without an English translation), London, 1896; further, *Last Gleanings from the Sinai Palimpsest*, *Expositor*, Aug. 1897, pp. 111–119; also, *An Omission from the Text of the Sinai Palimpsest*, *Expositor*, Dec. 1897, p. 472. On the discovery of the manuscript, see Mrs. Gibson, *How the Codex was found*, ... Cambridge, 1893, and Mrs. Lewis, *In the shadow of Sinai*, ... Cambridge, 1898; also Mrs. Bensly, *Our Journey to Sinai*, ... *With a chapter on the Sinai Palimpsest.* London, 1896. See also Mrs. Lewis, *The Earlier Home of the Sinaitic Palimpsest*, *Expositor*, June 1900, pp. 415–421. The text has been translated into German by Adalbert Merx, who has added a brief but valuable critical discussion. Berlin (Reimer), 1897. The second part, comprising the commentary, has not yet appeared. See also Gwilliam's notice of the editio princeps in the *Expository Times*, Jan. 1895, p. 157 ff.

4. On Tatian, the latest and best is Zahn, *Evangelienharmonie*, PRE[3], v. (1898), 653 ff.; also his *Forschungen*, i. (1881), *Tatian's Diatessaron*, ii. p. 286 ff. (1883), iv. (1891); *Gesch. des Kanons*, i. 387–414, ii. 530–556. J. H. Hill, *The earliest Life of Christ ever compiled from the Four Gospels, being the Diatessaron of Tatian* (c. A.D. 160), *literally translated from the Arabic Version.* Edinburgh, 1893. J. R. Harris, *The Diatessaron of Tatian, a Preliminary Study*. Cambridge, 1890. *The Diatessaron, a Reply*, in the *Con-*

temporary Review, Aug. 1895, in answer to W. R. Cassels, in the *Nineteenth Century*, April 1895; also by the same writer, *Fragments of the Commentary of Ephrem Syrus upon the Diatessaron.* London, 1895. . . . . J. H. Hill, *A Dissertation on the Gospel Commentary of S. Ephrem the Syrian* . . . . Edinburgh, 1896. J. A. Robinson, *Tatian's Diatessaron and a Dutch Harmony*, in the *Academy*, 24th March 1894. Hope W. Hogg, *The Diatessaron of Tatian, with introduction and translation*, in the *Ante-Nicene Library. Additional Volume* . . . . edited by Allan Menzies. Edinburgh, 1897, pp. 33–138. W. Elliott, *Tatian's Diatessaron and the Modern Critics.* Plymouth, 1888. I. H. Hall, *A Pair of Citations from the Diatessaron*, in the *Journal of Biblical Literature*, x. 2 (1891), 153–155. J. Goussen, *Pauca Fragmenta genuina Diatessaroniana*, appended to the *Apocalypsis S. Joannis Versio Sahidica*, 1895. See also Bäumer in the *Literarischer Handweiser*, 1890, 153–169; the article *Tatian* in the *Encyclopædia Britannica*, and Hastings' *Bible Dictionary*, vol. ii. p. 697 f.

5. On the later Syriac versions, see *Urt.*, 228, 236 f.; Gwynn, *The older Syriac Version of the four Minor Catholic Epistles*, *Hermathena*, No. xvi. (vol. vii.), 1890, 281–314. Merx, *Die in der Peschito fehlenden Briefe des Neuen Testamentes in arabischer der Philoxeniana entstammender Uebersetzung* . . . . *Zeitschrift für Assyriologie*, xii. 240 ff., 348 ff., xiii. 1–28. Bensly, *The Harklean Version of the Epistle to the Hebrews*, ... Cambridge, 1889. In this edition will be found the subscription mentioned above, connecting the manuscript with that of Pamphilus. See *Addenda*, p. xv.

6. On the Jerusalem Evangeliarium, see *Urt.*, 228, 237. Zahn, *Forschungen*, i. 329 ff. Lagarde, *Mitteilungen*, i. 111, iv. 328, 340. A. de Lagarde, *Erinnerungen an P. de Lagarde*, p. 112 ff. Lewis and Gibson, *The Palestinian Syriac Lectionary of the Gospels re-edited from two Sinai MSS. and from P. de Lagarde's edition of the Evangeliarium Hierosolymitanum*, London, 1899. The Lectionary published in the *Studia Sinaitica*, vi., contains, in the N.T., passages from Acts, Romans, 1 and 2 Cor., Gal., Ephes., Philip., Col., 1 Thess., 1 and 2 Tim., Heb., James. See notice in the *Expository Times*, Jan. 1898, p. 190 ff. *The Liturgy of the Nile*, published by G. Margoliouth, 1896 (*Journal of the Royal Asiatic Society*, Oct. 1896, 677–731, and also published separately), contains Acts xvi. 16–34. See also Woods, *The New Syriac Fragments* in the *Expository Times*, Nov. 1893.

(*b.*) LATIN VERSIONS.

Jerome.

The name most closely associated with the Latin Versions of the New Testament is that of **Jerome** (Hieronymus). This scholar was born at Stridon, on the borders of Dalmatia,[1] about the year 345, and educated at Rome. After leading for some time a hermit life in Palestine, Jerome returned to Rome, and it was during his residence there, in the year 382, that he was urged by Pope Damasus to undertake a revision of the Latin version of the New Testament then in use. This he did, and in 383 sent the Pope, who died in the following year, the first instalment of the work, the Four Gospels, accompanied with a letter beginning thus :—"Thou compellest me to make a new work out of an old ; after so many copies of the Scriptures have been dispersed throughout the whole world, I am now to occupy the seat of the arbiter, as it were, and seeing they disagree, to decide which of them accords with the truth of the Greek ; a pious task, verily, yet a perilous presumption, to pass judgment on others and oneself to be judged by all." He anticipates that everyone, no matter who, learned or ignorant, that takes up a Bible and finds a discrepancy between it and the usual text will straightway condemn him as an impious falsifier who presumed to add to or alter or correct the ancient Scriptures. But he comforts himself with the reflection that it is the High Pontiff himself that has laid this task upon him, and that the testimony of his jealous opponents themselves proves that discrepancies are an indication of error (verum non esse quod variat, etiam maledicorum testimonio comprobatur) ; for if they tell us we are to rest our faith on the Latin exemplars, they must first say which, because there are almost as many versions as manuscripts (tot enim sunt exemplaria paene quot codices) ; if it is to be the majority of these, why not rather go back to

[1] See F. Bulié, *Wo lag Stridon, die Heimat des h. Hieronymus?* in the *Festschrift für Otto Benndorf.* Vienna, 1898. Also *La patrie de S. Jerome* in *Analecta Bollandiana*, xviii. 3.

the Greek original which has been badly rendered by incompetent translators (a vitiosis interpretibus male edita), made worse instead of better by the presumption of unskilful correctors (a praesumptoribus imperitis emendata perversius), and added to or altered by sleepy scribes (a librariis dormitantibus aut addita sunt aut mutata). In a letter to his learned friend Marcella, written in the year 384, he gives instances of what he complains of, citing, *e.g.*, Romans xii. 11, where *tempori servientes* had hitherto been read instead of *domino servientes* (καιρῷ instead of κυρίῳ), and 1 Tim. v. 19, "against an elder receive not an accusation," where the qualifying clause, "except before two or three witnesses," was dropped, and also 1 Tim. i. 15, iii. 1, where *humanus sermo* was given in place of *fidelis.* In all three instances, our most recent critical editions decide in favour of Jerome, against the Old Latin Version. In the last instance cited, we know of only one Latin-Greek manuscript that has ἀνθρώπινος instead of πιστός, and that only in c. iii. 1, viz. D*. Jerome accordingly issued an improved version of the New Testament, beginning with the Gospels. For this purpose he made a careful comparison of old Greek manuscripts (codicum Graecorum emendata conlatione sed veterum). In his version he was also careful only to make an alteration when a real change of meaning was necessary, retaining in all other cases the familiar Latin wording. The Gospels were in the order which has been the prevailing one since his day—Matthew, Mark, Luke, John.

Augustine.

We learn from the great Church Teacher AUGUSTINE, who lived in Africa about the same time (354–430), that there was an endless variety and multitude of translators (latinorum interpretum infinita varietas, interpretum numerositas). He tells us that while it was possible to count the number of those who had translated the Bible—*i.e.* the Old Testament—from Hebrew into Greek, the Latin translators were innumerable; that in the early age of the Christian faith (primis fidei temporibus), no sooner did anyone gain possession of a Greek

Codex, and believe himself to have any knowledge of both languages, than he made bold to translate it (ausus est interpretari). The advice he himself gives is to prefer the *Italic* version to the others, as being the most faithful and intelligible (in ipsis autem interpretationibus Itala praeferatur; nam est verborum tenacior cum perspicuitate sententiae. *De Doctrina Christiana*, ii. 14, 15). On the ground of this passage, the pre-Jeromic versions have been comprehended under the title of the **Itala**, as distinguished from Jerome's own work, which is called the **Vulgate**, seeing that it became the prevailing text in the Church of the Middle Ages. By the Itala, Augustine himself, however, must have referred to a particular version, and, according to the usage of that time, the word cannot mean anything else than a version originating in or prevalent in Italy—*i.e.* the North of Italy, what is called Lombardy. It is not difficult to understand how it came to pass that Augustine used such a version in Africa, seeing that he was a pupil of Ambrose, Bishop of Milan. In recent times Burkitt has revived the opinion that by Itala Augustine means neither more nor less than Jerome's Revision of the Gospels. He demonstrates that Augustine's *De Consensu*, written about the year 400, is based on Jerome's revised text. In this, Zahn[1] agrees with him on grounds that admit of no question so far as this point is concerned. But Wordsworth-White[2] will not admit the inference that Augustine must have meant this Revision when he spoke of Itala in the year 397, seeing that in his letter to Jerome,[3] written in 403, he thanks God for the interpretation of the Gospel, "quasi de opere recenter cognito," while in his earlier letters to Jerome[4] he makes no mention of it: "quod mirandum esset si in opere ante sex annos publici iuris facto eam collaudasset."[5]

Itala.

Vulgate.

[1] *Einleitung*, ii. 195.

[2] *Epilogus ad Evangelia*, p. 656.

[3] No. 71; 164 in Jerome's letters.

[4] No. 56 (A.D. 394), 67 (397), 101 (402).

[5] Burkitt's view was expressed more than three-quarters of a century ago by C. A. Breyther, in a dissertation entitled, *De vi quam antiquissimae versiones*

(1.) LATIN VERSIONS BEFORE JEROME.

Old Latin Texts.

Where, when, and by whom was the New Testament, or at least were parts of it, first translated into Latin? From the passage in Augustine quoted above, we learn that it was done by all and sundry in the very earliest times of the Christian faith. Rome used to be regarded as the place where the Latin versions took their rise. But it was observed that Greek was very commonly employed as the written language at Rome, especially among Christians. The first Bishops of Rome have pure Greek names, and even the first representative of the Roman Church with a Latin name, the Clement that wrote the Epistle to the Corinthians about the year 95, even he wrote in Greek. Moreover, when the relics of the Old Latin Bibles began to be examined, it was observed that their language, both in vocabulary and grammar, entirely agreed with that found in African writers of that age, and in some things agreed with these alone. It is, of course, a fact that the majority of the writers of that age known to us are African. Till quite recently, therefore, it was held to be tolerably well made out that the birthplace of the Latin Bible is to be found in Africa. It was regarded by many as equally certain, that in spite of the statements of Jerome and Augustine, and in spite too of the various forms in which the Old Latin Bible now exists, these all proceed from a common origin, or at most from two sources, so that it was not quite correct to speak of a "multitude of translators" in the very earliest times. The settlement of this question is rendered more difficult by the fact that, while the extant copies of the pre-Jeromic Bible are undoubtedly very early, they are few in number, and for the most part mutilated. The reason of this is not far to seek. For, as time went on and Jerome's new version came to be more and more exclusively used, manuscripts of the earlier version lost their

African Latin.

quae extant latinae in crisin evangeliorum IV. habent (Merseburg, 1824). See v. Dobschütz, *ThLz.*, 1897, 135.

value, and were the more frequently used for palimpsests and book covers. One has also to take into account how liable the text of both was to be corrupted, either by the copyist of an Old Latin Bible inserting in the margin, or even interpolating in the text, various passages from Jerome's translation that seemed to him to be a decided improvement, or conversely, by the scribe who should have written the new rendering involuntarily permitting familiar expressions to creep in from the old. It is estimated that we have about 8000 manuscripts of Jerome's recension, of which 2228 have been catalogued by Gregory. Samuel Berger, the most thorough investigator in this field, examined 800 manuscripts in Paris alone. But on the other hand, only 38 manuscripts of the Old Latin Version of the New Testament are known to exist. The credit of collecting the relics of these pre-Jeromic versions of the Old and New Testament, so far as they were accessible at that time, belongs to Peter Sabatier the Maurist (Rheims, 1743, 3 vols. folio).

In critical editions of the New Testament the manuscripts of the pre-Jeromic versions are indicated by the small letters of the Roman alphabet. They are the following:—

1. Gospels.

a. Vercellensis: according to a tradition recorded in a document of the eighth century this manuscript was written by Eusebius, Bishop of Vercelli, who died in the year 370 or 371. Recent scholars, however, date it somewhat later. It is written on purple with silver letters. The order of the Gospels is that found in most of these Old Latin MSS.—viz. Matthew, John, Luke, Mark. The manuscript is defective in several places.

The codex was edited by Irico in 1748, and by Bianchini in 1749 along with some of the others in his Evangeliarium Quadruplex. This latter edition was reprinted, with some inaccuracies, in Migne's *Patrologia Latina*, vol. xii. The manuscript was again edited by

Belsheim; *Codex Vercellensis. Quatuor Evangelia ante Hieronymum latine translata ex reliquiis Codicis Vercellensis, saeculo ut videtur quarto scripti, et ex Editione Iriciana principe denuo ededit* (sic) *Jo. Belsheim.* Christiania, 1894.

b. Veronensis: of the fourth or fifth century, also written with silver on purple. In this Codex, John vii. 44–viii. 12 has been erased. The manuscript is defective.

Edited by Bianchini (see above). A Spagnolo, *L'Evangeliario Purpureo Veronese.* Nota (Torino, 1899. Estratta dagli Atti dell' Accademia Reale delle Scienze di Torino).

c. Colbertinus: in Paris, written in the twelfth century, but still containing the Old Latin text in the Gospels, though exhibiting Jerome's version in other parts.

Edited by Sabatier, and again by Belsheim; *Codex Colbertinus Parisiensis. Quatuor Evangelia ante Hieronymum latinè translata post editionem Petri Sabatier cum ipso codice collatam denuo edidit Jo. Belsheim.* Christiania, 1888.

d. The Latin part of Codex D; see p. 64 ff.

e. Palatinus: of the fourth or fifth century, written like a b f i j on purple with gold and silver letters: now in Vienna, with one leaf in Dublin.

Two other fragments were published in 1893 by Hugo Linke from a transcript made for Bianchini in 1762. The entire codex was edited by Belsheim, Christiania, 1896. See von Dobschütz in the *LCbl.*, 1896, 28.

f. Brixianus, of the sixth century, in Brescia. In their new edition of the Vulgate, Wordsworth and White printed the text of this manuscript underneath that of Jerome for comparison's sake as probably containing the text most nearly resembling that on which Jerome based his recension. But see Burkitt's Note in the *Journal of Theological Studies*, I. i. (Oct. 1899), 129–134, and the note to p. 139 in *Addenda.*

ff_1. Corbeiensis I., contains the Gospel according to Matthew alone. The manuscript formerly belonged to the Monastery of Corbey, near Amiens, and with others was transferred to St. Petersburg during the French Revolution.

ff_2. Corbeiensis II., written in the sixth century and now in Paris: contains the Gospels with several lacunæ.

On Belsheim's editions of ff_1 and ff_2 (1881 and 1887), see E. Ranke in the *ThLz.*, 1887, col. 566, and S. Berger, *Bull. Crit.*, 1891, 302 f.

g_1. Sangermanensis I., of the ninth century, in Paris, exhibits a mixed text. The manuscript was used by Stephen for his Latin Bible of 1538.

g_2. Sangermanensis II., written in an Irish hand of the tenth century, has a mixed text: in Paris (Lat. 13069).

h. Claromontanus, of the fourth or fifth century, now in the Vatican: has the Old Latin text in Matthew only. The manuscript is defective at the beginning down to Matt. iii. 15 and also from Matt. xiv. 33–xviii. 12.

Edited by Mai in his *Scriptorum Veterum Nova Collectio*, iii. 257–288, and by Belsheim, Christiania, 1892.

i. Vindobonensis, of the seventh century, contains fragments of Luke and Mark written on purple with silver and gold.

Edited by Belsheim, *Codex Vindobonensis membranaceus purpureus . . . . antiquissimae evangeliorum Lucae et Marci translationis Latinae fragmenta edidit Jo. Belsheim.* Lipsiae, 1885 (cum tabula).

j (z in *TiGr.*). Saretianus or Sarzannensis, of the fifth century, contains 292 verses from John written on purple. The manuscript was discovered in 1872 in the Church of Sarezzano, near Tortona, and is not yet completely edited.

Compare G. Amelli, *Un antichissimo codice biblico Latino purpureo conservato nella chiesa di Sarezzano presso Tortona.* Milan, 1872.

k. Bobiensis, of the fifth century, is perhaps the most important of the Old Latin manuscripts, but unfortunately contains only fragments of Matthew and Mark. It is said to have belonged to St. Columban, the founder of the monastery of Bobbio, who died in the year 615. It is now preserved at

Turin. See Burkitt on Mark xv. 34 in Codex Bobiensis in the *Journal of Theological Studies*, i. 2 (Jan. 1900), p. 278 f.

l. Rehdigeranus, in Breslau, purchased in Venice by Thomas von Rehdiger in 1569. Matthew i. 1–ii. 15 and a good deal of John wanting.

Edited by H. Fr. Haase, Breslau, 1865, 1866: *Evangeliorum quattuor vetus latina interpretatio ex codice Rehdigerano nunc primum edita.*

m. Does not represent any particular manuscript and should properly be omitted here. It indicates the *Liber de divinis scripturis sive Speculum*, a work mistakenly ascribed to Augustine, consisting of a collection of proof-passages (testimonia) from the Old and New Testaments. All the books of the latter are made use of except Philemon, Hebrews, and 3 John, but the Epistle to the Laodicæans is cited among the number.

Fragmenta Novi Testamenti in translatione latina antehieronymiana ex libro qui vocatur Speculum eruit et ordine librorum Novi Testamenti exposuit J. Belsheim. Christiania, 1899.

n o p. Are fragments at St. Gall: published in the Old Latin Biblical Texts, see below, p. 131 f.

n. Written in the fifth or sixth century, has probably been in the Library at St. Gall since its foundation. It contains portions of Matthew and Mark, with John xix. 13–42.

o. Written in the seventh century, possibly to take the place of the last leaf of n, which is wanting, contains Mark xvi. 14–20.

p. Two leaves of an Irish missal written in the seventh or eighth century.

a_2. Is part of the same manuscript as n. It consists of a leaf containing Luke xi. 11–29 and xiii. 16–34. It was found in the Episcopal archives at Chur, and is preserved in the Rhætisches Museum there.

q. Monacensis, written in the sixth or seventh century, came originally from Freising. Published in the Old Latin Biblical Texts.

r or r_1 and r_2. Usserianus I. and II., are both in Dublin. The former is written in an Irish hand of the seventh century, and has several lacunæ. r_2 belongs to the ninth or tenth century and has an Old Latin text in Matthew resembling that of r_1. It shows affinity with Jerome's text in Mark, Luke, and John, of which, however, only five leaves remain.

Edited by T. K. Abbott, *Evangeliorum versio antehieronymiana ex codice Usseriano (Dublinensi), adjecta collatione codicis Usseriani alterius. Accedit versio Vulgata. . . .* Dublin, 1884, 2 Parts.

s. Four leaves with portions of Luke, written in the sixth century. The fragments came originally from Bobbio, and are now in the Ambrosian Library at Milan. Published in the Old Latin Biblical Texts.

t. A palimpsest very difficult to decipher, containing portions of the first three chapters of Mark, written in the fifth century, and now at Berne. Published in the Old Latin Biblical Texts.

v. Bound in the cover of a volume at Vienna entitled, *Pactus Legis Ripuariæ*: exhibits John xix. 27–xx. 11. Published in the Old Latin Biblical Texts.

aur. Aureus or Holmiensis, written in the seventh or eighth century, exhibits the Gospels entire, with the exception of Luke xxi. 8–30. An inscription in old English states that the manuscript was purchased from the heathen (the Danes?) by Alfred the Alderman for Christ Church, Canterbury, when Alfred was King and Ethelred Archbishop (871–889). It was afterwards in Madrid, and is now at Stockholm. It is really a Vulgate text with an admixture of Old Latin readings. Published by Belsheim in 1878.

δ. Is the interlinear Latin version of Δ (see p. 72), and is interesting on account of its alternative readings given in almost every verse—*e.g.* *uxorem vel conjugem* for γυναῖκα, Matt. i. 20. Compare Harris, *The Codex Sangallensis*, Cambridge, 1891.

On the Prolegomena found in many Old Latin and Vulgate manuscripts of the Gospels, see Peter Corssen, *Monarchianische Prologe zu den vier Evangelien.* Leipzig, 1896 (*TU.*, xv. 1). This has been supplemented by von Dobschütz's *Prolog zur Apostelgeschichte.* See also Jülicher in the *GGA.*, 1896, xi. 841–851. J. S. in the *Revue Critique*, 1897, vii. 135 f. H. Holtzmann in the *Th. Lz.*, 1897, xii. col. 231 ff. A. Hilgenfeld, *Altchristliche Prolegomena zu den Evangelien* in the *ZfwTh.*, 1897, iii. 432–444.

2. ACTS.

d, m } As for the Gospels.

e. The Latin text of E. See above, p. 75.

g. Gigas Holmiensis, the immense manuscript of the entire Latin Bible preserved at Stockholm. The text is Old Latin only in the Acts and Apocalypse, the rest of the New Testament exhibiting Jerome's version. The manuscript was brought to Sweden from Prague as a prize of war in 1648, along with the Codex Argenteus.

The Acts and Apocalypse were edited by Belsheim, Christiania, 1879. On this see O. v. Gebhardt in the *ThLz.*, 1880, col. 185. A new collation of this manuscript was made for W.-W. by H. Karlsson in 1891.

g_2. In Milan, is part of a Lectionary written in the tenth or eleventh century, and contains the pericope for St. Stephen's day, Acts vi. 8–vii. 2, vii. 51–viii. 4.

Published by Ceriani in his *Monumenta Sacra et Profana*, i. 2, pp. 127, 128. Milan, 1866.

h. Floriacensis, a palimpsest formerly belonging to the Abbey of Fleury on the Loire, and now in Paris, written probably in the seventh century. It contains fragments of the Apocalypse, Acts, 1 and 2 Peter, and 1 John, in this order. (Tischendorf's reg.: Blass's f.)

The latest and best edition is that of S. Berger: *Le Palimpseste de Fleury.* Paris, 1889.

p_2, written in the thirteenth century, exhibits a text with an admixture of Old Latin readings in the Acts only. The manuscript came originally from Perpignan, and is now in Paris, No. 321. It was used by Blass.

Published by Berger: *Un ancien texte latin des Actes des Apôtres*, etc. Paris, 1895. See von Dobschütz in the *ThLz.*, 1896, 4; Haussleiter in the *Th. Lbl.*, no. 9; Schmiedel in the *L. Cbl.*, no. 33; E. Beurlier, *Bull. Crit.*, 1896, 32, p. 623.

s_2. Bobiensis, a palimpsest of the fifth or sixth century at Vienna, containing fragments of Acts xxiii., xxv.–xxviii., and of James and 1 Peter.

x_1. Written in the seventh or eighth century, contains the Acts with the exception of xiv. 26–xv. 32. The manuscript is preserved at Oxford and is not completely published.

w. Is the symbol given by Blass to a paper manuscript of the New Testament written, it seems, in Bohemia in the fifteenth century, and now at Wernigerode. In the main it exhibits Jerome's text even to a greater extent than p, but preserves elements of the Old Latin, particularly in the latter half of the Acts. The mixture is similar to that observed in the Provençal New Testament,[1] which is derived from a Latin manuscript of this nature, and to that in the pre-Lutheran German Bible. (See *Urt.*, p. 127 f.)

On Acts, see especially P. Corssen, *Der Cyprianische Text der Acta Apostolorum.* Berlin, 1892.

3. CATHOLIC EPISTLES.

h, m, s } As above.

ff. Corbeiensis, at St. Petersburg, of the tenth century, contains the Epistle of James.

Edited by Belsheim in the *Theologisk Tidsskrift for den evangelisk-lutherske Kirke i Norge* (N.S. Vol. ix. Part 2); also by J. Wordsworth, *The Corbey St. James*, etc., in *Studia Biblica*, i. pp. 113–150. Oxford, 1885.

[1] Photolithographed by Clédat from a MS. at Lyons.

q. Written in the seventh century, and preserved at Munich, contains fragments of 1 John, and of 1 and 2 Peter. The text exhibits the passage of the Three Heavenly Witnesses in 1 John v., but verse 7 follows verse 8.

Published by Ziegler in 1877, *Bruchstücke einer vorhieronymianischen Uebersetzung der Petrusbriefe.*

4. Pauline Epistles.

m. As for the Gospels.

d e f g. The Latin versions of the Greek Codices D E F G.

gue. Guelferbytanus, of the sixth century, contains fragments of Romans cc. xi.–xv., found in the Gothic palimpsest at Wolfenbüttel. See p. 69.

Published by Tischendorf in his *Anecdota Sacra et Profana*, 1855, pp. 153–158. See Burkitt, in the *Journal of Theological Studies*, i. 1 (Oct. 1899), p. 134, and compare the note to p. 139 in the *Addenda*, p. xv.

r. Written in the fifth or sixth century, came originally from Freising, and is now at Munich: contains portions of Romans, 1 and 2 Corinthians, Galatians, Ephesians, Philippians, 1 Timothy, and Hebrews.

Ziegler, *Italafragmente der paulinischen Briefe.* Marburg, 1876. Wölfflin, *Neue Bruchstücke der Freisinger Itala* (Münchener Sitzungsberichte, 1893, ii. 253–280).

r_2. Also at Munich, a single leaf, with part of Phil. iv. and of 1 Thess. i.

r_3. In the Benedictine Abbey of Göttweih on the Danube: fragments of Romans v. and vi. and of Galatians iv. and v., written on leaves used as a book cover.

Published by Rönsch in the *ZfwTh.*, xxii. (1879), pp. 234–238.

x_2. At Oxford, of the ninth century, contains the Pauline Epistles: defective from Heb. xi. 34–xiii. 25.

See also Fr. Zimmer, *Der Galaterbrief im altlateinischen Text, als Grundlage für einen textkritischen Apparat der Vetus Latina* in the

Theologische Studien und Skizzen aus Ostpreussen. Königsberg, i. (1887), pp. 1–81.

5. Apocalypse.

The only manuscripts are m as for the Gospels, and g and h as for the Acts. h exhibits only fragments of cc. i. and ii., viii. and ix., xi. and xii., and xiv.–xvi.

For the Old Latin Biblical Texts edited by Wordsworth and White, see below, p. 131.

Latin Fathers.

On account of the small number of these manuscripts the quotations of the Latin Fathers are valuable, especially those of *Cyprian* of Carthage,[1] and after them the recently discovered citations in *Priscillian*, who was the first to suffer death as a heretic in the year 385. In the Apocalypse we have the quotations of *Primasius*, Bishop of Hadrumet (ca. 550), who used in his commentary on the Apocalypse not only his own Old Latin Bible but also a revised version the same as that used by the African Donatist *Tyconius*. In attempting to classify these witnesses it was found that the text of certain manuscripts coincided with that of the Bible used by Cyprian—viz., in the Gospels k especially, in Acts h, and in the Apocalypse Primasius and h. This family has accordingly been designated the **African**.

Tertullian, a still earlier African Father, undoubtedly refers to the existence of a Latin Version in his time, but the quotations found in his Latin works cannot be taken into account, for this reason, that in citing the New Testament he seems to have made an independent translation from the Greek for his immediate purpose.[2]

[1] J. Heidenreich, *Der neutestamentliche Text bei Cyprian verglichen mit dem Vulgatatext. Eine textkritische Untersuchung zu den h. Schriften des Neuen Testamentes.* Bamberg, 1900.

[2] This is the view of Zahn. Others, however, have no doubt that Tertullian made use of a Latin version. Hoppe, in his treatise, *De sermone Tertullianeo Quaestiones Selectae* (1897), p. 6 (*de Graecismis Tertulliani*) says, "Permultas enim (constructiones) T. mutuatus est vel ex scriptoribus graecis, quibus assidue studuit, vel ex librorum sacrorum translatione latina graecismis abundante, qua

As for the quotations in Augustine, they are found to resemble the text of f and q in the Gospels, particularly the former, and that of q, r, and r_3 in the Epistles. To this group, therefore, the name **Italian** has been given. It has, however, been deemed necessary to regard this Italian family as being itself a revised and smoother form of a still earlier version styled the **European**, which is thought to be represented by g, g_2, and s in the Acts, by ff in the Epistles, and by g in the Apocalypse.

Old Latin Texts.

As illustrating the way in which the various forms deviate from each other, take the text of Luke xxiv., verses 4, 5, 11, and 13 as exhibited by a b c d e f and the Vulgate (vg).

v. 4.—All the seven agree in the opening words, Et factum est dum; but after that there follows:—

(1) stuperent a c, mente consternatae essent b, vg; mente consternatae sunt e, aporiarentur d, haesitarent f.

(2) de hoc a c f, de facto b, de eo d, de isto e, vg.

(3) ecce a c d f, vg; et ecce b e.

(4) viri duo a f, duo viri b c d e, vg.

(5) adstiterunt a f, astiterunt c, adsisterunt d, steterunt b e, vg.

(6) iuxta illas a f, secus illas b c e, vg; eis d.

(7) in veste fulgenti a f, vg; in veste fulgente b c e, in amictu scoruscanti d.

(8) v. 5: timore autem adprehensae inclinantes faciem ad terram a; cum timerent autem et declinarent vultum in terram b e f, vg; conterritae autem inclinaverunt faciem in terram c; in timore autem factae inclinaverunt vultus suos in terra d.

(9) v. 11: et visa sunt a b c (visae) e f, vg; et paruerunt d.

(10) illis a, ante illos b, vg; apud illos c e, in conspectu eorum d, coram illos f.

utebatur." And to this he adds, "Quam multa vocabula graeca in Tertullianeum sermonem ex Itala quae vocatur translatione redundaverint, discas ex Roenschii libro cum impigritate conscripto, qui inscribitur, *Itala und Vulgata*, ed. sec., p. 238." The Itala is cited for *sciant quia* (p. 18), *absque* (p. 44), and for the use of the superlative for the positive (p. 49). On this last the writer refers to Rönsch, p. 415, and adds, "ex Itala T. hunc usum aliquotiens assumpsisse videtur, quamquam in universum vitat." *Cf.* Westcott, *Canon*, Part I., c. iii. p. 251 ff.

(11) tanquam a, sicut b e, vg; quasi c d f.

(12) delira a, deliramentum b e f, vg; (b spells -lirr-, and f -ler-), deliramenta c, derissus d.

(13) v. 13: municipium a, castellum b c d e f, vg.

(14) stadios habentem LX ab hierusalem a, quod aberat stadia sexaginta ab hierusalem b, quod abest ab ierosolymis stadia sexag. c, iter habentis stadios sexag. ab hierus. d, quod est ab hierosolymis stadia septem e, quod aberat spatio stadiorum LX ab hierus. f, quod erat in spatio stadiorum sexaginta ab hierusalem vg.

(15) cui nomen a, nomine b c d e f, vg.

(16) ammaus a, cleopas et ammaus b, emmaus c f, vg; alammaus d, ammaus et cleopas e.

Is not this almost exactly as Jerome said: tot exemplaria, quot codices? And when we take into account that all this variety in the Latin manuscripts is not simply due to a difference in translation, but that a similar diversity exists in the Greek,[1] we can easily understand what a task it is to extricate the original text from out these conflicting witnesses. At the same time, we have evidence of the singular position in which D stands to all the others; while the last example also affords an illustration of the way in which mistakes might arise. The reading ᾗ ὄνομα in verse 13 would preclude any possibility of misunderstanding. But suppose the reader or the translator had before him a manuscript like D, in which the reading was ὀνόματι. What happened, we shall suppose, was this. The phrase, "Emmaus by name," was taken as referring, not to the village, but to the subject of the sentence;

[1] Thus we have, following the numbers given above, in verse 4 (1) *αποpειcθαι* and *διαπορειcθαι* (or *διαπορειν*), (2) *περι τουτου* and *περι αυτου*, (3) *ιδου* and *και ιδου*, (4) *ανδρες δυο* and *δυο ανδρες*, (5) *επεστησαν* and *παρειστηκεισαν*, (7) *εν εσθητι αστραπτουση* (or *λαμπρα*) and *εν εσθησεσιν αστραπτουσαις* (or *λευκαις*), (8) *εμφοβων* (or *εν φοβω*) *δε γενομενων και κλινουσων* and *ενφοβοι δε γενομεναι εκλειναν*, (9) *τα προσωπα* and *το προσωπον* (*αυτων*); in verse 11, (10) *ενωπιον αυτων* and its omission; in verse 13, (14) *εξηκοντα* and *εκατον εξηκοντα*, (15) *ᾗ ονομα* and *ονοματι*, (16) *Εμμαους* and *ουλαμμαους*. Of these (8), (15), and (16) are found only in D. In the case of (15) the very same variation is found at Tob. vi. 10 in the two recensions represented by *Codex Vaticanus* and *Codex Sinaiticus*.

the other name, Cleopas, was then inserted from verse 18, and in time placed even before Emmaus by a later copyist. And accordingly we find, even in Ambrose of Milan, that the two travellers are regularly called Ammaon et Cleopas. It was just as Jerome said: a vitiosis interpretibus male edita, a praesumptoribus imperitis emendata perversius, a librariis dormitantibus aut addita aut mutata.

(2.) THE LATIN VERSION OF JEROME.

It is a comparatively easy task to restore the work of Jerome; first of all because all our present manuscripts are derived from one and only one source, secondly because the number of existing manuscripts is very great, and lastly because some of them at least go back to the sixth century.

Codex Epternacensis.

There is a Codex in Paris which formerly belonged to the Church of St. Willibrord at Echternach, written by an Irish hand of the eighth or ninth century, and containing a subscription copied from its original to the following effect: proemendavi ut potui secundum codicem in bibliotheca Eugipi praespiteri quem ferunt fuisse sci Hieronymi, indictione VI. p(ost) con(sulatum) Bassilii u. c. anno septimo decimo. That must have been in the year 558.

Codex Amiatinus.

Codex Amiatinus, now in Florence, was formerly supposed to belong to the same time, but this turns out to be a mistake, because it has been proved that it was written for Ceolfrid, Abbot of Wearmouth, who died at Langres on the 25th September 716, on his way to Rome, where he intended to present this Codex to the Pope. One of the oldest and most valuable manuscripts of the Vulgate is at Fulda, where it has been preserved, perhaps, from the time of Boniface.

Codex Fuldensis.

This Codex Fuldensis was written between 540 and 546, by order of Bishop Victor of Capua, and corrected by himself. It contains the whole of the New Testament according to Jerome's version, only in place of the four separate Gospels it has a Harmony composed by Victor, who followed Tatian's plan, using the Latin text of Jerome. Victor's Harmony in turn became the basis of the so-called Old German Tatian.

Wordsworth and White.

The task of restoring the original text of Jerome's version has been undertaken in England by the Bishop of Salisbury, who has been at work on all the available material for more than fifteen years. The edition bears the title, *Novum Testamentum Domini nostri Jesu Christi secundum editionem sancti Hieronymi ad codicum manuscriptorum fidem recensuit Johannes Wordsworth in operis societatem adsumpto Henrico Juliano White.* Five parts of the first volume have already appeared, containing the four Gospels with an *Epilogus ad Evangelia.*[1] In France, J. Delisle, the Director of the Paris National Library, has rendered great service by his work upon the manuscripts under his care; while Samuel Berger has constituted himself pre-eminently the historian of the Vulgate by bringing fresh testimony from the early Middle Ages and the remotest provinces of the Church to bear upon the history of the Vulgate and its text as well as on the origin and dissemination of the different forms. In his compendious *Histoire de la Vulgate pendant les premiers siècles du moyen âge* (Paris, 1893), he has, *e.g.*, indicated no fewer than 212 different ways in which the books of the Old Testament were arranged in the manuscripts that he examined, and thirty-eight varieties in the order of the New Testament books. In Germany Bengel applied himself to the reconstruction of the Latin text of the Bible in the last century, and in this he was followed by Lachmann in the present century, while Riegler, van Ess, and Kaulen have added to our knowledge of the history of the Vulgate. Dr. Peter Corssen has followed up the labours of Ziegler and Rönsch in the particular field of the pre-Jeromic Bible and its text with a methodical examination of the earlier editions, and E. v. Dobschütz has begun to publish *Studies in the Textual Criticism of the Vulgate.* The valuable researches of Carlo Vercellone (1860–64) were concerned almost exclusively with

[1] 1889, 91, 93, 95, 98; cited in the sequel as W.-W.

the Old Testament, and do not seem to have been followed up in Italy. "Utinam Papa Leo XIII.," says Gregory, "tanta scientia tanta magnanimitate insignis curam in se suscipiat textus sacrosanctorum Bibliorum Latini edendi; cura, opus ecclesia et Papa dignum." Meanwhile Wordsworth and White appear to have accomplished as much as is possible at present in the field of the Gospels.[1]

MSS. used by Jerome.

The principles on which Jerome went in his revision of the text have been already referred to, but what the early Greek manuscripts were that he employed is not yet clearly made out. The relics of the material he used are as scanty as those of his own work. He must, however, have been able to make use of manuscripts that went back to Eusebius, seeing that he adopted the Eusebian Canons in his New Testament. But there are certain readings in Jerome which we have not yet been able to discover in any Greek manuscript that we know. For instance, he gives *docebit vos omnem veritatem* in John xvi. 13, where our present Greek editions read ὁδηγήσει ὑμᾶς ἐν τῇ ἀληθείᾳ πάσῃ, so that he would seem to have read διηγήσεται ὑμῖν τὴν ἀλήθειαν πᾶσαν. As a matter of fact, this reading does occur in two passages of Eusebius and in Cyril of Jerusalem, as well as in the Arabic version of Tatian, but it has not been discovered in any Greek manuscript.[2] In the other parts of the New Testament, the revision of which was perhaps completed by the year 386, Jerome inserted hardly any new readings from the Greek, but contented himself with improving the grammar and diction of the Latin. His work on the Old Testament was much more comprehensive, but does not fall to be discussed here.

History of the Vulgate.

It was only by degrees that Jerome's recension gained

[1] On the *Epilogus* to the first volume of their Oxford edition, see especially S. Berger in the *Revue Critique*, 1889, pp. 141–144; and on the whole, Burkitt, *The Vulgate Gospels and the Codex Brixianus*, in the *Journal of Theological Studies*, I. i. (Oct. 1899) pp. 129–134.

[2] Compare E. Maugenot, *Les manuscrits grecs des évangiles employés par Saint Jerôme*, in the *Revue des sciences ecclésiastiques*, January 1900.

ground. In Rome, Gregory the Great (d. 604) for one preferred it to the old, though at the same time he says expressly: sedes apostolica, cui auctore Deo praesideo, utraque utitur. Owing to the use of both forms the diversity of copies grew to such an extent that in 797 Charles the Great ordered **Alcuin** to make a uniformly revised text from the best Latin manuscripts for use in the Churches of his Empire. For this purpose Alcuin sent to his native Northumbria for manuscripts, by which he corrected the text of the Bible, and he was able to present the first copy to the Emperor at Christmas 801. A good many of the superb *Carolingian* manuscripts, as they are called, which are found in our libraries, contain Alcuin's Revision, as for instance the Bible of Grandval near Basel, which was probably written for Charles the Bald, and which is now in the British Museum (see Plate VII.); the Bible presented to the same monarch by Vivian, Abbot of St. Martin of Tours, which was sent by the Chapter of Metz from the Cathedral treasury there to Colbert in 1675, and is now in Paris (B. N., Lat. 1); another written in the same monastery of St. Martin, and now at Bamberg; and that in the Vallicellian Library of the Church of Sta. Maria in Rome, which is perhaps the best specimen of the Alcuinian Bible.

Alcuin.

Another revision was introduced into France by Alcuin's contemporary **Theodulf**, Bishop of Orleans (787–821). He was a Visigoth, born in the neighbourhood of Narbonne, and the type of text he introduced was taken essentially from Spanish manuscripts. We have his revision in the so-called Theodulfian Bible, which formerly belonged to the Cathedral Church of Orleans, and is now in Paris (Lat. 9380); in its companion volume, formerly in the Cathedral of Puy, and now in the British Museum (24142); and in the Bible of St. Hubert, which came from the monastery of that name in the Ardennes.

Theodulf.

A further revision was made by Stephen **Harding**, third Abbot of Citeaux. About the year 1109 he prepared a

Harding.

standard Bible for his congregation, in which the Latin text of the New Testament was corrected by the Greek. At the same time the Old Testament was revised from the Hebrew with the help of some Jewish scholars. Harding's copy of the standard Bible, in four volumes, is still preserved in the Public Library at Dijon. A similar work was done for his monastery by William, Abbot of Hirsau.

Correctoria. Attempts were also made to settle the text by means of the so-called **Correctoria Bibliorum,** in which those readings which were supposed to be correct were carefully collected and arranged. The University of Paris in particular did a great deal in this way, and such was its influence, that by the middle of the fifteenth century the Parisian text was the one most commonly followed in manuscripts, and the invention of printing gave it a complete ascendancy over the others.

Printed text. The first fruits of the printing press are understood to be the undated "forty-two line Bible," usually called the *Mazarin* Bible, seeing that it was the copy in the library of Cardinal Mazarin that first attracted the attention of bibliographers. The first dated Bible is of the year 1462. Copinger estimates that 124 editions were printed before the close of the fifteenth century, and over 400 during the sixteenth. The first edition in octavo, "for the poor man," was issued at Basel in 1491 from the Press of Froben, the same printer who prompted Erasmus to prepare the first Greek New Testament. The first edition in Latin with various readings was printed in 1504. In the following year Erasmus published the *Annotationes* which Laurentius Valla had prepared for the Latin Bible as early as 1444. The year 1528 saw the first really critical edition. It was brought out by Stephen, who used in its preparation three good Paris manuscripts—the Bible of Charles the Bald already referred to, that of St. Denis, and another of the ninth century, the New Testament portion of which has now disappeared. He afterwards published in 1538–40 another edition, for which he employed seventeen manuscripts, and which became the foundation of the present authorised Vulgate. About the same time John **Henten** published a very valuable edition [1547] on the basis of thirty-one manuscripts, in the preparation of which he was assisted by the theologians of Louvain. This was followed in 1573 and 1580 by two further editions containing important annotations by Lucas of Brügge. In the year previous to that in which Henten's edition appeared, the Council of Trent, in its fourth sitting of the 8th April 1546, decided "ut haec vetus et vulgata editio in publicis lectionibus, disputationibus, praedicationibus et expositionibus pro authentica habeatur," and at the same time ordained "posthac sacra scriptura, potissimum vero haec ipsa vetus et vulgata editio quam emendatissime imprimatur."

Henten.

Authorised Vulgate.

The latter part of this decree was carried into effect in the papacy of Sixtus V. His predecessor, Pius V., began the work of revising the text of the Bible, and a "Congregatio pro emendatione Bibliorum" gave twenty-six sittings to it in the year 1569. His successor seems to have allowed the work to lapse, but Sixtus V. appointed a new commission for the purpose under the Presidency of Cardinal Caraffa. The Pope himself revised the result of their labours, which was printed at the Vatican Press that he had founded. This edition, which takes its name from him, was issued under the Bull "Aeternus ille" of the 1st March 1589, and published in the following year. It is the first official edition of the Vulgate. Sixtus died on the 27th August 1590, and was succeeded by four Popes in the space of two years. His fourth successor in the Chair of Peter, Clement VIII., issued a new edition under the name of the old Pope, accompanied by the Bull "Cum sacrorum" of the 9th November 1592. This edition, containing a preface written by Cardinal Bellarmin, was substituted for the former, and has continued from that day without any alteration as the authorised Bible of the entire Roman

Sixtine.

Clementine.

Church. The text of this second edition approximated more closely to that of Henten, for which the Commission of Pope Sixtus had also expressed their preference, though their printed edition went rather by that of Stephen. The number of the variations between these two editions has been estimated at 3000. For our purpose both alike are superseded by the edition of Wordsworth and White. It may be added that the first edition to contain the names of both the Popes upon the title page is that of 1604. The title runs: "Sixti V. Pont. Max. iussu recognita et Clementis VIII. auctoritate edita." Those printed at Rome at the present day are entitled: "Sixti V. et Clementis VIII. Pontt. Maxx. iussu recognita atque edita." See below, p. 132.

An enumeration of all the manuscripts of the Vulgate mentioned by Tischendorf in his eighth edition, or even of the earliest and most important of them, cannot be attempted. Those, however, mentioned by Gebhardt in his *Adnotatio Critica* are given here, with the notation adopted by Wordsworth and White.

The best manuscripts, in the judgment of the English editors, are, Codex Amiatinus, Codex Fuldensis, and, the one in the Ambrosian Library at Milan (C 39 inf.), written in the sixth century. (M in W.-W.; not cited by Tischendorf.)

am. Amiatinus (*vide supra*, p. 122), written ca. 700, is an excellent manuscript, and particularly interesting as containing in the introduction a double catalogue of the Books of the Bible resembling that of the Senator Cassiodorus. See Westcott, *Bible in the Church*, Appendix B; *Canon*, Appendix D. (A in W.-W.) (See Plate VI.)

bodl. Bodleianus, of the seventh century, formerly belonging to the Library of St. Augustine at Canterbury. (O in W.-W.)

demid. Demidovianus, belonging to the thirteenth century, but copied from an earlier exemplar; formerly at Lyons; present locality unknown; not cited in W.-W.

em. Emeram, written in the year 870, in gold uncials with splendid miniatures: at Munich, Cimelie 55: not cited in W.–W.

erl. Erlangen, of the ninth century (Irmischer's Catalogue, 467): used only indirectly by Tischendorf, and not cited in W.–W.

for. Foroiuliensis, written in the sixth or seventh century, and now at Cividale, Friuli: fragments of it at Venice and Prague. (J in W.–W.)

fos. Of the ninth century: from St. Maur des Fossés, now in Paris. (Lat. 11959.)

fu. Fuldensis (*vide supra*, p. 122), written between 540 and 546: contains the Epistle to the Laodicaeans after Colossians: edited with facsimiles by E. Ranke. (F in W.–W.)

gat. Gatianus, from St. Gatien's in Tours: written in the eighth or ninth century: stolen from Libri: purchased by Lord Ashburnham and now in Paris: not cited in W.–W.

harl. Harleianus 1775, of the sixth or seventh century: in the British Museum, formerly in Paris 4582: stolen from there by John Aymont in 1707. (Z in W.–W.)

ing. Ingolstadt, of the seventh century, now in the University Library at Munich: defective. (I in W.–W.) See von Dobschütz, *Vulgatastudien* (with two facsimiles).

mm. Of the tenth or eleventh century, from Marmoutiers, near Tours: in the British Museum, Egerton 609. (E in W.–W.)

mt. Of the eighth or ninth century, from St. Martin's, and still at Tours: written in gold letters. (M in W.–W.)

pe. A very old purple manuscript of the sixth century at Perugia, containing Luke i. 1–xii. 7. (P in W.–W.)

prag. The fragments cited under *for.* (see above).

reg. Regius, of the seventh or eighth century, a purple manuscript inscribed in gold, containing Matthew and Mark, with lacunæ: at Paris 11955: not cited in W.–W.

rus. The so-called Rushworth Gospels, written by an Irish

scribe who died in the year 820: has an interlinear Anglo-Saxon version. (R in W.–W.)

san. At St. Gall, a fragment containing Matthew vi. 21–John xvii. 18, written by a scribe who says that he used two Latin and one Greek manuscripts. In the Epistles san. is a palimpsest at St. Gall containing Ephes. vi. 2 to 1 Tim. ii. 5, the Biblical text being the uppermost.

taur. Of the seventh century, at Turin, contains the Gospels beginning at Matthew xiii. 34: not cited in W.–W.

tol. Written in the eighth century: this manuscript, which was written by a Visigoth, was given by Servandus of Seville to John, Bishop of Cordova, who presented it to the See of Seville in 988: it was afterwards at Toledo, and is now at Madrid. It was collated for the Sixtine Recension by Palomares, but reached Rome too late to be of use. (T in W.–W.)

In addition to the eleven manuscripts mentioned above as cited by Wordsworth and White, twenty-one others are regularly used by them, and a great number are cited occasionally. For these reference must be made to their edition, and for further particulars to Berger's incomparable work.

On the Latin Versions compare *TiGr.*, 948–1108, 1313, and especially Scrivener. The chapter on *The Latin Versions* in the Fourth Edition of the latter work (c. iii.) was re-written by H. J. White, the collaborateur of Wordsworth. See also *Urt.*, 85–118, which deals with the Old Testament as well, and the article on the *Old Latin Versions* in Hastings' *Dictionary of the Bible*, iii. 47–62.

1. G. Riegler, *Kritische Geschichte der Vulgata*, Sulzbach, 1820; Lean. van Ess, *Pragmatisch-kritische Geschichte der Vulgata im Allgemeinen und zunächst in Beziehung auf das Trientische Decret*, Tübingen, 1824; Kaulen, *Geschichte der Vulgata*, Mainz, 1868; Berger, *Histoire de la Vulgate pendant les premiers siècles du moyen âge*, Paris, 1893 (List of the chief works dealing with the history of the Vulgate given on p. xxii. ff.).

2. On the subject of the Itala see Ziegler, *Die Lateinischen Bibelübersetzungen vor Hieronymus und die Itala des Augustinus*, Munich, 1879; Zycha, *Bemerkungen zur Italafrage*, in the *Eranos Vindo-*

bonensis, 1893, 177–184; Burkitt, *The Old Latin and the Itala* (*Texts and Studies*, vol. iv., No. 3, 1896).

3. On the language see Rönsch (d. 1888), *Itala und Vulgata*, 2nd Edition, 1875; also *Die ältesten lateinischen-Bibelübersetzungen nach ihrem Werthe für die lateinische Sprachwissenschaft*, by the same writer in the *Collectanea Philologa*, Bremen, 1891, 1–20; Kaulen, *Handbuch zur Vulgata, Eine systematische Darstellung ihres Sprachcharakters*, Mainz, 1870. Saalfeld, *De Bibliorum S. Vulgatæ Editionis Graecitate*, Quedlinburg, 1891.

4. Editions of the Text:—Among the earlier works the most important is that of Sabatier, which is not yet superseded, in the Old Testament at least, *Bibliorum sacrorum Latinæ Versiones antiquæ, seu Vetus Italica, et cæteræ quæcunque in codicibus MSS. et antiquorum libris reperiri potuerunt, etc., opera et studio D. Petri Sabatier*, 3 vols. folio,[1] Rheims, 1743. Jos. Bianchini (Blanchinus), *Evangeliarium Quadruplex*, 2 vols. folio, Rome, 1749 (copies now cost about £4). After a long interval work in this field has been resumed in the *Old Latin Biblical Texts*, published at the Clarendon Press, Oxford, of which four parts have appeared:—1. *The Gospel according to St. Matthew from the St. Germain MS.* (g_1), *now numbered Lat.* 11553 *in the National Library at Paris, with Introduction and five Appendices, edited by John Wordsworth, D.D.*, 1883 (6/-). 2. *Portions of the Gospels according to St. Mark and St. Matthew from the Bobbio MS.* (k), *now numbered G. VII.* 15 *in the National Library at Turin, together with other fragments of the Gospels from six MSS. in the Libraries of St. Gall, Coire, Milan, and Berne* (*usually cited as n, o, p, a_2, s, and t*). *Edited, with the aids of Tischendorf's Transcripts and the printed Texts of Ranke, Ceriani, and Hagen, with two facsimiles, by J. Wordsworth, D.D., ... W. Sanday, D.D., ... and H. J. White, M.A.*, 1886 (21/-). 3. *The Four Gospels, from the Munich MS.* (q), *now numbered Lat.* 6224 *in the Royal Library at Munich, with a Fragment from St. John in the Hof-Bibliothek at Vienna* (*Cod. Lat.* 502). *Edited, with the aid of Tischendorf's Transcript* (*under the direction of the Bishop of Salisbury*), *by H. J. White*,

[1] The New Testament is contained in vol. iii. The copy I use has the date 1743 on the title-pages of three volumes, but there is a note at the end, p. 1115, which says, "E prelo exiit hic tomus anno 1749." Romæ, 1713–19, in *TiGr.*, p. 1350, is a misprint. The imprimaturs of the first volume are dated 1737. The work was reprinted with new title-pages at Paris by Fr. Didot, 1751. Copies now cost from £15 to £25.

M.A., 1888 (12/6). 4. *Portions of the Acts of the Apostles, of the Epistle of St. James, and of the First Epistle of St. Peter from the Bobbio Palimpsest* (s), *now numbered Cod.* 16 *in the Imperial Library at Vienna. Edited, with the aid of Tischendorf's and Belsheim's printed Texts, by H. J. White, M.A., with a Facsimile*, 1897 (5/-). (See notice in the *Expository Times*, April 1898, p. 320 ff.)

5. Wordsworth and White's edition of the Vulgate is noticed by Berger in the *Bull. Crit.*, 1899, viii. 141–144. It may be added here, as that critic observes, that insufficient regard is paid to the later history of the Latin text in this edition. At least one representative of a recension so important as that of the University of Paris in the thirteenth century might have been collated, and perhaps also the first printed edition, "the forty-two line" Bible.

On the authorised edition of 1590 and 1592, see Eb. Nestle, *Ein Jubiläum der lateinischen Bibel. Zum 9 November* 1892, in *Marginalien und Materialien*, 1893; also printed separately.

An exact reprint of the Latin Vulgate has recently been published by M. Hetzenauer from his Greek-Latin New Testament (see above, p. 25), entitled *Novum Testamentum Vulgatae Editionis. Ex Vaticanis Editionibus earumque Correctorio critice edidit Michael Hetzenauer.* Oeniponte, 1899. As an introduction to this edition reference may be made to the same writer's *Wesen und Principien der Bibelkritik auf katholischer Grundlage. Unter besonderer Berücksichtigung der offiziellen Vulgataausgabe dargelegt.* Innsbruck, 1900.

(*c.*) EGYPTIAN VERSIONS.

Next in importance to the Syriac versions from the East and the Latin from the West are the **Egyptian** versions from the South. Here too we find not one early version but several.

Dialects. What used till lately to be called Coptic[1] is merely one of the dialects into which the language of ancient Egypt was divided. And here we must distinguish three main branches—the Bohairic, the Sahidic, and the Middle Egyptian.

Bohairic. (1) **Bohairic**[2] is the name given to the dialect that was spoken in the Bohaira—*i.e.* the district by the sea and therefore Lower Egypt, the neighbourhood of Alexandria. It was

[1] The word Coptic is not derived from the town in Upper Egypt called Coptos, but is a modification of the Greek word Αἰγύπτιος.

[2] The spelling Bahiric is due to a wrong vocalisation of the word.

the principal dialect, and being that used for ecclesiastical purposes over the whole country, and, moreover, that with which European scholars first became acquainted, the versions written in it were described as the Coptic simply. The term Memphitic, which was preferred for a time, is incorrect, because it was not till the eleventh century that the Patriarchate was transferred to Cairo—*i.e.* the district of Memphis, and in early times a different dialect was spoken there.

Sahidic.

(2) **Sahidic** is the name used to describe the dialect of Upper Egypt. It is sometimes and not improperly spoken of as the Thebaic in distinction to the Memphitic.

Middle Egyptian.

(3) Under the **Middle Egyptian**[1] we have to distinguish—

(*a*) The *Fayumic*, spoken in the Fayum—*i.e.* the district to the S.W. of the Delta, watered by the Joseph Canal, and separated from the valley of the Nile by a narrow strip of the desert. It was in this district that those recent papyrus discoveries were made which have enriched the libraries and museums of Europe.

(*b*) The *Middle Egyptian proper*, or Lower Sahidic, a dialect which has its home on the site of ancient Memphis.

(*c*) The dialect of *Achmim*, which preserves a more primitive form of early Egyptian than any of those already referred to.

In the eleventh century the Coptic Bishop Athanasius specifies three dialects of the Coptic language—the Bohairic, the Sahidic, and a third which he says was already extinct, and to which he gives the name of Bashmuric; but whether this last is to be identified with the dialects included above under the name of Middle Egyptian, is not quite certain.

(1.) *The Bohairic Version.*

Bohairic.

This version, formerly designated as the Coptic, was first used for the New Testament by Bishop Fell of Oxford, who was indebted for his knowledge of it to Marshall. It was afterwards employed by Mill for his edition of 1707. It was first published in 1716 by Wilkins (or rather Wilke), a

[1] On the Middle Egyptian, see W. E. Crum in the *Journal of Theological Studies*, I. 3 (April 1900), pp. 416 ff.

Prussian who had settled in England, with the title, "Novum Testamentum Aegyptium vulgo Copticum." His edition was accompanied with a Latin translation. In 1734 Bengel obtained a few particulars regarding this version from La Croze, the Berlin Librarian. An edition of the Gospels by Moritz Schwartze appeared in 1846–47, and after his death the Acts and Epistles were published (1852) by Paul Boetticher, afterwards distinguished under his adopted name of de Lagarde. About the same time Tattam prepared a wholly uncritical edition of the entire New Testament, including the Apocalypse which did not originally form part of this version.[1] Steindorff is of opinion that the Bohairic version originated in the Natron Valley during the fourth or fifth century, but others affirm that it is older, or at all events rests on an older foundation. The order of the New Testament books was originally: (1) the Gospels, in which John stood first, followed by Matthew, Mark, Luke, (2) the Pauline Epistles, with Hebrews between 2 Thess. and 1 Tim., (3) the seven Catholic Epistles, and (4) the Acts. More than fifty Bohairic manuscripts are preserved in the libraries of Europe, and from these an edition has been prepared for the Clarendon Press in two volumes, with exhaustive Introduction by G. Horner (1898).

The Greek text on which this version is based is regarded by present critics as particularly pure, and free from so-called Western additions.

(2.) *The Sahidic Version.*

Sahidic.

It was a long time before this version attracted any attention. In his New Testament, Wilkins mentioned two manuscripts, "lingua plane a reliquis MSS. Copticis diversa," and Woide in 1778 announced his intention of editing certain fragments of the New Testament "iuxta interpretationem superioris Aegypti quae Thebaidica vocatur," which were afterwards published by Ford in 1799. At the close of last century and the beginning of this, various other fragments

[1] Westcott, *Canon*, Part II., chapter ii., § 1 *sub finem*.

were issued by Tuki, Mingarelli, Münter, Zoega, and Engelbreth, but it was not till more recent times that really important parts of the Old and New Testaments were published by Amélineau, Ciasca (in two vols.), Bouriant, Maspero, Ceugney, and Krall. In 1895 Goussen gave us a large part of the Apocalypse.[1] This version, like the former, contained the entire New Testament, with the exception of the Apocalypse, and originally exhibited the Gospels in the same order—John, Matthew, Mark, Luke. Hebrews, however, stood between 2 Corinthians and Galatians. Its Greek original was quite different from that of the Bohairic version. (See Plate VIII.)

(3.) *The Middle Egyptian Versions.*

Middle Egyptian.

Of these only fragments are as yet known to exist. Portions of Matthew and John, and of 1 Cor., Ephes., Phil., Thess., and Hebrews in the Fayumic, or, as it used to be called, the Bashmuric dialect, were first published by Zoega in 1809, by Engelbreth in 1811, and especially by Bouriant (1889) and Crum (1893).

Fragments in the Lower Sahidic have been published in the *Mitteilungen aus der Sammlung der Papyrus des Erzherzogs Rainer.*

In the Achmim dialect, James iv. 12, 13 and Jude 17–20 are the only fragments that have been discovered as yet, and these have been published by Crum. Whether these fragments are really parts of a separate version, or merely dialectical modifications of the Sahidic, is not quite certain.[2]

As to the date of these versions we have no definite information. It has been understood from certain passages in the Life of St. Anthony, who was born about the year 250, that in his boyhood he heard the Gospel read in Church in the language of Egypt, but that need not imply the existence of a written version, as the translation may have been made by a

[1] H. Hyvernat, *Un fragment inédit de la version sahidique du Nouveau Testament* (Ephes. i. 6–ii. 8*b*). *Revue Biblique*, April 1900, pp. 248–253. The fragment is of the eighth or ninth century.

[2] See also the Greek and Middle Egyptian manuscript published by Crum and Kenyon, referred to above, p. 70.

reader who interpreted as he read. In the third century, however, versions may have arisen, and it was certainly in the South that the first attempts at translation were made. Our oldest known manuscripts, a Sahidic containing 2 Thess. iii., and one in Middle Egyptian of Jude 17–20, date from the fourth or fifth century. The Sahidic version seems to have been made first, then the Middle Egyptian, and finally the Bohairic. To what extent the one influenced the other is a question requiring further investigation.

A correct edition and a critical application of these Egyptian versions is, next to a fresh examination of the minuscules, the task of most importance at present for the textual criticism of the New Testament. For the Sahidic version in particular represents a type of text found hitherto almost exclusively in the West, and looked upon as the outcome of Western corruption and licence, whereas it may really bear the most resemblance to the original form. In the Acts especially its agreement with the text of Codex D is remarkable. One might instance, *e.g.*, the mention of Pentecost in Acts i. 5, the insertion of the Golden Rule in its negative form in xv. 20, 29, the relation of the vision in xvi. 10, and the description of the stone which twenty men could not roll away in Luke xxiii. 53, all of which are now found in a Greek-Sahidic manuscript. The Sahidic version, like the Bohairic, is well represented in European libraries, and the manuscripts are dated as a rule in the Egyptian fashion according to the years of the Martyrs—*i.e.* according to an era reckoned from August or September 284 A.D.

TiGr., 859–893. Scrivener[4], ii. 91–144, revised by Horner, with additions by Headlam. H. Hyvernat, *Étude sur les Versions Coptes de la Bible* (*Revue Biblique*, v. (1896) 427–433, 540–569; vi. 1 (1897) 48–74. *Urt.*, 144–147. Forbes Robinson, *Egyptian Versions*, in Hastings' *Dictionary of the Bible*, vol. i. (1898) 668–673. W. E. Crum, *Coptic Studies* from the *Egypt Exploration Fund's Report* for 1897–1898, 15 pp. 4to. For the Gospels, Horner's edition eclipses all others. It is entitled, *The Coptic Version of the New Testament in the*

Northern dialect, otherwise called Memphitic or Bohairic, with Introduction, Critical Apparatus, and literal English Translation. Vol. I. Introduction, Matthew and Mark, cxlviii. 484. Oxford, Clarendon Press, 1898; *Vol. II. Luke and John*, 548 pp., 1898. See notice by Hyvernat in the *Revue Biblique*, 1899, pp. 148–150, and also W. E. Crum, *lib. cit.*, where reference is also made to the *Manuscrits Coptes au Musée . . . . à Leide*, 1897. As Horner's edition as yet only covers the Gospels, the remaining portions of the New Testament must still be sought in the two parts published by Lagarde after Schwartze's death, *Acta Apostolorum coptice* (1852), and *Epistulae Novi Testamenti coptice* (1852). On Brugsch's *Recension* in the *Zeitschrift der deutschen morgenländischen Gesellschaft*, vii. (1853) pp. 115–121, see *ibid.*, p. 456, and Lagarde, *Aus dem deutschen Gelehrtenleben*, pp. 25–65, 73–77. Tattam's Bohairic-Arabic edition was published by the Society for Promoting Christian Knowledge.

The first fragments of the New Testament in Sahidic appeared in Tuki's *Rudimenta* in 1778, and Woide's editio princeps, announced in the same year, was brought out after his death by Ford in 1799. Amélineau's *Fragments Thébaines inédits du Nouveau Testament* were published in vols. xxiv.–xxvi. of the *Zeitschrift fur ägyptische Sprache* (1886–1888). Considerable portions of the Apocalypse were issued in facsimile by Goussen in the first Fasciculus of his *Studia Theologica* (Lipsiae, 1897). Apocryphal and Pseudepigraphical writings have also been discovered in recent times, as, for example, the *Acta Pauli* in a manuscript of the seventh century, written in Sahidic consonants with Middle Egyptian vocalisation. These are to be published by A. Schmidt. See *Addenda*, p. xv.

See also Amélineau, *Notice des manuscrits coptes de la Bibliothèque Nationale renfermant des textes bilingues du Nouveau Testament*, in the *Athenæum*, No. 3601, p. 599.

The foregoing versions are those of most importance in the criticism of the text. There are, however, one or two others which, though inferior in value, are still interesting. Among these is—

(*d.*) THE GOTHIC VERSION.

This is the work of **Ulfilas**—*i.e.* Wölflin—a Cappadocian by descent, who in the year 340 succeeded Theophilus, the first Gothic.

Bishop of the Goths.[1] While the tribe was still settled in the Crimea, he is said to have invented an alphabet, and translated both the Old and the New Testament for their use. In the Old Testament Ulfilas followed the Septuagint according to the Recension of Lucian of Antioch (d. 312), which circulated in the diocese of Constantinople. In the New Testament the text is likewise essentially that of Chrysostom. The traces of Latin influence which were supposed to be discernible in the version, and which may either have existed from the first or been introduced at a later time, relate at most, perhaps, to matters of orthography.

(1) The Gothic version first became known through the so-called Codex Argenteus which Ant. Morillon, Granvella's secretary, and Mercator the geographer saw in the Monastery of Werden in the sixteenth century. It was afterwards seen at Prague by Richard Strein (d. 1601). In 1648 it was brought to Sweden as a prize of war, and presented to Queen Christina, or her librarian, Isaac Voss. It was purchased by Marshall de la Gardie in 1662, bound in silver, and deposited in the library at Upsala, where it has since remained. Ten leaves were stolen from the manuscript between 1821 and 1834, but restored, after many years, by the thief upon his deathbed. This magnificent Codex was written in the fifth or sixth century on purple with gold and silver lettering. It now comprises 187 leaves out of 330, and contains fragments of the four Gospels in the order, Matthew, John, Luke, Mark. It was published for the first time in 1665, from a transcript made by Derrer ten years before.

(2) Codex Carolinus, the Wolfenbüttel palimpsest already referred to as Q of the Gospels (see p. 69 above) and the Old Latin gue of Paul (see p. 118), contains some forty verses of the Epistle to the Romans. It was first published in 1762.

[1] The dates of Ulfilas' birth and death are uncertain. He certainly lived till autumn 381 or 383. The date of his life is variously given as 310–380 or 318–388. According to Kauffmann, the Synod at which Ulfilas was consecrated Bishop was that of Antioch, *De Encaeniis*, 341.

(3) Fragments of seven palimpsests in the Ambrosian Library at Milan, discovered by Cardinal Mai in 1817. Like Codex Carolinus, they are in all probability from the Monastery of Bobbio. They exhibit part of the Pauline Epistles and fragments of the Gospels. A few quotations from Hebrews are also found in a theological work. No portion of Acts, (Hebrews), Catholic Epistles, or Apocalypse has as yet been discovered. Editions of the Gothic version have been published by Gabelentz and Löbe (1836–1843), Stamm (1858), Heyne [5](1872) [9](1896), Bernhardt (Halle, 1875, 1884), and Balg (Milwaukee, 1891). St. Mark was edited by Müller and Höppe in 1881, and by Skeat in 1882.

LITERATURE.—On Ulfilas, see Scott, *Ulfilas, the Apostle of the Goths*, Cambr., 1885. Bradley, *The Goths*, in the "Story of the Nations" Series, 1888. Gwatkin, *Studies of Arianism*, 1882. *Urt.*, pp. 119–120, where see literature, to which add Eckstein, *Ulfilas und die gothische Uebersetzung der Bibel*, in Westermann's *Illustr. Monatshefte*, Dec. 1892, 403–407; Jostes, *Das Todesjahr des Ulfilas und der Uebertritt der Gothen zum Arianismus* (*Beiträge zur Geschichte der deutschen Sprache*, xxii. i. 158 ff.). Jostes gives 383 as the date of Ulfilas's death. On the other side, see Kauffmann, *Der Arianismus des Wulfila* in the *ZfdPhil.*, xxx. (1897) 93–113; Luft, *Die arianischen Quellen über Wulfila* in the *ZfdAltert.*, xlii. 4; Vogt, *Zu Wulfila's Bekenntnis und dem Opus imperfectum*, *ibid.* Kauffmann, *Beiträge zur Quellenkritik der gotischen Bibelübersetzung* in the *ZfdPhil.*; (ii.) *das N. T.* (xxx., 1897, 145–183); (iii.) *das gotische Matthäusevangelium und die Itala*; (iv.) *die griechische Vorlage des gotischen Johannesevangeliums* (xxxi., 1898, 177–198): also by the same author, *Aus der Schule des Wulfila. Auxentii Dorostorensis epistula de Fide, Vita, et Obitu Wulfila im Zusammenhang der Dissertatio Maximini contra Ambrosium herausgegeben.* Strassburg, 1899. P. Batiffol, *De quelques homilies de St. Chrysostome et de la version gothique des écritures* (*Revue Biblique*, Oct. 1899, pp. 566–572), see also *ThLz.*, 1900, No. i.; *LCbl.*, 1900, No. 28. On the relation of the Gothic version to the codex Brixianus (f), see Burkitt in the *Journal of Theological Studies*, i. p. 131 ff., and compare *Addenda*, p. xv.

On the Gothic language and writing, see Douse, *Introduction to the Gothic of Ulfilas.* London, 1886; the grammars of Braune and Skeat, and the dictionaries of Schulze, Heyne, and Bernhardt; see also Luft, *Studien zu den ältesten germanischen Alfabeten*, Gütersloh, 1898, viii. 115, who traces eighteen characters to the Greek alphabet and nine to the Latin and Ulfilas's own invention. On R. Löwe's *Reste der Germanen am schwarzen Meer* (Halle, 1896), see the story told by Melanchthon according to Pirkheimer (*Th. St. und Kr.*, 1897, 784 ff.).

To what extent the remaining ancient versions were taken directly from the Greek or influenced by one or other of those already described is still subject of dispute.

(*e.*) THE ETHIOPIC VERSION.

According to the tradition of the Abyssinian Church, the **Ethiopic** version of the New Testament was made from the Greek previous to the fifth century. Dillmann accepts this as correct, but Gildemeister would assign it to the sixth or seventh century, and thinks that traces are discernible of Syrian Monophysitism. Guidi decides for the end of the fifth or beginning of the sixth century. In addition to the usual twenty-seven books, the Ethiopic New Testament has an Appendix consisting of a work on Canon Law in eight books called the Synodos, so that the Ethiopian Church reckons in all thirty-five books in the New Testament. In later times the version was undoubtedly corrected from Arabic and Coptic texts. The first edition appeared in Rome in 1548–1549, but neither it nor those issued since are of any real critical worth.

At least a hundred Ethiopic manuscripts, mostly of late origin, exist in the libraries of Europe. What is perhaps the oldest is preserved in Paris. It dates from the thirteenth century, and exhibits the Gospels in an unrevised text.

LITERATURE.—See *TiGr.*, 894–912. Scrivener, ii. 154 ff. re-written by Margoliouth. *Urt.*, 147–150 (F. Praetorius). R. H. Charles, *Ethiopic Version* in Hastings' *Dictionary of the Bible*, i. 791–793. C. Conti Rossini, *Sulla Versione e sulla Revisione delle Sacre Scritture in Etiopico*, in the *Z. für Assyriologie*, x. 2, 3 (1895). The view of

Lagarde (*Ankündigung*, 1882, p. 28; *cf.* also *Gesammelte Abhandlungen*, lxi. 113), that this version may have been made from the Arabic or Egyptian in the fourteenth century, is now generally rejected.

(*f.*) THE ARMENIAN VERSION.

La Croze, the Berlin Librarian, thought this the "Queen of the Versions."

Till the fifth century of the Christian era Syrian influence was supreme in Armenia, and the inhabitants of that region first received the Scriptures of the Old and New Testaments in the form of a translation from the Syriac. But in the year 433 two pupils of Mesrob, returning from the Synod of Ephesus, are said to have brought back with them from Constantinople a Greek Bible, and having learned Greek in Alexandria, to have translated it into Armenian. According to another account this was done by St. Sahak (390–428) about the year 406. The first edition of the Armenian New Testament was brought out in Amsterdam in the year 1666[1] by Osgan of Eriwan, who had been sent to Europe four years previously by the Armenian Synod. It was edited from a defective manuscript, the missing portions of which Osgan supplied from the Vulgate. A better edition was published in 1789 by Zohrab, who used twenty manuscripts, and especially a Cilician Codex of the year 1310. He was of opinion that the Armenians did not receive the Apocalypse before the eighth century. Zohrab's text was collated for Tregelles by Rieu, whom Tischendorf seems to have drawn upon in his editions.

The Armenian manuscripts display variations of several sorts. In some John's Gospel precedes the Synoptists, in others it is followed by the Apocryphal "Rest of St. John." The Apocalypse was not read in church prior to the twelfth century. In the oldest manuscript of the entire New Testament, at Venice, which dates from the year 1220, the order of

[1] Or 1115 according to the Armenian reckoning.

the other books is Acts, Catholic Epistles, Apocalypse, Pauline Epistles, with the Epistle of the Corinthians to Paul. In Moscow there is a manuscript of the year 887, in Venice one dated 902, in Etschmiadzin one written in the year 986 and bound in ivory covers of the third or fourth century. In the last-mentioned Codex the words, "of Ariston the Presbyter," are found after Mark xvi. 8, as the heading of what follows. (*See Plate IX.*) We learn from this, what is evidently correct, viz., that the present conclusion of Mark's Gospel is due to a certain Ariston, who may perhaps be identified with Aristion, the teacher of Papias in the second century. The earlier Armenian version also contained the two verses Luke xxii. 43, 44, which were omitted in the later.

LITERATURE.—*TiGr.*, 912–922. Scrivener, ii. 148–154. F. C. Conybeare, *Armenian Versions of N. T.*, in Hastings' *Bible Dictionary*, i. 153 f. See also J. A. Robinson, *Euthaliana*, c. v.; *The Armenian Version and its supposed relation to Euthalius*, in *Texts and Studies*, vol. iii. (1895). On Aristion see *Expositor*, 1894, p. 241, and below, p. 295.

(*g.*) THE GEORGIAN VERSION.

This version, called also the Grusinian or Iberian, is thought to have been made from the Greek in the sixth century, though it may also be derived from the Armenian. It contains the pericope adulteræ (John vii. 53–viii. 11), but places it immediately after ch. vii. 44, which is the more remarkable, seeing that in the Old Latin Codex b, the passage from vii. 44 onwards has been erased. The Georgian version was first printed at Moscow in 1743.

Scrivener, ii. 156–158; re-written by F. C. Conybeare. *TiGr.*, 922 f.

(*h.*) THE ARABIC VERSIONS.

Some of these were made directly from the Greek, others from the Syriac and the Coptic, while there are also manuscripts exhibiting a recension undertaken at Alexandria in the thirteenth century. The New Testament was even cast into that form of rhymed prose made classic by the Koran. As early as the eighth century we find Mohammedan scholars quoting various passages of the New Testament, particularly the sayings regarding the Paraclete in John xv. 26, 27, xvi. 13, which they understood of Mohammed. He himself, however, knew the Gospel narrative from oral tradition only. The oldest known manuscript is perhaps one at Sinai, written in the ninth century, from which Mrs. Gibson edited the text of Romans, 1 and 2 Cor., Gal., and Ephes. i. 1–ii. 9, in the *Studia Sinaitica*, ii. The four Gospels were published in 1864 by Lagarde from a Vienna manuscript, in which a number of various readings were cited from the Coptic, Syriac, and Latin, this last, *e.g.*, being adduced in support of a reading hitherto found only in D, one Old Latin (g), and the Lewis-Syriac: οὐκ εἰσιν δύο ἢ τρεῖς συνηγμένοι . . . . παρ' οἷς οὐκ εἰμι ἐν μέσῳ αὐτῶν (Matthew xviii. 20). The first edition of the Gospels appeared at Rome in 1591. In common with the remaining versions of the New Testament, *Persic*, *Old High German*, *Anglo-Saxon*, *Bohemian*, and *Slavonic*, these secondary Arabic versions are not only exceedingly interesting from the point of view of the history of language and culture, but they are also valuable here and there for the restoration of the original text. In the present work, however, we cannot enter more fully into them.

Other versions.

LITERATURE.—*TiGr.*, 928–947. Scrivener, ii. 161–164. *Urt.*, 150–155. F. C. Burkitt, *Arabic Versions*, in Hastings' *Dictionary of the Bible*, i. 136–138, where see literature. Burkitt thinks that the oldest monument of Arabic Christianity is the manuscript formerly belonging to the Convent of Mar Saba, now known as Cod. Vat. Arab. 13, and numbered 101 in *TiGr.*, which is generally assigned to the eighth century. It originally contained the Psalter, Gospels, Acts, and Epistles, and is derived from the Syriac. Fragments of Matthew, Mark, and Luke, and of the Pauline Epistles, are all that now remain. From the same convent come two manuscripts of the ninth century, containing a version made directly from the

Greek, and perhaps ultimately derived from the Greek-Arabic manuscript cited as Θ^{h}, of which only four leaves have been preserved (see above, p. 72). On a Græco-Arabic MS. connected with the Ferrar Group (211^{ev}), see Lake in the *Journal of Theological Studies*, i. 117 ff. Most of the Coptic manuscripts are accompanied by an Arabic version. The one contained in Cod. Vat. Copt. 9 of the year 1202 is the best, and forms the basis of our printed editions. The first revision was undertaken in the year 1250, at Alexandria, by Hibat Allâh ibn el-Assâl, and a second towards the end of the thirteenth century, from which the variants in Lagarde's edition are derived. An Arabic version of the Acts and all seven Catholic Epistles, found in a ninth century manuscript at Sinai, and numbered 154 in Mrs. Gibson's Catalogue, is published by her in *Studia Sinaitica*, vii. (1899).

For the remaining versions of the N. T., see Scrivener, ii. pp. 158–166 (Slavonic, Anglo-Saxon, Frankish, Persic). These minor versions will be treated in vol. iv. of Hastings' *Bible Dictionary*, under the general heading of Versions. See also *Urtext und Uebersetzungen der Bibel.*

3. QUOTATIONS.

Our third source of material for the restoration of the text of the New Testament is **Quotations** found in other books. These are of great value, because they represent, for the most part, definite manuscripts existing in certain places at the time of the writer quoting them, and also because a large number of them belong to a time from which no codices have come down to us. The value of their testimony depends, of course, on the conditions already mentioned (p. 32)—viz., that the author quoted accurately, and the copyist copied faithfully, and the editor edited correctly. Quotations made by *Jewish* writers as well as by Christian will fall to be considered, only it is doubtful if in their case we have more than one or two uncertain allusions to Matthew v. 17. So, too, will the quotations made by *pagan opponents* of Christianity, particularly those of *Celsus* in the second century, and of the Emperor Julian. But here again we are not in possession of their complete works, which can only be restored by a similar process and with more or less uncertainty from the quotations from them found in the writings of the Apologists.[1] The books of those Christian Churches which were isolated from the main church will also be valuable. Even a verse of Scripture carved upon a stone in an old ruin may have something to tell us.

Brief quotations were usually made from memory. It was not so convenient to turn up the passage in an old manuscript as it is now in our handy printed editions.[2] In the case of longer passages and verbal quotations generally, indolent copyists were sometimes content with simply adding *καὶ τὰ ἑξῆς*. In the *Apostolic Constitutions*, ii. 22, for example, where the entire prayer of Manasses was meant to be given, the copyist of a certain manuscript,[3] after writing the opening words from Κύριε down to *δικαίου*, omitted all the rest, amounting to thirty-one lines of print, substituting simply *καὶ τὰ ἑξῆς τῆς εὐχῆς ἃ ὑμεῖς οὐκ ἀγνοεῖτε.* (See further, *Apost. Const.*, i. 7, Lagarde, p. 8, 23; ii. 14, p. 28, 7. 11; 29, 2). This, however, is not without its parallel in modern times. As late as 1872, an Oxford editor, in bringing out Cyril of Alexandria's Commentary on the Gospel according to St. John, wrote down only the initial and final words of the quotations in his manuscript, and allowed the compositor to set up the rest from a printed edition of the Textus Receptus. Another editor in Vienna, in preparing an edition of Cyprian's Works, preferred those very manuscripts in which the Scriptural quotations had been accommodated to the current text of later times. Only when a quotation is given by an author

[1] Celsus's polemic against Christianity has perished, but considerable fragments are embedded in Origen's Reply. See *Ante-Nicene Christian Library*, vol. xxiii., (Clark, Edin.).

[2] Clement of Alexandria cites Matt. xviii. 3 in four different ways. He quotes Matt. v. 45 six times, and only once accurately.

[3] Petropol. gr. 254, formerly cited as Paris. coisl. 212, written in the year 1111, the oldest manuscript that Lagarde was able to use for his edition of the *Apostolic Constitutions*. Further examples of the untrustworthiness of manuscripts and printed editions will be found in the small print at the end of this section.

several times in exactly the same form is it safe to depend on the actual wording, or when in a Commentary, *e.g.*, the context agrees with the quoted text. Collections of Scriptural passages like the *Testimonia* of Cyprian and the so-called *Speculum* of Augustine are also taken directly from manuscripts of the Bible.

Francis Lucas of Brügge was the first to explore the writings of the Church Fathers for the express purposes of textual criticism. They are referred to in four notes found in the Complutensian Polyglot. In his edition of 1516, Erasmus cites a whole series of Patristic witnesses — Ambrosius, Athanasius, Augustine, Cyprian, Gregory of Nazianzen, Origen, and Theodoret. Since that time all judicious critics have paid attention to them. Valuable service has been rendered for Tertullian by Rönsch, and for Origen by Griesbach. For Augustine, Lagarde is specially to be mentioned. Most of the Fathers were thus cared for by Burgon, who indexed the New Testament quotations in sixteen large volumes, which were deposited in the British Museum after his death. The only pity is that the works of those very Fathers that are of most importance are not yet satisfactorily edited. All the more welcome, therefore, is the appearance of the Vienna Academy's *Corpus Scriptorum Ecclesiasticorum Latinorum*, of which forty volumes have been issued since 1867, and of the Berlin Academy's edition of the Ante-Nicene Greek Fathers, of which one volume of Hippolytus and two of Origen have made their appearance.[1]

The earliest Fathers are valuable chiefly for the history of the *Canon*. That is to say, their evidence must be taken simply as showing what New Testament writings they were acquainted with, and here the *argumentum ex silentio* is to be applied with caution. This is the case with *Barnabas* and *Clement*[2] in the first century, and *Ignatius* and *Hermas* in the

[1] See extended note (2) at the end of the chapter, p. 149.

[2] On the question whether Clement of Rome knew the second Epistle of Paul to the Corinthians, see J. H. Kennedy, *The Second and Third Epistles of St. Paul to the Corinthians.* London, 1900, p. 142 ff.

first half of the second. Even with the much more extensive writings of *Justin*, there is still considerable dispute—*e.g.*, as to what Gospels he made use of.[1] *Irenæus* of Lyons is valuable on account of his extreme carefulness, and would be particularly so if it could be proved that he brought his New Testament with him from Smyrna[2] and if his writings were extant in Greek, and not, as is the case with most of them, in Latin only. In Egypt *Clement of Alexandria* holds a prominent place, but by far the most distinguished of all is the great Biblical scholar of antiquity, *Origen* (d. 248). Already we find these writers appealing to manuscripts, and distinguishing them by such epithets as "good," "old," "emended," "most," or "few." In the case of the Ante-Nicene Fathers their locality is an important consideration, whether Antioch, Cæsarea (*Eusebius*), Egypt, Constantinople (*Chrysostom*), or Cappadocia (*Theodore*), etc. Their expositions of Scripture are preserved in the so-called **Catenæ**, or continuous commentaries, in which the interpretations of different Fathers are arranged continuously like the links of a chain. It not unfrequently happens in these Catenæ that the words of one writer are cited under the name of another. The evidence afforded by the writings of the Heretics is no less valuable, if we except those passages, which are not numerous, in which they are understood to have altered the text of the Scriptures. The works of *Marcion* have been preserved for the most part in Latin by *Tertullian*. They have recently been collected and restored by Zahn. The Latin translator of Irenæus also belongs, in all probability, to the time of Tertullian, and not to the fourth century. This unknown translator seems to have preserved the Scriptural quotations of Irenæus with greater fidelity than the later Church Fathers who cite them in the Greek. Of Latin writers contemporary with or subsequent to Tertullian, those of most importance for the text of the Old Latin Bible are *Cyprian*, *Hilary of Poictiers*, *Ambrose of Milan*, *Augustine* and

[1] Westcott, *Canon*, Part I., c. ii. 7.
[2] *Ibid.*, Part II., c. i. 1.; c. ii. 4.

his opponent *Pelagius*, and for the Apocalypse, *Tyconius* and *Primasius*. From the works of Augustine Lagarde collected no fewer than 29540 quotations from the New Testament in addition to 13276 from the Old.

Valuable testimony is also afforded by Syrian and Armenian writers. It is only with their assistance, *e.g.*, that it has been possible to restore one of our oldest authorities—the Diatessaron of Tatian—which dates from the second century.

(1) Further examples might be adduced of the unreliable nature of manuscripts and printed editions.

We find, *e.g.*, in the voluminous commentary of the so-called Ambrosiaster,[1] the following note on the quotation in 1 Cor. ii. 9:—"Eye hath not seen, etc."—"hoc est scriptum in Apocalypsi Heliae in apocryphis." In place of the last five words, two manuscripts and all the printed editions previous to that of St. Maur—*i.e.* prior to the year 1690—have "in Esaia propheta aliis verbis."

Compare also what Zahn says in his *Einleitung*, ii. 314. "A comparison of the quotations in Matthew with the LXX. is rendered more difficult by the fact that in manuscripts of the latter written by Christians, and especially in Cod. Alexandrinus, the text of the O. T. has been accommodated to the form in which it is cited in the N. T. *Cf.*, also, p. 563 on the quotation from Zechariah xii. 10, found in John xix. 37. The same writer says (p. 465): "In the Chronicle of Georgios Hamartolos (circa 860), all the manuscripts save one assert the peaceful death of John (ἐν εἰρήνῃ ἀνεπαύσατο), but this one says the very opposite, μαρτυρίου κατηξίωται, and goes on to make certain other additions." On the other hand, we must not forget in this connection the testimony preserved by

[1] Ambrosiaster is the name given to the unknown writer of a Commentary on the Pauline Epistles, which till the time of Erasmus was attributed to Ambrose. In recent times Dom G. Morin has raised the question whether the writer may not be one Isaac, who is known to have lived in the papacy of Damasus. He was a Jewish convert to Christianity, and afterwards returned to his former faith. See Dom G. Morin, *L'Ambrosiaster et le juif converti Isaac, contemporain du pape Damase*, in the *Revue d'Histoire et de Littérature religieuses*, iv. 2 (1899), 112. This writer informs us that a new edition of the whole of Ambrosiaster will be brought out by A. Amelli on the basis of a very old manuscript from Monte Cassino. Morin believes that the text of this manuscript, in spite of its age, is "fortement retouché, dont on a éliminé la plupart des traits vraiment intéressants" (*ibid.*, p. 121).

Eusebius to the scrupulous care taken by Irenæus for the propagation of his writings in the identical form in which he wrote them. According to that historian, he wrote at the end of one of his works the following note:—Ὁρκίζω σε τὸν μεταγραψόμενον τὸ βιβλίον τοῦτο κατὰ τοῦ Κυρίου ἡμῶν Ἰησοῦ Χριστοῦ καὶ κατὰ τῆς ἐνδόξου παρουσίας αὐτοῦ, ἧς ἔρχεται κρῖναι ζῶντας καὶ νεκρούς, ἵνα ἀντιβάλλῃς ὃ μετεγράψω καὶ κατορθώσῃς αὐτὸ πρὸς τὸ ἀντίγραφον τοῦτο ὅθεν μετεγράψω ἐπιμελῶς, καὶ τὸν ὅρκον τοῦτον ὁμοίως μεταγράψῃς καὶ θήσεις ἐν τῷ ἀντιγράφῳ.[1]

(2) It was Lagarde who most clearly recognised and pointed out the unsatisfactory way in which the Fathers had previously been edited. How much care is necessary in the matter of the text is shown by the discussions connected with the treatment of Scriptural quotations in the new Vienna edition of Augustine (see *Urt.*, 76, 94; Preuschen, in the *ThLz.* for 1897, 24, col. 630). Even in the new Berlin edition one cannot absolutely rely on the form of the Scriptural quotations exhibited in the text, but must always verify it by means of an independent examination of the apparatus. A few passages from the first volume of Origen recently published will show this, and prove at the same time how faulty the editions have been hitherto. This first volume of Koetschau's new edition of Origen opens with the *Exhortation to Martyrdom* (εἰς μαρτύριον προτρεπτικός), a work which is to be assigned to the year 235. The text of previous editions is grounded solely on a manuscript at Basel written in the sixteenth century (No. 31, A. iii. 9), which is itself a copy, and a not altogether correct copy, of a Parisian manuscript written in the year 1339, not known to the first editors of Origen (P = suppl. grec. 616). Moreover, the Basel manuscript was not transcribed with sufficient accuracy, or the print was not superintended with sufficient care by the scholar who prepared the first printed edition of 1674. With the help of a fresh manuscript (M = Venetus Marc. 45, of the fourteenth century) it is now established that the writer of P arbitrarily altered the text in a great number of passages, and, above all, abridged it mainly by the excision of Scriptural quotations. Where Origen, *e.g.*, in citing a passage gives all three Synoptists, P quite calmly drops one of them. The *Panegyric* of Gregory Thaumaturgus is treated in the same way, this manuscript omitting about 100 out of some 1200 lines of print. And

[1] This reminds us of how Luther used to entreat the printers to let his writings stand as he wrote them.

these were the texts to which till the present we were referred for our Patristic quotations! To take an example:

On τοὺς ἐμοὺς λόγους, Luke ix. 26, Tischendorf, who in his seventh edition gave τοὺς ἐμούς (=my followers) as the correct reading, observed that this reading, without λόγους, was supported by D a e l Or., i. 298. But he added—and this is a proof of the carefulness with which the quotation from Origen is employed here—sed præcedit ουτε επαισχυντεον αυτον η τους λογους αυτου. But if we turn up this passage in the new edition, we find that it now reads (i. 34, 9 ff.): ουτ' επαισχυντεον αυτον η τους οικειους αυτου η τους λογους αυτου, and then the three parallel passages are quoted in the order frequently found in Origen—viz., Matthew x. 33 = Luke ix. 26 = Mark viii. 38. Previous editions entirely omitted this last quotation, as well as the words in the context, η τους οικειους αυτου. But now everything is in order. The words ουτ' επαισχυντεον αυτον refer to οστις δ' αν απαρνησηται με in Matt. x. 33; η τους οικειους αυτου to ος γαρ αν επαισχυνθη με και τους εμους in Luke ix. 26; and η τους λογους αυτου to ος γαρ αν επαισχυνθη με και τους εμους λογους, in Mark viii. 38. So that whereas, on the ground of previous editions, Tischendorf was obliged to point out a discrepancy between Origen's context and his peculiar quotation from Luke, the context of the new edition serves to confirm this peculiar quotation, and shows at the same time that we can accept it on the authority of this very passage, as against a former passage (p. 296 = 31, 7), where the verse in Luke is found in the newly-employed manuscript also with the words τους εμους λογους. That the editor should have put λογους in the first passage within brackets, or at least have pointed out the discrepancy between it and the quotation further down, would have been too much to expect, seeing that his manuscripts of Origen gave no manner of ground for doing so; it is the duty of those who investigate the Scriptural quotations in Origen to pay attention to such things. But there are also passages where the editor has actually gone in the face of his manuscripts, and wrongly altered the text of his Scriptural quotations, having evidently allowed himself to be influenced by the printed text of the N. T., and paying too little respect to the manuscripts.

An attentive reader will have observed that the reading in Luke ix. 26, τους εμους = my followers, which is now established for Origen, is at present supported by D alone of the Greek manuscripts and by three Old Latin witnesses. (It is also found in the Curetonian

Syriac, but unfortunately the corresponding words in the Sinai-Syriac could not be made out with certainty by Mrs. Lewis; see *Some Pages*, p. 72 = p. 168 in the first edition). Now, look at the passage in Origen's work, i. 25, 26 ff. (p. 293 in De la Rue's edition): ο μεν γαρ Ματθαιος ανεγραφε λεγοντα τον κυριον . . . . ο δε Λουκας . . . . ο δε Μαρκος· ἀββᾶ ὁ πατὴρ, δυνατά σοι πάντα· παρένεγκε κ.τ.λ. The passage is printed thus by Koetschau, agreeing exactly with the earlier printed editions and our texts of the N. T. in Mark xiv. 36. But in this he is far wrong. Because, as his own apparatus shows us, the Venetian manuscript, which he rightly follows elsewhere, reads the words in the order δυνατὰ πάντα σοί, which is exactly the order of the words (Mark xiv. 36) in D, but again in no other Greek manuscript with the solitary exception of the cursive 473.[1] But there are even passages where Koetschau follows the printed text of the N. T. in the scriptural quotations in despite of both his manuscripts. In i. 29, 13 (i. 295 De la Rue), where Matt. x. 17–23 is quoted, he inserts after πῶς ἢ τί λαλήσητε the clause δοθήσεται γὰρ ὑμῖν ἐν ἐκείνῃ τῇ ὥρᾳ τί λαλήσητε from Matt. x. 19, on the supposition that these words may have dropped out of the archetype of M P on account of the homoioteleuton. But they are also omitted in Cod. D of the N. T. And this, moreover, is not the only point of agreement between this manuscript and the text given in this quotation. There is, *e.g.*, the omission of δέ in v. 17, the reading παραδώσουσιν in v. 19, which Koetschau has altered to the more grammatical παραδῶσιν, again without sufficient reason and in defiance of both his manuscripts, and the omission of ὑμῶν in v. 20, of which there is no mention in Tischendorf (see the Collation of D in my *Supplementum*). Origen also agrees with D, though not verbally, in reading κἂν ἐκ ταύτης διώκωσιν φεύγετε εἰς τὴν ἄλλην further down (v. 23), where again Koetschau seems to me to have unnecessarily inserted τὴν, which is omitted in his principal manuscript and also in D. Compare, also, i. 22, 12, where Origen agrees with D in reading φέρωσιν (Luke xii. 11) instead of

[1] Called 2[pe] by Tischendorf, and numbered 81 in Westcott and Hort, and 565 in *TiGr.* Mark of this manuscript was edited by Belsheim in 1885, with a collation of the other three Gospels. It is a valuable cursive, as appears from what is said of it in W–H: "The most valuable cursive for the preservation of Western readings in the Gospels is 81, a St. Petersburg manuscript called 2[pe] by Tischendorf, as standing second in a list of documents collated by Muralt. It has a large ancient element, in great measure Western, and in St. Mark its ancient readings are numerous enough to be of real importance." See above, under Codex N, p. 68.

εἰσφέρωσιν, read by our critical editions on the authority of ℵ B L X; or προσφέρωσιν by the *textus receptus* with A Q R, etc. Both concur, also, in the omission of the first ἢ τί in the same verse.

What is here said as to the close affinity of Origen's Bible with Codex D is corroborated by the testimony of the Athos manuscript discovered by von der Goltz (see above, p. 90). This manuscript confirms what we knew before—viz. that Marcion's text had χριστὸν and not κύριον or θεὸν in 1 Cor. x. 9. But it also tells us what we did not know—viz. that χριστὸν was the only reading known to Origen, and that κύριον in the *Synodical Epistle* addressed to Paul of Samosata, published by Turrianus (in Routh's *Reliquiæ Sacræ*, iii.[2] 299), is not the original reading but a later substitute for χριστόν. This is made out by Zahn in the *ThLbl.*, 1899, col. 180, who concludes by saying that Clement, *Ecl. Proph.*, 49, should not be omitted in a proper apparatus, and that κύριον ought never again to be printed in the text. Our most recent editors, Tischendorf, Westcott and Hort, Weiss, and Baljon, put κύριον in their text without so much as mentioning χριστόν in the margin, or among the Noteworthy Rejected Readings, or in the list of Interchanged Words (Weiss, p. 7). In the Stuttgart edition the text is determined by a consensus of previous editions, and I was obliged to let κύριον stand in the text, but I have put χριστόν in the margin, as Tregelles also did. In this instance the *textus receptus* is actually better than our critical editions. The rejected reading is again the Western, and Zahn, in commenting on the newly-discovered testimony as to the text of 1 John iv. 3 (see below, p. 327), pertinently remarks that "here again it is perfectly evident, as any discerning person might have known, that many important readings which were wont to be contemptuously dismissed as Western, were long prevalent in the East as well, not only among the Syrians but also among the Alexandrians, and were only discarded by the official recensions of the text that were made subsequent to the time of Origen." These illustrations will serve to show that not only is the editing of the Patristic texts no easy matter, but also that the employment even of the best editions is not unaccompanied with risks. See Koetschau, *Bibelcitate bei Origenes*, ZfwTh., 1900, pp. 321–378.

(3) The Rev. Prebendary Ed. Miller is at present at work on a *Textual Commentary upon the Holy Gospels*, on the ground of Burgon's Collection and his own researches. A specimen of this work (Matthew v. 44) is given in his *Present State of the Textual Controversy respecting the Holy Gospels*, which was printed for private

circulation, and may be had of the author.[1] In this little pamphlet he takes up the question (p. 30) whether Origen in the *De Oratione* 1 (De la Rue, i. 198; Koetschau, ii. 299, 22) quotes from Luke (vi. 28) or Matthew (v. 44), and decides for the latter. Koetschau is of the opposite opinion, giving "Luke vi. 28 (Matthew v. 44)." In the case of Patristic quotations, it will be seen that matters are frequently very complicated. It must be borne in mind, too, that the various writers did not use the same copy of the Scriptures all their life long. At different times and in different localities they must necessarily have had different copies before them.

(4) It is further to be observed that in the case of controversial writings, such as those of Origen against Celsus, and Augustine against the Manichæans, the question must always be considered whether the Scriptural quotations found in them are quotations made by Origen and Augustine themselves, or taken by them from the writings they assail or refer to; and also whether the quotations have been made directly from a manuscript of the Bible, or from the works of a previous writer. Borrowing from an author without acknowledgment may have been a much more common thing in olden times than it is even at present.

In Clement of Rome (c. 13), in Clement of Alexandria (*Stromata*, ii. p. 476), and partly also in the *Epistle of Polycarp* (c. 2), we find the following quotation:—"Be ye merciful that ye may obtain mercy: forgive that ye may be forgiven: as ye do, so shall it be done to you: as ye give, so shall it be given to you: as ye judge, so shall ye be judged: as ye are kind, so shall kindness be shown to you: with what measure ye mete, it shall be meted unto you." We find also in Clement of Rome (c. 46), and in Clement of Alexandria (*Stromata*, iii. p. 561), the quotation: "Woe to that man: it were good for him if he had never been born, rather than that he should offend one of my elect: it were better for him that a millstone were hanged about his neck and he be drowned in the depth of the sea, than that he should offend one of my little ones." Neither of these quotations is found literally in our canonical Gospels. Accordingly, Rendel Harris concludes from the testimony of these various witnesses that they must have been taken from an Urevangelium, now perished (*Contemporary*

[1] The First Part has been issued: *A Textual Commentary upon the Holy Gospels.* Part I. St. Matthew, Division I., cc. i.–xiv. (London, Bell, 1899). See notice by Gwilliam in *The Critical Review*, May 1900. In this work Origen is also cited for Matt. v. 44.

Review, Sept. 1897). This view is combated, it seems to me rightly, by H. T. Andrews in the *Expository Times* for November 1897, p. 94 f. He thinks it probable that Clement of Alexandria and Polycarp are both dependent on Clement of Rome.[1]

(5) In spite of all these difficulties, a systematic examination of the Patristic quotations remains one of the most important tasks for the textual criticism of the N. T. We have most useful collections, both ancient and modern, of passages from the Fathers to illustrate the history of the Canon, and their use of the Scriptures has been scrutinised in the interests of dogmatic history, but there are not yet, so far as I know, any collections of Patristic quotations to elucidate the history of the text. Two things are specially wanted at present. One is a collection, arranged according to time and locality, of all the passages in which the Fathers appeal to ἀντίγραφα. In the new volumes of Origen, *e.g.*, we find two such references—κατά τινα τῶν ἀντιγράφων τοῦ κατὰ Μάρκον εὐαγγελίου (i. 113), and κατὰ τὰ κοινὰ τῶν ἀντιγράφων (ii. 52).[2] The other desideratum is a collection of all the passages in the biographies of the Saints where mention is made of the writing of Biblical manuscripts. It is said of Evagrius, *e.g.*, in the *Historia Lausiaca* (c. 28 in Preuschen, *Palladius*, p. 111), εὐφυῶς γὰρ ἔγραφε τὸν ὀξύρυγχον χαρακτῆρα, and the preparation of Biblical manuscripts is also referred to in the *Vita Epiphanii* (ed. Petav. ii.), and in Cassiodorus, *De Institutione Divinarum Literarum* (see above, p. 50). On the use hitherto made of Patristic testimony see the section *De Scriptoribus Ecclesiasticis* in *TiGr.*, 1129–1230. An abridged list of those mentioned there will be found in Baljon's *New Testament*, pp. xv.–xxiii. A catalogue of the names and dates of the Patristic writers most frequently cited in critical editions of the

[1] In the *Expository Times* for October 1897, p. 13 ff., I have called attention to another instance in which a Scriptural quotation (Isaiah lii. 5) is given with remarkable similarity in the *Apostolic Constitutions*, with its original (i. 10, iii. 5, vii. 204), in Ignatius (*Ad Trallianos*, viii.), and in 2nd Clement (c. xiii.). Similar things are to be observed even in the N.T., as, *e.g.*, in Mark i. 2, where a quotation from Malachi iii. 1 is inserted between the heading, "In the prophet Isaiah," and the words taken from that book. But they are found also in the writings of Paul, which has led to the view that he may possibly have used some sort of dogmatic anthology of the O. T. Clement of Alexandria has a good many quotations from Philo. On his quotations from the Gospels, see P. M. Barnard, *The Biblical Text of Clement of Alexandria in the Four Gospels and the Acts of the Apostles. Texts and Studies*, v. 5, Cambridge, 1899.

[2] See below, Appendix II., Ἀντίγραφα.

N. T. is given in Scrivener, ii. pp. 172–174.[1] See also *Urt.*, p. 22, 56 f., 94. On the Old Latin *Didascalia*, see Ed. Hauler in the *W.S.B.*, 1895, vol. cxxxiv. p. 40 ff., and the *Mitteilungen* of B. G. Teubner, 1897, ii. p. 52.[2] On the Biblical text of Filastrius (*C.S.E.*, vol. xxxviii., 1898), see Kroll in the notice of Marx's edition in the *Berlin. Phil. Wochenschrift*, 1898, 27. On Jovinian, see *TU.*, New Series, ii. 1, etc. On the quotations from the Gospels in Novatian (Pseudo-Cyprian) see Harnack in *TU.*, xiii. 4.

[1] *Vide infra*, Appendix I.
[2] Fasciculus i., edited by Hauler, 1900.

CHAPTER III.

THEORY AND PRAXIS OF THE TEXTUAL CRITICISM OF THE NEW TESTAMENT.[1]

THERE is no special theory of the textual criticism of the New Testament. The task and the method are the same for all literary productions. The task is to exhibit what the original writer intended to communicate to his readers, and the method is simply that of tracing the history of the document in question back to its beginning, if, and in so far as, we have the means to do so at our command. Diversity of treatment can only arise when the fortunes of one written work have been more chequered and complicated than those of another, or when we have more abundant means at our disposal to help us in the one case than in the other. The task is very simple when we have only one completely independent document to deal with, as in the case of several of the recently discovered papyri, but this occurs very seldom with literary texts. In this case all that we have to do is to see that we read the existing text correctly, and then by means of the

[1] I could desire no better motto for this third section than the words of Augustine: Codicibus emendandis primitus debet invigilare sollertia eorum qui scripturas nosse desiderant, ut emendatis non emendati cedant (*De Doctrina Christiana*, ii. 14, 21, where the saying about the interpretum numerositas, cited on page 108, is also found). Or if not these words, then those of our Lord himself, γίνεσθε δόκιμοι τραπεζῖται, which Origen applied to the verification of the canon, but which, taken in the sense of 1 Thess. v. 21, are equally applicable to the work of the "lower" criticism. Apollos, the pupil of Marcion, also vindicated the right of Biblical criticism with these same words. Epiphanius, *Haeres.*, xliv. 2 (Zahn, GK., i. 175).

Internal Criticism.

so-called internal criticism to determine whether the text so received can be correct. Even when several witnesses are at our command, we cannot altogether dispense with this internal criticism in the matter of sifting and weighing their testimony, only it would be unfortunate were we left with such a subjective criterion alone. For not only in such a case would different scholars come to very different conclusions, but even one and the same scholar would not be able to avoid a certain amount of uncertainty and inconsistency in most cases. The principle laid down in the maxim, *lectio difficilior placet*, or, as Bengel more correctly and more cautiously puts it, *proclivi scriptioni praestat ardua*, is perfectly sound; that reading is correct, is the original reading, from which the origin of another or of several others can be most easily explained. But how seldom can this be established with certainty! Take an illustration:—

Conclusion of the Apocalypse.

How does the Apocalypse, and the New Testament with it, conclude? Leaving out of account additions like "Amen" or "Amen, Amen," and variations like "The grace of the Lord Jesus," and "our Lord Jesus," and "the Lord Jesus Christ," and "Christ" simply, we find that the following forms are given:—

(1)	μετὰ	πάντων	ὑμῶν			
(2)	μετὰ	πάντων		ἡμῶν		
(3)	μετὰ	πάντων			τῶν	ἁγίων
(4)	μετὰ	πάντων				
(5)	μετὰ				τῶν	ἁγίων

How are we to decide without external evidence which is the correct form? Even supposing we know that the first two are out of the question, and why they are so, it is very difficult on internal grounds alone to decide between the other three. Lachmann, who did not know of (5), decided in favour of (4). But so does Tischendorf, Weizsäcker, and Weiss, the latter giving as his reason for doing so that (5), τῶν ἁγίων, is explanatory of (4), πάντων, which is manifestly too general, and that (3) is the result of a combination of these two. On the other hand, Tregelles and Westcott and Hort favour (5), without so much as mentioning (4) in their margin; while Bousset, the latest expositor of the Apocalypse, regards (3) as the correct reading, and thinks that in all probability both (4) and (5) are due to a transcriptional error. Who is to decide when doctors disagree? Manifestly one might argue on quite as good if not better grounds than those of Weiss to the very opposite conclusion—viz. that a later writer who wished the Apocalypse, and with it the New Testament, to conclude with as comprehensive a benediction as possible, substituted the words "Grace be with all" in place of the restricted and somewhat strange expression "Grace be with the saints." I did not observe that Bousset still defends the third form when I said in the first edition of this work that this reading does not fall to be considered at all. But my reason for saying so was not "because this form proves to be a combination of the other two," or "because the authorities for it are later," but because it could be shown that its supporters follow a corrected text in other places as well as this; and I concluded with observing that the decision between (4) and (5) could not be made to depend solely on internal criteria either, but depended on the decision come to regarding the general relationship between the witnesses that support each one, in this instance between A, as supporting (4), and ℵ, as supporting (5).

(1) It may be stated here, merely by way of comment, that the first form of the benediction, "with you all," was clearly translated into Greek by Erasmus from his Latin Bible, without the authority of a single Greek manuscript. But in spite of this, it is still propagated in the *textus receptus* by the English Bible Society, and even in the last revision of Luther's German Bible it was allowed to stand without demur. The English Authorised Version had it in this form, but the Revised Version adopts the fifth form "with the saints," and puts (4) in the margin, with a note to the effect that "two ancient authorities read 'with all.'"

The second form, "with us all," which was adopted by Melanchthon in his Greek Bible of 1545, published by Herwag, is just as arbitrary an alteration. The third form, "with all the saints," is read by the Complutensian with Q, with more than forty minuscules, and the Syriac, Coptic, and Armenian versions. The fourth, "with all," is found in A and Codex Amiatinus, while the fifth, "with the saints," is given by א and the Old Latin g. In the Syriac version of the Apocalypse, edited by Gwynn in 1897, a sixth form seems to have been brought to light, which Baljon, who himself decides for (5), cites as μετὰ πάντων τῶν ἁγίων αὐτοῦ: Syr^{gwynn}. But the pronoun, which in Syriac is indicated by a suffix only, is employed now and again merely to represent the Greek definite article, so that this new Syriac manuscript does not give us a sixth form but only another witness to the third. On the other hand, Gwynn mentions the omission of the entire verse in Primasius, a fact that neither Tischendorf nor Weiss takes the least notice of, and he adduces lastly that a manuscript of the Vulgate reads "cum omnibus *hominibus*." One sees from an illustration like this what an amount of pains is required seriously to apply, even in a single point, Bengel's principle that the smallest particle of gold is gold, but that nothing must be passed as gold that has not been proved to be such (*Introductio in Crisin Novi Testamenti*, § 1, p. 572).

(2) LITERATURE.—See especially Gebhardt (*Urt.*, p. 16). Ed. Reuss, *Geschichte der h. Schriften des N. T.*, Braunschweig, 1887, § 351 ff. S. P. Tregelles, *An Introduction to the Textual Criticism of the N.T.* (=vol. iv. of Horne's *Introduction*, 1877). F. H. A. Scrivener (see above, p. 6); also *Adversaria Critica Sacra*, edited by Miller, Cambr. 1893. B. F. Westcott, *The New Testament* in Smith's *Dictionary of the Bible*, vol. ii., London, 1863. C. E. Hammond, *Outlines of Textual Criticism*, Oxford, 1890. Westcott-Hort, vol. ii. (see p. 21). B. B. Warfield, *Introduction to the Textual Criticism of the N. T.*, New York, 1887; London, 1893. J. W. Burgon, *Last Twelve Verses of the Gospel according to St. Mark*, Oxford and London, 1871; also *The Traditional Text of the Holy Gospels vindicated and established*, edited by Miller, London, 1896; also, *The Causes of the Corruption of the Traditional Text of the Holy Gospels*, edited by Miller, London and Cambridge, 1896. *The Oxford Debate on the Textual Criticism of the N. T. held at New College on May* 6, 1897; with a preface (by Miller) explanatory of the Rival Systems, 1897, pp. xvi. 43. Ed. Miller, *The Present State*

of the Textual Controversy respecting the Holy Gospels (see above, p. 152).

Martin (Abbé J. P.), *Introduction à la Critique textuelle du N.T.*, in five volumes, with plates and facsimiles: vol. i. pp. xxxvi. 327, Paris, 1884, 25 fr.; vol. ii. pp. ix. 554, 1884, 40 fr.; vol. iii. pp. vi. 512, 1885, 40 fr.; vol. iv. pp. vi. 549, 1886, 40 fr.; vol. v. pp. xi. 248 and 50 pp. of facsimiles, 1886, 20 fr. Also by the same author, *Description technique des manuscrits grecs relatifs au N.T. conservés dans les Bibliothèques de Paris.* Supplement to the foregoing, Paris, 1884, pp. xix. 205, with facsimiles, 20 fr.; *Quatre manuscrits importants du N.T. auxquels on peut en ajouter un cinquième*, Paris, 1886, pp. 62, 3 fr.; *Les plus anciens mss. grecs du N.T., leur origine, leur véritable caractère*, in the *Revue des Quest. Hist.*, 1884, No. 71, pp. 62–109; *Origène et la Critique textuelle du N.T.*, Paris. Reprinted from the *Rev. des Quest. Hist.* for Jan. 1885, No. 73, pp. 5–62.

Th. Zahn, *Geschichte des N.T. Kanons*: vol. i., *Das N.T. vor Origenes*, Part 1, 1888; Part 2, 1889. Vol. ii., *Urkunden und Belege zum ersten und dritten Band*, Part 1, 1890; Part 2, 1892. The third vol. has not yet appeared. The order of the books of the N.T. is discussed in vol. ii. p. 343 ff., and the conclusion of Mark's Gospel in the same vol., p. 910 ff.

Salmon (Geo.), *Some thoughts on the Textual Criticism of the N.T.*, London, 1897, pp. xv. 162. Blass, *Philology of the Gospels*, London, 1898, pp. viii. 250. Ada Bryson, *Recent Literature on the text of the N.T.* in the *Expository Times* for April 1899, pp. 294–300. M. Vincent, *History of the Textual Criticism of the N.T.*, 1900. G. L. Cary, *The Synoptic Gospels, with a chapter on the Textual Criticism of the N.T.*, New York, 1900. See also Prof. Jannaris in the *Expositor*, vol. viii. of Series V. There is an article in the *American Journal of Theology*, 1897, iv. p. 927 ff., entitled *Alexandria and the N.T.*, which I have not been able to consult.

In attempting to restore the text of the New Testament as nearly as possible to its original form, it is essential to remember that the New Testament, as we have it to-day, is not all of one piece, but consists of twenty-seven separate documents now arranged in five groups, and that every several document and every several group has had its own peculiar history. Of these groups the most complicated, perhaps, is the one with which the New Testament opens—viz. the Gospels.

It is quite uncertain when our four Gospels were first written together in one volume and arranged in the order that is now common. The Muratorian Fragment on the Canon [1] is defective at the beginning, but seems to imply this arrangement. It was supposed that the Gospels were written in the following order—viz. Matthew first and John last. The order, Matthew, Mark, Luke, John, which is found in nearly all the Greek and Syriac manuscripts, was made popular by Eusebius and Jerome. The former followed it in his *Canons*, which were afterwards adopted by Jerome in his Latin Bible. According to Eusebius (*Eccl. Hist.*, vi. 25),[2] Origen knew this order, though he very frequently cites the Gospels in the order Matthew, Luke, Mark. Gospels.

The following arrangements are also found:—

(2) Matthew, Mark, John, Luke, in the earlier (Curetonian) Syriac and in the Canon Mommsenianus, a catalogue of the Books of the Bible and of the works of Cyprian, originating in Latin Africa about the year 360, and first published by Mommsen.[3]

(3) Matthew, Luke, Mark, John, in the so-called Ambrosiaster and in a Catalogue of the Sixty Canonical Books.

[1] The fragment was edited by Tregelles with a facsimile in 1867. It is given in Westcott's *Canon of the N. T.*, Appendix C, where also see the section on the Muratorian Canon, Part i. c. ii. It will be found also in Preuschen's *Analecta, Kürzere Texte* . . . . pp. 129–137 (the eighth number of G. Krüger's *Sammlung ausgewählter kirchen- und dogmengeschichtlicher Quellenschriften*, Freib. and Leipzig, 1893).

[2] Quoted in Westcott, *Canon*, part ii. c. ii. § 1, and in Zahn's *Einleitung*, ii. 179.

[3] Given in Preuschen. In the manuscripts it is entitled "Indiculum Veteris et Novi Testamenti et Caecili Cipriani." It was first made known from a MS. at Cheltenham in 1886. As it is mostly assigned to the year 365 (see also Jülicher, *Einleitung*, p. 336) the words of W.-W. may be repeated here: "S. Berger tamen aliter sentit, rationibus commotus quarum una certe nobis satis vera videtur. Concordant enim numeri in Veteri Testamento cum codicibus Hieronymianis, *e.g.* in libris Regum quattuor, Esaiae, Jeremiae, et duodecim Prophetarum, Tobiae, et Macchabeorum secundo. Indiculus tamen sine dubio antiquus est" (p. 736).

L

(4) Matthew, John, Mark, Luke—*i.e.* the two Apostles put before the two pupils of Apostles, in the Codex Claromontanus.[1] This order occurs also in the Arabic writer Masudi's *Meadows of Gold*.[2]

(5) Matthew, John, Luke, Mark, in Codd. D and X, in the *Apostolic Constitutions*, in Ulfilas, and especially in the Old Latin Manuscripts; see Corssen, *Monarchianische Prologe*, p. 65, in *TU*. xv. 1.[3]

(6) John, Luke, Mark, Matthew, in Codex k.

(7) John, Matthew, Mark, Luke, in the Vocabularies of the Egyptian versions.

(8) John, Matthew, Luke, Mark, in Tertullian and cod. 19. See Arthur Wright, *Some New Testament Problems*, p. 196 ff.[4]

This very variety shows that for a long time, perhaps till the third century, at all events much longer than the Pauline Epistles, the Gospels were propagated singly, perhaps on rolls, and only afterwards incorporated in a codex. And this makes it probable that the text of our manuscripts was not taken from a single copy of the first Tetraevangelium. More than probable we cannot call it, seeing that a copyist may have had any sort of reasons of his own for disarranging the order of the books given in his exemplar, as may still be gathered luckily from the position occupied by Hebrews in Codex B. The probability is heightened, however, by the fact that our manuscripts display a considerably greater amount of textual variation in the Gospels than in the Pauline Epistles, though not in all to the same extent as in D which contains an entirely peculiar recension, especially in Luke. One of the most remarkable indications of this is afforded by the discovery made by E. Lippelt, a pupil of Professor Blass. The order of the books in D is Matthew, John, Luke, Mark, Acts, where it will be seen that the two portions of the book

[1] Catalogus Claramontanus given in Westcott, *Canon*, Appendix D, p. 563.

[2] Translated into French, *Prairies d'or*, i. 123: one volume into English by Sprenger. 1841; Sayous, *Jésus Christ d'après Mohammed*, p. 34.

[3] See Zahn, *Einl.*, ii. 176; *GK.*, ii. 364–375, 1014.

[4] See *Addenda*, p. xvi.

inscribed to Theophilus are separated by Mark. Now Lippelt observed that while the name Johannes is regularly spelt with two ν's (Ἰωάννης) in Matthew, John, and Mark, it is just as regularly spelt with one (Ἰωάνης) in Luke and Acts, sundered though these two books are by Mark, where the other spelling prevails.[1] This shows an accuracy of tradition which is surprising, but till now it has only been traced in this one manuscript. The others write the name throughout with two ν's and B as consistently with one. In this connection the question naturally arises whether certain liberties were not taken with the books on the occasion of their collection and arrangement. Resch, *e.g.*, thinks that it was then that the second Gospel received the conclusion or appendix which is found in most of our manuscripts, and Rohrbach holds a similar opinion.[2] I have elsewhere expressed the idea that the peculiar opening of Mark is to be accounted for in this way.[3] Zahn, however, doubts whether the use of ἀρχή and τέλος for ἄρχεται and ἐτελέσθη, *incipit* and *explicit*, can be established for early times.[4] I have found it in Greek Psalters, though not very early, I admit, where αρχη των ωδων occurs instead of ωδαι as the superscription of the Hymns at the end of the Psalter.[5] However, there is no need to dwell

[1] The numbers are as follows :—

	-ν-	-νν-
Matthew,	2	24
John,	7	17
Luke,	27	1
Mark,	2	24
Acts,	21	2

See Blass, *Lucae ad Theophilum liber prior*, p. vi. f., *Philology of the Gospels*, p. 75 f., where three of Lippelt's numbers are corrected with the help of Harris. See also *Expository Times*, Nov. 1897, p. 92 f. I cannot understand why Wendt, in the new edition of his Commentary on the Acts, should take not the slightest notice of this far-reaching discovery. On the spelling in the Latin manuscripts, see W.-W., *Epilogus*, 776.

[2] *Der Schluss des Markus-Evangeliums, der Vier-Evangelien-Kanon, und die kleinasiastischen Presbyter* (Berlin, 1894).

[3] *Expositor*, Dec. 1894.

[4] *Einleitung*, ii. 221.

[5] See Coxe's *Catalogue of Greek MSS. in the Bodleian Library*, 1854.

further on this point. Zahn (p. 174) is quite right in his contention that the usual titles κατὰ Μαθθαῖον, etc.,[1] imply a collection of the Gospels of which Εὐαγγέλιον is the general title.

If, then, for the sake of simplicity, we take as our goal the first manuscript of the Tetraevangelium, one would think it must be possible with the means at our command gradually to work back to it. Even the latest of our manuscripts is surely copied from an earlier one, and that one from another, and so on always further and further back, so that all we have to do is to establish their genealogy, pretty much as Reuss has done for the printed editions of the New Testament; and seeing we have manuscripts as old as the fourth and fifth century, that means that the entire period of a thousand years prior to the invention of printing is bridged over at once, so that the task would appear to be simply that of throwing a bridge over the first few centuries of the Christian era. And by going on comparing the witnesses and always eliminating those that prove unreliable, it must be possible, one would suppose, in this way to arrive at the original. But a little experience will shortly moderate our expectations.

At the outset it is very much against us that we have no really serviceable text for comparison. The text of our present critical editions is a patchwork of many colours, more wonderful than the cloak of Child Roland of old. In fact it is a text that never really existed at all. In the preparation of my *Supplement*, which I undertook with the object of making the text of Codex Bezae easily accessible to every one, I compared the text of that manuscript with that of Tischendorf-Gebhardt's edition, and I saw clearly that my work would necessarily present a very confused appearance indeed. I also issued an interleaved edition of my Stuttgart New Testament with a similar object—viz. to furnish a convenient means of

[1] On *cata* or *kata* in the subscriptions, titles, prefaces, etc., of Latin manuscripts, see the index in W.-W., to which add the remarkable phrase *cata tempus*, which codex e gives in John v. 4, in place of *secundum tempus* in the other manuscripts.

comparing the text of manuscripts and of Patristic quotations, but that, too, labours under the same disadvantage. Whoever intends really to further the textual criticism of the New Testament will have to issue a copy of a single manuscript printed in such a way as will make it practically convenient for the comparison of different texts, something like Tischendorf's edition of Codex Sinaiticus (*Novum Testamentum Sinaiticum*, 1863), which, however, is of little use for other purposes, or like Schjøtt's edition of the New Testament (see above, p. 24). But as these are in the hands of very few, there is nothing for it at present but to take one of our most common texts, always bearing in mind its composite character. This feature of the text appears at the very outset in the title. In ℵ B (D) it is *κατα* Μαθθαιου. Codex D is defective at the beginning down to c. i. 20, but *κατ* Μαθθαιου is found regularly as the title at the top of the pages, a fact which Tischendorf has overlooked. Most other manuscripts, C E K M etc., have Ευαγγελιον *κατα* Ματθαιου. If this latter is held as incorrect, then all these manuscripts should for the future be dropped out of account and ℵ B D alone be regarded as authoritative.

Again, in verse 2, ℵ* has Ισακ twice, while the others have Ισαακ, so that ℵ too would drop out, leaving B standing alone. But then in verse 3 our editors forthwith reject B, which reads Ζαρε, and decide in favour of the others which have Ζαρα. Whether this may not be a little premature, seeing that there are other places where ε is found for final ח,[1] and that one manuscript, 56, has deliberately corrected Ζαρα into Ζαρε in Gen. xxxviii. 30, where a third has Ζαρε, we do not pause to determine. The point is simply this, that in these first three verses there is no manuscript that is always right in the judgment of our editors. True, the cases we have been considering are trifling, the differences being of an orthographical nature merely, and one must not be too particular in such matters, though at the same time the oft-quoted maxim, *minima non curat praetor*, is nowhere less

[1] See Field, *Hexapla*, i. p. lxxii.

applicable than in textual criticism. But the same state of things reappears immediately where we have differences involving important matters of fact. What is the fact in verse 11? Did Josias beget Jechoniah, or did he beget Joachim and Joachim Jechoniah? Verse 16 has already been referred to: in this case our oldest Greek manuscripts would give no occasion to mention the verse. But in verse 25 we have again to ask which is correct, ἔτεκεν υἱόν or ἔτεκεν τὸν υἱὸν αὐτῆς τὸν πρωτότοκον? And when we hear Jerome say—Ex hoc loco quidam perversissime suspicantur et alios filios habuisse Mariam, dicentes primogenitum non dici nisi qui habeat et fratres, we learn already how dogmatic motives may have some influence upon the form of the text. And, moreover, when we call to mind the words of Luke ii. 7, we are made aware of another thing that may exert a disturbing influence in the Gospels—viz. the tendency to alter the text in conformity with the parallel passage. Apart from the stylistic peculiarities of Codex D, we meet with no materially important variants in our Greek manuscripts of Matthew till we come to the Sermon on the Mount. The only thing is in iii. 15, where two Latin witnesses have an addition which is evidently taken from a Greek source: et cum baptizaretur, lumen ingens circumfulsit de aqua ita ut timerent omnes qui advenerant (congregati erant). This interpolation, however, does not concern the criticism of the text of the New Testament, seeing that it is derived from some source outside the Canon.

Dogmatic influence.

Parallel passages.

On the other hand, there is a great question as to the order of the first three Beatitudes in Matthew v. 3–5, whether they are to be read in the order given in the common text, πτωχοί . . . . . πενθοῦντες . . . . πραεῖς . . . . , or as our recent editors prefer πτωχοί . . . . πραεῖς . . . . πενθοῦντες.[1] The latter arrangement is attested by only two Greek manuscripts —D and 33. Now, if their evidence is accepted here in spite of

[1] The order, πραεῖς . . . . πτωχοί . . . . πενθοῦντες, in Baljon is due to a strange oversight which is not corrected in the Addenda et Corrigenda.

its apparent weakness, how can we justify the refusal to acknowledge the authority of D in other similar cases? Verse 22, but a short way down, is a case in point. Here D, with most authorities, exhibits the sorely-contested εἰκῇ. But our modern critics will have nothing to do with it, going by ℵ B, Origen, Jerome, and Athanasius. Merx (*Die vier kanonischen Evangelien*, pp. 231–237) has recently come forward as a strong supporter of it, on the ground that Syr^{sin} also has it,[1] but how is its omission, especially by Jerome, to be explained? The Vulgate itself shows that it was easier to insert it than to omit it, because out of twenty-four manuscripts collated in W.–W. three have it, though it certainly does not belong to the text of the Vulgate.[2]

In view of these illustrations, which serve to show the somewhat haphazard way in which the text of our editions hitherto has been arrived at, the question becomes very important how the original text is to be restored in disputed or doubtful cases.

Conjectural emendation.

The first case, or, if we like to call it, the last, but at all events the one most easy of settlement, is when the correct reading is no longer found in any of our witnesses, neither in Greek manuscript, version, nor patristic quotation. Here we must simply have recourse to **conjecture.** Not long ago philologists evinced such a fondness for conjectural emendation that the question might not unreasonably be asked why they did not rather themselves write the text that they took in hand to explain. At the same time, the aversion to this method of criticism which till recently prevailed and still to some extent prevails, especially in the matter of the New Testament text, is just as unreasonable. Tischendorf, *e.g.*, did not admit a single emendation of this nature into his text, while Westcott and Hort consider it to be necessary in only a

[1] To the passages which may be adduced in support of the reading, add Clement, *Hom.* η 32 (Lagarde, 92, 35), ια 32 (118, 31).

[2] Codex D and Syr^{sin} also agree in omitting v. 30, but this is probably no more than a remarkable coincidence.

very few cases, such as Colossians ii. 18, though they also decline to adopt any conjectural readings in their text. For ΑΕΟΡΑΚΕΝΕΜΒΑΤΕΥΩΝ in this passage, which Weizsäcker renders "pluming himself upon his visions," they would read ΑΕΡΑ ΚΕΝΕΜΒΑΤΕΥΩΝ, which is obtained by the omission of a single letter and a different division of the words. In Holland conjectural criticism is freely indulged in,[1] the example of Cobet and his school being followed by such critics as S. A. Naber, W. C. van Manen, W. H. van de Sande-Bakhuyzen, van de Becke Callenfels, D. Harting, S. S. de Koe, H. Franssen, J. M. S. Baljon, J. H. A. Michelsen, and J. Cramer.[2] Baljon has adopted a great number of such conjectural emendations in his edition of the text published in 1898 (see above, p. 24). In place of *πολλοὶ διδάσκαλοι*, *e.g.*, in James iii. 1, Lachmann would read *πῶλοι δύσκολοι*, Naber *πλανοδιδάσκαλοι*, while Junius, de Hoop-Scheffer, and Bakhuyzen prefer *πολυλάλοι* on the ground that m[64] has *nolite multiloqui esse*.[3] So far, therefore, this last is not pure conjecture. For *κρινέτω* in Col. ii. 16 Lagarde wished to read *κιρνάτω*, because the verb דוד found in the Peshitto at this place is elsewhere used to translate *θροεῖν* (Matt. xxiv. 6), *ταράσσειν* (John xiv. 1, 27), *ἐγκόπτειν* (Gal. v. 7), and also *διαστρέφειν* (Eccl. vii. 18; xii. 3). My proposal to read *ἐπὶ πόντον* in Apoc. xviii. 17, a reading adopted by Baljon in his text, instead of *ἐπὶ τόπον* or *ἐπὶ πλοίων* as given in our manuscripts, was a pure conjecture, but it has the support of *super mare* in Primasius.[4] There is therefore no objection on principle to the method of con-

[1] See *Urt.*, 55 ff, where works on this subject are cited.

[2] See also Linwood, *Remarks on Conjectural Emendations as applied to the New Testament*, 1873.

[3] On the symbol m, see above, p. 114.

[4] The converse occurs in Eusebius, *Eccl. Hist.*, iv. 15, in the address of Polycarp's *Martyrium*. There the reading *κατὰ Πόντον*, which is also found in the Syriac, should, according to Harnack's *Chronologie der altchristl. Lit.*, i. 341, be replaced by *κατὰ πάντα τόπον*, or rather by *κατὰ τόπον* which is found in 1 Macc. xii. 4; 2 Macc. xii. 2. Compare also the variation found in the manuscripts in 2 Cor. x. 15 between *κοποις*, *πονοις*, and *τοποις*, and between *ποτος* and *τοπος* in Judith vi. 21. See also Eusebius, *Eccl. Hist.*, v. 15, 23.

jecture, nor to the adoption of conjectural readings in the text, though it is only to be resorted to as the *ultima ratio regis* and with due regard to all the considerations involved, transcriptional, linguistic, and otherwise.[1] There is no essential difficulty in supposing, *e.g.*, that κιρνάτω in Col. ii. 16 was first corrupted into κρινάτω and then into κρινέτω. Such a transposition of the liquid is quite common in all languages.[2] But we must see if κιρνάτω has the sense required in the passage. There is no doubt a reference to drinking here, and so far, therefore, the word seems to suit the context better. It is also true that evidence is not wanting of the metaphorical use of the word proposed to be inserted. Passow, *e.g.*, gives τὸ τῆς φύσεως σκληρὸν κιρνᾶν from Polybius iv. 21, 3, and τὴν πόλιν κιρνᾶν from Aristophanes i. 1. In spite of this, however, I have considerable misgivings whether this sense of the word is in harmony with Pauline usage and is suitable to the context of the passage. If it is sought to justify a conjectural reading on transcriptional grounds, then, as has been observed (p. 82), a strict account must be taken of the manner of writing

[1] The opposite view is expressed in Scrivener, ii. 244: "It is now agreed among competent judges that Conjectural Emendation must never be resorted to, even in passages of acknowledged difficulty"; and he quotes from Roberts (*Words of the New Testament*): "conjectural criticism is entirely banished from the field . . . . simply because there is no need for it." With this, however, he does not quite agree. He admits that there are passages respecting which we cannot help framing a shrewd suspicion that the original reading differed from any form in which they are now presented to us. He notes as passages for which we should be glad of more light, Acts vii. 46, xiii. 32, xix. 40, xxvi. 28; Rom. viii. 2; 1 Cor. xii. 2, where Ephes. ii. 11 might suggest ὅτι ποτέ; 1 Tim. vi. 7; 2 Pet. iii. 10, 12; Jude 5, 22, 23. G. Krüger expresses himself to the same effect. He would have no conjecture, however well founded, received into the text. See his notice of Koetschau's Origen in the *L. Cbl.*, No. 39, 1899. I find that Swete has had no objection to adopt a conjecture of mine in his second edition of the last volume of the Cambridge Septuagint (Enoch xiv. 3). If such a thing is permissible in the case of Enoch, why should it not be allowable in the New Testament? As clever suggestions may be noted ἐκολάφισαν for the hapax legomenon ἐκεφαλίωσαν, Mark xii. 4 (Linwood, Van de Sande-Bakhuyzen) and λανθάνουσι for μανθάνουσι, 1 Tim. v. 13 (Hitzig). Lagrange (*Revue Biblique*, 1900, p. 206) cautions us against "prêter de l'esprit à l'Esprit Saint."

[2] Compare my conjecture of מְפַתְּרִם for מִתְרַפֵּס, Ps. lxviii. 31, and see below, p. 236.

prevalent at the time when the corruption is supposed to have originated. Luke's handwriting must have been very bad indeed if we are to suppose that the scribe of D or the parent manuscript mistook ἠρνήσασθε for the enigmatical ἐβαρύνατε in Acts iii. 14, though it is quite conceivable how he came to write δόξῃ instead of δεξιᾷ in v. 31, or conversely wrote ἐδέξαντο instead of ἐδόξασαν in xiii. 48, or that ΚΑΙΤΟΥΤΩΣΥΝΦΩΝΟΥΣΙΝ was made into ΚΑΙΟΥΤΩΣΣΥΝΦΩΝΗΣΟΥΣΙΝ or *vice versa.*[1] A slight experience in the reading of ancient manuscripts shows how easy it is to make mistakes of this sort. And if we wish to see what mistakes of this sort actually do occur in Codices Vaticanus, Alexandrinus, Sinaiticus, and Ephraemi, we have only to look into Morrish's *Handy Concordance of the Septuagint,*[2] though of course the examples there are all from the Old Testament. We have, *e.g.*, ἀγαπάω for ἀπατάω; ἀγάπη for ἀπάτη; ἁγιάζω for ἀγοράζω; ἅγιος for αἴγειος, ἀγγεῖον, ἀγρός, γῆ; ἀδιάλυτος for διάλυτος; βάλλω and its compounds for λαμβάνω and its compounds; λαός for ναός, etc.

Eclectic method.

It is more difficult to answer the question how the text is to be restored in cases where there is no lack of external evidence. We have already seen that critics have hitherto adopted an eclectic mode of procedure. In general, whenever Vaticanus and Sinaiticus agree, editors, Tischendorf as well as Westcott and Hort, give the preference to their testimony. But if they do not agree, what is to be done? And what if a third reading seems on internal grounds to be better than either? In his *Thoughts on the Textual Criticism of the New Testament,* Salmon very pungently, but not altogether incorrectly, describes Westcott and Hort's method on the lines of an anecdote told of Cato by Cicero: "To the question what authorities should be followed, Hort answers, Follow B א. But if B is not supported by א? Still follow B, if it has the

[1] Meyer-Wendt[8], p. 51. For an example of Σ repeated by mistake, *cf.* ΈΙΣΣΤΕΛΟΣ in B, Mark xiii. 13. Its erroneous omission is quite common.

[2] Bagster, London, 1887.

support of any other manuscript. But suppose B stands quite alone? Even then it is not safe to reject B unless it is clearly a clerical error. But suppose B is defective? Then follow ℵ. And what about D? What about killing a man!" Lagarde has said that the gag is the modern equivalent of the stake. Codex D has not been gagged outright, to be sure, but it has been shoved aside, and only now and then with remarkable inconsistency has its evidence been accepted as trustworthy. For one must surely call it inconsistent to follow one side as a rule and then all at once to take sides with that which is diametrically opposed to the first. In his *Introduction*, Hort, in the most brilliant manner one must admit, has established the principle that the restoration of the text must be grounded on the study of its history, and no one has studied that history as carefully as Hort has done. But the question remains whether he has not interpreted the history wrongly, whether what he calls the Neutral text is really the original, and whether that which he rejects as a Western Corruption is really to be regarded as such.

History of transmission.

I cannot presume to judge; but I have the feeling that the history of the transmission of our New Testament text must be studied in quite another way from that in which it has been done hitherto, and in a twofold direction:—

(1) The manuscripts and their relation to each other must be subjected to a still more searching investigation, and

(2) The works of the ecclesiastical writers, especially the Commentaries and the Catenæ, must be thoroughly explored for any information they may have to give regarding the history of the text of the New Testament, and these two results must then be set in relation with each other.

With regard to the former task, it might not be essential to make such a minute collation of the manuscripts as Ferrar, Hoskier, and other investigators deemed necessary, and as is certainly the right thing to do in the case of the oldest documents. With such a mode of procedure, the task could not be accomplished in any conceivable time. But suppose the work was organised the way that Reuss did with the printed editions, by selecting say a thousand passages for comparison, it would be possible, and in a very short time we should be much better informed than we are at present as to the state of the text in our manuscripts, and especially in the minuscules.

Such a task, moreover, must be preceded by a fresh scientific statement of the way in which the text was propagated previous to the invention of printing, on the lines laid down by Hort in the first fourteen paragraphs of his *Introduction.*[1] A necessary preliminary to this is the study of genealogy, in which we have an excellent guide in Ottokar Lorenz's *Lehrbuch der gesamten wissenschaftlichen Genealogie* (Berlin, 1898). See especially the first chapter of Part I. on the distinction between Genealogical Tree (Table of genealogy) and Table of Ancestors, and the third chapter of Part II. on the problem of Loss of Ancestors.

All the ideas pertaining to the genealogy of living creatures, such as crossing, heredity, and so forth, fall to be considered also in the genealogy of manuscripts, the only difference being that in the latter case new features make their appearance. It has been asserted somewhere that if an Englishman, a Dutchman, a German, a Frenchman, and an American meet in a company, the nationality of each is at once recognisable, but it is impossible to determine their exact genealogical relationships, and that the same impossibility exists in the case of the manuscripts of the New Testament. That is perhaps an exaggeration, but it is certainly a surprising fact that so few even of our latest manuscripts can be proved with certainty to be copies of manuscripts still in existence, or at least to be derived from a common original.

Analogous works.

It will be a very great help, particularly to those beginning

[1] See Isaac Taylor's *History of the Transmission of Ancient Books to Modern Times* (1827); and compare also the text-books on Hermeneutics, *e.g.* in I. v. Müller's *Handbuch der klassischen Altertumswissenschaft.*

work in this field, to compare the method and results of investigations pursued in similar and perhaps easier departments of study. Apart from the works of classical philologists, or works like the new edition of Luther's writings, a great deal of most valuable research has been carried on of late years in the matter of textual criticism, some of it very extensive, some of it less so. Ed. Wölfflin, *e.g.*, devoted his attention to the Rule of St. Benedict of Nursia, who died some time after the year 542. His Rule, which extends only to eighty-five pages of the Teubner size, is extant in manuscripts dating as far back as the seventh and eighth centuries. By a comparison of these, Wölfflin was convinced that we still possess the Rule essentially in the identical wording of the original vulgar Latin, that Benedict himself had afterwards made certain alterations and additions, and that we have therefore to distinguish several (fortasse tres) editions.[1] Wölfflin purported to give the text of that recension which he took to be the earliest. But we had no more than time to congratulate ourselves on the satisfactory result arrived at by this experienced philologist, when behold, another totally different conclusion was announced by a younger worker in the same field. Wölfflin had done little more than compare the manuscripts, but Lud. Traube applied also the external evidence afforded by the history of the text, and discovered that certain manuscripts that Wölfflin had thrown aside possessed a greater claim to originality.[2] Rule of Benedict.

Similarly, E. C. Richardson gave several years to an examination of all the accessible manuscripts of the *De Viris Illustribus* of Jerome and Gennadius, a work not much larger than the Rule of Benedict. These manuscripts, about 120 in De Viris Illustribus.

[1] *Benedicti regula monachorum. Recensuit Ed. Wölfflin*, Lipsiae, Teubner, 1895, pp. xv. 85, 8vo. See also his article on the Latinity of Benedict in the *Arch. f. Lat. Lexikogr.* ix. 4, 1896, pp. 493–521.

[2] *Textgeschichte der Regula S. Benedicti* (*Abh. d.* 3 *Cl. d. k. Ak. d. Wiss.*, vol. xxi., Munich, 1898). Compare also *The Text of St. Benedict's Rule* by Dom C. Butler, O.S.B. Reprinted from the *Downside Review*, December 1899, 12 pp.

number, he grouped, and then framed his text in accordance with them.[1] While his work was in the press, an edition was published by C. A. Bernoulli, based on some of the manuscripts that Richardson also had used.[2] But from the very first sentence onwards, the two editors follow contradictory authorities, so that while one gives *parvam* as the correct reading, the other reads *non parvam.* But more than that, the same Part of *Texte und Untersuchungen* that gave us Richardson's laborious work contained a second piece of work on the same material—viz., O. v. Gebhardt's edition of the so-called Greek Sophronius, which is an old version of Jerome's book. And the last chapter of this version, which is autobiographical, contains indications, according to v. Gebhardt's Introduction, that Jerome issued two editions of his book, so that, if this be so, an entirely new grouping of the manuscripts becomes necessary.

In the case of Holl's researches on the *Sacra Parallela* of John Damascene, published in the same Collection,[3] matters are too complicated for beginners in textual criticism, but of non-biblical texts mention may be made of the *Recherches sur la tradition manuscrite des lettres de l'Empereur Julien* by S. Bidez and Fr. Cumont (Brussels, 1898), as showing how much can be attained by combining the internal and external history of the transmission of literary texts.[4] In the field of Biblical texts, and particularly of the New Testament, the study of Wordsworth and White's *Epilogus* to the first volume of their *Novum Testamentum Latine* is to be specially recommended, particularly c. iv. *De Patria et Indole Codicum nostrorum*, c. v. *De Textus Historia*, and c. vi. *De Regulis a nobis in Textu constituendo adhibitis.* As was said before, Jerome undertook his revision of the Gospels in the year 383; his work was of an entirely uniform texture, apart from a few

Julian's Letters.

Latin New Testament.

[1] *TU.* xiv. 1, 1896.

[2] Krüger's *Sammlung*, Heft xi., Freiburg and Leipzig, 1895.

[3] *TU.*, New Series, i. 1, 1897.

[4] Compare also the differences between the editions of Josephus, published by Niese and Naber.

passages where a correction may have occurred even in the original manuscript; and there is a sufficiency of manuscripts extant, some of them going back to the sixth century. One of these, which formerly belonged to the Church of St. Willibrord at Echternach, contains a note dated 558, and copied into it from the parent manuscript, to the effect: proemendavi ut potui secundum codicem in bibliotheca Eugipi presbyteri, quem ferunt fuisse sancti Hieronymi. (See above, p. 122.) In these circumstances it must surely be possible, one would think, to arrive at some satisfactory conclusion. And yet, in spite of all this, and in spite of long years of labour, many a problem remains to perplex the editor of the Vulgate. To begin with, there is one striking circumstance. Jerome executed his work at Rome, in obedience to the commission of Pope Damasus. One would therefore expect to find the best manuscripts in Rome, or at least originating from Rome. But that is by no means the case: "praeter expectationem accidit ut pauci vel nulli ex codicibus optimis et antiquissimis originem Romanam clare ostendant." The manuscript that editors consider the best—viz. Codex Amiatinus, now at Florence—was certainly at Rome for a long time, but it was sent there as a present from beyond the Alps; indeed, it came from England. And on the other hand it was not from Rome that the Latin Bible came to England, or to Canterbury in particular, although Augustine was sent thither by Pope Gregory the Great, but from the South of Italy; in fact, it was from Naples. Codex Fuldensis, which may have been brought to Fulda by Boniface, formerly belonged to Bishop Victor of Capua; the Echternach manuscript referred to above came from the Lucullan Monastery at Naples, while the manuscript from which Codex Amiatinus was copied was written by Cassiodorus of Vivarium, and therefore came from Calabria. The history of the transmission of the Latin Bible reveals many other facts as strange as these in connection with the locality to which manuscripts belong. We must be prepared, therefore, for similar surprises in the case of Greek manuscripts also, and need not be astonished to hear that the Greek-Latin Codex Bezae, so much decried as "Western," takes us back to Smyrna or Ephesus by way of Lyons and by means of Irenæus.[1]

Families. It is also very instructive to observe that after long years of the most thorough study of their manuscripts, Wordsworth and White refrain from constructing **stemmata** or genealogies of these. All they venture to do is to distinguish certain large classes or **families**, and within these again to bring certain manuscripts into somewhat closer relationship with each other. They distinguish two main classes. In the first they reckon five, or it may be four, Italian-Northumbrian manuscripts, A Δ H* S Y, two Canterbury O X, three Italian J M P, the two mentioned already from Capua-Fulda F and Lucullan-Echternach EP, and the Harleian Z, so called from a former possessor and now in the British Museum. To the second class belong five Celtic D E L Q R, three French B BF G, and two Spanish C T. After these come the witnesses to the history of the text in the stricter sense of the term, the recensions made by Theodulf (H^c Θ) and Alcuin (KV MT), and, for the form which the text assumed in the later manuscripts and in the printed editions, the Salisbury Codex W. We should have great reason to congratulate ourselves, could we arrive at like certain results in the region of the far older and more diversified history of the transmission of the Greek text, but there too we shall encounter the same general features—viz., a form of the text in the printed editions, in the later manuscripts, in the Recensions, the dates of which are still to be determined (Lucian, Hesychius ?, Pamphilus), and in the families, which are only to be classified in a general way.

It is also instructive to find that in the case of several manuscripts, Wordsworth and White are obliged to observe that they seem to have been corrected from the Greek, H*

[1] See, however, the two articles by Lake and Brightman, *On the Italian Origin of Codex Bezae* in the *Journal of Theological Studies*, i. 441 ff.

(p. 709), M (p. 711), EP* (p. 712), D R L (pp. 714, 716), which suggests the possibility of Greek manuscripts also having been influenced by one of the versions, be it Latin or Syriac.

Finally, when we enquire as to the relationship between Jerome and the Greek manuscript or manuscripts used by him, we find that that manuscript must have been most nearly related to the Sinaiticus, while it had no sort of connection with Codex D. Whether this result tells in favour of ℵ or the reverse, we will not pronounce at present: Jerome certainly avers that he made use of a Graecorum codicum emendata conlatione . . . . sed veterum (p. 108), only *veterum* is a comparative term, and it might quite well happen that to Jerome that form of text appeared to be the best which was most recent or most widely circulated in his neighbourhood, and that he would have nothing to do with such a singular form of text as D exhibits, even supposing he was acquainted with it, a point we cannot decide. The intimate connection in various passages between his text and that of the cursive 473 (2^{pe}) is remarkable, and especially the many points of resemblance between the Irish manuscripts (D L R) and the members of the Ferrar Group.

And this brings us back from our survey of the history of the Latin text to that of the Greek, where we seem to have got at least one fixed point to begin with in this perplexing chaos, for that is the first impression we gain on glancing at the mass of Greek manuscripts before us. But here again our too sanguine hopes are likely to be disappointed, and we shall learn only too soon that even this is no Archimedean point from which we are able to regulate this world of disorder.

Ferrar Group.

If we find that in a certain number of manuscripts the passage usually indicated as John vii. 53–viii. 11 occurs in Luke, and in exactly the same place in each one—viz. after Luke xxi. 38—we must needs conclude that the manuscripts exhibiting this common peculiarity are intimately connected with each other. This is the case with the cursives 13, 69,

124, 346, 624, 626. Whether the others that are reckoned in this group have this same peculiarity, I am not perfectly sure. Now one would naturally expect that these manuscripts would also coincide in the other peculiarities characteristic of this group. But on the contrary, they part company over the very first and most conspicuous of these—viz. Matthew i. 16. Here, unfortunately, 13 and 69 are defective, but we can compare 124 and 346. And we find that whereas the former has the usual text, the latter, with the support of 556, 624, 626, exhibits in place of τὸν ἄνδρα . . . . Χριστός, the reading already mentioned, ᾧ μνηστευθεῖσα παρθένος Μαριὰμ ἐγέννησεν Ἰησοῦν τὸν λεγόμενον Χριστόν. Which of these readings is right, or whether both of them may not be wrong, we need not enquire at present. It is sufficient to point out that one and the same mother may give birth to very different children. The specific difference will be inherited from the other of the two parents, in this case represented by the copyist, and will depend on whether he is painstaking, careless, violent, arbitrary, well-informed, or the reverse. But the mother herself has a great number of hereditary or acquired peculiarities which, the latter no less than the former, may be transmitted to the children in a variety of ways. There is perhaps no manuscript in existence which is entirely free from corrections, while, on the other hand, there are many so overlaid with corrections that the original writing is scarcely now recognisable. Codex B, on the whole, is in a very good state of preservation, but it was supposed lately (see *ThLz.*, 1899, col. 176) that its first hand wrote in John viii. 57, "and Abraham saw thee" instead of "and hast thou seen Abraham," as all our editors read in that passage.[1] The supposition proved to be incorrect, but if that could possibly happen with B, what must have happened in the case of manuscripts that are so full of corrections as ℵ and D, if they came to be copied in later times? Suppose that one scribe took the trouble to copy the text of the first hand, while

Variation.

[1] See below on John viii. 57, p. 289.

another thought it his duty to follow the corrections, the result would be two manuscripts whose common origin would be scarcely recognisable. And in the course of centuries how often may not this process have been repeated. No wonder, therefore, that so few manuscripts have as yet been clearly made out to be the descendants of our oldest codices, so as to permit of their being removed from the board with one sweep, as having no independent testimony to contribute, as is the case with E_3 which is merely a bad copy of D_2 (p. 77), or that scholars cannot agree as to the relationship existing between two manuscripts like F_2 and G_3 (p. 77).[1] Nor need we be surprised to find that some of our most peculiar witnesses seem to have remained absolutely childless, while a less valuable race is perpetuated in many copies. The words of Homer—*οἵη περ φύλλων γενεή, τοίη δὲ καὶ ἀνδρῶν*—may be applied conversely to the leaves to which we entrust our immortality: habent sua fata libelli. The only unfortunate thing is that we are so little able to follow the course of these fates by means of external testimony.

External testimony.

When the Emperor Constantine *e.g.* asks Eusebius to supply him with fifty copies of the Scriptures at once, we cannot but suppose that these became authoritative over a large area. But in which of the classes into which our manuscripts have hitherto been divided are we to look for these now?[2] And conversely if, in another locality, heathen per-

[1] An instructive discussion of the relationship between D_2 and E_3 is given in Hort's *Introduction*, §§ 335–337. It is possible that one copyist in Rom. xv. 31–33 took *ἵνα ἡ διακονία μου ἡ εἰς Ἱερουσαλὴμ . . . . διὰ θελήματος Θεοῦ*, and the other *καὶ ἡ δωροφορία μου ἡ ἐν Ἱερ . . . . διὰ θελήματος Χριστοῦ Ἰησοῦ*—*i.e.* two entirely different recensions.

[2] Zahn very properly remarks (*Th. Lbl.*, 1899, 16, 179): "One must not, at least as regards the N. T., confound Eusebius with Pamphilus, or, if I might say so, with the firm of Pamphilus and Eusebius. If the fifty Bibles that Eusebius provided at the bidding of the Emperor for the use of the churches of the capital had contained a text of the N. T. prepared on the basis of the previous works and commentaries of Origen, the entire subsequent history of the text of the N. T. in the region of Constantinople, revealing as it does the extensive propagation of the Antiochean text, would be perfectly incomprehensible. As in the matter of the canon so also of the text of the N. T., Eusebius emancipated himself from the

secution was directed specially against the Bibles of the Christians, this cannot have been without some effect. According to C. Hülsen (*Bilder aus der Geschichte des Kapitols*, Rome, 1899), even the Roman Bishop Marcellinus, with his deacons Strabo and Cassianus, in the year 304, burned, in front of the temple of Juno Moneta, those Gospels which ten years later were made the law of Christian Rome by the Emperor Constantine. These scattered notices must be much more carefully collected and considered than hitherto, and combined with the results obtained from the collation of the manuscripts.

Recensions.

Most of our information with respect to the **recensions** of the Bible comes from the Syrian Church, and is concerned rather with the Old Testament than with the New; but the recensions of the former may throw some light on those of the latter.

Lucian.

(*a*) As the result of their researches, Westcott and Hort have made it very probable, on internal grounds, that a recension of an official nature was undertaken in Syria, perhaps at Antioch, about the fourth century, and that to this recension are due the origin and propagation of that form of the text of the New Testament which was widely disseminated in the Byzantine Empire, now represented in our later minuscules, and made the *textus receptus* by means of the first printed editions.

Lucian, the celebrated founder of the Antiochean school of exegesis, suffered martyrdom in the year 311 or 312, most probably the latter. Of all the names that we know, none has a better claim than his to be associated with such a recension, and the conjecture derives some support from the passage of Jerome cited above (p. 85).[1] It is, perhaps, even better supported by what we know of Lucian's recension of the Old Testament. In his preface to the Chronicles, Jerome wrote: "Alexandria et Aegyptus in Septuaginta suis Hesychium laudat

school of Origen, and attached himself to that of Antioch, at least in this particular instance fraught with such important consequences for the history of the Bible."

[1] See Hort, *Introduction*, §§ 188, 189.

auctorem, Constantinopolis usque Antiochiam Luciani martyris exemplaria probat, mediae inter has provinciae Palaestinae (*v.l.* Palaestinos) codices legunt, quos ab Origene elaboratos Eusebius et Pamphilus vulgaverunt; totusque orbis hac inter se trifaria varietate compugnat." Now it is true that the words of a man like Jerome must not be pressed too far, and what may have been true in his day might be quite different in a comparatively short time—think *e.g.* of the fifty copies of the Bible that Eusebius Pamphili had sent to Constantine, or the Bible or Bibles sent by Athanasius to Constans[1]—at the same time it has been established beyond all doubt by Field and Lagarde, that it is to Lucian we must refer a peculiar recension of the Greek Old Testament preserved in a good many manuscripts, the one found in the unfortunately small remnant of the Gothic Old Testament and especially in the numerous Biblical quotations of the famous theologian John of Antioch, better known as Chrysostom of Constantinople, who was a pupil of Lucian. The probability, therefore, is very great that the same thing will hold good of the New Testament portion of the Bible of Ulfilas and Chrysostom. As regards the former, Kauffmann has expressed a decided opinion to this effect in his work on the Gothic Bible cited above (p. 139). The supposition would be converted into something like certainty if it could be proved on palæographic grounds that this or that New Testament manuscript belongs to this or that Old Testament manuscript of Lucianic derivation as part of what was originally one and the same complete Bible. This is a point which I am not in a position personally to investigate, and I must therefore content myself with throwing out this suggestion, and with adding in support of it that we have the express testimony of the Menologies for saying that Lucian bequeathed to his pupils a copy of the Old *and New* Testaments written in three columns with his own hand.

[1] Athanasius, writing to Constans, says in his first Apology: *τῷ ἀδελφῷ σου οὐκ ἔγραψα ἢ μόνον ὅτε . . . . καὶ ὅτε πυκτία τῶν θείων γραφῶν κελεύσαντος αὐτοῦ μοι κατασκευάσαι, ταῦτα ποιήσας ἀπέστειλα.*

There is a statement in the Pseudo-Athanasian Synopsis,[1] which seems, however, to refer only to the Old Testament portion, to the effect that it was discovered in a concealed cupboard (πυργίσκος) in the house of a Jew at Nicomedia in the time of Constantine. Long ago Hug and Eichhorn attributed the "Asiatic" or "Byzantine" recension to Lucian, and no decided objection can be established to the view of Hort, which Gregory also is inclined to accept (*TiGr.*, p. 814).[2]

[1] It is given in Syriac in Abbé Martin's *Introduction à la critique textuelle du N. T.*, Plate XX. No. 35 (1883), from the MS. de Paris, 27, f 88 b, and also in Lagarde's *Bibliotheca Syriaca*, 259, 22–27. From the Greek πυργίσκος, which becomes פרדיסקא in the Semitic, the Syriac forms another diminutive פרדסקונא, which is still omitted n the *Thesaurus Syriacus*, 3240; *cf.* Bar Bahlul, 1606, 9 (App. p. 64). In place of πυργίσκῳ, Oikonomos would read the genitive πυργίσκου (περι των ὁ ερμηνευτων, iv. 500).

[2] Not only does the Old Testament promise to shed some light upon an obscure problem in the New, but the converse may also be true—viz. that the history of the text of the New Testament may contribute to a better understanding of that of the Old. It was long observed that many peculiarities of the Lucianic revision of the Septuagint occur also in the witnesses to the Old Latin version (see especially Driver, *Notes on Samuel*, p. li; *Urt.*, 78). No proper explanation of this phenomenon could be given so long as the Old Latin version of the Old Testament was looked upon as homogeneous and of great antiquity. But the New Testament, for which we have far more Old Latin manuscripts than for the Old, shows that the Old Latin pre-Jeromic version had a chequered history, and in particular that at a certain time a revision was undertaken, the result of which is found especially in Codex Brixianus (f, see p. 112), and which "non solum interpretationem veterem stilo elegantiori emendabat, sed etiam lectiones novas protulit. Notatu certe dignum est, in ista emendatione Itala eminere lectiones quae in maiori parte codicum Graecorum apparent, *quas Recensioni Syrae vel Antiochenae adiudicant Westcott et Hort.*" So say Wordsworth and White, p. 654. If the same thing holds good of the Old Testament, then the relationship between the Old Latin and Lucian at once becomes evident, and the supposition is not so absurd that the marginal glosses of Codex Legionensis,[a] which are particularly striking on this view of the case, may have been translated into Latin from Lucian. These considerations, moreover, may possibly throw fresh light on the question that I have raised elsewhere (*Urt.*, p. 78), whether Lucian may not also have used the Peshitto in his recension of the Old Testament. I see that it has been taken up by J. Méritan, in his little book, entitled, *La Version grecque des Livres de Samuel, précédée d'une Introduction sur la critique textuelle* (Paris, 1898). On pp. 96–113 he discusses the same question—whether Lucian knew and used the Peshitto. He answers the question in the affirmative: "It is therefore probable that as regards certain passages of the Books of Samuel, in his work of revision, or rather of correction, Lucian did not

[a] Called Codex Gothicus in Hastings' *Bible Dictionary*, iii. p. 50*b*.

(*b*) It is, on the other hand, somewhat difficult to make out how matters stand with regard to the recension of **Hesychius.** Jerome commends it with that of Lucian for the Old Testament, but contemptuously rejects it for the New; and accordingly, in the decree of Pope Gelasius, we hear of Gospels "quae falsavit Lucianus, apocrypha, evangelia quae falsavit Hesychius, apocrypha" (c. vi. 14, 15). Considering the important position of Alexandria and Egypt, and the vast number of manuscripts referred with more or less certainty to that locality, it is the more remarkable that so few unmistakable traces have as yet been discovered of the recension of which "Alexandria et Aegyptus . . . . Hesychium laudat auctorem," and that till the present moment the most divergent views have been held with regard to it. And this is true of the Old Testament no less than of the New. One view, for which a good deal can be said, has already been referred to (p. 61 f.)—viz. that we have the recension of Hesychius in Codex B. Rahlfs, who was the first to connect B with the Canon of Athanasius, says (*lib. cit.*, p. 78, note 7); "If we care to trust ourselves to pure hypothesis, we might hazard the conjecture that our superb Codex, manifestly written for one of the principal churches of Egypt, was prepared at the instigation of St. Athanasius himself. The

Hesychius.

Codex B.

follow the Hebrew text as his sole and infallible guide, but availed himself of others also, and that one of those principal authorities was the Syriac version." We often enough find ὁ Σύρος cited as an authority in the Greek Commentaries on the Old Testament. Whether it is also mentioned for the New Testament is a point that seems not yet to be looked into.

I may add that Bickel concludes his short article in the *Zeitschrift für kath. Theol.*, iii. 467–469, entitled, "Die Lucianische Septuagintabearbeitung nachgewiesen," by saying: "In establishing the recensions of Lucian and Hesychius for the Septuagint, we may be held as settling the question whether traces of these may not also be found in the New Testament."

In his *Einleitung*, ii. 240, Zahn says: "Without a doubt many readings which had a considerable circulation in the second and third centuries, some of them being of no small importance and extent, were gradually ousted from their place in the text from the fourth century onwards, and some of them dropped out of the later tradition altogether. And it is equally true that many interpolations were current in these later centuries which were unknown in the second. But whatever our judgment be in doubtful cases, we are still always in a position to support it with extant documents."

locality in which the manuscript was produced supports this conjecture, while the time is not inconsistent with it." I am not aware if Rahlfs knew that Athanasius had executed πυκτία τῶν θείων γραφῶν for Constans, and I am not sufficiently acquainted with the minutiæ of the ecclesiastical history of that time, and with the life of Athanasius in particular, to hazard the assertion that Codex B was prepared by Athanasius for the Emperor Constans. It is certainly the case, as every Church History records, that Constans was Prefect of Illyricum and Italy, and that Athanasius fled to Rome to Julius II., which would help to explain how Codex B comes to be in that city.[1] I cannot ascertain however from the books at my command, whether any particular resemblance has been observed between the text of this manuscript and the Biblical quotations found in those writings of Athanasius that belong to this period of his life, that is, prior to the year 350. And, besides, one has always to take into consideration how very little reliance can be placed as yet on the text of the Biblical quotations in our editions of the Fathers. In the Book of Judges B certainly exhibits quite a peculiar form of text which is not used by the earlier Egyptian teachers, Clement and Origen, nor even by Didymus (d. 394 or 399), but was employed first by Cyril of Alexandria, and which is the basis of the Sahidic version. This fact may have an important bearing on the question as to the text of the New Testament as well.[2] As early as 1705 Grabe expressed the opinion that the Sahidic version was the work of Hesychius, but we have very little information indeed regarding that Church Father, and in particular as to his connection with the lexicographer of that name. Here also, the evidence afforded by palæography would need to be examined with a view to ascertaining whether or not any of the manuscripts agreeing with B in the

[1] Rahlfs cannot, of course, assent to this supposition, seeing that he regards Codex B as depending on the Festal Letter containing the Canon of Athanasius, which was not written till the year 367.

[2] See especially Lagarde, *Sept.-Studien*, 1892, and Moore's *Commentary on Judges*, 1895, p. xlvi.

Book of Judges—viz. G (Brit. Mus., 20,002), 16, 30, 52, 53, 58, 63, 77, 85, 131, 144, 209, 236, 237, Catena Nicephori—has a counterpart in some manuscript of the New Testament. On Codex G see Rahlfs (p. 35, n. 2), and compare v. Dobschütz (*ThLz.*, 1899, 3, 74) on the two New Testament manuscripts Λ and 566$^{evv.}$ (Greg).[1] According to the latter, the difference in size precludes the supposition that Λ and 566 are the New Testament portion of the manuscript described by Rahlfs (*loc. cit.*). But if they are not written by the same scribe, they both undoubtedly come from the same school of copyists. At most, however, Λ–566 would only possess importance for the recension of Hesychius if the text they, or rather it, follows were different from that with which it was collated. Its subscription shows that it belongs to those exemplars which were collated with the Codex of Pamphilus. This fact has an important bearing on the Gospel of the Hebrews. See Zahn, *GK.* ii. 648.

Eusebius-Pamphilus.

(*c*) We have nearly as little certain information regarding the third, and perhaps most important, of the recensions mentioned by Jerome in connection with the Old Testament, that of **Eusebius** and **Pamphilus**, which goes back to Origen.[2] So far as I know, the references which Origen makes in his extant writings to his own labours in the field of textual criticism, relate only to the Old Testament. At the same time

Origen.

[1] See above under Λ, p. 72.

[2] There is no need to discuss here the other expressions used by Jerome in his letter of the year 403 to the Gothic priests Sunnia and Fretela, seeing that these relate only to the Old Testament. But the words themselves may be quoted: "Breviter admoneo ut sciatis, aliam esse editionem, quam Origenes et Caesariensis Eusebius omnesque Graeciae tractatores κοινὴν, id est communem appellant, atque vulgatam, et a plerisque nunc Λουκιανός dicitur, aliam septuaginta interpretum quae in ἑξαπλοῖς codicibus reperitur, et a nobis in latinum sermonem fideliter versa est, et Jerosolymae atque in orientis ecclesiae (so Lagarde, *Librorum V. T. can. pars prior*, p. xiii. from *Vallarsi*, i. 635?) decantatur . . . . κοινὴ autem ista, hoc est communis, editio ipsa est quae et septuaginta, sed hoc interest inter utramque quod κοινὴ pro locis et temporibus et pro voluntate scriptorum vetus corrupta editio est, ea autem quae habetur in ἑξαπλοῖς et quam nos vertimus, ipsa est quae in eruditorum libris incorrupta et immaculata septuaginta interpretum translatio reservatur" (*ibid.*, 637). For Λουκιανός Oikonomos (iv. 499) would read Λουκιανὶς.

his complaint as to the evil condition of the manuscripts of his day refers to the New Testament, and to the Gospels in particular. Νυνὶ δὲ δηλονότι, he says, in his *Commentary on Matthew*, Bk. xv. 14, πολλὴ γέγονεν ἡ τῶν ἀντιγράφων διαφορά, εἴτε ἀπὸ ῥᾳθυμίας τινῶν γραφέων, εἴτε ἀπὸ τόλμης τινῶν μοχθηρᾶς τῆς διορθώσεως τῶν γραφομένων, εἴτε καὶ ἀπὸ τῶν τὰ ἑαυτοῖς δοκοῦντα ἐν τῇ διορθώσει προστιθέντων ἢ ἀφαιρούντων.[1] He tells us in the same place how, θεοῦ διδόντος, he found ways and means of remedying the evil by the employment of the critical symbols of Homeric commentators, the obelus and asterisk, τὴν μὲν οὖν ἐν τοῖς ἀντιγράφοις τῆς παλαιᾶς διαθήκης διαφωνίαν, θεοῦ διδόντος, εὕρομεν ἰάσασθαι. According to his own express declaration, supposing it to have been correctly preserved, for it is only extant in Latin, his work in textual criticism at that time at least was confined to the Old Testament: in exemplaribus autem Novi Testamenti hoc ipsum me posse facere sine periculo non putavi. Von Gebhardt consequently says (*Urt.*, 25) that this statement from Origen's own mouth should have kept anyone from ascribing a formal recension of the New Testament text to him, alluding to Hug's system of recensions; but at the same time he will not deny that the works of Origen, who was a man of conspicuous critical accuracy, are of the highest importance for the criticism of the text of the New Testament. As a matter of fact, later church teachers appeal chiefly to Origen's manuscripts of the Old Testament, but several references are also found to his New Testament manuscripts. On Gal. iii. 1, Jerome remarks (ii. 418): legitur in quibusdam codicibus, Quis vos fascinavit non credere veritati? Sed hoc (meaning, of course, the last three words only) quia in exemplaribus Adamantii non habetur, omisimus. The words are a gloss interpolated from ch. v. 7, but they are also found in Origen, though only in the Latin

[1] A. D. Loman would emend this passage by reading εἴτε ἀπὸ μοχθηρίας τῆς διορθώσεως τῶν γραφομένων εἴτε καὶ ἀπὸ τόλμης τινῶν τῶν τὰ ἑαυτοῖς δοκοῦντα (*Leiden. Theol. Tijdschr.*, vii., 1873, 233).

translation of Rufinus, and they appear, among our Greek manuscripts, in C D[c] E K L P, and likewise in most codices of the Vulgate (see Wordsworth and White, p. 659). The same writer says on Matthew xxiv. 36 (ii. 199): in quibusdam latinis exemplaribus additum est "neque filius," quum in Graecis et maxime Adamantii et Pierii exemplaribus hoc non habeatur additum; sed quia in nonnullis legitur, disserendum videtur (W. and W., p. 658). Pierius is no doubt the Presbyter of Alexandria who lived at Rome after the Diocletian persecution. He was styled "the younger Origen" on account of his learning, and was perhaps the teacher of Pamphilus (Jerome, *Viri Ill.*, 76; Eusebius, *Eccl. Hist.*, vii. 32). Adamantius, like Chalkenteros, is a surname of honour given to Origen. Here again, it is a strange fact that the words which Jerome says were omitted in Origen's exemplar are found in a certain passage of his works also extant only in Latin, and there expounded so fully that there cannot be the slightest doubt that he had them in his text, and, moreover, had no conception of their omission in other copies. What explanation, if any, can be given of this fact we need not pause to enquire. Nor need we take up the question where Jerome obtained access to the exemplars of Pierius. I suppose it would be in Caesarea, where he also saw the (Bible?) volumes of Origen transcribed by Pamphilus with his own hand, and actually obtained possession of his copy of the commentary on the Minor Prophets.[1] Even supposing that what is meant by *exemplaria Adamantii* is not really a recension of the text of the Bible but simply

[1] What he says is (*Viri Illust.*, c. 75): Pamphilus presbyter, Eusebii Caesariensis episcopi necessarius, tanto bibliothecae divinae amore flagravit, ut maximam partem Origenis voluminum sua manu descripserit, quae usque hodie in Caesariensi bibliotheca habetur. Sed et in duodecim prophetas vigintiquinque ἐξηγήσεων Origenis volumina manu eius (*i.e.* Pamphili) exarata repperi, quae tanto amplector et servo gaudio, ut Croesi opes habere me credam. Si enim laetitia est unam epistulam habere martyris, quanto magis tot milia versuum, quae mihi videntur suis sanguinis signasse vestigiis. The above is Richardson's text. Bernoulli (Krüger's *Sammlung*, Heft xi. 1895) reads *habentur*, *Sed in*, and *videtur*, and also omits *volumina*.

the copy that Origen used most or used last, that copy might have been authoritative for Pamphilus if not for Eusebius, and so far, therefore, it becomes necessary for us to try and discover the Origenic text in the New Testament as well as in the Old. At all events a good many of our manuscripts go back to Pamphilus, and particularly H of the Pauline Epistles. In addition to a very practical suggestion as to the lending of books,[1] and a notice of its preparation and of the original writer, this manuscript has also the following note: *ἀντεβλήθη δὲ ἡ βίβλος πρὸς τὸ ἐν Καισαρίᾳ ἀντίγραφον τῆς βιβλιοθήκης τοῦ ἁγίου Παμφίλου χειρὶ γεγραμμένον (αὐτοῦ).* From this subscription Field (*Hexapla*, i. p. xcix) has concluded that the library of Pamphilus was still in existence in the sixth century, but it is doubtful whether the subscription may not have been found in the original of H and copied into it along with the text, as is the case with a similar note copied into the minuscules 15, 83, 173. In any case this manuscript is our principal witness for the recension of Pamphilus, or, as it used to be called, the recension of **Euthalius.**[2] I have no intention of discussing the question whether it should be Euthalius or Evagrius: Von Dobschütz (*Euthaliusstudien*, p. 152 n. 1) has promised to give us further particulars

Euthalius.

[1] Προσφώνησις· κορωνίς εἰμι δογμάτων θείων διδάσκαλος· ἄν τινί με χρήσῃς ἀντίβιβλον λάμβανε, οἱ γὰρ ἀποδόται κακοί· Ἀντίφρασις· θησαυρὸν ἔχων σε πνευματικῶν ἀγαθῶν καὶ πᾶσιν ἀνθρώποις ποθητὸν ἁρμονίαις τε καὶ ποικίλαις γραμμαῖς κεκοσμημένον—νὴ τὴν ἀλήθειαν—οὐ δώσω σε προχείρως τινὶ οὐδ᾽ αὖ φθονέσω τῆς ὠφελείας, χρήσω δὲ τοῖς φίλοις ἀντίβιβλον λαμβάνων. The last seven words, which are erased in H, are supplied by the minuscule 93[paul] and the Armenian version. On ἀντίβιβλον = "borrowing-receipt" or "voucher," see *ThLz.*, 1895, 283, 407. See also Robinson, *Euthaliana, Texts and Studies*, iii. 3.

[2] To the literature referred to on p. 79 should be added the second section of Bousset's *Textkritische Studien* (*TU.* xi. 4, 1894), entitled, *Der Codex Pamphili*, pp. 45–73. Bousset affirms the close connection between the Corrector of Sinaiticus indicated by Tischendorf as [c] and Codex H. I have established the connection of this corrector in the Psalter with Eusebius by means of the latter's Commentary on the Psalms (see above, p. 58). As yet no one appears to have examined the New Testament quotations in Eusebius. *Cf.* however Bousset, *ThLz.*, 1900, 22, 611 ff.

as to the Syriac texts relating to the subject. I would merely call attention to two facts, viz.—

(1) That the subscription testifying to a collation with the exemplar of Pamphilus is found also at the end of the Harklean Syriac published by Bensly (see above, pp. 79, 106). **Harklean.**

(2) That the name **Evagrius**, which Ehrhard proposes to read in place of Euthalius in Codex H, is actually found associated with the library of Pamphilus in another manuscript of the Old Testament. In his *Notitia editionis codicis Bibliorum Sinaitici* (Lipsiæ, 1860), pp. 73–122, Tischendorf published "Ex Codicibus Insulae Patmi, Ineditum Diodori Siculi; Origenis Scholia in Proverbia Salomonis." The latter he took from a manuscript which, according to H. O. Coxe's *Report . . . . on the Greek MSS. yet remaining in the Levant* (1858, p. 61), professed to contain "Origenis Hexapla cum Scholiis" after the Philocalia. In reality they are Origen's Scholia on the Proverbs which Angelo Mai had published in a different form from the Vatican Catena 1802, in the *Nova Patrum Bibliotheca*, 1854. In the Patmos manuscript the scholia proper are prefaced by two (or three) explanatory notes on the use of the obelus and the asterisk, and on the different arrangement of the chapters in the Hebrew and Greek texts, followed by another explanation of the same sort under the title Εὐαγρίου σχόλιον.[1] Who they are that are referred to in the scholion as having collated the book (τῶν ἀντιβεβληκότων τὸ βιβλίον) we learn from the subscription, which says: *μετελήφθησαν ἀφ' ὧν εὕρομεν ἐξαπλῶν καὶ πάλιν αὐτὰ χειρὶ* (*leg.* *αὐτόχειρι*) Πάμφιλος *καὶ* Εὐσέβιος *διορθώσαντο.* This subscription, which Oikonomos published fully fifty years ago

Evagrius.

[1] It runs: *Εἰσὶν ὅσα προτεταγμένον ἔχουσι τὸν ἀριθμὸν ὧδε, ὅσα 'Ωριγένην ἐπιγεγραμμένον ἔχει τούτῳ τῷ μονοσυλλάβῳ* $\frac{\text{P}}{\Omega}$*· εἰσὶ δὲ μάλιστα ἐν τῷ 'Ιώβ· ὅσα δὲ περὶ διαφωνίας ῥητῶν τινῶν τῶν ἐν τῷ ἐδαφίῳ ἢ ἐκδόσεών ἐστιν σχόλια, ἅπερ καὶ κάτω νενευκυῖαν περιεστιγμένην ἔχει προτεταγμένην, τῶν ἀντιβεβληκότων τὸ βιβλίον ἐστίν· ὅσα δὲ ἀμφιβόλως ἔξω κείμενα ῥητὰ ἔξω νενευκυῖαν περιεστιγμένην ἔχει προτεταγμένην, διὰ τὰ σχόλια προσετέθησαν κατ' αὐτὰ τοῦ μεγάλου εἰρηκότος διδασκάλου ἵνα μὴ δόξῃ κατὰ κενοῦ τὸ σχόλιον φέρεσθαι, ἐν πολλοῖς μὲν τῶν ἀντιγράφων τῶν ῥητῶν οὕτως ἐχόντων, ἐν τούτῳ δὲ μὴ οὕτως κειμένων ἢ μηδ' ὅλως φερομένων καὶ διὰ τοῦτο προστεθέντων.*

from that Patmos manuscript,[1] should be added to those usually cited—viz. those appended to Ezra and Esther in א, to Isaiah and Ezekiel in Codex Marchalianus, to 3 and 4 Kings in the Syriac Hexapla, and to Ezekiel in Codex Chisianus 88.

With what has been said the student should compare what Von der Goltz tells us of a critical work upon the text of the New Testament belonging partly to the tenth and partly to the sixth century.[2] This, too, goes back to Origen, and in a scholion on James ii. 3, the greater part of which is unfortunately erased, the work mentions "a manuscript written by the hand of St. Eusebius." As Zahn elsewhere shows, the writer of the Athos manuscript did not base his own work on this Codex of Eusebius, and in one passage he expressly contrasts it with the text of Origen which he follows. In spite of this, however, this Athos manuscript must be taken into account in dealing with the recension of Pamphilus. Still more so must the Armenian and Syriac texts, according to Conybeare and von Dobschütz.[3] Even the Latin manuscripts may contain traces of this recension. E. Riggenbach has shown that the table of chapters in Hebrews given in Codex Fuldensis and in a manuscript indicated as Cod. Vat. Reg. 9, is nothing but a translation of the corresponding part of "Euthalius."[4] Unfortunately the relics of the literary activity of Pamphilus, that devoted student of the Scriptures,[5] are exceedingly scanty, and what little is left is extant only in a Latin translation. In these circumstances the attempt to specify more closely than hitherto his manuscripts of the Bible by means of his quotations does seem rather hopeless.

Later revisers.

(*d*) As we are now dealing with the question how to arrive at the oldest form of the Greek text, it is unnecessary to take

[1] Περι των ό ερμηνευτων, iv. 904. Athens, 1844–1849.

[2] *Texte und Untersuchungen*, xvii. (N.F. ii.) 4. See above, p. 90.

[3] *Euthaliusstudien*, pp. 111–115; 115 ff.

[4] *Neue Jahrbücher für deutsche Theologie*, ii. 3, 3 (1894), pp. 360–363. Compare also von Dobschütz, *lib. cit.*, 111.

[5] μάλιστα δὲ παρὰ τοὺς καθ' ἡμᾶς πάντας διέπρεπε τῇ περὶ τὰ θεῖα λόγια γνησιωτάτῃ σπουδῇ. Euseb., *Eccl. Hist.*, viii. 11.

account of the labours of any later individuals in the formation of the Greek New Testament. Among these were Emperors and Empresses like Constantine and Constans, who exerted themselves in the dissemination of the Scriptures, and perhaps even made copies of them with their own hands, but these we may disregard.[1] The work of *Andreas* and *Arethas* on the Apocalypse will be noticed when we come to speak of that book. One naturally turns here to Krumbacher's *History of Byzantine Literature*, but the index to the first edition of that work contains only two references to the New Testament, neither of them bearing on our present subject. The matter is one which may be commended to those who have the time and the opportunity and the willingness to investigate it, and considering the ardour with which the study of Byzantine antiquities is being prosecuted at present, it may suffice merely to throw out this hint.

Pre-Origenic texts.

(*e*) So far as we have gone, therefore, it appears that much uncertainty prevails regarding the text formations we have already considered—those of Lucian, Hesychius, Pamphilus, and the Ferrar Group. Considering the amount of evidence at our command—how the external testimony points in the same direction as the manuscripts themselves, and, indeed, how probable is the whole nature of the operation in question—one would expect these to be the most easily distinguishable of all. Indeed, even so cautious an enquirer as Zahn speaks without any hesitation of "the official recensions originating subsequent to the time of Origen" (*ThLbl.*, 1899, 180). The vagueness of our conclusions with respect to these recensions does not look very promising for the result of our investigation of the text prior to the time of Origen, when activity in this field was more disconnected and might be said to run wild and unrestrained. And there is this further

[1] See above, p. 87 ff., on Evan. 473, Act. 246, 419, Evl. 286, and compare Zahn, *ThLbl.*, 1899, 181: Would that some one with the time and opportunity to work in the Monasteries of Mount Athos applied himself to the Codex written in the year 800 by the unhappy Empress Maria (Lambros 129, S. Pauli 2). Since the above was written the manuscript has been collated by Von der Goltz.

difficulty that some of the writers who fall to be considered in this period came in later times more or less justly under the imputation of heresy, with the consequence that the results of their labours were less widely disseminated, if not deliberately suppressed. In circumstances like these any attempted revision of the text must have been equally mischievous, whether it proceeded from the orthodox side or from the opposite. That there were *διορθωταί* who were supposed to correct the text in the interests of orthodoxy we have already learned from Epiphanius. Indeed, from our point of view the action of the orthodox correctors must be thought the more regrettable of the two, since the books without a doubt parted at their hands with many vivid, strange, and even fantastic traits of language. Even in the matter of style it seems to me incontestable that it was at their hands that the Gospels received that reserved and solemn tone which we would not now willingly part with, and which can be compared to nothing so much as to those solemn pictures of Christ that we see painted on a golden background in Byzantine churches. For myself, at least, I have not the slightest doubt that the Gospel, and the Gospel particularly, was originally narrated in a much more vivacious style. Just consider this, for example. In all our present authorities—Greek manuscripts, ancient versions, Syriac, Egyptian, and so forth, and in all the Church Fathers without exception, so far as I am aware—we read the beautiful words: "your Father knoweth what things ye have need of before ye ask Him," *πρὸ τοῦ ὑμᾶς αἰτῆσαι αὐτόν* (Matt. vi. 8). Compare with this what we find singly and solely in Codex D and the Old Latin h, *πρὸ τοῦ ἀνοῖξαι τὸ στόμα*, antequam os aperiatis, "before ever you open your mouth." To me it is a striking indication to what an extent the instinctive sense of originality is wanting, that a reading like this is not inserted by Westcott and Hort among their Noteworthy Rejected Readings, nor even cited by Baljon in his critical apparatus, and that our commentators have not a single syllable about it, so that our students and preachers know nothing whatever of this form of the words of Jesus. If my edition of the New Testament did no more than bring such things to the notice of those who previously were unacquainted with them, I should consider it had done no small service. But take another illustration from the parable of the Barren Fig Tree. "Cut it down, why cumbereth it the ground,"—that is how our ordinary texts give the commandment of the justly indignant husbandman in Luke xiii. 7: *ἔκκοψον αὐτήν· ἱνατί καὶ τὴν γῆν καταργεῖ.* Here again, the great majority of our witnesses of every sort exhibit no variation worth mentioning, except that a good many (A L T etc.) insert a very prosy *οὖν* after the imperative, while B 80 read *τὸν τόπον* for *τὴν γῆν.* And in the answer of the vine-dresser (verse 8), "till I shall dig about it and dung it," there is again no various reading in our ordinary witnesses of all kinds except the insignificant interchange of (*βάλω*) *κόπρια, κοπρίαν,* and *κόπρον.* What a difference do we find here also in the text of D: "bring the axe," *φέρε τὴν ἀξίνην,* adfers securem; and, "I will throw in a basket of dung," *βάλω κόφινον κοπρίων,* mittam qualum (=squalum) stercoris d, or cophinum stercoris a b c f ff² i l q, from which it was taken into the Codex of Marmoutier, a copy of the Alcuinian recension of the Vulgate written in gold.[1] Here again, our editors and commentators for the most part take no notice. "Bring the axe" is omitted by Weiss, father and son, Westcott–Hort, Tregelles, and also by Baljon, while Holtzmann ignores both variants. It stands to reason, of course, that greater vivacity of style is not of itself an actual proof of greater originality. But the whole question is raised as to the principles by which we are to be guided in estimating the comparative value of the witnesses. One might be inclined to regard such peculiarities as due to the caprice

[1] On *κόφινον κοπρίων,* see Chase, *Syro-Latin Text,* p. 135 f. It may be observed in passing how variously *καταργεῖ* is rendered in the different Latin manuscripts—viz. by *evacuat* in b ff² l q, by *detinet* in ff²ᶜ i r, by *intricat* in e, and by *occupat* in d and the Vulgate.

of some scribe by whom D or its parent manuscript was written. As a matter of fact, Westcott and Hort, and most recent editors with them, do so regard them, seeing they cite the reading of D neither in Matt. vi. 8 nor in Luke xiii. 7. In the latter passage one might be inclined to take that view of the case, because as yet we have no other testimony to φέρε τὴν ἀξίνην than D d. But it is not so likely in the case of Matt. vi. 8, seeing that here the testimony of D is supported by that of h. To justify our neglect of these witnesses, we should require to prove either that h is derived from D or D from h.[1] So far as my knowledge goes, no one has yet maintained the latter view. The derivation of h from D is an impossibility, for this reason alone that h belongs either to the fourth, or, what is perhaps more likely, to the fifth century (see p. 113).[2] The truth is, rather, that we have in h a second and independent witness to the fact that at a very early date the text of Matt. vi. 8 read, "before you open your mouth." But it is quite impossible to ignore the evidence of D in Luke xiii. 8 (κόφινον κοπρίων). Here too, of course, one might take exception and say that as D is bilingual, its Greek text might be derived from the Latin. Fortunately, however, it happens that the Latin of D, that is, d, differs from all the other eight Latin witnesses in reading not *cophinus* but *qualus*, and it is *cophinus* that is a loan word from the Greek[3]; so that this objection, actually raised against D in the case of other readings, does not apply to this one. There is this to be observed, moreover—a point not given in Tischendorf, but noticed in Westcott and Hort—viz., that Origen also seems to have read "basket." The passage is again one that is extant only in

[1] The evidence of d in this passage cannot be had, unfortunately, as eight leaves (a quaternio) containing the Greek of Matt. vi. 20–ix. 2, and the Latin of vi. 8–viii. 27, have gone amissing.

[2] Unfortunately h exhibits only the text of Matthew, otherwise I might simply have referred to the list of variants on p. 120. I am not aware if what Wordsworth and White (vol. i. p. xxxii) say of this manuscript is still true: Codex hodie, ut fertur, in bibliotheca Vaticana inveniri non potest.

[3] See Index in Wordsworth and White, p. 751.

the Latin translation of Rufinus, and Tischendorf cites Or. 3, 452 among the witnesses supporting *κόπρια*; but Westcott and Hort expressly mention that Origen's context appears to support the reading *κόφινον* ("Lev. lat. Ruf., 190, apparently with context").

Here, then, we have these three stages:—

(1) D d alone, *φέρε τὴν ἀξίνην*—*i.e.* one solitary Greek manuscript.

(2) D supported by h, *ἀνοῖξαι τὸ στόμα*—*i.e.* the same solitary Greek manuscript with the addition of one representative of a version.

(3) D supported by eight Latin manuscripts and Origen, *κόφινον κοπρίων*—*i.e.* the same solitary Greek manuscript with the addition of eight representatives of one version and one not absolutely certain quotation.

What then? Can it be allowable to judge a reading's claim to be mentioned and considered from the number of the witnesses supporting it, and like Westcott and Hort and Baljon to mention the third only, and take no notice of the other two? I think not. For just as in certain circumstances the correct reading may no longer appear in any manuscript, but must be determined by conjecture, so in another case the truth may have only one solitary representative left to support it against a whole world of adversaries (Heb. xii. 3), and this solitary witness either a manuscript, a version, or a quotation. On the other hand, it may have a whole cloud of witnesses accompanying it and supporting it. In matters of this kind numbers have nothing to do with the case whatever. To speak of majorities is nonsense. The true man is willing and able to stand alone, and to many a witness of this sort we must apply the words of Socrates: *ἃ μὲν συνῆκα γενναῖα· οἶμαι δὲ καὶ ἃ μὴ συνῆκα.* If we have been able to verify the word of a witness once, several times, frequently, then we shall be willing to trust him even in cases where we cannot check his evidence. Of course we must make allowance for human fallibility—quandoque bonus dormitat Homerus; least of all in matters of this kind must we look for inerrancy. A manuscript whose testimony was decisive on every point would be even a greater miracle than a book printed without a single error at the time of the Incunabula, which the printers of that age would have regarded as an eighth wonder of the world. But how to estimate the character of such a witness, seeing that the subjective feeling, the instinctive perception of what is original, is as little to be trusted as the number of the witnesses—that is the difficulty. And what is the point that our discussion has brought us to? From the "official recensions of the text" made in the later centuries, we sought to get back to similar works of earlier times, and we found that the original text may have suffered as much at the hands of orthodox revisers and correctors, who toned down and obscured the fresh colouring of the ancient records, as at the hands of heretics who inserted foreign and extraneous elements.[1]

Unfortunately very little definite information has come down to us from those early times, and as that relates more to the history of the canon than of the text, reference must be made here to the monumental work of Zahn.[2] Two figures, however,

[1] At the same time it must be pointed out here that not only in Luke and Acts, but in all the books of the N. T., it is wrong in principle to present the alternative "original or later alteration" or even forgery. The dilemma can be wrongly stated. Blass was not the first to express the opinion, "Lucam bis edidisse Actus." De Dieu did so before him, and by an examination of those passages of the Gospels in which the original text has been preserved in purely "Western" witnesses Hort (§ 241) was led to suppose that the Western and non-Western texts may have "started respectively from a first and a second edition of the Gospels, both conceivably apostolic." Similarly Wordsworth and White are unable to explain the origin and propagation of several readings in the manuscripts of the Vulgate otherwise than by supposing that the primitive document itself contained certain variants (corrections) in the passages in question.

[2] *Geschichte des neutestamentlichen Kanons* (Erlangen): I. Band, *Das N. T. vor Origenes*, 1 and 2 Hälfte, 1888–89; II. Band, *Urkunden und Belege zum ersten und dritten Band*, 1890–92. It is to be hoped that the third volume will not be long in making its appearance. Along with this we must take his

emerge from this chaos who have left their traces on the history of the text as well, **Tatian** and **Marcion**, the former chiefly in connection with the Gospels, the latter with the Pauline Epistles. Both have been already referred to more than once in the chapter on the "Materials" (Tatian, p. 97 f.; Marcion, pp. 76, 87), and both will require careful consideration here in our treatment of the principles involved in the reconstruction of the text. How much would be achieved could we but restore the original work of Tatian upon the Gospels, or the *Gospel* and the *Apostle* of Marcion!

(*f*) Before speaking of their work, however, there are still a few less important notices to be gleaned from their own and the preceding time. Heretics.

Nearly all the **heretics** were in turn accused of falsifying the Scriptures. In this sense, also, the Dutch proverb is true, "jedere ketter heeft zijn letter" (every heretic has his letter, his text of the Scriptures). In early times Justin charged the Jews with such falsification in the Old Testament, and Lagarde was sometimes inclined to suspect that the Massoretic numbers in Genesis had been manipulated by the opponents of Christianity. Such complaints were most frequently made against the Gnostics, particularly the Valentinians, and when we glance over the long lists of apocryphal and pseudepigraphical writings,[1] it is abundantly evident that at various times there was a good deal of falsification—*i.e.*, a good deal written under false names. At the same time it cannot be denied that alterations were also made on early Christian works and the books of Scripture in the interests of dogma. These alterations are of all sorts, ranging from quite harmless changes made in all innocence to supposed corrections,

Forschungen zur Geschichte des neutestamentlichen Kanons und der altkirchlichen Literatur, of which six volumes have been published (1881–1900). Meanwhile Zahn's *Einleitung in das Neue Testament* (Leipzig, I., 1898; II., 1899, 2nd ed., 1900) cannot be too strongly recommended. It contains a great deal of valuable material for the criticism of the text. Needless to say, textual criticism is the basis on which all sound exegesis rests.

[1] A small selection will be found in Preuschen, *Analecta*, pp. 152–157.

and, it may be, even wilful corruptions.[1] But most assuredly the heretics are not alone in being chargeable with this offence: Iliacos intra muros peccatur et extra.

As Jülicher (*Einl.*, 378) points out, the orthodox Church teachers were very fond of making this charge against the heretics: *παραλλάσσειν, παραχαράσσειν, ῥᾳδιουργεῖν, διαφθείρειν, ἐξαιρεῖν, ἀφανίζειν, κατορθοῦν* (ironically), *ἀποκόπτειν, παρακόπτειν, περικόπτειν, μετατιθέναι, προστιθέναι,* interpolare, adulterare, violare, corrodere, dissecare, auferre, delere, emendare (ironically), eradere, subvertere, extinguere, these are some of the expressions we hear in this connection. Marcion gave occasion to the reproach by his edition of the Gospel of Luke and the Epistles of Paul, but against the rest of the Gnostics, especially the Valentinians, against the Artemonites, Novatians, Arians, and Donatists, and against the Nestorians, the same accusation is made as was formerly brought against the Jews. Even within the pale of the Church one party attributed such practices to the other. Ambrosiaster, *e.g.*, believed that in the case of important discrepancies between the Greek and Latin manuscripts, the variations were due to the presumption of the Greek writers who had interpolated spurious matter. Jerome was afraid this would be said of him if he ventured to make the slightest alteration: quis doctus pariter vel indoctus non statim erumpat in vocem, me falsarium, me, clamans, esse sacrilegum qui audeam aliquid in veteribus libris addere, mutare, corrigere! The curse in Apoc. xxii. 18 f. was also referred to the "falsifiers," who thought it more convincing and more reverent to observe the rules of grammar and logic than to abide by all the peculiar expressions in the Scriptures. At a meeting of Cyprian bishops, about the year 350, when one of them, in quoting the verse John v. 8, substituted for *κράβαττος* the better Greek word *σκίμπους*, another shouted to him in the hearing of all the multitude, "Art thou better than he who said

[1] Here again, unfortunately, we have no collection of notices referring to the history of the text as distinguished from that of the canon.

κράβαττος that thou art ashamed to use his words?"[1] And it is a well-known fact that in the time of Augustine there was very nearly an uproar in an African congregation over Jonah's "gourd" (cucurbita) or Jonah's "ivy" (hedera). A few references at least may be collected here:—

(1) On a certain Sunday[2] in the year 170 or thereabouts, Dionysius, Bishop of Corinth, wrote a letter to the Church at Rome through their Bishop Soter, of which Eusebius has preserved the following among other passages (*Eccl. Hist.*, iv. 23):—Ἐπιστολὰς γὰρ ἀδελφῶν ἀξιωσάντων με γράψαι ἔγραψα. Καὶ ταύτας οἱ τοῦ διαβόλου ἀπόστολοι[3] ζιζανίων γεγέμικαν, ἃ μὲν ἐξαιροῦντες, ἃ δὲ προστιθέντες. Οἷς τὸ οὐαὶ κεῖται.[4] Οὐ θαυμαστὸν ἄρα,[5] εἰ καὶ τῶν Κυριακῶν ῥᾳδιουργῆσαί τινες ἐπιβέβληνται γραφῶν, ὁπότε καὶ ταῖς οὐ τοιαύταις ἐπιβεβουλεύκασι. The κυριακαὶ γραφαὶ are in all likelihood the Gospels (the Syriac renders "the writings of our Lord"), but may also include the Pauline Epistles and the O.T. If we are to take the words of Dionysius in their strict sense, it would appear that these writings, like his own letters, had been corrupted by means of "additions" and "omissions." The last sentence, if it is put correctly, and if it has been faithfully transmitted, leads us to infer that in his letter to Corinth Soter had expressed his surprise that the writings of the Lord should have been falsified. To which Dionysius replies that certain letters of his own had been falsified also, and that it was therefore no wonder if they did the same to the writings of the Lord, seeing they tampered also (or, *even*) with those that were inferior to them. The simplest explanation of the words is, undoubtedly, that Dionysius sought to console himself over the fate that

[1] Jülicher, *loc. cit.*, from Sozomen, *Hist. Eccl.*, i. 11. On the Latin form *grabattum*, see W.-W., Index, p. 756, σκίμπους occurs as early as Clem. Al. *Paed.*, 1, 2, 6. In the parallels to Mark ii. 6, Matthew has κλίνη (ix. 6), and Luke κλινίδιον (v. 24). *Cf.* the passage cited by Lagarde (*De Novo Test.*, 20 = *Ges. Abh.*, 118) from Lucian's *Philopseudes*, 11; ὁ Μίδας αὐτὸς ἀράμενος τὸν σκίμποδα ἐφ' οὗ ἐκεκόμιστο ᾤχετο εἰς ἀγρὸν ἀπιών.

[2] Τὴν σήμερον οὖν Κυριακὴν ἡμέραν διηγάγομεν, ἐν ᾗ ἀνέγνωμεν ὑμῶν τὴν ἐπιστολήν· ἣν ἕξομεν ἀεί ποτε ἀναγινώσκοντες νουθετεῖσθαι, ὡς καὶ τὴν προτέραν ἡμῖν διὰ Κλήμεντος γραφεῖσαν.

[3] *Cf.* Matt. xiii. 27, δοῦλοι τοῦ οἰκοδεσπότου, and also the superscriptions of the N. T. Epistles, particularly those of Paul, where δοῦλος Ἰησοῦ Χριστοῦ is varied by ἀπόστολος Ἰ. Χ.

[4] "is reserved"—Syr.

[5] "but"—Syr.

had befallen his letters, by reflecting that it was not surprising that they had falsified his letters of less importance, seeing they had presumed to do the same *even* to the writings of the Lord. On the first interpretation, one would certainly expect Dionysius to use a stronger expression to describe his feelings at the manipulation of the sacred writings than the mere *οὐ θαυμαστόν*. Who are meant by *τινές*? One most naturally thinks of Marcion. According to a later account, Soter, whom Jerome does not mention among the writers, composed a book against the Montanists.

Artemonites. (2) In the last chapter of the Fifth Book of his Ecclesiastical History (c. xxviii.), entitled Περὶ τῶν τὴν Ἀρτέμωνος αἵρεσιν ἐξαρχῆς προβεβλημένων· οἷοί τε τὸν τρόπον γεγόνασι καὶ ὅπως τὰς ἁγίας γραφὰς διαφθεῖραι τετολμήκασιν, Eusebius quotes the following complaint from an earlier source, entitled the *Little Labyrinth* (± 235):—Γραφὰς μὲν θείας ἀφόβως ῥερᾳδιουργήκασιν, πίστεως δὲ ἀρχαίας κανόνα ἠθετήκασι, Χριστὸν δὲ ἠγνοήκασιν, οὐ τί αἱ θεῖαι λέγουσι γραφαὶ ζητοῦντες, but occupying themselves with Logic, Geometry, Euclid, Aristotle, Theophrastus, and Galen, ταῖς τῶν ἀπίστων τέχναις, τὴν ἁπλῆν τῶν θείων γραφῶν πίστιν καπηλεύοντες . . . . διὰ τοῦτο ταῖς θείαις γραφαῖς ἀφόβως ἐπέβαλον τὰς χεῖρας, λέγοντες αὐτὰς διωρθωκέναι. Καὶ ὅτι τοῦτο μὴ καταψευδόμενος αὐτῶν λέγω, ὁ βουλόμενος δύναται μαθεῖν. Εἰ γάρ τις θελήσει συγκομίσας αὐτῶν ἑκάστου τὰ ἀντίγραφα ἐξετάζειν πρὸς ἄλληλα, κατὰ πολὺ ἂν εὕροι διαφωνοῦντα. Ἀσύμφωνα γοῦν ἔσται τὰ Ἀσκληπιάδου τοῖς Θεοδότου. Πολλῶν δὲ ἔστιν εὐπορῆσαι διὰ τὸ φιλοτίμως ἐγγεγράφθαι τοὺς μαθητὰς αὐτῶν τὰ ὑφ' ἑκάστου αὐτῶν, ὡς αὐτοὶ καλοῦσι κατωρθωμένα τουτέστιν ἠφανισμένα. Πάλιν δὲ τούτοις τὰ Ἑρμοφίλου οὐ συνᾴδει. Τὰ γὰρ Ἀπολλωνίδου οὐδὲ αὐτὰ ἑαυτοῖς ἐστι σύμφωνα. Ἔνεστι γὰρ συγκρῖναι τὰ πρότερον ὑπ' αὐτῶν[1] κατασκευασθέντα τοῖς ὕστερον πάλιν ἐπιδιαστραφεῖσι, καὶ εὑρεῖν κατὰ πολὺ ἀπᾴδοντα. Ὅσης δὲ τόλμης ἐστὶ τοῦτο τὸ ἁμάρτημα, εἰκὸς μηδὲ ἐκείνους ἀγνοεῖν. Ἢ γὰρ οὐ πιστεύουσιν Ἁγίῳ Πνεύματι λελέχθαι τὰς θείας γραφάς, καί εἰσιν ἄπιστοι· ἢ ἑαυτοὺς ἡγοῦνται σοφωτέρους τοῦ Ἁγίου Πνεύματος ὑπάρχειν, καὶ τί ἕτερον ἢ δαιμονῶσιν; Οὐδὲ γὰρ ἀρνήσασθαι δύνανται ἑαυτῶν εἶναι τὸ τόλμημα, ὁπόταν καὶ τῇ αὐτῶν χειρὶ ᾖ γεγραμμένα, καὶ παρ' ὧν κατηχήθησαν μὴ τοιαύτας παρέλαβον τὰς γραφάς· καὶ δεῖξαι ἀντίγραφα, ὅθεν αὐτὰ μετεγράψαντο, μὴ ἔχωσιν. Ἔνιοι δὲ αὐτῶν οὐδὲ παραχαράσσειν ἠξίωσαν αὐτάς, ἀλλ' ἁπλῶς

[1] This reading is confirmed by the Syriac as against ὑπ' αὐτοῦ read by Christophorson and Savil.

ἀρνησάμενοι τόν τε νόμον καὶ τοὺς προφήτας ἀνόμου καὶ ἀθέου διδασκαλίας προφάσει χάριτος, εἰς ἔσχατον ἀπωλείας ὄλεθρον κατωλίσθησαν.

The passage is very instructive. We learn that copies of the writings of these heretics were to be found in abundance, because their disciples eagerly inserted their emendations in their texts, "each one's emendations, as they style them, but in reality they are corruptions," as the Syriac has it. At the same time, it is not quite certain that κατωρθωμένα really means corrected manuscripts of the Bible, and not the heretics' own works—*i.e.*, whether we should understand ἀντίγραφα τῶν θείων γραφῶν after τὰ Ἀσκληπιάδου, τὰ Θεοδότου, τὰ Ἑρμοφίλου, τὰ Ἀπολλωνίδου and not rather γράμματα or συντάγματα. In the former case we shall have to search for a recension of Asclepiades, of Theodotus, of Hermophilus, and in the case of Apollonides for a double recension, an earlier and a later. This interpretation of the words does certainly receive support from the positive way in which the historian argues from the conduct of these heretics, that they either did not believe in any inspiration of the holy Scriptures, or thought they could write better themselves, and also from his remark that they did not receive τὰς γραφάς in that form (τοιαύτας) from their (Christian) instructors, and were not able to show any older copies from which their own were transcribed. From the mention of the Law and the Prophets, we may conclude that the reference is mainly to the O. T. Epiphanius mentions the Theodotians as appealing to Deut. xviii. 15, Jer. xvii. 9, Isa. liii. 3, Matt. xii. 31, Luke i. 35, John viii. 40, Acts ii. 22, 1 Tim. ii. 5; while Hippolytus argues against them on the ground that in John i. 14, it is not τὸ πνεῦμα but ὁ λόγος σάρξ ἐγένετο. No sure traces, however, can be discovered in any of these N. T. passages of their supposed trenchant criticism of the text. The most probable instance is Luke i. 35. "If we may trust the statement of Epiphanius," says Harnack (*Monarchianismus*, PRE³, x. 188), "Theodotus wished to separate the second half of the sentence from the first (διὸ καὶ τὸ γεννώμενον ἐκ σοῦ ἅγιον κληθήσεται, υἱὸς Θεοῦ),[1] as

[1] The passage is a conspicuous example of the importance of punctuation. Bengel punctuates ἅγιον, κληθήσεται υἱὸς Θεοῦ, and Westcott and Hort ἅγιον κληθήσεται, υἱὸς Θεοῦ. Weiss is accordingly not quite right in citing Bengel along with Bleek and Hoffman as supporting the view of Tertullian (see Bengel's *Gnomon*). It will be difficult to prove that Tertullian's construction is impossible "on account of the position of κληθήσεται." Westcott and Hort surely know Greek, and Tertullian knew it better than any of us.

if the words διὸ καὶ were wanting, which makes the sentence imply that the divine Sonship of Christ rests on his approving himself. But perhaps Theodotus omitted διὸ καὶ altogether, just as he seems to have read πνεῦμα κυρίου instead of πνεῦμα ἅγιον, in order to obviate all ambiguity." The latter reading is not mentioned in Tischendorf, and the remark of Epiphanius in my opinion amounts to this, that whereas he understood ἅγιον to be the subject of the sentence, Theodotus made it the predicate and separated it from γεννώμενον.[1]

Marcosians.

(3) Speaking of the Marcosians,[2] Irenæus says (92):—Ἔνια δὲ καὶ τῶν ἐν Εὐαγγελίῳ κειμένων εἰς τοῦτον τὸν χαρακτῆρα μεθαρμόζουσιν . . . . ἀλλὰ καὶ ἐν τῷ εἰρηκέναι· πολλάκις ἐπεθύμησα ἀκοῦσαι ἕνα τῶν λόγων καὶ οὐκ ἔσχον τὸν ἐροῦντα, ἐμφαίνοντός φασι δεῖν διὰ τοῦ ἑνὸς τὸν

[1] It seems worth while to quote here Harnack's words on these notices of the earliest attempts at textual criticism. He says (*ibid.*, p. 189): "The charge preferred against the disciples of that erudite Tanner (Theodotus) by the author of the Little Labyrinth is threefold. He complains of their formal and grammatical exegesis of Scripture, of their arbitrary system of textual criticism, and of the extent to which they were engrossed in Logic, Mathematics, and empirical Science. At the first glance, therefore, it would appear that these people had no interest to spare for Theology. But the very opposite is the case. The complainant himself has to confess that they employed the method of grammatical exegesis 'with the object of establishing their godless conclusions,' and textual criticism in order to correct the manuscripts of the holy Scriptures. In place of the allegorical method of exposition, the grammatical is the only right one, and we have here an attempt to discover a text more nearly resembling the original instead of simply accepting the traditional form. How inimitable and charming really are these notices! . . . . These scholars had to be generals without an army, because their grammar and textual criticism and logic might only discredit in the eyes of the churches that christological method which long tradition had invested with admiration and respect. . . . . As 'genuine' scholars—this is an exceedingly characteristic description that is given of them—they also took a jealous care that none of them lost the credit of his conjectures and emendations. No remnants have been preserved of the works of these the first scholarly exegetes of the Christian Church (the Syntagma knows of the existence of such; *cf.* Epiph. lv. c. 1)." So writes Harnack. Nothing, however, is said in the text of Eusebius of a jealous watch over the priority of the conjectures. In the sentence which Harnack renders "for their disciples have with an ambitious zeal recorded what each one has corrected as they call it, that is corrupted (deleted?)," φιλοτίμως ἐγγεγράφθαι is to be understood simply of a diligent record of "corrections" undertaken solely out of an interest in their contents. According to the Syriac ἠφανισμένα is not to be rendered by "deleted," but as Harnack translates it: *cf.* the various Syriac versions in Matthew vi. verse 16 (Syr^{p}), verses 19 and 20 (Syr^{pc}). On the validity of the charge of inventing false Scriptures, see Zahn, *GK.* 1, 296 f.

[2] Westcott, *Canon*, Pt. I. c. iv. § 8, p. 308 ff.

ἀληθῶς ἕνα Θεόν. This seems to contain a reference to Matt. xiii. 17, but what is complained of is a false interpretation of the words of Scripture rather than an actual alteration of the text itself.[1] The still earlier passage, Polycarp vii. 1, is also to be taken as referring to this practice, ὃς ἂν μεθοδεύῃ τὰ λόγια τοῦ Κυρίου πρὸς τὰς ἰδίας ἐπιθυμίας καὶ λέγῃ μήτε ἀνάστασιν μήτε κρίσιν [εἶναι], οὗτος πρωτότοκός ἐστι τοῦ Σατανᾶ. For the exposition of the passage see Zahn, *GK.* i. 842.

(4) That Basilides[2] altered the text of the Gospels as received by the Church in accordance with his own religious and ethical views, and incorporated them in their altered form in his *Evangelium*, is shown by Zahn on Matt. xix. 10–12 (*GK.* i. 771). He shows also that the form into which Basilides cast the Synoptic narrative may have prepared the way for the belief that Simon the Cyrenian was crucified instead of Jesus, if this was really his doctrine. Basilides

(5) Hippolytus says of Noëtus (Lagarde's edition, 45, 19): ὁπόταν γὰρ θελήσωσιν πανουργεύεσθαι, περικόπτουσι τὰς γραφάς. He means by this, according to Zahn, that the Noetians garbled their quotations, and made selections of Scriptural sayings without paying regard to the context. But compare *ibid.*, line 7 ff., αἱ μὲν γὰρ γραφαὶ ὀρθῶς λέγουσιν, ἀλλὰ ἂν καὶ Νόητος νοῇ· οὐκ ἤδη δὲ εἰ Νόητος μὴ νοεῖ, παρὰ τοῦτο ἔκβλητοι αἱ γραφαί. Noëtus

(6) Heracleon,[3] the Valentinian, is said to have read πέντε instead of ἕξ in John ii. 20, but whether he made the alteration himself or found the former reading in his exemplar is not clearly made out. There is no notice of the variant in Tischendorf, Baljon, or in our commentaries. It is mentioned by Scrivener, *Introd.*, ii. 260, n. 3, where reference is made to Lightfoot's *Colossians*, p. 336, n. 1. Origen, commenting on John i. 28, cites Heracleon in support of the reading "Bethany," which, he says, "is found in almost all the manuscripts." Valentinians.

In contrast to the Marcionites and their practice of mutilating the Scriptures, Irenæus says of the Valentinians (iii. 12, 12): scripturas quidem confitentur, interpretationes vero convertunt, quemadmodum ostendimus in primo libro. There we read (i. 3, 6): καὶ οὐ μόνον ἐκ τῶν εὐαγγελικῶν καὶ τῶν ἀποστολικῶν πειρῶνται τὰς ἀποδείξεις ποιεῖσθαι παρατρέποντες τὰς ἑρμηνείας καὶ ῥᾳδιουργοῦντες τὰς ἐξηγήσεις, ἀλλὰ καὶ ἐκ νόμου καὶ προφητῶν. But in i. 11, 9 he says of them: Illi vero qui sunt a Valentino . . . . suas conscriptiones proferentes, plura habere

[1] Westcott, *Canon*, Pt. I. c. iv. p. 310. [2] *Ibid.*, p. 291.

[3] *Ibid.*, p. 303 ff. Cf. *Texts and Studies*, vol. i. 4: *The Fragments of Heracleon*, by A. E. Brooke, M.A.

gloriantur quam sint ipsa evangelia, siquidem in tantum processerunt audaciae, uti quod ab his non olim scriptum est, "veritatis evangelium" titulent, in nihilo conveniens apostolorum evangeliis, ut nec evangelium sit apud eos sine blasphemia. For the continuation and discussion of the passage, see Zahn, *GK.* ii. 748. See also Westcott, *Canon*, p. 298 ff.

Zahn (*GK.* ii. 755) endeavours to show that they corrected the text of the manuscripts, by the omission of ὑπὲρ αὐτῶν, *e.g.*, in 1 Cor. xv. 29, and the insertion of θεότητες in Col. i. 16.

In i. 8, 1, Irenæus accuses them of ἐξ ἀγράφων ἀναγινώσκοντες καὶ τὸ δὴ λεγόμενον ἐξ ἄμμου σχοίνια πλέκειν ἐπιτηδεύοντες. The proverb is from Ahikar.

The well-known charge made by Celsus (*Orig. con. Cels.*, 2, 27; Koetschau, i. 156) and the answer of Origen refer partly to the re-writing of manuscripts and partly to their alteration: Μετὰ ταῦτά τινας τῶν πιστευόντων φησὶν (Celsus) ὡς ἐκ μέθης ἥκοντας εἰς τὸ ἐφεστάναι αὑτοῖς μεταχαράττειν ἐκ τῆς πρώτης γραφῆς τὸ εὐαγγέλιον τριχῇ καὶ τετραχῇ καὶ πολλαχῇ, ἵν' ἔχοιεν πρὸς τοὺς ἐλέγχους ἀρνεῖσθαι. Μεταχαράξαντας δὲ τὸ εὐαγγέλιον ἄλλους οὐκ οἶδα ἢ τοὺς ἀπὸ Μαρκίωνος καὶ τοὺς ἀπὸ Οὐαλεντίνου οἶμαι δὲ καὶ τοὺς ἀπὸ Λουκιάνου. Τοῦτο δὲ λεγόμενον οὐ τοῦ λόγου ἐστὶν ἔγκλημα ἀλλὰ τῶν τολμησάντων ῥᾳδιουργῆσαι τὰ εὐαγγέλια. Καὶ ὥσπερ οὐ φιλοσοφίας ἔγκλημά εἰσιν οἱ σοφισταὶ ἢ οἱ Ἐπικούρειοι ἢ οἱ Περιπατητικοὶ ἢ οἵτινές ποτ' ἂν ὦσιν οἱ ψευδοδοξοῦντες, οὕτως οὐ τοῦ ἀληθινοῦ χριστιανισμοῦ ἔγκλημα οἱ μεταχαράττοντες τὰ εὐαγγέλια καὶ αἱρέσεις ξένας ἐπεισάγοντες τῷ βουλήματι τῆς Ἰησοῦ διδασκαλίας.

Gnostics. (7) Clement (*Strom.*, iii. 39) complains that the Gnostics corrupted the sense of the Scriptures both by arbitrarily misplacing the emphasis (in oral delivery) and by altering the punctuation (in copying manuscripts?); see Zahn, *GK.* i. 424. On Tertullian's complaint as to the way in which Marcion construed Luke xx. 35, see below, p. 276.

(8) Clement (*Strom.*, iv. 41) quotes Matt. v. 10*a*, to which he annexes the reason found in verse 9*b*, and then goes on to say, ἢ ὥς τινες τῶν μετατιθέντων τὰ εὐαγγέλια, Μακάριοι, φησίν, οἱ δεδιωγμένοι ὑπὲρ τῆς δικαιοσύνης, ὅτι αὐτοὶ ἔσονται τέλειοι. Zahn (*GK.* i. p. 411) makes the surmise that when Clement spoke of certain persons who "transposed" or altered the Gospels—*i.e.*, took liberties with the text, he may have been thinking of Tatian, whose personal intercourse he may have enjoyed for a length of time, and with whose Greek writings he shows himself to be familiar.

(9) In an Arabic Introduction to a collection of alleged Nicene Canons particular stress is laid upon the falsification of the Scriptures by heretics. The Emperor Constantine is represented as addressing the Fathers at Nicæa, and enjoining them, in dealing with heretics, to distinguish between those who reject and falsify the holy Scriptures and those who merely interpret them falsely. The arch-heretic Simon Magus already appears as a fabricator of spurious Scripture. His sect possessed an Evangelium in four books, to which they gave the title "Liber quatuor angulorum et cardinum mundi." The Phocalites (Kukiani) retained the Old Testament, but in place of the Church's New Testament they had one manufactured by themselves, in which the twelve Apostles bore barbaric names. It is said of the Marcionites: Sacras scripturas quibusdam in locis commutarunt addideruntque Evangelio et Epistolis Pauli apostoli quibusdam in locis, quaedam vero loca mutilarunt. Apostolorum Actus e medio omnino sustulerunt, alium substituentes Actorum librum, qui faveret opinionibus ac dogmatibus, illumque nuncuparunt "Librum propositi finis." See Zahn, *GK.* ii. 448, where reference is made to Mansi, *Conc. Coll.*, ii. (Flor., 1759), 947–1082; Hefele, *Conciliengeschichte*, 2nd. ed., i. 361–368, 282 f.; Harnack, *Der Ketzer-Katalog des Bischofs Maruta von Maipherkat*, *TU.* (New Series), iv., 1899; *ThLz.*, 1899, 2.

Simon Magus and the Marcionites.

(10) Ambrose says on John iii. 6 (*De Spiritu*, iii. 10): Quem locum ita expresse, Ariani, testificamini esse de Spiritu, ut eum de vestris codicibus auferatis. Atque utinam de vestris et non etiam de Ecclesiae codicibus tolleretis. Eo enim tempore quo impiae infidelitatis Auxentius Mediolanensem Ecclesiam armis exercituque occupaverat, vel a Valente atque Ursatis nutantibus sacerdotibus suis incursabatur Ecclesia Sirmiensis, falsum hoc et sacrilegium vestrum in Ecclesiasticis codicibus deprehensum est. Et fortasse hoc etiam in oriente fecistis.

Arians.

(11) Ambrosiaster has the following note on Rom. v. 14 (Migne, xvii. 100 f.): Et tamen sic (*i.e.* μὴ ἁμαρτήσαντες) praescribitur nobis de graecis codicibus, quasi non ipsi ab invicem discrepent, quod facit studium contentionis. Quia enim propria quis auctoritate uti non potest ad victoriam, verba legis adulterat, ut sensum suis quasi verba legis asserat, ut non ratio sed auctoritas praescribere videatur. Constat autem porro olim quosdam latinos de veteribus graecis translatos (esse) codicibus, quos incorruptos simplicitas temporum servavit et probat: postquam autem a concordia animis discedentibus et haereticis perturbantibus torqueri quaestionibus coeperunt, multa immutata

Greeks.

sunt ad sensum humanum, ut hoc contineretur in litteris quod homini videretur, unde etiam ipsi Graeci diversos codices habent. Hoc autem verum arbitror, quando et ratio et historia et auctoritas observatur: nam hodie quae in latinis reprehenduntur codicibus, sic inveniuntur a veteribus posita, Tertulliano, Victorino, et Cypriano. The correction "hodie quae" for "hodieque" in the last sentence is due to Haussleiter, *Forschungen*, iv. 32. The passage is also interesting as being the earliest instance known to me of the collocation of *ratio* and *auctoritas* as the two arbiters in theological disputes. Compare the frequent combination of the two by Luther in his earlier polemics — *e.g.* against Prierias, and also later in his protest at Worms.

Again, Ambrosiaster says on Gal. ii. 1, with reference to Acts xv. 20, 29: Quae sophistae Graecorum non intelligentes, scientes tamen a sanguine abstinendum *adulterant* scripturam, quartum mandatum addentes "et a suffocatis observandum," quod puto nec ne Dei nutu intellecturi sunt, quia iam supra dictum est, quod addiderunt.

Marcion.

(*g*) **Marcion.**—We have more exact information in regard to Marcion's great undertaking than to these slender attempts at textual criticism. Here there is a fuller stream of testimony both in the Greek and Latin Fathers. It must be confessed, however, that hitherto attention has been directed more to his position in the matter of the Canon generally than to his work on the text of the New Testament. Here again, the works of Zahn throw most light upon the subject; in other works, like the PRE *e.g.*, this side of Marcion's activity is very superficially treated. Several points have already been referred to here and there in the previous part of this work, but the question must now be treated as a whole.[1]

[1] On the literature of the subject, *cf.* Zahn, *GK.* i. 585–718, *Das N. T. Marcions*; ii. 409–529, *Marcions N. T.* All other works are superseded by this, but mention may still be made of A. Hahn, *Das Evangelium Marcions in seiner ursprünglichen Gestalt* (1823); Thilo, *Codex Apocryphus Novi Testamenti* (1832: for this work Hahn attempted to restore the text of Marcion, pp. 401–486); A. Ritschl, *Das Evangelium Marcions und das kanonische Evangelium des Lucas* (1846); Hilgenfeld, in the *Z. f. hist. Theol.*, 1855, pp. 426–484; Sanday, *The Gospels in the Second Century*, c. viii.

In the opening sentence of his examination of Marcion's New Testament, Zahn avers that no church teacher of the second century occupies such an important position in the history of the ecclesiastical canon as does that early writer. If this is really so, it becomes all the more important for us to inquire whether traces of his influence may not be discoverable also in our witnesses to the text of the New Testament.

His New Testament.

Marcion's New Testament, which was at the same time his entire Bible, consisted of two books of moderate compass—viz. a *Gospel-Book*, which he seems to have called Εὐαγγέλιον simply, and a collection of *ten Pauline Epistles* called, probably by himself, τὸ Ἀποστολικὸν (*sc.* βιβλίον). The Epistles were arranged in an order which was evidently thought to correspond to that of their composition—viz., Gal., 1 and 2 Cor., Rom., 1 and 2 Thess., Laodicenos (=Ephes.), Col., Phil., Phm. He was unanimously accused by the Church teachers of having mutilated the ecclesiastical Bible in the manufacture of his own, and also of having corrupted the text here and there by means of interpolations, particularly in the case of Luke, which was the only Gospel he admitted. They complained that he used not the pen but the knife (only he used it for a purpose the opposite of that for which the scissors are employed nowadays), and the sponge, and also that he deleted not words merely but whole pages. They compared his work upon the manuscripts to that of a mouse.[1] And as for his disciples! Every day they were improving their Gospel. Seeing that he himself had not gone so far as to erase the writings of Paul altogether, his disciples continued his work, and removed whatever did not concur with their views.[2]

[1] The proof passages will be found in Zahn, *GK.* i. 620, 626, 663: machaera non stilo: erubescat spongia Marcionis (Tert., v. 4, p. 282. Is it permissible to infer from this that minium was already used in manuscripts of the Bible at that time?—*cf.* Augustine, *Con. Jul.*, iii. 13: ipsum libri tui argumentum erubescendo convertatur in minium): non miror si syllabas subtrahit, quum paginas totas plerumque subducet. Quis tam comesor mus Ponticus quam qui evangelia corrosit (*con. Marc.*, i. 1): tuum apostoli codicem licet sit undique circumrosus (Adamantius).

[2] See the passage from Tertullian (cotidie reformant illud (*sc.* evangelium), prout a nobis cotidie revincuntur), and from Adamantius (*Pseudo-Origenes*, de la Rue, i. 887=Lat. in *Caspari Anecdota*, i. 57) in Zahn, *GK.* i. 613.

But according to testimony extending over a long stretch of time, their text of the Scriptures seems to have undergone fewer alterations during that period than that of the Catholic Church (Zahn, *GK.* i. 613). In comparing the text of these two collections "it should be clearly understood that the Church's text, whose treatment by Marcion is in question, is not to be identified with that of our Bible Societies, or of Tischendorf, or of Epiphanius, but was such a text as Marcion found in the Catholic Church or in the Roman community about the year 150. The text of the ecclesiastical exemplar on which Marcion based his labours can no longer be restored in every word, but sufficient means are at our command to give us a general idea of the form which the text of the Pauline Epistles presented in the second century, and at the same time to ascertain in many separate instances what text Marcion had before him. It turns out in many cases that what seems strange in Marcion's text to one who compares it with the *textus receptus*, or with one of our modern critical editions, without knowing much about the history of the text, is by no means peculiar to Marcion, but was pretty common in the West in early times. Now it is quite inconceivable, in view of the implacable hostility of the Church to Marcion, that his text, condemned as it was unceasingly as being heretical and spurious, should have exerted any positive influence on that of the Church.[1] It follows, accordingly, that all those things in Marcion's Bible that seem to the uninitiated to be peculiar to it alone, but which are attested by Catholic manuscripts, versions, and Patristic writers, were not invented by Marcion, but taken by him from the Church's Bible of that time, or from one such Bible at all events, and were only gradually ousted from the text used by the Church."[2] All this, which is taken word for word, with

[1] *Cf.* also *GK.* p. 681.

[2] *Cf.* Westcott, *Canon*, Pt. I. c. iv. § 9, Marcion: "Some of the omissions can be explained at once by his peculiar doctrines, but others are unlike arbitrary corrections, and must be considered as various readings of the greatest interest,

the exception of a slight change in the last sentence, from Zahn's dissertation of the year 1889 (p. 636), should even at that time have been self-evident, but, like Zahn's further statements in the same place, has not yet been sufficiently attended to, especially in our commentaries on Luke and the Pauline Epistles. He points out, *e.g.*, that Tertullian, in speaking of the change of the address "ad Ephesios" to "Laodicenos," credits Marcion with the intention of being "et in isto diligentissimus explorator," so that it is possible that he compared several manuscripts in order to discover the original wording.[1] In such cases, therefore, the question may be asked whether Marcion may not really have preserved the original text, and whether his text, so far as it is corroborated by any independent tradition, should not be estimated much higher than it is by the textual critics of the present.[2] Zahn deserves all the more credit for giving such careful attention to questions relating to the text, seeing that the subject of his investigation was merely the history of the canon. He has dealt chiefly with those passages in which Marcion's intentional alterations have been preserved. Reference may be made, *e.g.*, to the pages in the first volume of his History, entitled *Minor Emendations*, wherein it is shown how Marcion, in his hostility to the Old Testament with its God of Righteousness, omitted the quotations from the Old Testament altogether, or dropped the introductory formula of quotation in Rom. i. 17, xii. 19, 2 Cor. iv. 13; excluded all the references to Abraham

His "Emendations."

dating as they do to a time anterior to all other authorities in our possession" (p. 315). See also note at the end of the paragraph, where certain readings peculiar to Marcion are cited.

[1] *Cf.* also *ibid.*, p. 684, and see below, p. 313.

[2] *Cf.* also *ibid.*, p. 682: "I repeat that readings which are proved to be earlier than Marcion by their simultaneous occurrence in his text and that of the several Catholic witnesses deserve greater consideration both in the Gospels and Epistles than has generally been accorded them. It is much more important to ascertain whether a certain reading has the support of Marcion than to observe that it occurs in this or that uncial manuscript. In spite of this, however, the critical notes in our commentaries hardly ever refer to Marcion, not to speak of their doing so systematically."

in Galatians except in iv. 22; altered ἀγνοοῦντες τὴν τοῦ θεοῦ δικαιοσύνην in Rom. x. 3 to ἀγνοοῦντες τὸν θεόν; removed the words γενόμενον ἐκ γυναικὸς, γενόμενον ὑπὸ νόμον from Gal. iv. 4; changed the active construction into the passive in 1 Cor. iii. 17; and elsewhere strove after greater condensation, lucidity, and brevity of expression. Marcion, says Zahn, had good grounds for believing that the text of the Scriptures had not remained unchanged during the century that had elapsed since their composition, though that might be said with more truth of the Gospels and the Acts than of the Epistles; but to attempt to rid the Apostle's text of all supposed corruptions with no regard to any sort of critical material whatever, but depending simply and solely on his own instinctive sense of what was genuinely Christian and apostolic, was the undertaking of a giant, as Irenæus calls Marcion. And his disciples, in a blind veneration of his authority, seem to have exceeded the intention of the master and editor, "just as many Lutherans at the present day look upon Luther's translation, with all its faults, as the very word of God, and hardly capable of improvement."

In the Appendices to his second volume Zahn has gone still more carefully into the questions relating to the criticism of the text.[1] His main conclusions will hardly be contested. Among these are the following:—

Marcion and the Western Text.

1. That Marcion based his Gospel on that of Luke, although his text displays various elements belonging to Matthew and Mark;

2. That this mixture is found in those passages wherein the ecclesiastical texts, and especially the Western, exhibit the same or similar features;

3. That Marcion's text shows[2] none of those small "apocryphal additions" which we find combined with the contents of our Gospels in Justin and Tatian.

[1] Pp. 409–449, on the criticism of the sources; pp. 449–529, the restoration of the text. On p. 449 f. he gives his verdict on the earlier works of Hilgenfeld, Volkmar, and van Manen in this direction.

[2] Zahn interjects "as yet."

Zahn also calls attention frequently to the different manuscripts which still exhibit a text agreeing with that credited to Marcion, and which are precisely the Western witnesses, the Old Latin manuscripts, and D of the Greek.[1] Compare, *e.g.*, on Luke v. 14, 34, 39; vi. 25 f., 31, 37; viii. 45; ix. 6, 16, 22; x. 22, 25; xi. 20, 41; xii. 14, 31, 58 f.; xviii. 35; xx. 36; xxi. 27, 30; xxiv. 6, 26, 37. But there are also passages where Marcion parts company with D and its associates—*e.g.*, vi. 22, 26, 29; xi. 4. In Paul, too, the number of passages displaying agreement between Marcion and D_2 G_2 preponderates: Gal. ii. 5; iii. 14*b*; v. 1, 14, 24; 1 Cor. i. 18; 2 Cor. v. 4; 1 Thess. iv. 16; Eph. i. 9, 13; iii. 10; iv. 6; v. 28 ff. The agreement between Marcion's text and that of the minuscule 157 was previously emphasised by Zahn—*e.g.*, in Luke xvi. 12, where the reading τὸ ἐμόν instead of τὸ ὑμέτερον (ἡμέτερον B L) is supported as yet by this Greek manuscript alone and three old Latin (e i l), and in xxi. 30, where only one other of the minuscules collated by Scrivener supports D 157 in reading προβάλωσιν τὸν καρπὸν αὐτῶν.[2] In Luke xxiv. 26, D and Marcion are our only witnesses for the reading ὅτι instead of οὐχί. How is this to be explained? Zahn, *e.g.*, holds that it is a mere coincidence that Marcion's reading, "prophetas suos,"[3] in 1 Thess. ii. 15 agrees with τοὺς ἰδίους προφήτας read by D_2 E_2 K_2 L_2, *i.e.*, the representatives of the Antiochean recension, with which Marcion elsewhere very seldom agrees, seeing he founds throughout upon a Western text. In the great majority of cases the explanation seems to be simple enough.

[1] We have not yet discovered a manuscript containing exactly Marcion's text. The chances of our still doing so are very small in view of the hatred with which Marcion was pursued. But when the libelli of certain libellatici have been found, and also a great part of the Gospel of Peter, we need not despair of finding other lost works as well. Codex 604 is interesting as exhibiting the Marcionite reading, ἐλθέτω τὸ πνεῦμά σου ἐφ' ἡμᾶς καὶ καθαρισάτω ἡμᾶς, in the Lord's Prayer, Luke xi. 2. The same manuscript omits με λέγετε εἶναι in Luke ix. 20, and λέγουσα in verse 35. Compare also Jülicher, *Gleichnisreden Jesu*, ii. 5: "Marcion, who perhaps created the Roman text of Luke xxi. 30."

[2] On this passage W.-W. observe: "D ex Latinis forsan correctus."

[3] "Licet *suos* adiectio sit haeretici." Tertullian.

Marcion began his career at Rome, so that we may naturally expect him to give us a Western text. So far, therefore, one might be tempted simply to ignore that text as hitherto, although a text attested by Marcion and the Church in common is surely entitled, even in respect of its antiquity, to much more consideration than has been paid to it heretofore. The importance, and at the same time the difficulty, of the problem is increased by the fact that we find the same text as his, or at all events one of a similar sort, represented in a totally different quarter—viz. in Tatian.[1]

Tatian.

(*h*) **Tatian**[2] has already been referred to in a general way above (p. 97 ff.): we shall now give the testimony of the early church regarding him verbatim. If we leave out of account the somewhat doubtful reference in Hegesippus (p. 96), and an equally uncertain allusion to the title of his Harmony in Origen,[3] the testimony from purely Greek sources is confined to a few sentences in Eusebius,[4]

[1] In the critical notes at the end of this chapter I have cited a number of Marcion's readings from Zahn's work, with the hope that these will now earn a fuller recognition in our theological commentaries. See *e.g.* on Luke xviii. 20; xxiii. 2; xxiv. 37; 1 Cor. vi. 20; xiv. 19.

[2] See Literature on p. 105 f., to which add Westcott, *Canon*, Part I. c. iv. § 10.

[3] Defending the plurality of the canonical Gospels against the Marcionites, he says: *τὸ ἀληθῶς διὰ τεσσάρων ἕν ἐστιν εὐαγγέλιον* (*Philocalia*, ed. Robinson, 47; Zahn, *GK.* i. 412; PRE[3], v. 654). From what Origen says, *Contra Celsum*, vi. 51, it would seem that he himself heard Tatian.

[4] Euseb., *Hist. Eccl.*, iv. 29, with reference to the Encratites: *Χρῶνται μὲν οὖν οὗτοι Νόμῳ καὶ Προφήταις καὶ Εὐαγγελίοις* (Syriac has אונגליון), *ἰδίως ἑρμηνεύοντες τῶν ἱερῶν τὰ νοήματα γραφῶν . . . . βλασφημοῦντες δὲ Παῦλον τὸν ἀπόστολον ἀθετοῦσιν αὐτοῦ τὰς Ἐπιστολάς, μηδὲ τὰς Πράξεις τῶν ἀποστόλων καταδεχόμενοι. ὁ μέντοι γε πρότερος αὐτῶν ἀρχηγὸς ὁ Τατιανὸς συνάφειάν τινα καὶ συναγωγὴν οὐκ οἶδ' ὅπως τῶν Εὐαγγελίων συνθεὶς Τὸ Διὰ Τεσσάρων τοῦτο προσωνόμασεν· ὃ καὶ παρά τισιν εἰσέτι φέρεται. Τοῦ δὲ Ἀποστόλου φασὶ τολμῆσαί τινας αὐτὸν μεταφράσαι φωνὰς ὡς ἐπιδιορθούμενον αὐτῶν τὴν τῆς φράσεως σύνταξιν. Καταλέλοιπε δὲ οὗτος πολύ τι πλῆθος γραμμάτων κ.τ.λ.* In the Syriac version it runs: But this Tatian, their first head, collected and combined and framed a (*or*, the) אונגליון and called it ריטסרון, that is "the combined," which is in the possession of many till this day. And it is said of him that he ventured to alter certain phrases of the Apostle (the plural points in the Syriac are to be omitted) as with the object of amending the composition of the phrases. And he has left many writings, etc.

a notice in Epiphanius,[1] and a scholion in a manuscript of the Gospels.[2]

For more exact information we are indebted solely to the Syrian church. The Greek writer Theodoret gives us most details.[3] The notices contained in Syriac and Arabic sources are more numerous than the Greek, but they are shorter and must be omitted here.[4] It becomes necessary, therefore, to consider very carefully whether any vestiges of Tatian's work are preserved in our witnesses for the text, and how these may, and indeed must, be used in its criticism. I assume as having been demonstrated by Zahn, that Tatian's Diatessaron was a Syriac work, and I take it as very probable that the Curetonian Syriac and the Lewis Syriac present us with two works based on, or at least influenced by, that of Tatian. To what extent the same is true of the Peshitto as well need not be considered here, the main problem being to elucidate the connection between Tatian and the *Western* witnesses. And here we are at once confronted with a matter of great uncertainty — viz., whether there might not also have been a *Greek* Harmony of the Gospels either antecedent to

[1] Epiphan., *Haeret*, 46, 1 (Pet. 391): λέγουσι δὲ τὸ διὰ τεσσάρων Εὐαγγέλιον ὑπ' αὐτοῦ γεγενῆσθαι, ὅπερ κατὰ Ἑβραίους τινὲς καλοῦσι.

[2] Minuscule Evan. 72 (Harleianus 5647 of the eleventh century) on Matt. xxvii. 48: σῃ[μείωσαι] ὅτι εἰς τὸ καθ' ἱστορίαν εὐαγγέλιον Διοδώρου καὶ Τατιανοῦ καὶ ἄλλων διαφόρων ἁγίων πατέρων τοῦτο προσκεῖται. Instead of Διοδώρου, Harnack–Preuschen (i. 493), read Διαδώρου, whether rightly or not I do not know. Nothing being known of the historical Gospel of one Diodorus, it is natural enough to conjecture (Zahn, *Forsch.*, i. 28) that the reading should be διὰ δ', but what becomes then of ωρου καὶ? Harnack suggests διὰ δ' Σύρου Τατιανοῦ, but see Zahn, *Forsch.*, ii. 298. The omission of the article before διὰ δ' is a difficulty.

[3] In his Ἐπιτομὴ αἱρετικῆς κακομυθίας (i. 20; vol. iv. 312), written in the year 453, he says at the end of the chapter on Tatian:—οὗτος καὶ τὸ διὰ τεσσάρων καλούμενον συντέθεικεν εὐαγγέλιον, τάς τε γενεαλογίας περικόψας καὶ τὰ ἄλλα ὅσα ἐκ σπέρματος Δαβὶδ κατὰ σάρκα γεγεννημένον τὸν κύριον δείκνυσιν, ἐχρήσαντο δὲ τούτῳ οὐ μόνοι οἱ τῆς ἐκείνου συμμορίας, ἀλλὰ καὶ οἱ τοῖς ἀποστολικοῖς ἑπόμενοι δόγμασι, τὴν τῆς συνθήκης κακουργίαν οὐκ ἐγνωκότες, ἀλλ' ἁπλούστερον ὡς συντόμῳ τῷ βιβλίῳ χρησάμενοι. Εὗρον δὲ κἀγὼ πλείους ἢ διακοσίας βίβλους τοιαύτας ἐν ταῖς παρ' ἡμῖν ἐκκλησίαις τετιμημένας, καὶ πάσας συναγαγὼν ἀπεθέμην καὶ τὰ τῶν τεττάρων εὐαγγελιστῶν ἀντεισήγαγον.

[4] See Hamlyn Hill, *Earliest Life of Christ*, etc., p. 324; Hope W. Hogg, Ante-Nicene Library, Additional Volume.

the Diatessaron or contemporary with it, which Tatian himself made or employed. Zahn thinks not, mainly because from the side of the Greek Church we have almost no notice whatever of the existence of anything of this sort, nor of Tatian's own work either. Harnack seems not to be convinced of the correctness of Zahn's position.[1] He even declares that Harris's *Preliminary Study*[2] has only confirmed his "conviction that Tatian composed a Greek Harmony of the Gospels."[3] That treatise is accompanied by a facsimile of the fragment of Mark in Codex W^{d}, "the contents of which display an affinity with the text of the Diatessaron (with the original text?)."[4] At all events Harnack is of opinion that Harris's conclusions with regard to a Pre-Tatian and a very early Harmony of the narrative of the Passion are very premature, and in his judgment should either not have been put forward at all in a *Preliminary Study* or suggested with more deliberation. G. Krüger also puts "this Combined Gospel written in Syriac (Greek?)" in his *History of Early Christian Literature*, § 37. On the other hand, Hogg in § 12 of his Introduction,[5] *Non-Syriac Texts of the Diatessaron*, says nothing of a Greek text, and in § 19, where he raises the question, "In what language was it written?", he speaks only of the "view favoured by an increasing majority of scholars, that it was written in Syriac," and then asks, on this view, "was it a translation or simply a compilation?" and lastly, which is the main question, "what precisely is its relation to . . . . the Western text generally?"

In his first work, written prior to the publication of the Arabic text, Zahn very frequently pointed to the fact that the so-called Western witnesses—*i.e.*, Codex D and the Old

[1] See *Die Ueberlieferung der griechischen Apologeten*, 1882, pp. 196–218, and, on the other side, Zahn, *Forschungen*, ii. 292 ff.

[2] *The Diatessaron of Tatian: a Preliminary Study*, 1890.

[3] See *ThLz.*, 1891, col. 356.

[4] It is not clear whether Harnack gives this as his own opinion or not. For a reading of cod. W^{d}, akin to that of Tatian, see below on Mark vii. 33, p. 264.

[5] Ante-Nicene Christian Library, Additional Volume, p. 38.

Latin manuscripts, agree so often with Tatian.[1] His explanation of this phenomenon is very simple—viz., that Tatian returned from Rome to his old home in Syria about the year 172, and took with him from the West his text, which was just the Western text. This view would present no difficulty if it were only the case that the Diatessaron shared the peculiarities of the Western text, but is the fact not rather the converse of this—viz., that D, the leading representative of that text, shares the peculiarities of a Harmony of the Gospels, might we say, in short, of the Diatessaron? Not only are certain readings the same in both texts, but the Western text seems actually to exhibit features which can scarcely be regarded otherwise than as the outcome of a Harmony. I have given expression to this opinion ere now; it struck me forcibly when I was collating the Codex Bezae for my *Supplementum Novi Testamenti Graeci.* In order to afford a more convenient survey of the vast number of variants, I followed the paragraphing of Westcott and Hort's edition. Now look at the variants there. Whereas the majority consist of quite separate and disconnected readings, I was obliged at the beginning of the pericopæ regularly to copy half a line or even a whole line from D, its text differed so much from that of our present editions at the beginnings of the pericopæ, and there only to the same extent. See, *e.g.*, Luke v. 17, 27; vii. 1, 18; ix. 37; x. 1, 25; xi. 14; xii. 1 to the end; xxiv. 13. It is true this phenomenon is most frequently observed in Luke, where I had previously explained its appearance in another way by supposing like Blass that it was due to the author having issued two editions of that Gospel. But neither is it altogether absent from the other Gospels. It occurs most seldom, as might be expected, in Matthew, but examples may be seen in xvii. 22, 24; xx. 29. In Mark see iii. 19; iv. 1; vi. 7. There are other features besides this which are difficult of explanation on any other grounds. For these I may briefly refer to the second of

Tatian and the Western Text.

[1] See *Forschungen*, i. 130, 140, 216, 228 f., 237, 248, 263.

the works relating to this part of the subject, *The Syro-Latin Text of the Gospels*, by F. H. Chase,[1] in which a special chapter is devoted to the question of "Harmonistic Influence." (pp. 76–100). The writer calls attention there to three points, viz.:—

1. "The text of Codex Bezae shows constant indications of harmonistic influence." This, however, is nothing new. Jerome, *e.g.*, complains of amalgamations of this sort. But then,

2. "In such harmonized passages readings occur which we are justified by other evidence in considering as Tatianic readings."

3. "There are other signs of the influence of Syriac phraseology in, or in the neighbourhood of, such readings due to harmonistic influence."

I waive consideration of this last point, but as regards the second it is noteworthy, and bears out what I have said above, that Chase in this connection goes almost entirely by passages from Luke with the exception of Matt. xxi. 18; xxiv. 31 f.; xxvi. 59 ff.; and Mark viii. 10; xiii. 2; x. 25 ff. From Luke he instances iii. 23–38; iv. 31; v. 10 f., 14 f.; vi. 42; viii. 35; xi. 2; xx. 20; xxi. 7; xxiii. 45 ff.; xxiv. 1.

I should like, however, to call attention here to one passage to which Chase refers in another connection—viz., the extensive interpolation after Matt. xx. 28 (Chase, pp. 9–14). It is true, as Zahn expressly points out,[2] that neither Ephraem nor Aphraates, who were our only sources for the Diatessaron prior to 1881, "shows any traces of this long and in part apocryphal interpolation, nor yet of Luke xiv. 7–10, from which the most of it is taken." But in the Arabic Tatian,[3] Luke xiv. 1–6 and xiv. 7–11, 12–15 are found after Matt. xx. 1–16 at the end of § 29 and the beginning of § 30 respectively. The verse Matt. xx. 28, regarding which Zahn was uncertain

[1] London, Macmillan, 1895.

[2] *Forschungen*, i. 179.

[3] This will be found most conveniently in Hogg's translation—Ante-Nicene Library, Additional Volume.

whether it was in Tatian or not, seeing that neither Ephraem nor Aphraates mentions it, is found in § 31, 5 between Mark x. 44 and Luke xiii. 22, while Matt. xx. 29*a* (+Mark x. 46*a*) follows a little further down in § 31, 25. So far, indeed, this result is not favourable to our theory. But I ask myself in vain how else this interpolation is to be explained except as an attempt at harmonising. Now, seeing that its text is found in one Syriac, two Greek, and half a dozen Latin witnesses (the particulars are given in the critical note, p. 255), the further question arises, Whence comes it? The most ready answer will be, "it comes from the Greek, whence it passed to the Latin on the one side and to the Syriac on the other." As for the Latin, it is certain that the majority, perhaps even all, of the Latin forms are derived from the Greek. But are the Syriac as well? Or is not rather the converse true, however strange it may seem at the first glance, that the Greek is a translation of the Syriac? There is the word δειπνοκλήτωρ, *e.g.*, which strikes me as it did Chase, as being particularly strange. I admit that I should not care to build a hypothesis of this magnitude on this one word and this one passage alone. I would merely submit it generally as a question to be kept in view in further investigations. And I would supplement it by another question whether, in the case of the first being negatived, it may not be true after all, *pace* Zahn, that there was a Greek Harmony alongside the Syriac and probably going back to the same author. May not the close resemblances traceable between Tatian and the Western text be also accounted for on the supposition that instead of Tatian being influenced by the latter, it really goes back to Tatian?

I would ask this question specially in regard to the Western text of the *Pauline Epistles*. What is meant by the statement of Eusebius cited above as to Tatian's treatment of these Epistles? Μεταφράσαι may certainly mean to translate, but then one translates an entire text and not φωνάς τινας merely, and, moreover, one does not translate ὡς ἐπιδιορθούμενος αὐτῶν τὴν τῆς φράσεως σύνταξιν "with a view to improving the phraseology and syntax." Do not our Western witnesses present us with a work of this description? I am well aware that such hypotheses are like that regarding the author of the *Nibelungenlied* where there was a great poem without a name and one or two great names without poems, and so various combinations were made, for each of which something could be said, while none of them could be said to be proved. That may be the case here too. But at present I feel disposed to attribute a considerable share in this peculiar "Western" text to Tatian. And as this name "Western," the inappropriateness of which has long been recognised, becomes on this supposition more inappropriate still, I am inclined to recommend the freer adoption of the nomenclature familiarised by the work of Chase, I mean that of "Syro-Latin." In his preface Chase puts in a plea for its use, citing a sentence from the *Dublin Review* of July 1894, p. 52, in which H. Lucas says: "The time is, we hope, not far distant, when the term Western will give place to the term Syro-Latin, the only one which truly represents, in our opinion, the facts of the case." Just as when we wish to indicate those languages and tribes that extend from the Indian to the German and Keltic we say Indo-Germanic, or Indo-Keltic, if we wish to be more exact and avoid wounding the sensibilities of the French, so the term Syro-Latin would be the best designation for a form of text whose characteristics are as distinctly traceable among the Syrians in the East as among the Greeks in the centre and the Latins in the West. But be that as it may, one thing is clear, that many problems here await solution. But they will not for ever defy methodical investigation.

Syro-Latin.

The foregoing was all written before I saw the analysis given by Zahn in his *Geschichte des Kanons*, i. 383 ff. Reading it, I am surprised that his conclusions have not been followed up by a thorough investigation of the subject long ere now. Personally, I am precluded at this moment from even making an attempt in this direction. Zahn says: "The quotations of Aphraates frequently presuppose a different Greek text (of the Pauline Epistles) than that lying at the foundation of the Peshitto. The repeated resemblances to Western texts, Claromontanus, Boernerianus (D G), Tertullian, and other Latin witnesses are particularly striking. In the earliest Syriac Gospel the same phenomenon appears even more conspicuously. How is it to be explained? Shall we suppose that this type of text was dispersed equally throughout *all* parts of the Church during the second century? In that case we should have to regard it as the earliest form at which we can arrive, on the principle laid down by Tertullian: quod apud multos unum invenitur, non est erratum sed traditum. But," says Zahn, "even those who venerate the Western tradition of the text—*i.e.* those who, like myself, are of opinion that it does not get nearly its due share of attention from present-day critics—will decline to assent to this proposition. Because the result of this view would be to establish the rule that the so-called Western tradition *invariably* deserves the preference over those others, even over our oldest Greek manuscripts themselves. Even if we limited it to those elements of the text in which the furthest East agrees with the furthest West, the result would still be a text to which no cautious critic would pin his faith. A more natural explanation of this striking condition of things is required." Zahn finds this in the supposition that there was formerly a close intimacy between the Syrian Church and Rome. "Just as the Princes of Edessa had much direct intercourse with Rome, so to all appearance had the Church there." In proof of this, he points to the early intrusion of Marcion's doctrines and Bible into Mesopotamia, to the participation of the Church of Edessa in the Easter controversy and its agreement in that matter with Victor of Rome, and to the Abgar Legend which connects Edessa with Zephyrinus of Rome (199–216) by way of Antioch, and represents Peter as sending the Epistles of Paul from Rome to Edessa. "Considering the anachronisms that legends usually exhibit, may we not take this to be the expression of an historical fact, viz. that a text written in the West formed the basis of the earliest Syriac version of the Pauline Epistles? This supposition is confirmed by the earliest history of the Gospel among the Syrians—viz. by the Diatessaron." [1] After a most thorough discussion of all the questions relating to that book (pp. 387–422), Zahn

[1] *Cf.* p. 393: "To judge from Ephraem's Commentary, the Diatessaron contains scarcely as much apocryphal matter as Codex Cantabrigiensis of the Gospels and Acts."

discovers in this part also (the Gospels) an intimate connection between the text on which it is based, and the form assumed by the text of the Gospels in the West during the second century. And he believes that it will be difficult to find a more feasible explanation of the remarkable agreement evidenced by these two texts in the very matter of their textual corruption and licence than this, that this text came from Rome to Syria. And so the final question arises, "whether a connection does not exist between the first Gospel and the first text of Paul and the Acts in the Syriac, and whether the *entire* N. T., as the *Doctrine of Addai* says, was not a present which Tatian brought with him from Rome to his countrymen, and adapted for their use by means of a free translation and revision?" Zahn thinks that a positive answer cannot be given, but he refers pointedly to what Eusebius says regarding Tatian's treatment of the Pauline Epistles, and is led to suppose that those changes were introduced on the occasion and in the form of a translation from the Greek into Syriac, and that the reason why Eusebius had such hazy notions regarding it as well as the Diatessaron, is most likely that both the books were in Syriac, and used only in the Syrian Church. A closer investigation of the Pauline Epistles in the Syriac is needed to decide these questions.

To these propositions of Zahn I have but the one objection stated above, that the expressions used by Eusebius point far too plainly to a revision of the phraseology of the Pauline Epistles, which could have been done only on the original Greek.[1] Zahn himself points out that the words of Eusebius remind us of what is elsewhere said of the Theodotians (*Eccl. Hist.*, v. 28, 15. 18; see above, p. 200).[2]

[1] In his *N.T. um* 200, p. 108, Harnack treats Zahn's interpretation of the words of Eusebius as a bad blunder. The latter defends himself by saying among other things that it is not quite clear whether Eusebius himself was aware of the double meaning of the word μεταφράσαι which was employed in the tradition (he says φασι) reported to him. He thinks that Rufinus might be said to have "paraphrased" certain commentaries of Origen, correcting his thought and phraseology in many places. True, but in Eusebius it is φωνάς τινας τοῦ ἀποστόλου, not whole epistles, that Tatian is said to have "metaphrased."

[2] On the words of Jerome (*ad Tit. praef.*, vii. 686), "Sed Tatianus Encratitarum patriarches, qui et ipse nonnullas Pauli epistolas repudiavit, hanc vel maxime, hoc est ad Titum, apostoli pronuntiandam credidit, parvipendens Marcionis et aliorum qui cum eo in hac parte consentiunt assertionem," compare Zahn, *Forsch.*, i. 6, *GK.* i. 426.

Western Text.

(*i*) **The Western Text.**—We thus find ourselves face to face with what has been called the only burning question of the textual criticism of the New Testament—the question, namely, of the place to be assigned to the so-called Western text. Our treatment of the external testimony has led us back through Lucian, Pamphilus, Hesychius, and Origen, to Marcion and Tatian, that is, into the middle of the second century. But the question is now whether we must stop here, or whether it is not possible to ascend with certainty even somewat higher by means of an investigation of the material afforded by the manuscripts themselves. The "Higher Criticism," *e.g.*, seeks to get behind the Synoptic Gospels to the documents which the authors or editors used in their composition; is it not possible for the "Lower Criticism" to recover with certainty at least the primitive text of the New Testament books? And is that not most readily found in the so-called Western text? We have been obliged to make frequent reference to it already; the question for us now is, "What is the value of Codex Bezae and its associates?"

It was observed by Theodore Beza himself, the scholar whose name the Codex justly bears, that the text of this manuscript differed in so many respects from that of others, especially in Luke and Acts, that he could give no explanation of it satisfactory to himself. He was not led to suppose that the alterations were due to heretics; nevertheless, like a cautious man, he thought it more advisable to preserve the Codex than to publish it. Eight hundred years before, Bede was similarly impressed by the Codex which we now know by the name of Laudianus, E_2. He indicated "quaedam quae in Graeco sive aliter seu plus aut minus posita vidimus." He was uncertain "utrum negligentia interpretis omissa vel aliter dicta, an incuria librariorum sint depravata sive relicta . . . . namque graecum exemplar fuisse falsatum suspicari non audeo." When the manuscripts began to be more systematically collated, Bengel declared that the criticism of the text would be much simplified if one were not bound to trouble himself with these codices, which, as being written in Greek and Latin, he called *vere bilingues*. Old students of the Maulbronn College have told me that Ephorus Bäumlein the most distinguished philologist of our Institute in this century, and editor of *Disquisitions on the Greek Particles* and similar works, was always referring to the Codex Cantabrigiensis, though they themselves never rightly understood about this Codex, or indeed about such things at all. I do not know who it was from whom I myself first heard of it; certainly there was no particular importance attributed to it in my student days or at the college where I was. On the other hand, Tischendorf admitted its claims in opposition to all the other Greek manuscripts in several passages, such as Mark ii. 22; xi. 6; Luke xxiv. 52, 53, etc. In other places he did so at first, but changed his opinion afterwards—*e.g.*, in Acts xi. 12, while in others again, like Acts xiii. 45, he was inclined to accept its testimony, asserting expressly: Ceterum D quantopere passim inter omnes testes excellat constat. One of the things for which Westcott and Hort deserve credit is the attention they have directed to Codex Bezae and its associates. Some of their remarks upon it will be found in the note below.[1]

[1] *Introd.*, ii. § 170, p. 120. On all accounts the Western text claims our attention first. The earliest readings which can be fixed chronologically belong to it. As far as we can judge from extant evidence, it was the most widely-spread text of Ante-Nicene times; and sooner or later every version directly or indirectly felt its influence. But any prepossessions in its favour that might be created by this imposing early ascendancy are for the most part soon dissipated by continuous study of its internal character. The eccentric Whiston's translation of the Gospels and Acts from the Codex Bezae, and of the Pauline Epistles from the Codex Claromontanus, and Bornemann's edition of the Acts, in which the Codex Bezae was taken as the standard authority, are probably the only attempts which have ever been made in modern times to set up an exclusively, or even predominantly, Western Greek text as the purest reproduction of what the Apostles wrote. This all but universal rejection is doubtless partly owing to the persistent influence of a whimsical theory of the last century, which, ignoring all non-Latin Western documentary evidence except the handful of extant bilingual uncials, maintained that the Western Greek text owed its peculiarities to translation from the Latin; partly to an imperfect apprehension of the antiquity and extension of the Western text as revealed by Patristic quotations and by versions. Yet even with the aid of a true perception of the facts of Ante-Nicene textual history, it would have been strange if this text,

That peerless scholar, P. de Lagarde, has even greater claims to honourable mention in this connection, though but Lagarde.

as a whole, had found much favour. A few scattered Western readings have long been approved by good textual critics on transcriptional and to a great extent insufficient grounds; and in Tischendorf's last edition their number has been augmented, owing to the misinterpreted accession of the Sinai MS. to the attesting documents. To one small and peculiar class of Western readings, exclusively omissions, we shall ourselves have to call attention as having exceptional claims to adoption.

§ 202 (p. 149). In spite of the prodigious amount of error which D contains, these readings, in which it sustains and is sustained by other documents derived from very ancient texts of other types, render it often invaluable for the secure recovery of the true text; and, apart from this direct applicability, no other single source of evidence, except the quotations of Origen, surpasses it in value on the equally important ground of historical or indirect instructiveness. To what extent its unique readings are due to licence on the part of the scribe rather than to faithful reproduction of an antecedent text now otherwise lost, it is impossible to say; but it is remarkable how frequently the discovery of fresh evidence, especially Old-Latin evidence, supplies a second authority for readings in which D had hitherto stood alone.

§ 240 (p. 175). On the other hand there remain, as has been before intimated (§ 170), a few other Western readings of similar form, which we cannot doubt to be genuine in spite of the exclusively Western character of their attestation. They are all omissions, or, to speak more correctly, non-interpolations of various length, that is to say, the original record has here, to the best of our belief, suffered interpolation in all the extant non-Western texts. . . . . With a single peculiar exception (Matt. xxvii. 49), in which the extraneous words are omitted by the Syrian as well as by the Western text, the Western non-interpolations are confined to the last three chapters of St. Luke.

§ 241. These exceptional instances of the preservation of the original text in exclusively Western readings are likely to have had an exceptional origin.

In the edition of 1896, the surviving editor (Westcott) appends an Additional Note which contains a further exceedingly valuable admission in the same direction. It is as follows:—

Note to p. 121, § 170 (p. 328): "The Essays of Dr. Chase on *The Syriac Element in Codex Bezae*, Cambridge, 1893, and *The Syro-Latin Text of the Gospels*, Cambridge, 1895, are a most important contribution to the solution of a fundamental problem in the history of the text of the N.T. The discovery of the Sinaitic MS. of the Old Syriac raises the question whether the combination of the oldest types of the Syriac and Latin texts can outweigh the combination of the primary Greek texts. A careful examination of the passages in which Syr^{sin} and k are arrayed against ℵ B, would point to the conclusion." [The proper title of Chase's Essays is The Old Syriac, under which shorter (outside) title Zahn also quotes them (*Einl.*, ii. 348).] This statement by Westcott sounds strange after the remark made in the Preface. "For the rest," he says there, "I may perhaps be allowed to say that no arguments have been advanced against the general principles maintained in the Introduction and illustrated in the Notes since the publication of the First Edition, which were not fully considered by Dr. Hort and little regard was paid to his representations during his lifetime. As early as 1857, he said of Codex Cantabrigiensis: facile patet, quum similibus libris careamus et ultra Evangelia et Actus nondum cogitem, totius editionis meae quasi fundamentum futurum esse hunc codicem Cantabrigiensem, sed eum eis librarii vitiis purgatum quae vitia esse agnita fuerint (*Gesam. Abh.*, p. 98). His chief merit, however, lies not in his having estimated Cantabrigiensis so highly, but in having assigned a lower value to the other manuscripts. By comparing D with the earlier versions, and particularly by relying on the testimony of Epiphanius, he recognised in it a representative of an "editio emendatorum orthodoxorum temeritate corrupta" (*ibid.*, p. 96). Compare also his *Uebersicht über die Bildung der Nomina*, p. 213, where he instances ἔταξαν ἀναβαίνειν of the "emendati" for παρήγγειλαν ἀναβαίνειν of D.[1]

Blass. General attention was first directed to the question of the Western text, when Blass came forward with his view that it was quite wrong to present the problem in the shape of an alternative between D and A B, because both groups were right, D and its associates representing a first edition of the Acts and a second of Luke, and the other group conversely. I hailed this solution of the difficulty at once as a veritable Columbus Egg, and to this day I am firmly persuaded that Blass's theory is nearer the mark than the previous estimate of the Western text. Readers may, perhaps, be struck by the fact, which Zahn has since made public (*Einl.*, ii. 348), that in his practical class at Erlangen, in the winter of 1885–6, he set as the subject of the prize essay an "Investigation of the materially important peculiarities of Codex D in the Acts," and made a note at the time of the result which he hoped to see the investigation arrive at—viz., "either the author's first

Zahn.

myself in the long course of our work, and in our judgment dealt with accurately. —Auckland Castle, March 27, 1896. B. F. D."

[1] See my *Philologica Sacra*, p. 3, where I have cited this passage of Lagarde. His book may not be very accessible to textual critics.

draft before publication or his hand copy with his own marginal notes inserted afterwards." Zahn himself got no further, but he was not surprised when Blass came forward with his clearly-defined and thoroughly-elaborated hypothesis. In one point, certainly, Zahn does not agree with Blass, and that is in the application of the hypothesis to Luke. He holds that the text which Blass restored as the Roman form or second edition of Luke is essentially nothing but a bold attempt to restore what is called the Western text; that the question to which such different answers have been made as to the value of this type of text—for it is not to be spoken of as a recension in the proper sense of that term—is by no means confined to the Third Gospel, but touches the others as well and the Pauline Epistles also; that the reason why the divergence of the Western text from that exhibited in the oldest manuscripts and the great majority of Greek witnesses is more conspicuous in Luke, is simply that we have the additional testimony of Marcion for that Gospel, but the question is essentially the same in all the cases; that whereas in Acts we have two parallel texts both possessing equal authority, in Luke the case is different, where in determining what the evangelist actually wrote, we have to choose one or the other of two mutually exclusive propositions; that this verdict on the text of Luke, however, in no way invalidates the conclusion come to as regards the text of the Acts. But further, Zahn, who even before this had avowed himself an "admirer of the Western text," stands up determinedly for the view that this same Western text, which I shall, like Zahn and Blass, indicate henceforward as β, contains much that is original. He says that just as we must beware of a superstitious idolatry of what are styled the best manuscripts,[1] which goes hand in hand with a disparagement of much older tradition (Marcion, Irenæus), so we have equally to be on our guard against a morbid preference for every interest-

[1] "Thou shalt worship no manuscripts" was one of the ten commandments that Lehrs gave philologists.

ing and fanciful excrescence of the riotous tradition of the second and third centuries. Such a preference would logically imply that the scholars who took in hand to revise the text about the beginning of the fourth century simply corrupted it, somewhat after the fashion of those who set themselves to "improve" our Church hymns in the age of Rationalism. More than twenty years ago, when I was a Tutor at Tübingen, I had the impression to which I frequently enough gave utterance in debate with my colleagues, that modern textual criticism is going altogether on the wrong tack. The textual study of the New Testament was out of my province at that time, and is really so still, were it not that, as Augustine says, it is necessary for everyone who devotes himself to the holy Scriptures to take up such studies. Nor am I inclined thus far to fall foul of the system to which Westcott and Hort devoted the labours of a lifetime, and in the building up of which they had at their command such an apparatus as is far beyond the reach of a German, especially of one who is not attached to any University. And as for the results of Zahn's researches, I prefer to look upon myself here as a mere learner and admirer. In the presence of such doughty warriors I feel like a spectator upon the battlefield of New Testament textual criticism, and I would beg that what follows, as well as what has been already said, be regarded as but suggestions, the acceptance or rejection of which by others may perchance serve to bring a younger generation nearer to the goal. In this spirit I have in my *Philologica Sacra* (1–15th March 1896) taken as a starting-point the reading in Luke xxii. 52, *λαου=ναου=ιερου*, which is not mentioned at all by Tischendorf, and have sought by means of one or two analogous cases to show "how frequently D preserves the correct reading." I have instanced *ἑπταπλασίονα*, Luke xviii. 30; *φάντασμα*, xxiv. 37; *δέρριν καμήλου*, Mark i. 6; *ἠνοιγμένους*, i. 10, which might, however, be inserted from Matt. iii. 16, Luke iii. 21; *ὀργισθείς*, Mark i. 40; *ὁμοιάζει*, Matt. xxvi. 73.

In the first sketch of this Introduction, written in the year 1895, I referred to the addition found in Matt. xxvii. 49, which is manifestly taken from John xix. 34, and is read by many authorities, among these being ℵ B C.[1] I said then: "Only two possibilities are conceivable. Either the passage stood here originally, and was removed at an early date on account of its variance with John xix. 34, or it is an interpolation. In the latter case, it must have been inserted at a very early date, and all the witnesses containing it, which elsewhere are so frequently and so widely divergent, must then go back to one and the same exemplar. Because the third possibility—viz. that the same sentence was inserted in different copies in the same place quite independently of each other, no one will consider to be at all likely. But if the second supposition is to be held as correct, then we see just what amount of importance is to be attached to the concurrence of our oldest witnesses, particularly our chief manuscripts ℵ B C L. They are not streams flowing independently from the same fountain of Paradise: they flowed together for a good part of their course, and were considerably polluted before they parted company."

Two years later, when the first edition was issued, I added: "This too must now be asserted with far greater emphasis, that the concurrence of B ℵ, on which so much stress has been laid hitherto by almost all textual critics, proves nothing at all. In Sirach the common archetype of B ℵ was younger than the origin of the Latin version, manifestly a good deal younger, because it already contained errors that had not yet made their appearance in our other manuscripts (or in their sources). Salmon (p. 52) is of opinion that the text which Salmon.
Westcott and Hort have restored is one 'that was most in favour in Alexandria in the third century, and that came

[1] This passage was the subject of a heated discussion between Severus and Macedonius at Constantinople in the year 510. On this occasion the superb copy of Matthew's Gospel, which had been discovered in the grave of Barnabas in the reign of the Emperor Zeno, was brought upon the scene.

there, perhaps, in the century previous. This is not far from Bousset's view that B perhaps contains the recension of Hesychius. Salmon calls the results of Westcott and Hort 'an elaborate locking of the stable door after the horse has been stolen.' Burgon's paradox, that the reason why B and ℵ have survived is that they were the worst, seemed to Salmon at first to be a joke, but he now thinks it not improbable that they were set aside on account of their divergence from the form of text that acquired ascendancy *at a later time.* If that be so, then they met the same fate that they themselves prepared for the primitive form they supplanted; and just as they, with the help of Tischendorf and Westcott and Hort, dislodged the *Textus Receptus* of the sixteenth and seventeenth centuries from the hands of theologians, and made themselves the *Textus Receptus* of the end of the nineteenth century, so perchance will Codex D, which the builders despised, become the foundation-stone of a new structure. In *Urtext*, p. 54, Oscar v. Gebhardt alludes to the objections raised partly against the entire method of Westcott and Hort, partly against their particular estimate of Codex Vaticanus, and partly also against the position they have assigned to what they call the Western text, and he too says: 'If these objections are valid, then the sure foundation which they seemed at last to have secured for the text of the New Testament begins once more to totter.'"

Since this was written, my impressions have been greatly confirmed, particularly by Zahn's *Einleitung*; only I must admit that I am now less in a position than ever to make any definite proposals as to the way in which the goal of the textual criticism of the New Testament is to be reached. To follow one witness or one group of witnesses through thick and thin, which would really be the only consistent course, will seemingly not do.[1] And the "eclectic method" to which

[1] Compare what Westcott and Hort say of Whiston and Bornemann, cited above, p. 222, and particularly the section on the twofold recension of the Acts in Zahn's *Einleitung*, ii. § 59, pp. 338–359. See also Burkitt's Introduction to

Bousset was led in his work on the Apocalypse as the only possible one, is surely the opposite of the genealogical, which we must acknowledge to be in theory the only correct method. But first of all, a fresh application of it would require to be made. And as the task is too great for any single worker, might it not be well if, in the exegetical classes of our Theological Faculties, the separate witnesses were either examined anew, or, conversely, selected passages of the text, quite small passages—a single chapter, or a single epistle like 2 or 3 John or Philemon—were given out to different students to examine thoroughly all the witnesses for each passage, and the results then compared with one another? Furthermore, the critical apparatus would require at once to be lightened of all those manuscripts which are unmistakeably recognised to be the representatives of a definite recension, and the Lucianic recension printed separately with or without an apparatus, just as was done by Lagarde himself for half of the Old Testament. Finally, the Western text would require to be much more thoroughly examined than has hitherto been the case. It is true that Weiss has given a special part of *Texte und Untersuchungen* to an examination of Codex D in Acts, but without prejudice one may be quite sure that a solution of the problem is not to be found in the way in which Weiss seeks it. No doubt he establishes among other things the fact, that in the Speeches of Peter β displays almost no variation, but then he makes no attempt to explain this fact or make any use of it. It is an indication of considerable progress to find Zahn going so carefully into matters of the text in an Introduction to the New Testament, and his appreciation of the Western text is most gratifying. At the same time the reader will naturally ask whether Zahn's verdict on the β text in Luke is not fatal to his own conclusions with

Luke and Acts in D.

Barnard's *Biblical Text of Clement of Alexandria* (*Texts and Studies*, v. 5), especially p. xviii: "Let us come out of the land of Egypt, which speaks, as Clement's quotations show, with such doubtful authority, and let us see whether the agreement of East and West, of Edessa and Carthage, will not give us a surer basis upon which to establish our text of the Gospels."

regard to Acts. Is it not true in this connection that "he who says A must also say B"? If you admit that there were two editions of Acts, you must make the same admission in the case of Luke. And conversely, if there was no second edition of the Gospel, must you not then look for some other explanation of the variations in Acts? For it seems quite certain that the variants in Luke xxiv. are most closely related to the text of Acts i. Or how else are the readings in Luke xxiv. 51–53 to be explained? Westcott and Hort have one way of explaining them. They say that *καὶ ἀνεφέρετο εἰς τὸν οὐρανόν* "was evidently inserted from an assumption that a separation from the disciples at the close of a Gospel must be the Ascension. The Ascension apparently did not lie within the proper scope of the Gospels, as seen in their genuine texts; its true place was at the head of the Acts of the Apostles as the preparation for the Day of Pentecost, and thus the beginning of the history of the Church." That is all very well, and it may also be the case that *προσκυνήσαντες αὐτόν* in v. 52 is the natural result of the insertion of *καὶ ἀνεφέρετο εἰς τὸν οὐρανόν*. But how then are we to account for the interchange of *εὐλογοῦντες* and *αἰνοῦντες* in the next verse, which is found in precisely the same groups of witnesses?[1]

If this explanation then is insufficient on account of verse 53, it may be confidently asserted that the omission of the Ascension and the Worship of the Exalted Lord by any later scribe is all but inconceivable from the moment that Luke was separated from Acts and placed among the Gospels. If such a

[1] Attention may be directed in passing to the interesting way in which the witnesses are distributed. Thus we have in verse 51, for the omission of *καὶ ἀνεφερ. εἰς τ. οὐρ.* ℵ* D Syr^{sin} a b d e ff l*, Aug. 1/2; verse 52, omit *προσκυν. αὐτόν*, D Syr^{sin} a b d e ff l, Aug. 1/1; verse 53, *αἰνοῦντες* for *εὐλογοῦντες* D a b d e ff l r (Aug.); (Syr^{sin} here has מברכין, not משבחין which represents *αἰνοῦντες* in Luke ii. 13, 20, xix. 37, and, therefore, must have read *εὐλογοῦντες* in this passage). Now I ask, is it right to accept the testimony of D and its associates in verse 52, only to reject it in verse 53? And what amount of weight is added to the testimony of D by the addition of that of ℵ*? Schiller says in *Tell*: "The strong is mightiest alone: united e'en the weak are strong"—how far are both these notions true in textual criticism?

thing were possible at all, it would be in the case of προσκυνήσαντες αὐτόν, as there is no express mention in Acts i. of the disciples worshipping. On the other hand, the omission becomes quite conceivable as soon as the author added a δεύτερος λόγος to the πρῶτος. So far these variants appear to me to fit in very well with Blass's theory and with no other. Zahn, as far as I can see, has nowhere expressed any opinion regarding them, certainly he says nothing of the variation between αἰνοῦντες and εὐλογοῦντες, which is the one of most importance critically, though it is of least consequence materially.

Graefe, following on the lines of Birt and Rüegg, supposes that the shorter form was due to want of space, that Luke was glad to get the shorter form all into his roll at the foot the first time he wrote it out, and sent off the book to Theophilus in that form, hoping to deal with the Ascension in the second of his books. In the second edition he had sufficient space to admit of the insertion of καὶ ἀνεφέρετο εἰς τὸν οὐρανόν, then of προσκυνήσαντες αὐτόν, and finally of εὐλογοῦντες.[1] These additions he made, feeling, rightly enough, that there could be no more fitting conclusion to his Life of Jesus than a brief allusion to the Ascension, which he had already described more particularly in the Acts. At the same time he substituted ἕως εἰς for ἔξω πρὸς. Graefe thinks that all these changes are connected with the alterations made also in the introduction to the Acts, though he omits to say what the connection is.

Weiss, father and son, omit the words καὶ ἀνεφέρετο εἰς τὸν οὐρανόν as "a gloss derived from Acts i.," and "likewise" the words προσκυνήσαντες αὐτόν in verse 52 (is this also a gloss from Acts i.?). Which text they hold to be correct in verse 53 they do not say.[2]

[1] So Graefe, but it is not apparent whether the καὶ that belongs to this reading is to be supplied before it or after. Evidently he intends to read αἰν. καὶ εὐλογ. with the great majority of witnesses, and not εὐλογ. καὶ αἰν. with the Ethiopic version. See *Th. St. Kr.*, 1898, i. 136 f. The passage is regarded by Westcott and Hort as a good example of "conflation," § 146.

[2] See now *Textkritik der vier Evangelien*, pp. 48, 181.

Αἰνεῖν[1] is the specifically Lucan word for "to praise," while εὐλογεῖν in this sense does not occur in Acts at all, and only in the first two chapters of Luke. Further, as any concordance will show, αἰνεῖν is the regular equivalent of הלל and εὐλογεῖν of ברך, while αἰνεῖν is rarely used for ברך or εὐλογεῖν for הלל. This confirms the supposition that αἰνοῦντες, which is preferred by Tischendorf but rejected by Westcott and Hort, is the original reading.

In order to show the full extent of the difficulty of the problem, we shall take along with this passage from the end of the Gospel a single instance from the Acts. How does the Apostolic Decree read in ch. xv.? "To judge any matter before knowing the facts of the case is inadmissible." So Hilgenfeld says in his magazine, adding that the matter of the Apostolic Council, as it is called, and the Decree have been so judged. He himself restores the whole text in this passage to the form that Blass has adopted as the *Forma Romana*—*i.e.*, to confine ourselves to this point of main importance, he omits "things strangled."[2] On the other hand, Harnack, in the article to which reference will be made below, comes to the conclusion that the Eastern, *i.e.* the common, text is the original, and the Western a later correction made subsequent to the *Didache*, and not earlier than the first decade of the second century.[3] The same conclusion is reached by Zahn in his extremely careful discussion of the question (*Einl.*, ii. 344 ff.): "The two texts are here mutually exclusive, and therefore cannot both be derived from the same author (xv. 20, 29, xxi. 25)." But he immediately adds: "The fact

[1] Αἰνεῖν is not given in Cremer's *Dictionary* among the synonyms of εὐλογεῖν, and is only cited on p. 610 with the reading αἰνοῦντες καὶ εὐλογοῦντες from this passage.

[2] See Hilgenfeld, *Das Apostel-Concil nach seinem ursprünglichen Wortlaute* in the *ZfwTh.*, 42 (1899), 1, 138–149.

[3] Harnack, *Das Aposteldecret* (Acta xv. 29) *und die Blass'sche Hypothese*, Berlin, 1899. From the *Sitzungsberichte der preuss. Akad. der Wiss.* Noticed in the *Expository Times* for June 1899, p. 395 f. See also the *Berliner philologische Wochenschrift* of the 13th May 1899.

that Blass, in this important point, as in many another of less consequence, declares a certain thing to be an original element of the text which turns out to be simply an early corruption in no wise detracts from the correctness of his hypothesis." That is quite true and must be borne in mind in connection with the objection raised by Wendt, that "manifest clerical errors are found in the actual β text." The passages are also used by Corssen as an argument against Blass. The remarks of the latter in reply to the strictures of Corssen (*Evang. sec. Lucam*, p. xxvi) seem to me to be not without reason, but in any case it is strange that alterations should have been made in an official document like the Decree in Acts xv., no matter whether these were due to the writer himself or a later intermediary. That there was some method in the alteration is shown by its recurrence in three places. But again I must emphasise the superiority of Codex D. Whereas in ch. xv. 20, 29 the shorter text is represented by other witnesses as well, in ch. xxi. 25 it is supported by D with the sole addition of Gigas Holmiensis.[1] I have not to decide the question here; I simply commend it to a searching investigation, in which attention must be paid to the apparently meaningless differences in the use of particles and synonyms, of simple and compound words, and such-like seeming minutiæ. I can only repeat how frequently the thought occurred to me when I was comparing Scrivener's edition with that of v. Gebhardt for my *Supplement*, that here was no alteration of a later scribe, and what then? The simplest explanation was that both readings were due to the author himself, who on the one occasion purposely set down the one reading and on the other the other.

There is another question in connection with the Western text which has been even more neglected than the former—viz. the amount of importance to be attached to it in the case of the Pauline Epistles. What about Eusebius's reference to Tatian's work on these Epistles? I frankly confess that not

[1] See critical note in the *Expositor's Greek Testament* (Knowling), *in loco.*

till the printing of this work was begun did I become aware, mainly from Zahn's *Einleitung*, how many problems are here waiting to be solved, and for this reason as well as others I must for the present forbear making any attempt in this direction.

Here I can only indicate a few of the most general rules of textual criticism, and thereafter adduce a number of New Testament passages which are of interest from a critical point of view.

Rules of criticism.

(*k*) **General Rules of Textual Criticism.**—In its essence the task of the textual critic resembles that of the physician, who must first of all make a correct diagnosis of the disease before attempting its cure. Manifestly the first thing to do is to observe the injuries and the dangers to which a text transmitted by handwriting is liable to be exposed. A correct treatment must be preceded by a correct diagnosis.

The injuries which a text receives will vary according as it is multiplied by **Dictation** or by **Copying.** The fifty Bibles which Eusebius prepared at once for Constantine would be written to dictation. In the early times of the Church, copying, as has been already mentioned, would doubtless be the more usual method of multiplication. Here, however, we must make a single exception in the case of Paul, who for the most part did not write his Epistles with his own hand. He evidently dictated them. He certainly did not have them simply written out from his own rough draft.

Illegibility.

(1) In the case of copying, errors originate first of all, though not most frequently, in a word or group of letters being **illegible,** or in their being read for some psychological reason otherwise than as they were intended. However attentive the copyist may be, he may still be in doubt as to the way in which a word or passage should be read, and may decide wrongly. Proper names, *e.g.*, are often very doubtful.[1] More frequently however the mistake will be due to inattention. The context may lead the copyist to expect a certain word; he sees one like it, and inserts the former in its place.

[1] *Cf.* the passage of Hermas cited above, p. 47.

Homoioteleuton.

(2) It frequently happens, particularly in copying the old *scriptio continua*, that the eye of the scribe jumps from one word or group of letters to another the same or similar to it, either before or after it. In the former case the intervening words will be repeated, in the latter they will be omitted. Scholars designate these errors as **dittography** and **elision** respectively; printers know them under the name of a marriage and a funeral. The former mistake is not so serious, because it is at once detected on reading over the copy. A peep into any manuscript will show how frequently this error occurs, the repeated words being enclosed in brackets or surmounted with dots.[1] In Codex B such passages give us an opportunity of observing the beauty of the original writing, because the painstaking man who retraced the old writing with fresh ink in the eighth, or tenth, or eleventh century, or whenever it was, adding at the same time accents and punctuation marks, left these untouched. This kind of mistake very often happens in passages where a group of characters catches the eye for any reason, such as the occurrence of the abbreviation mark, $\overline{\Theta\Sigma}$, $\overline{\mathrm{I}\Lambda\mathrm{HM}}$, $\overline{\mathrm{AN}\mathrm{O}\Sigma}$, etc., and at the transition to a new page or leaf. The omission of a piece of the text of various length by homoioteleuton is as common, and is more serious.[2] Any critical apparatus will show the frequency of its occurrence. We often find there the note "a voce alterutra . . . . ad

[1] A good example is seen in Ezek. xvi. 3. In the Sixtine edition of 1586 a new page (692) occurs in the middle of the sentence *διαμαρτυρον τη Ιερουσαλημ τας ανομιας αυτης ταδε λεγει κυριος τη Ιερουσαλημ*, with the result that the eight words from the first *Ιερουσαλημ* to the second are printed twice by a recessive homoioteleuton, while in Codex 62 they have dropped out altogether owing to a forward error of the same sort. The former mistake is tacitly corrected in all reprints, but the latter could not be detected from the context alone without other testimony. Compare also Mark ix. 10 in codex T of the Vulgate and ff of the Old Latin. In the former the passage from *resurrexit* to *resurrexit* is repeated, in the latter it is omitted.

[2] I had a teacher once who invariably tried to get over any difficulty in the Greek classics by saying that the text was corrupted by homoioteleuton. We did not always agree with him; he was perhaps a little too ready with this way out of a difficulty, but any one with experience knows how very apt this mistake is to occur.

alterutram desunt" or "a voce 1° ad vocem 2° (3°) transilit," or "vox . . . . alterutra et intermedia desunt." Compare, *e.g.*, Codex D, Matt. xviii. 18 from γῆς to γῆς; x. 23; xxiii. 14–16. The result is worst when the mistake is not discovered till afterwards and the two fragments are patched together in some way with more or less success. Lacunæ that have not been doctored are very helpful in determining the relationship between different texts.[1]

Confusion. (3) As errors of the tongue and the memory[2] rather than of the eye may be reckoned the **Transposition** and **Confusion** of particular combinations of letters or entire words. The former occurs so frequently in connection with a liquid, that in some cases it ceases to be a mistake. Thus we have on the one hand the confusion of κορκοδειλος with κροκοδειλος, Καρχηδων with Carthago, and on the other, εβαλον with ελαβον, βηθαραβα with βηθαβαρα, John i. 28; κιρνατω with κρινετω, πουτον with τοπον, ככרין, *talent*, Matt. xxv. 14–30, with כרכין, *cities*, Luke xix. 17, 19. Akin to this is the confusion of vowels with a similar sound, to which are to be ascribed all cases of **itacism**, as it is called—ἔγειρε and ἔγειραι, —εσθε and —εσθαι, ἑταίροις and ἑτέροις, χρηστὸς ὁ κύριος and χριστὸς ὁ κύριος, 2 Cor. xii. 1; φορέσωμεν and φορέσομεν, ἔχωμεν and ἔχομεν, Rom. v. 1; μετὰ διωγμῶν and μετὰ διωγμόν. Manifestly mistakes of this sort would occur more readily in dictation than in copying.

A third class of errors of a more conscious or semi-conscious description is due to the **substitution** of words or forms of similar meaning. Thus, for λέγει we may have εἶπε or ἔφη or ἀπεκρίνατο, or the simple form may be replaced by the compound or *vice versa*, or one preposition may be substituted for

[1] This applies to printed editions as well as to manuscripts. Van Ess's reprint of the Sixtine Septuagint (1824) is very carefully done, yet five words have dropped out in Joel iii. 9. These are omitted in all the later editions of 1835, 1855 (novis curis correcta), 1868, and 1879, and were only supplied by myself in 1887 on the occasion of the third centenary of the Sixtine edition. They are omitted in Tischendorf's first edition of 1850, and also in the second of 1856.

[2] In ancient times people always read aloud, even when reading by themselves.

another.[1] Separate words are very frequently transposed without seriously affecting the sense. Thus, in Acts iv. 12, we find nearly all the possible permutations of the three words *ονομα εστιν ετερον* actually represented—viz., in addition to this (2) *ονομα ετερον εστιν*; (3) *ετερον ονομα εστιν*; (4) *εστιν ετερον ονομα*; (5) *εστιν ονομα ετερον*.[2] On Luke xvii. 10, Merx says (*Die vier kanonischen Evangelien*, p. 246): "Let it be observed that the position of ἀχρεῖοι fluctuates between (1) δοῦλοι ἀχρεῖοί ἐσμεν; (2) δοῦλοί ἐσμεν ἀχρεῖοι D, and (3) ἀχρεῖοι δοῦλοί ἐσμεν. Such fluctuations are due to the different arrangement of a word that did not originally belong to the text, but was appended as a note and after-

[1] Scrivener would explain the "remarkable confusion" of the two prepositions *προ* and *προσ*, when compounded with verbs, which we meet *e.g.* in Matt. xxvi. 39; Mark xiv. 35; Acts xii. 6; xvii. 5, 26; xx. 5, 13; xxii. 25, by saying that the symbol $\overset{\text{P}}{\Pi}$ is used indifferently for *προ* and *προσ* in the Herculanean rolls, and here and there in Codex Sinaiticus. Seeing that it has become a bad habit in Hebrew Grammars to speak of Aleph *prostheticum* instead of *protheticum*, and that the practice is still defended (Gesenius-Kautzsch[26], p. 64, n. 3, "rightly so") after my notice of it (*Marginalien*, p. 67), I have given some little attention to this confusion, and could cite dozens of examples. Others, of course, have noticed it as well as myself. In his *N.T.*, i. 20, B. Weiss says: "The compounds with *προ* and *προσ* are interchanged quite heedlessly," and he cites in proof of this eight passages from the Acts. He writes similarly in ii. 34. I shall instance only one or two cases in connection with this same word πρόθεσις. Pitra on *Apost. Const.*, 5, 17 (p. 325): πρόθεσιν restituimus cum Vatican. 2, 3, 4, 5, vulgo πρόσθεσιν; Excerpta Περὶ Παθῶν, ed. R. Schneider (*Programme of Duisburg*, 1895), where the manuscripts deviate in five passages, pp. 5, 14. 20; 6, 5; 13, 7. 13, and we read in § 10, ἀντίκειται δὲ πρόσθεσις μὲν ἀφαιρέσει, etc., and in § 11, πρόσθεσις μὲν οὖν ἐστὶ προσθήκη στοιχείου κατ' ἀρχήν, οἷον σταφίς, ἀσταφὶς καὶ ὀσταφίς. Both times, of course, it should be πρόθεσις, as the better manuscripts have it. Wherever mention is made of the "shewbread," D invariably turns it into "extra bread," by reading προσθέσεως instead of προθέσεως. Tischendorf first called attention to this in Luke vi. 4, but it occurs also in Matt. xii. 4. I have no doubt myself that in the case of verbal forms, the σ was inserted in order to avoid the hiatus before the augment. Compare προσέθηκεν for προέθηκεν, Ex. xxiv. 23; προσέθηκας, Ps. lxxxix. 8, Symmachus; προανεθέμην or προσανεθέμην, Gal. i. 16. In Wisdom, vii. 27, the first hand of Sinaiticus even writes προσφήτας for prophets. It is disputed whether the title of one of Philo's books is προπαιδεύματα or πρὸς [τὰ] παιδεύματα. Etc. etc. *Sapienti sat.*

[2] We find all the possible permutations of the words αὐτοῖς ἐλάλησεν ὁ Ἰησοῦς in John viii. 12. See my note on Codex Purpureus Petropolitanus (N) in Hilgenfeld's *Zeitschrift für wissenschaftliche Theologie*, 42 (1899), p. 623.

wards incorporated with the text. Such fluctuations point to the interpolation of the fluctuating word." This judgment has to be accepted with caution. For one thing, it is not at all clear which word it is that fluctuates. In this particular case, one might say that δοῦλοι fluctuates as much as ἀχρεῖοι, and the copula still more. Moreover such an interpolation becomes at once an integral part of the text, and its insertion is no longer visible. Only if several copies were made of that exemplar in which the interpolation was first introduced could fluctuation of this sort originate. Such transpositions are much more frequently of a harmless order, as each one may perceive for himself. The writer's thoughts fly faster than his pen and anticipate a word that should not come in till later. One of the most frequent cases of transposition is that of Ἰησοῦς Χριστός and Χριστὸς Ἰησοῦς in the Pauline Epistles.

Additions.

(4) Akin to this last is a class of mistakes originating in the border region between the unconscious and the conscious or intentional—viz. that of **Additions.** One can readily understand how easy it was to insert a κύριος or ὁ κύριος ἡμῶν, a μου after πατήρ on the lips of Jesus, the subject at the beginning of a sentence, especially of the first sentence of a pericope, or the object in the form of a pronoun. Bengel proposed to omit the name of Jesus in some twenty-five places, for which he was ridiculed by Wettstein, as may be learned from my work on Bengel, p. 74. Now, everyone admits that Bengel was right. Under the head of "Interpolationes breviores," Wordsworth and White first give examples "de nomine Jesus," then of "Christus, Dominus, Deus," and then of "Pronomina." It is evident that in this way the wrong word may be supplied now and again. Perhaps one of the most interesting cases is Luke i. 46. All our present Greek witnesses make Mary the composer of the Magnificat, but Elisabeth's name is attached to it in three Old Latin manuscripts, in the Latin version of Irenæus, according to the best manuscripts, and in some manuscripts

known to Origen (or to his translator, Jerome: the passage, unfortunately, is found as yet only in the Latin).[1]

(5) To the category of conscious alterations belong first of all **grammatical corrections**, then **assimilations** to parallel passages, **liturgical changes** introduced from the Evangeliaria, as, *e.g.*, the addition at the close of a pericope of the words ὁ ἔχων ὦτα ἀκουέτω which occurs in all sorts of manuscripts in the most diverse passages, or indications of time, such as ἐν τῷ καιρῷ ἐκείνῳ at the beginning of a pericope,[2] and lastly, alterations made for **dogmatic** reasons, if any such can be established. It is impossible to deny that dogmatic conceptions had some influence on the propagation of certain readings if not on their origin—as, *e.g.*, on the form assumed by the words in Matt. xix. 17, τί με λέγεις ἀγαθόν, or on the omission of the words οὐδὲ ὁ υἱός in Mark xiii. 22; compare also above, p. 106. On the whole, however, there is no real ground for the scepticism that was for a time entertained with respect to our texts in this connection. A sober criticism will be able in most cases to restore the correct form. Its conditions will be apparent from what has been said in the foregoing.

Corrections.

Gerhard von Maestricht laid down forty-three Critical Canons, and Wettstein set forth in his New Testament his *Animadversiones et Cautiones ad examen variarum lectionum Novi Testamenti necessariae* (vol. ii. 851–874). In 1755 J. D. Michaelis added to his *Curae in versionem Syriacam Act. Apost.* his *Consectaria critica de . . . . usu versionis Syriacae tabularum Novi Foederis.*[3] Bengel reduced all the rules to a single one. Quite recently Wordsworth and White compre-

Canons of Criticism.

[1] See Harnack, *Das Magnificat der Elisabeth* (Lukas i. 46–55) in the *Berliner Sitzungsberichte* of the 17th May 1900, p. 538 ff. A good example of how glosses may creep into the text is afforded by Philo "Quod det." 11 (Cohn, 1, 266).

[2] On the influence of a system of pericopæ on the text of Codex D, see Scrivener's Introduction to his edition of the manuscript, p. li, and Zahn, *Einl.*, ii. 355.

[3] See Semler's edition of *J. J. Wetsteinii libelli ad crisin atque interpretationem N.T.*, Halae, 1766.

hended the rules they followed in the preparation of the text of their Latin New Testament in four sentences. Of these the first two apply to a version only, and therefore do not concern us here;[1] while the fourth (*brevior lectio probabilior*) is but another form of Bengel's canon. The third alone may be regarded as new and deserving of attention—viz., *vera lectio ad finem victoriam reportat.* That is to say, if a phrase is repeated in several passages in the same or similar terms, and displays variants in the earlier passages, the reading of the later passage will, as a rule, be the correct one, the reason being that copyists are apt to consider a certain reading to be an error the first time it occurs, and therefore to alter it, but come in the end to admit it as correct.

I would once more briefly emphasize the following propositions:—

(1) The text of our manuscripts must not be regarded as homogeneous, but must be examined separately for each part of the New Testament. A manuscript that exhibits a very good text in one book does not necessarily do the same in the others. The same thing holds good of versions and quotations.

(2) The text is preserved with less alteration in the versions than in the manuscripts.[2]

(3) In the Gospels that reading is the more probable which differs from that of the parallel passages.

(4) The influence of the ecclesiastical use of the Scriptures on the text must be more carefully attended to than heretofore.[2]

[1] (1) Lectio quae in veteribus latinis non apparet probabilior est. (2) Codices qui cum graecis ℵ B L concordant plerumque textum Hieronymianum ostendunt.

[2] In view of the frequency with which the witnesses fluctuate between ἡμῶν and ὑμῶν, ἡμῖν and ὑμῖν, etc., it is impossible to adjust their claims on any mere arithmetical principle. Zahn (*Einl.*, ii. 61) calls attention to an important consideration in support of the reading ὑμῖν in 2 Peter i. 4, which applies to other passages as well—viz., "that when the New Testament epistles were read at divine service, ἡμεῖς would very readily and very frequently be substituted for ὑμεῖς, which

(5) One of the most valuable aids in estimating the importance of the witnesses is the proper names, particularly those of less frequent occurrence.

(6) "Proclivi scriptioni praestat ardua."

Of these propositions only the last two need be illustrated further, particularly the second last. For it is really remarkable to what extent this consideration has been neglected hitherto. To the best of my knowledge there is as yet no monograph in which the **proper names** are treated from a critical point of view. And yet these are for the critic frequently the only points of light in vast regions of darkness. They are to him what the lighthouse is to the mariner or the fossil to the geologist. This makes their neglect all the more strange. Had there been a systematic examination of the proper names of the New Testament, Lippelt's important discovery with regard to the spellings Ἰωάνης and Ἰωάννης might have been made long ere now (see above, p. 162 f.). Weiss's critical studies in Acts deserve honourable mention in this connection. But Westcott and Hort, who have paid attention to these things with their usual exactitude, were

Proper names.

excluded the reader or preacher." Compare Acts iv. 12: ἐν ᾧ δεῖ σωθῆναι—, ἡμᾶς or ὑμᾶς?

It might be laid down as a second rule in this connection, that particular importance attaches to those versions in which the distinction of the persons does not depend simply on a single letter but on a separate word (*nobis* : *vobis*, etc.). In versions of this sort the original reading is preserved from the first; in the case of the others, the change could be made at any point of the transmission, especially when it was helped by the nature of the writing, which must also, of course, be taken into account.

A glance over the verse enumeration in the margin of one of the modern editions of the text will reveal, perhaps, most clearly how strong is the tendency to interpolation. Of the verses into which Stephen divided the Greek N.T. (1551), the Stuttgart edition omits entirely the following from the Synoptic Gospels—viz., Matt. xviii. 11 (xxi. 44, Tischen.), xxiii. 14; Mark vii. 16; ix. 44, 46; xi. 26; xv. 28; Luke xvii. 36 (xxi. 18, W–H margin); xxiii. 17 (xxiv. 12, 40, Tisch.). Compare also Matt. xx. 28; xxvii. 35, 38, 49; Mark vi. 11; xiii. 2; Luke vi. 5; ix. 55; xii. 21; xix. 45; xxi. 38; xxii. 19 f., 43 f., 47; xxiii. 2, 5, 34, 48, 53; xxiv. 5, 36, 51, 52. In the case of several verses this or that part had to be omitted. Luke xx. 30, *e.g.*, is reduced to the three words, καὶ ὁ δεύτερος, with the result that it becomes the shortest verse in the N.T.

simply on the wrong tack in this case when they asked whether the various persons who bore this name might not have spelt it differently, as in the case of Smith, Smyth, Smythe, etc. Similarly the genealogies give rise to a whole host of problems of which no account has been taken hitherto. See above, p. 165, for the reading *Ζαρέ* exhibited by B in Matt. i. 3; and compare Sela, given by Syr[sin] in verses 4 and 5, with Σαλά in Luke iii. 32. Tischendorf omits the testimony in Matt. i. 5, while Baljon passes over both the variants, though they are certainly of more importance than the variation in the spelling of Βοές, Βοός, Βοόζ. In Luke iii. 27 the word רֵאשָׁא is converted into a proper name Ῥησά. From this fact some very interesting conclusions might be drawn with regard to the sources of Luke's Gospel, but this is a matter lying outside the scope of this chapter. On the other hand, the fact that in the fourth Gospel the traitor is called not Ἰσκαριώτης, or anything like it, but ἀπὸ Καρυώτου by ℵ in ch. vi. 71, where his name first occurs, and by D in every other place in that Gospel (xii. 4; xiii. 2, 26; xiv. 22), raises a very strong presumption in favour of these two manuscripts and indeed of the fourth Gospel. On this see my *Philologica Sacra*, p. 14, and my notes, with Chase's unconvincing replies, in the *Expository Times* for December 1897, and January, February, and March 1898. I am very glad to see that Zahn now inclines to the same view (*Einl.*, ii. 561). Considerable weight is given to it by the fact that these two manuscripts seem to be the only ones that have preserved the correct reading in the case of other names as well.

What is Apollos called in Acts? He is mentioned by D only in ch. xviii. 24, where he is called Ἀπολλώνιος. ℵ* calls him Ἀπελλῆς in xviii. 24 and xix. 1. This reading is supported in the former passage by the minuscules 15 and 180, and in the latter by 180 alone. Wendt now agrees with Blass in thinking it probable that the original form in Acts was Ἀπελλῆς, which was altered in the main body of manuscripts in conformity with 1 Corinthians, just as ἀπὸ Καρυώτου in John was accommodated to Ἰσκαριώτης given by the Synoptics. But what about D? I must ask with Salmon. Even Weiss says in this connection (*Codex D*, p. 18): "The most that can be said for Ἀπολλώνιος is that this form, differing as it does from that prevailing in the Pauline Epistles, has the presumption of originality, seeing that there was always a temptation for the scribes to accommodate it to the latter."[1] In his earlier work on the text (p. 9) he seems not to have considered this point.

I cannot understand how Weiss could at first explain Ἰωνάθας, which is found in D (Acts iv. 6) in place of Ἰωάν(ν)ης read by the other witnesses, as a "clerical error," whereas now (*Cod. D*, p. 108) he deems it more natural to suppose that a corrector inserted the name of the son of Annas and the successor of Caiaphas mentioned by Josephus (*Antiq.* xviii. 4, 3) in place of that of the entirely unknown John, than that the name of Jonathan, even supposing it was unknown to the copyist, which applies equally to that of Alexander mentioned along with him, was replaced by John, which was a very common name, the name of the Apostle so frequently mentioned before. It could, therefore, be only a purely accidental clerical error. Headlam, in his article on John (Hastings' *Dictionary of the Bible*, ii. 676) seems to know nothing of all this. But perhaps Weiss sees on the same page of the aforesaid book that the mistake of Johanan and Jonathan occurred elsewhere also, and remembering Bengel's principle, considers that Ἰωνάθας is the *scriptio ardua*, and, therefore, the *praestantior*.[2]

In 2 Peter ii. 15 the father of Balaam is called Βοσόρ, which is quite peculiar. Westcott and Hort and Weiss, in their fondness for B, write Βεώρ. But this is most certainly

[1] The best discussion of the form Ἀπελλῆς will again be found in Zahn, *Einl.*, i. 193.

[2] See my note in the *Expository Times* for July 1900, p. 478, where I have brought forward a new witness for the reading Jonatha—viz., Jerome's *Liber interpretationis Hebraicorum nominum*. He explains the word as "*columba dans* vel *columba veniens*."

a correction which is combined with the original to form *βεωρσόρ* in א. The only thorough discussion of the passage that I know is in Zahn's *Einleitung*, ii. 109. The only thing that might be added to his data in the LXX. is that, according to Holmes-Parsons, the Georgian version has *υἱὸν τοῦ βοσόρ* in Jos. xiii. 22. *Σεπφώρ*, as the name of Beor, has crept into various manuscripts in several places from Jos. xxiv. 9—*e.g.* into the Armenian in Gen. xxxvi. 32, Codex 18 in Num. xxii. 5, Codex 53 in Num. xxiv. 15, where Cod. 75 has *Σεβεώρ*, and into Lucian in 1 Chr. i. 43. There seems to me to be a confusion between Gen. xxxvi. 32 (=1 Chr. i. 43) and the following verse, in which Bosra occurs. In Gen. xxxvi. 33 one manuscript observes, *ἡ βοσὸρ πόλις τῆς 'Αραβίας ἡ νῦν καλουμένη βόσρα.* Jerome also renders "ex Bosor."[1] Βοσόρ also occurs as the name of a place in Deut. iv. 43; 1 Sam. xxx. 9; 1 Macc. v. 26. On this last passage see *ZdPV.*, 12, 51; 13, 41. For other interpretations (Hebrew pronunciation of the Aramaic פתורה)[2] see Pole's *Synopsis* on 2 Peter ii. 15.

It is worth observing that minuscule 81 displays a close agreement with B in other places as well as this.

On the names in the catalogue of the Apostles, see Zahn, *Einl.*, ii. 263; on 'Ιερουσαλήμ and 'Ιεροσόλυμα, ii. 310; on Jesus Barabbas, ii. 294; on Barachias in Matt. xxiii. 35, i. 454, ii. 308. On the confusion between Isaiah and Asaph in Matt. xiii. 35, and between Jeremiah, Zechariah, and Isaiah in other passages, compare Ambrosiaster's note on 1 Cor. ii. 9 cited above, p. 148.

"He who seeks in the wild fir wood, will still find many a cudgel good."

[1] Volck has an article of four and a half pages on Balaam in the PRE[3], iii. 227 ff., but he says not a syllable about the form *βοσόρ*, which is too bad. In Hastings' *Dictionary of the Bible* it is at least mentioned though not explained.

[2] בער is explained as the Hebrew form of the Aramaic בעור by C. B. Michaelis (*De Paronomasia*, § 30); Hiller, *Onomasticum*, 1706, p. 536; and Bernardus (in Marck, *In praecipuas quasdam partes Pentateuchi Commentarius*, Leyden, 1713, 366). Marck himself makes it the equivalent of פתור. M. M. Kalish, *Bible Studies*, i. *The prophecies of Bileam*, London, 1877, contributes nothing to the solution of the question.

The rule that the **shorter text** is the more original is a subdivision of Bengel's canon. It is specially the case when two longer forms are opposed to it which are mutually exclusive and whose origin can be explained from the shorter. As examples of this Zahn adduces, in addition to the double conclusion of Mark's Gospel, the following:— Textus brevior.

John vi. 47: πιστεύων, ℵ B L T, + "in God," Syr^{cu. sin}, + εἰς ἐμέ A C D Γ Δ Λ Π. . . . .

John vii. 39: πνεῦμα, ℵ K T Π, + ἅγιον L X Γ Δ Λ, + δεδομένον it vg^{cle}, + ἅγιον ἐπ' αὐτοῖς, D f goth, + ἅγιον δεδομένον, B 254 Syr^{sin. hark}. . . .

James v. 7: πρόϊμον, B 31, pr. ὑετὸν A K L P, pr. καρπὸν ℵ 9 ff etc.

It is equally clear that a reading is incorrect which proves to be a mixture of two others (**conflate readings**). The respective claims of these others must be adjudged on other considerations. Thus we have—

Luke xxiv. 53:	αἰνοῦντες, D a b e.
	εὐλογοῦντες, ℵ B C* L.
	αἰνοῦντες καὶ εὐλογοῦντες, A C² X Γ Δ Λ Π.
	εὐλογοῦντες καὶ αἰνοῦντες, Ethiop.
Acts vi. 8:	πλήρης χάριτος, ℵ A B D.
	πλήρης πίστεως, H P.
	πλήρης χάριτος καὶ πίστεως, E.

In general that reading will have the best claim to originality which stands first in the combination. Further illustrations are unnecessary.

In order to fulfil the promise of the title of this chapter, the foregoing exposition of the Theory of New Testament criticism should be succeeded by a further part dealing with its Praxis. Such a part would contain particular illustrations of the way in which the criticism of the text has been handled by our authorities hitherto and the way in which it must be treated in accordance with the foregoing principles. The following notes do not and cannot claim to be a complete fulfilment of this great task, more especially as in the preceding part we were unable to arrive at a finished system of textual criticism. I have therefore contented myself with bringing together a series of passages of interest from a critical point of view. In doing so I have freely drawn upon Zahn's Introduction. For this I feel sure the reader will thank me, while at the same time I trust that the author will pardon the liberty I have taken. I have made use, as far as possible, of the additional material afforded by editions later than those of Tischendorf and Westcott and Hort, particularly of the Sinai-Syriac. This collection may therefore serve in some degree to supplement our commentaries, which, though their merits in other directions are to be freely conceded, still leave much to be desired in the matter of textual criticism. A purely critical commentary on the New Testament is a great desideratum. The following notes are to be regarded not as the commencement of such a work, but simply as a stimulus thereto. I myself felt it to be a defect in the small Stuttgart edition of the New Testament that want of space obliged me to omit all references to the origin and significance of the various readings selected from manuscripts. For many of these an Annotatio Critica in an Appendix like that in the larger edition of v. Gebhardt would scarcely have been sufficient. What information, *e.g.*, would it have imparted to a reader to have given the numbers of the two minuscules 346, 556 after the reading in Matt. i. 16? What he needs is an Apparatus Criticus or a Commentarius Criticus such as Bengel appended to his edition, or like that which Burk published separately in his second issue. Ed. Miller has promised to give us one for the Gospels, only it will proceed on principles which very few of us will be able to accept.

CRITICAL NOTES ON VARIOUS PASSAGES OF THE NEW TESTAMENT.

THE GOSPEL.

Matthew.

WITH regard to the title, Westcott and Hort say (*Introduction*, § 423, p. 321): "In prefixing the name ΕΥΑΓΓΕΛΙΟΝ in the singular to the quaternion of 'the Gospels,' we have wished to supply the antecedent which alone gives an adequate sense to the preposition ΚΑΤΑ in the several titles. The idea, if not the name, of a collective 'Gospel' is implied throughout the well-known passage in the third book of Irenæus, who doubtless received it from earlier generations. It evidently preceded and produced the commoner usage by which the term Gospel denotes a single written representation of the one fundamental Gospel." Compare Zahn, *GK.*, i. 106 ff.; *Einleitung*, ii. 172 ff., 178 f.: "Of recent editors, Westcott and Hort have most faithfully interpreted the original idea by setting Εὐαγγέλιον on the fly-leaf, and κατὰ Μαθθαῖον, etc., over the separate books." I have followed the same principle in the Table of Contents prefixed to the Stuttgart edition of the New Testament. Compare above, pp. 164, 165. On the spelling Μαθθαῖος, instead of Ματθαῖος, compare on the one hand the LXX. manuscripts, which exhibit the forms Μαθανιά, Μαθθανιά, Ματθανιά; Ματταθίας, Ματθαθίας, Μαθθάθίας (see Supplement I. to Hatch and Redpath's *Concordance to the*

Septuagint), and on the other, Blass's *Grammatik des neutestamentlichen Griechisch*, § 3, 11 (English Trans. by Thackeray, 1898, p. 11).

i. 16. There are three forms of the text here—

(1) Ἰωσὴφ τὸν ἄνδρα Μαρίας, ἐξ ἧς ἐγεννήθη Ἰησοῦς ὁ λεγόμενος Χριστός: all our Greek uncials and almost all the minuscules.

(2) Ἰωσήφ, ᾧ μνηστευθεῖσα παρθένος Μαρία ἐγέννησεν τὸν Ἰησοῦν (τὸν λεγόμενον) Χριστόν: most of the Old Latin (a d g_1 k q, with b c similarly), Curetonian Syriac, Armenian, and four minuscules—viz., 346, 556, 624, 626, with slight divergencies.

(3) Ἰωσήφ· Ἰωσὴφ δὲ, ᾧ μνηστευθεῖσα (or μεμνηστευμένη?) ἦν παρθένος Μαρία, ἐγέννησεν τὸν Ἰησοῦν Χριστόν: the form underlying the newly-discovered Sinai-Syriac.[1]

These readings are discussed in the "Additional Note" to *Notes on Select Readings*, Westcott and Hort, *Introduction* (1896), p. 140 ff. Reading (2) is dismissed on external grounds as displaying the characteristic features of the "Western" type of text. Reading (3) is regarded as independent of (2), neither confirming it nor confirmed by it. Taken therefore on its own merits, it must yield to the received text (1), as it is easier to suppose that (3) is derived from (1) than *vice versa.*

Zahn goes fully into these various forms (*Einleitung*, ii. 291–293). He begins by saying that it is impossible, except on a very loose view of the facts, to conclude that the Sinai-Syriac here preserves the original text, which was gradually displaced for dogmatic reasons by the modified form presented in (2), and ultimately by that given in (1). On the contrary, the Curetonian-Syriac preserves an early form of text, and one that had a pretty wide circulation, so that it cannot be due to an orthodox alteration of the Sinai-Syriac.

[1] See Mrs. Lewis, in the *Expository Times*, November 1900, p. 56 ff., *What have we gained in the Sinaitic Palimpsest? I. St. Matthew's Gospel*, where a number of important variants are cited from that manuscript.

"If it be the case that the latter, like the former, is derived from a Greek original, and that these two earliest versions of the 'Distinct' Gospel are not independent of each other but are two recensions of a single version, then it follows that the recension which agrees exactly with a demonstrably old Greek text (in this case the Curetonian Syriac) preserves the original form of the Syriac version; while, on the other hand, the one which deviates from all the Greek, Latin, and other forms of the transmitted text (in this case the Sinai-Syriac) is derived from the other by a process of intentional alteration." There would be nothing to object to this reasoning were it not that, as it seems to me, there is a flaw in the second of the premises stated above, which of course vitiates the conclusion. In the main, it is true that the Sinai-Syriac and the Curetonian are not independent, but two recensions of a single version, but their common original was, as Zahn himself was the first to suggest, Tatian's Diatessaron, which did not contain the first chapter of Matthew's Gospel. So that the Sinai-Syriac may also go back to a Greek text (such as has been discovered in the *Dialogue of Timothy and Aquila*, see above, p. 99), and be earlier than the Curetonian.

Zahn concludes his examination of this passage by saying: "We may give up all hope of finding in early manuscripts and versions any indication that Joseph was regarded as the natural father of Jesus by the writers of lost Gospels which may have been employed in the composition of the canonical Matthew and Luke. A writer like Matthew, whose purpose was to silence the calumnies raised against the miraculous birth of the Messiah, and who knew how to utilise the smallest details of an intractable genealogy to this end, cannot at the same time have accepted in his narrative statements directly contradicting his view of that occurrence. Any text of Matthew's Gospel containing such features would be pre-condemned as one that had been tampered with in a manner contrary to the conception of the author."

i. 18. The reading γένεσις is now supported by the newly-discovered Oxyrhynchus Papyrus. It was adopted in the text by Vignon (Geneva, 1574). Origen knew no other reading than γέννησις, which is also attested by L (Codex D is defective here). Westcott and Hort have accordingly given it a place in their Appendix. Weiss explains it as an alteration made in conformity with the verbal forms ἐγέννησε, ἐγεννήθη, occurring in the previous part of the chapter. Zahn (*Einleitung*, ii. 270, 289) thinks it is probably original. The two oldest and the latest Syriac have a different word here from that in i. 1. These agree with Irenæus in the omission of Ἰησοῦ. Zahn thinks this is probably correct.

i. 25. On πρωτότοκον, see above, p. 166, and the *Oxford Debate*, p. 4 ff.

v. 25. On ἀντίδικος = בעלדינא, see Lagarde, *De Novo*, 20 (*Ges. Abhdl.*, 188); quem Matthaei locum quum imitaretur et rideret Lucianus in Navigio 35, ἀντίδικος non ferebat: ἕως ἔτι καθ' ὁδόν εἰσιν οἱ πολέμιοι, ἐπιχειρῶμεν αὐτοῖς.

vi. 1. δικαιοσύνην, ℵ* B D Syr[sin]: ἐλεημοσύνην, most authorities: δόσιν ℵ[a]: "your gifts," Syr[cu]. Zahn (*Einl.*, ii. 311) asks whether these variants may not go back to a time when the Aramaic Gospel was interpreted orally in these different ways? The agreement exhibited between ℵ[a] and Syr[cu] is particularly strange.

vi. 13. There is a considerable amount of unanimity now with regard to the doxology which used to be so much discussed. Among the witnesses supporting its insertion are Syr[cu], which, however, omits καὶ ἡ δύναμις, and the Sahidic, which omits καὶ ἡ δόξα. Syr[sin] is unfortunately lost here. In addition to the testimony previously known for the insertion of the Doxology, there is now that of the *Teaching of the Apostles*, one of the earliest Church writings. But the very fact that the *Teaching* is a Church work reveals the source of the Doxology—viz. liturgical use. The Conclusion was early added in Church worship from Old Testament analogies; in the First Gospel it is out of place. The Greek manuscripts from which Jerome made his version knew nothing of it, and accordingly the Catholic Church omits it to this day. Luther also passed it over in his Catechism, in which the exposition of the Conclusion is limited to the word "Amen," and says, "it is added that I may have the assurance that my prayer will be heard." In the Greek Church the Amen was explained as equivalent to γένοιτο, "so may it be."

viii. 7. Fritzsche (1826) took this verse as a question of surprise. This view has been renewed by Zahn (*Einl.*, ii. 307).

viii. 24. The words "erat enim ventus contrarius eis," which are found in one manuscript of the Vulgate in W–W after "mari," and in four after "fluctibus," are an interpolation from Mark vi. 48. Tischendorf cites two Greek minuscules in support of it. Lagarde's Vienna Arabic manuscript (see p. 143) mentions it as an addition of the "Roman" version.

xi. 19. Schlottman and Lagarde explain the variation between ἔργα and τέκνα as a confusion of the Aramaic עַבְדָּא (*servant*: παῖς) and עֲבָדָא (*work*). See Zahn, *Einl.*, ii. 311 f., and compare also Salmon, *Some Thoughts etc.*, p. 121 f. It is still to be shown, however, that τέκνα is ever used as the equivalent of עַבְדָּא. Hilgenfeld (*ZfwTh.*, 42. 4, p. 629) refers to 4 Esdras vii. 64 (134), where the Latin and the first Arabic version read "quasi suis *operibus*," the Ethiopic "quasi *filiis* suis," and the Syriac "quia *servi* eius sumus."

xii. 36. See on xviii. 7.

xiii. 35. διὰ Ἠσαΐου τοῦ προφήτου is now attested only by א*, two members of the Ferrar group, and some other minuscules, but Eusebius and Jerome found it in several manuscripts, and it was used still earlier by Porphyrius as a proof of Matthew's ignorance. It is certainly, therefore, genuine, although it is omitted by Syr^{sin}, Syr^{cu}, by the "accurate" manuscripts according to Eusebius,[1] and by the "vulgata editio" according to Jerome. The conjecture of the latter, that Ἀσάφ was the original reading, which was changed to Ἠσαΐου by some unintelligent copyist and then dropped as incorrect, only serves to show what sort of ideas

[1] Corderius (*Caten. Psal.*, ii. 631) substitutes "ancient" for "accurate."

he had with regard to textual criticism. The assertion of the *Breviarium in Psalmos*, p. 59 f., that all the old manuscripts read "in Asaph propheta" is pure fiction. Compare Ἰερεμίου in Matt. xxvii. 9, where one would expect *Ζαχαρίου*, and where we find that Ἰερεμίου is omitted by some witnesses and replaced in others by *Ζαχαρίου* or "Esaiam." "Esaiam" has also crept into the Vulgate manuscript rus (W–W's R). On the insertion, omission, and interchange of such names, see W–H's discussion of this passage, and the "Supplementary Note" by Burkitt on Syr[sin] in the edition of 1896, p. 143. For an interesting exchange of names (Jonah and Nahum), see Tobit, xiv. 8. Asaph is called ὁ προφήτης in 2 Chron. xxix. 30. Compare Zahn, *Einl.*, ii. 313 f. Weiss[9] would omit the word on the ground of insufficient testimony as being simply introduced from iii. 3, iv. 14, viii. 17, and xii. 17.

xiv. 3. Zahn (*Einl.*, ii. 309) thinks it extremely improbable that D and certain important Latin witnesses should have removed the (wrong) name, Philip, from this passage on the ground of their better knowledge, while allowing it to stand without exception in Mark vi. 17. He believes rather that they have preserved the original text, and that Φιλίππου is here an interpolation from the passage in Mark. Weiss[9], on the other hand, sees no reason why it should be either bracketed or omitted. The possibility of its being inserted is shown by the fact that it also crept into six or seven manuscripts of Jerome, collated by W–W. This is one of the passages where Tischendorf in his seventh edition frankly preferred Codex D to all the other Greek witnesses.

xv. 4*b*. For θανάτῳ τελευτάτω, Syr[cu] has נתקטל, evidently in accordance with Exod. xxi. 17. In the Arabic Diatessaron (§ 20, 23) the second half of this verse seems to be replaced by Mark vii. 10*b*. After "morte moriatur" in this passage, Ephraem adds "et qui blasphemat Deum *crucifigatur*," which Zahn (*Forsch.*, i. 157) thinks he must have found in his original. This apocryphal addition, which has no other testimony than that of Ephraem, does not seem to Zahn like a passage that had been afterwards removed from the text of the New Testament with complete success (*Forsch.*, i. 241). The correct explanation of the words is given by Harris: they are the Peshitto rendering of Deut. xxi. 23. Compare Driver's *Deuteronomy* on the passage, and the reference there made to Lightfoot's *Galatians* (Extended Note on iii. 13, ninth edition, p. 152 f.). Symmachus also renders the words: "propter blasphemiam Dei suspensus est," while Onkelos says על דחב קדם יי אצטליב, and Siphre מביני שקלל את השם. This should be noted in connection with Matt. xxvi. 65, and still more so with John xix. 7. The only passage usually cited there is Levit. xxiv. 16, according to which Jesus should have been *stoned*. Our commentators pass too hastily over the question why the Jews insisted on crucifixion instead of stoning.

xvi. 18*b*, 19. So far as the criticism of the text is concerned, there is no occasion for entering on the discussion whether this passage, like the one resembling it in xviii. 15–18, is original or not. There may, however, be cases in which one cannot overlook the fact that where the "lower" criticism ends the "higher" begins. Compare, on the one side, Zahn, *Forsch.*, i. 244 ff., and on the other, Resch, *Logia*, p. 55; *Paralleltexte*, ii. 187–196, 441.

xvi. 22. The peculiar reading, "compatiens," which is found in the Arabic Tatian (J. H. Hill, p. 137, § 23. 42: Zahn, *GK.*, ii. 546), and which Sellin has also traced in Ephraem, is now explained by the Syr^{sin} of Mark viii. 32: see my note in Lewis, *Some Pages*, p. xiii. The very same play upon the words חוס, "to pity," and חס, "to be far from," is found as late as in the *Histoire de Mar-Jabalaha, de trois autres patriarches*, ed. Bedjan, 1895, p. 407, line 14; p. 408, line 4. For a moment I thought of *ὀργισθείς* and *σπλαγχνισθείς* in Mark i. 41.

xviii. 7. The Dictum Agraphum *τὰ ἀγαθὰ ἐλθεῖν δεῖ, μακάριος δὲ δι' οὗ ἔρχεται*, which, according to the *Clementine Homilies* (xii. 29), *ὁ τῆς ἀληθείας προφήτης ἔφη*, was known also to Ephraem (*cf.* Zahn, *Forsch.*, i. 241 f. on § 50. 4). An exact parallel to this "harmless expansion of the canonical text" is seen in the form which Matt. xii. 36 assumed in Codex C of the Palestinian Syriac Evangeliarium: that "for every *good* word that men do *not* speak they shall give account" (see Lewis, *In the Shadow of Sinai* (1898), pp. 256–261; and thereon, *ThLz.*, 1899, col. 177).

xviii. 20. On the form in which this saying is found in the Oxyrhynchus Logia, compare Ephraem (Moesinger 165), "ubi unus est ibi et ego sum." Zahn believes that Ephraem found this in his text, but that Aphraates, who also has it, arrived at it by way of a "spiritual interpretation" of the canonical words. After quoting the comments of Aphraates on these words, Zahn says: "It appears certain, therefore, that Aphraates did not find in his text the apocryphal sentence given in Ephraem, but by way of interpretation reached the same thought that Ephraem found in his text as a word of comfort spoken by Jesus to the lonely. (Ephraem introduces the saying with the words: 'He comforted them in His saying.') The interpretation, which may not have been original in Aphraates, became first a gloss and then part of the text of Tatian's Harmony." This should be noticed in connection with the Oxyrhynchus Logion. See Burkitt in the Introduction to Barnard's *Biblical Text of Clement* (*Texts and Studies*, v. 5, p. xiv).

xx. 13. The peculiar form of the householder's reply given in Syr^{cu}, *μὴ ἀδίκει με* (Baethgen, *μή μοι κόπους πάρεχε*) is ignored by Tischendorf. Our commentators also err in not taking note of the variant *συνεφώνησά σοι* for *συνεφώνησάς μοι*. Compare the similar variation in John viii. 57; also Luke xviii. 20, *τὰς ἐντολὰς οἶδα*, read by the Marcionites instead of *οἶδας*; and Ephes. v. 14, *ἐπιψαύσεις τοῦ Χριστοῦ*, derived through a presupposed reading, *ἐπιψαύσει σοι ὁ Χριστός*. *Συνεφώνησά σοι* in Matt. xx. 13 is also attested by Syr^{sin}, which agrees with the common text in the first member of the verse. It is also found in the newly-discovered purple manuscript in Paris. The Arabic Tatian agrees with the usual text in both members. On the strange mixture of this verse and Luke xvi. 25 in Petrus Siculus (*ἑταῖρε, οὐκ ἀδικῶ σε· ἀπέλαβες τὰ σὰ ἐν τῇ ζωῇ σου· νῦν ἆρον τὸ σὸν καὶ ὕπαγε*) see Zahn, *GK.*, ii. 445.

xx. 16. The concluding member of this verse is now rightly omitted with ℵ B L Z and the Egyptian versions. All the Syriac versions have it, including the newly-discovered Syr^{sin}. It is worth observing that the verse with this addition forms the close of a lection in Syr^{hier}.

xx. 28. Westcott and Hort devote one of their "Notes on Select Readings" to the addition to this verse, and in the edition of 1896 Burkitt adds that it cannot have stood in Syr^{sin}, because there was not room for it on the leaf that is missing between Matt. xx. 24 and xxi. 20. According to W-H the passage is Western, being attested by D Φ among the Greek manuscripts and by the Latin and Syriac versions. "The first part only, *ὑμεῖς—εἶναι*, is preserved in m, ger, and apparently Leo, who quotes no more; the second part only, *εἰσερχόμενοι—χρήσιμον*, in ger_2 and apparently Hilary. The first part must come from an independent source, written or oral; the second probably comes from the same, but it is in substance identical with Luke xiv. 8–10." Tischendorf states that of the Old Latin, four (f g_2 l q) omit the section, which, however, is found in c d e $ff_{1,2}$ g_1 h (m) n, two manuscripts of the Vulgate (and. emm.), the Old German, and the Saxon. To these W-W add also the Old Latin r, two manuscripts of the Vulgate not usually employed by them, and, of those forming the basis of their edition, H^{mg} Θ O—*i.e.* the Theodulfian Recension. A hand of the tenth century has written on the margin of O, "mirum unde istud additum: cum Lucas parabolam de invitatis ad nuptias et primos accubitus eligentibus decimo canone, ubi M(atthaeu)s sua non communia dicit referat." This resembles the marginal note attached to the passage by Thomas of Heraclea (not given by Jos. White, but by Adler, from *Cod. Assem.*, 1):

Haec quidem in exemplis antiquis in Luca tantum leguntur capite 53: inveniuntur autem in exemplis graecis[1] hoc loco: quapropter hic etiam a nobis adiecta sunt.

The word δειπνοκλήτωρ, which Resch took from this passage into the text of his *Logia Jesu*, for ὁ σὲ καὶ αὐτὸν καλέσας, found in Luke xiv. 9, should itself have provoked investigation. The only Latin witnesses which render it in a substantive form are d, which has *coenae invitator* both times, and m, which has *invitator* the first time. The others give it as a relative clause (*qui vocavit, invitavit*), so that they may have read it in the form in which it stands in our present text of Luke.[2] It is impossible not to believe that some connection exists between these substantive expressions and the Syriac מרא אחשמיתא, "master of the feast," which is found in Syr^{cu} and Syr^{sin}, and is also given by Aphraates, for τῷ κεκληκότι αὐτόν in Luke xiv. 12 (Aphr. 388, 12–19; Zahn, *Forsch.*, i. 85, note). Syr^{cu} has it both times in this passage of Matthew.[3]

Bengel, like our modern expositors, says nothing of the interpolation in his *Gnomon*, and his view with respect to it

[1] Or "exemplo graeco," according as the plural points are inserted or not. The passage is printed in Syriac by Cureton, p. xxxvi, who says that it is also found in the margin of the London manuscript of the Peshitto, 14456. He also gives the verses in which Juvencus paraphrases this text.

[2] The other variations of the Latin witnesses are extremely instructive—viz.:

locis eminentioribus	superioribus g_2 emm.	honorificis m
clarior	dignior d m g_2 emm.	honoratior e
deorsum	inferius g_2 emm.	infra m
inferior	humilior	minor
superius	sursum	in superiori loco.
utilius	utile	gloriam.

This variety is an indication of the early age at which the text was translated into Latin.

[3] The *Thesaurus Syriacus* does not contain the word either in col. 1405 under חשמיתא, or in col. 2205 under מרא.

It may also be observed in passing, that the passage is one of those whose sense is entirely changed by the insertion or omission of the negative in this or that witness (see below on Gal. ii. 5). Instead of καὶ ἐκ μείζονος, Syr^{cu} reads καὶ μὴ ἐκ μείζονος. Moreover, it takes ζητεῖτε as imperative, a fact that Tischendorf has failed to notice.

has, therefore, to be gathered from his apparatus. "Interjicit cod. Lat. vetustissimus Vos autem, etc. . . . . Vid. Rich. Simon, *Obs. Nouv.*, p. 31. Et sic fere Cant. (*i.e.*, D) cuius lectio passim exstat. Idem vero Codex Graeca sua ad Latina haec, quae modo exscripsimus, confecit: Latina autem sua, sub manu, vehementius interpolavit, magno argumento licentiae suae. Eandem periocham legit Juvencus, Hilarius: habentque praeterea codd. Lat. aliquot, et inde Sax. Ex. Luc. xiv. 8 f., interveniente forsan Evangelio Nazaraeorum . . . . Priorem duntaxat partem, 'Vos autem . . . . minui' habet alius cod. Lat. antiquiss. ut si Librarius, cum describere coepisset, non scribendum agnosceret: eandémque Leo M. sic exhibet. Et tamen . . . . porro ab hoc loco ad Luc. xxii. 28, verbum *crescendi* protulit Cant. *coenaeque invitator* ei dicitur δειπνοκλήτωρ."

The truth is, of course, the very opposite of this, as is shown by the indicative *quaeritis* and the imperative of the Syriac, which are both derived from the ambiguous ζητεῖτε. There cannot be the slightest doubt of this, seeing that the discovery of Codex Beratinus (Φ) has added a second Greek witness in support of the interpolation. It reads ἐλάττων (*cf. minor*, c), omits the καὶ before ἐπέλθῃ just as m does with *et*, has ἄγε in place of σύναγε (*accede*: d, *collige*), and the comparative χρησιμώτερον (*utilius*) for the positive read by D d. The word δειπνοκλήτωρ also occurs in Φ.[1] It is not found in Bekker's *Pollux* or in Schmid's *Hesychius*, and the only instance that ancient lexicons are able to cite for its usage is that of Athenæus, who observes (4. 171 B) that Artemidorus calls the ἐλέατρος by that name. The note appended in Hase-Dindorf's *Stephanus* was not correct at the time of its publication: Quidam codices Matt. xx. 27, Hesych., Wakef. Eust. *Od.*, p. 1413, 3; nor the quotation from Ducange: Δ. in Lex. MS. Cyrilli exp. ἑστιάτωρ. In the same work δειπνοκλητόριον is cited from Eust., *Il.*, 766, 58, and as an explana-

[1] I see that Chase, who discusses the passage in pp. 9–14 of his *Syro-Latin Text*, has the same impression: "the compound Greek word in D, ὁ δειπνοκλήτωρ, seems intended to represent the Syriac expression 'the lord of the supper.'"

tion of ἑστιατόριον from the Lex. MS. Cyrilli. The word therefore belongs to the later popular language. The question is whether it may not also belong to the vocabulary of Tatian. Moreover, it reminds us of the equally rare word κτήτωρ in Acts iv. 34.

On the occurrence of the passage in Tatian, see Zahn, *Forsch.*, i. 85, 179. On the questions connected with its interpolation see Chase and p. 216 above.

xxii. 23. We have in this verse an illustration of the difference caused by the insertion or omission of the article. If we read οἱ λέγοντες with ℵ[c] E F G etc., then the words introduce the creed of the Sadducees (" who say," Weizsäcker: " members of that sect who deny the resurrection," Stage); if we omit οἱ with ℵ* B D and Syr[sin], we have then what they actually said to Jesus. But as this would be the only place where Matthew gave an explanation of this sort regarding Jewish affairs, the article should be omitted. See note *in loco*, *Expositor's Greek Testament*, and compare the margin of the Revised English Version.

xxiii. 35. ℵ[1] omits υἱοῦ βαραχίου, which is replaced in the Gospels of the Hebrews by "filium Joiadae." Zahn (*Einl.*, ii. 308) refers to the view of Hug, adopted by Eichhorn and many others, that the author, or redactor, or translator of Matthew made this Zechariah, who is rightly called the son of Jehoiada in the Gospel of the Hebrews, the son of Barachiah in order to identify him with the Zechariah, son of Baruch, who was murdered by the Zealots (Josephus, *Bell.*, iv. 5. 4). He points out that this would involve a prediction on the part of Jesus, and that, moreover, the scene of the murder is different in the two cases: that the locality in Matt. points to 2 Chron. xxiv. 21, and that Matthew's mistake in calling him the son of Barachiah is due to a confusion with the Zechariah mentioned in Isa. viii. 2, or that in Zech. i. 1. It should be observed, however, that Lucian alone calls the murdered person in Chronicles by the name of Zechariah; the LXX calls him Azariah.

xxv. 41. See on Luke xx. 35.

xxvi. 73. Ὁμοιάζει was formerly attested by D alone, but has now the further support of Syr^{sin}. The clause καὶ ἡ λαλιά σου ὁμοιάζει has crept into a great number of manuscripts, including even A, in Mark xiv. 70. There Tischendorf remarks, "Omnino e Mt. fluxit," in which he is quite right. But he is wrong when he says "ipsum ὁμοιάζει glossatoris est." Because the glossator must then have been earlier than Tatian (Ciasca, p. 87), and the parent of all those manuscripts. The converse is the truth—viz., that D alone preserves the original reading, and that δῆλόν σε ποιεῖ is the voice of the διορθωτής.

xxvii. 9. The name of the prophet, which was omitted in some manuscripts, according to Augustine, is now omitted only by a b and the two minuscules 33 and 157. Augustine also observes that Matthew himself would have noticed his mistake or had his attention called to it by others. On this compare my notes on ἐβαρύνατε in Acts iii. 14, which I have explained by supposing that the author read כברתם or כבדתם instead of כפרתם (*Philologica Sacra*, p. 40; above, p. 170). Origen, Eusebius, and Jerome evidently still found Ἰερεμίου in all the manuscripts. Ζαχαρίου is supplied only by 22 and *Esaiam* by 1. See on Matt. xiii. 35, and compare *Expository Times*, November 1900, p. 62.

xxvii. 16. Zahn (*Einl.*, ii. 294) points out that Origen also found *Jesus* given as the prenomen of Barabbas "in very ancient manuscripts," but that in all probability Tatian did not have it, seeing that Bar-Bahlul cites it expressly as the reading of the "Distinct" (*i.e.*, not harmonised) Gospel. Jerome says that in the Gospel of the Hebrews he was called by a name meaning "filius magistri eorum," so that he must have been thinking not of *Bar-'abbam* but of *Bar-rabbam*.

xxvii. 49. See above, p. 227, and compare Burkitt, *Texts and Studies*, v. 5, p. xix.

xxviii. 18. Compare Dan. vii. 14*b* (LXX), καὶ ἐδόθη αὐτῷ ἐξουσία, and also Dan. vii. 13 (=Matt. xxvi. 64), vii. 14 f. (=Matt. xxviii. 18). See the *English Revised Version with marginal References* (Oxford, 1899).

According to the subscriptions found in various minuscules, the Hebrew Matthew was translated into Greek "by John," or "by James," to which some add "the Brother of the Lord," or "by Bartholomew, the celebrated Apostle (*πανευφήμου*), but as others say by John the Theologian, *οἱ καὶ ἀληθῶς εἰρήκασιν*." See Tischendorf, and Zahn, *Einl.*, ii. 267.

Mark.

As if to enforce the desire to which I have given expression above (p. 246), there has come into my hands Blass's *Textkritische Bemerkungen zu Markus*. If the statements contained in the introductory remarks are correct, and scarcely any other view is possible in the circumstances described, then the textual criticism of the first and second Gospels is a hopeless matter. "An evangelist or teacher who obtained possession of the originally anonymous Commentarius could not feel bound to respect the external form, but considered himself justified in correcting it if it seemed to him to be defective, and even felt called to correct or complete its subject matter." Blass reminds us that we have whole classes of documents, legends of saints *e.g.*, which were treated with the utmost possible freedom by the copyists, who in fact were in this case editors and revisers. But he says that no one has treated Mark quite so drastically as all this. His summing up of the matter is, that the critic can often do no more than recognise and admit the early multiplicity, and that in such a case it were best to print the text in parallel columns. At the same time he is able to distinguish some of the variants as later falsifications or corruptions. Universally trustworthy authorities there are none; here one group is right, there another, and we no sooner give them credence than they mislead us with some fresh error.

We are far removed, truly, from the confidence displayed by Tischendorf in the treatise he published shortly before his death in 1873 in answer to the question, "Have we the genuine text of the Evangelical and Apostolical writings?" All the more urgently, therefore, do we need fresh studies in textual criticism, and their appearance in Germany is the more gratifying on that account. The *Markus-Studien* of Dr. H. P. Chajes (Berlin, 1899), however, are quite beside the point. They are purely imaginary, having neither substance nor method.

i. 1. On the title, see above; Zahn, *Einl.*, ii. 220 ff., 235; Swete, *in loco*; and on this last, S. D. F. Salmond, in the *Critical Review*, April 1899, 206 f.: "We do not see, however, why Professor Swete should regard the opening verses as probably not a part of the original work. One might say the same of the whole paragraph with which the Gospel opens, or, for that matter, the whole chapter. The documentary evidence is substantially the same in each case, and the internal considerations are much too indeterminate." It may be pointed out, as remotely analogous to this, that before Matt. i. 18 the margin of harl (Z in W–W) contains a note in a hand of the ninth or tenth century to the effect, "genealogia hucusque: incipit evangelium secundum Matthaeum," while Y has the words "incipit evangelium secundum Matthaeum" in the text, and eight manuscripts begin verse 18 with capital or red letters. Compare Scrivener, I. c. iii., on the divisions of the text in B and other manuscripts.

For the way in which the opening sentences are to be construed, reference must be made to the commentaries. It may be said here, however, that parallels may be cited from the New Testament for each of the three possible constructions. These are (1) Ἀρχὴ . . . . , καθὼς . . . . αὐτοῦ, ἐγένετο; (2) Ἀρχὴ . . . . Καθὼς . . . . αὐτοῦ. Ἐγένετο; (3) Ἀρχὴ . . . . Καθὼς . . . . αὐτοῦ, ἐγένετο. For (1) and (2) compare Luke iii. 1 ff., and for (3) 1 Tim. i. 1 ff. Origen favours the first construction (*Contra Celsum*, ii. 4; vol. i. p. 131). As regards the text it need only be said that καὶ is read before ἐγένετο (v. 4) by א[1], and that δὲ is found after it, not only in the Coptic, but also in Syr[hier].

i. 2. Origen here read ἐγὼ and ἔμπροσθέν σου (i. 131). But

the former should be omitted with B D etc., and the latter with all the good authorities. It follows that Matt. xi. 10 is not taken from Mark i. 2 (Zahn, *Einl.*, ii. 316, 332). One can see how important the so-called "lower" criticism may be for the "higher."

i. 11; ix. 7. See on "Punctuation" above, p. 52.

i. 29. "B here has ἐξελθὼν ἦλθεν, and D b c e q Pesh. have substantially the same. This is not an improvement, because it excludes Peter and Andrew. The reading of Syr^{sin} is peculiar, 'and He went out of the synagogue and came into the house of Simon Cephas (Andrew and James and John were with him), and the mother-in-law etc.'" See Zahn, *Einl.*, ii. 252, and below on ix. 14.

i. 41. The remarkable "Western reading" ὀργισθείς is dismissed by Swete with a reference to W–H, who call it "a singular reading, perhaps suggested by v. 43 (ἐμβριμησάμενος), perhaps derived from an extraneous source." In my *Philologica Sacra*, p. 26, I have expressed the opinion that it is impossible to suppose a copyist altered σπλαγχνισθείς to ὀργισθείς, even though ἐμβριμησάμενος does follow two verses further down.[1] Either ὀργή, ὀργίζεσθαι has another meaning in Biblical Greek, which is quite possible, or we have here an instance of a difference in translation. The confusion of the gutturals, *e.g.*, is very common. Compare Ps. xii. 6, יפיח, Gr. יפיע; Ps. xiv. 6, עני = liii. 6, חנך; וישמח in Isa. xxxix. 2 for וישמע in 2 Kings xx. 13; Ps. xxii. 25, ענות, where Gr. has δέησις = תחנות; Ps. xcvii. 11, זרע, Gr. ἀνέτειλεν = זרח; and especially Mark ix. 19 in the recently-published Evangeliarium Hierosolymitanum of Lewis–Gibson, where Cod. B has מרחית for מרעת found in A B. Compare also חר, Matt. vii. 11 (p. 68), and ער (p. 135). A glance at the *Thesaurus Syriacus* 3953 shows that רעם is used, not only for βροντᾶν, but also for σπλαγχνίζεσθαι, στέργειν, and συμπαθεῖν, while אתרעם stands for χαλεπαινειν, ἀγανακτεῖν, and γογγύζειν. Payne-Smith gives no instance of ὀργίζεσθαι. The usual Syriac word for it even in Syr^{sin} and Syr^{hier} is רגז

[1] The case is quite different in 1 Macc. v. 2, where the first hand of ℵ wrote ὠργίσθησαν for ἐβουλεύσαντο. Here ὠργίσθη occurs immediately before it.

or אתחמת; both verbs are found together in 1 Macc. vi. 59 for the simple ὠργίσθησαν (אתחַמתו ורגזו). It is worth noting that in Col. iii. 13, ὀργήν is read by F G, where D* has μέμψιν, and the other authorities μομφήν.

On the reading in Mark i. 41, see Harris, *Fragments etc.* (1895), p. 6. He shows that Ephraem had ὀργισθείς in his text alongside of σπλαγχνισθείς. The Arabic Diatessaron, in which the pericope does not come till § 22, follows the usual text, and so, too, does $\mathrm{Syr}^{\mathrm{sin}}$.

ii. 14. Zahn (*Einl.*, ii. 263) holds that "Levi son of Alphaeus" is the original reading here and not "James," and that it was taken from Mark into the Gospel of Peter. The reading "Jacobum" was also taken into the first hand of the Vulgate manuscript G from D 13, 69, 124, a b c d e ff_2 r. In Koetschau's new edition of Origen, the name is no longer spelt Λεβής but Λευής (i. 113, 19; Cod. P: Λευίς).

iii. 17. Our expositors might tell us where Luther got his "Bnehargem," which is retained in the German Revised Version. On Daniel ii. 7 Jerome has "Benereem." I have looked in vain in Lyra, Pole's *Synopsis*, Calov, and Wolf.

iii. 31. We have here to choose between καλοῦντες (ℵ B C L etc.), φωνοῦντες (D etc.), and ζητοῦντες (A): Δ leaves a space. I am inclined to think that φωνοῦντες is the original reading, which was improved by the substitution of the more usual word καλοῦντες, just as οὐ φωνεῦντος ἀκούω was altered to λαλέοντος in the Delphic Oracle in Herodotus i. 47. Compare a similar variation in Heb. xi. 13, where the original reading κομισάμενοι (ℵ* P) was thought to be improved by the substitution of λαβόντες ($\aleph^{c}$ D E K) or προσδεξάμενοι (A). Here, too, A stands alone. Was it never copied?

vi. 16. There is a discrepancy in the Eusebian Canons in this verse which has not been explained. Both Tischendorf and Wordsworth and White number this verse $\frac{58}{2}$. But according to the table in *TiGr.*, p. 152, W–W, p. 10, pericope 58 belongs to the *tenth* Canon as being one that is peculiar to

Mark. As a matter of fact it is not so, unless Eusebius meant ἀκούσας δέ at the beginning of the verse. It is remarkable that Eusebius did not make the whole of verses 14–20 one pericope of the second canon, but numbered 14, 15 as $\frac{57}{2}$ and 17–20 as $\frac{59}{2}$. He must therefore have found something peculiar in verse 16 to make it 58.

vi. 20. This passage is very instructive from a textual point of view. Most authorities read that "Herod had put John in prison, heard him and did much," or "heard much of what he did," ἀκούσας αὐτοῦ πολλὰ (ἃ) ἐποίει. But in place of this last word ℵ B L and the Bohairic version alone read ἠπόρει, "was much perplexed when he heard him." The great majority of expositors decide at once in favour of the latter reading, setting aside ἐποίει as the *scriptio proclivior.* But in that case should it not have been ἠπορεῖτο? In classical Greek it should undoubtedly, but in Biblical Greek we find ἠπόρει in *Wisd.* xi. 5, 17, for example, and what is specially worth noting, διηπόρει in the parallel passage Luke ix. 7, for which D, it is true, has ἠπορεῖτο. The passage may therefore be taken as showing that the correct reading has been preserved in a very few witnesses. Strict logic, moreover, would lead us to infer that not one of our 1300 manuscripts is derived from any one of these three, but that ℵ B L continued childless. Is that likely? Field, it may be added, decides in favour of ἐποίει (*Otium Norvicense*; see *Expository Times,* August 1899, p. 483), and so, too, does Burkitt (*Texts and Studies,* v. 5, p. xix). In Philo, i. 264, line 8 (ed. Cohn), the manuscripts vary between μετεωροπολειν, —πορειν, —ποιειν, and —λογειν.

vii. 33. Codex W^d, published by Harris in facsimile (1896), here exhibits a very peculiar reading which Harnack (*ThLz.*, 1891, p. 356) thinks has affinity with Tatian. It reads: ἔπτυσεν εἰς τοὺς δακτύλους αὐτοῦ καὶ ἔβαλεν εἰς τὰ ὦτα τοῦ κωφοῦ καὶ ἥψατο τῆς γλώσσης τοῦ μογιλάλου. This gives us quite another view of the occurrence than most of the authorities do. It seems much more natural certainly to moisten the fingers before putting them in the ears than before touching the tongue. It reads somewhat similarly in Syr^{sin}, which says that "he put his fingers and spat in his ears, and touched his tongue."[1] This manuscript exhibits other noteworthy readings, which will be found most conveniently in Swete.

ix. 14. The singular, ἐλθὼν . . . . εἶδεν, has the support of D, while Syr^{sin} takes the side of the plural, ἐλθόντες . . . . εἶδον. Zahn decides for the latter. He explains the plural by saying that the original narrator was evidently one of the three disciples who were with Jesus on the Mount, in all probability Peter, as tradition has it. Peter, of course, in telling the story, used the first person and the plural number, "When we came down from the mountain we saw, etc." Mark, reporting the words of Peter, turned the first person into the third, retaining the plural number. Zahn explains in the same way the somewhat peculiar expressions in Mark i. 29. Here Peter said, "*we* (*i.e.* Jesus, Andrew, and himself) came into *our* house with James and John." In reporting Peter's words Mark paraphrases "we" and "our," and says, "they came into the house of Simon and Andrew with James and John." See Zahn, *Einl.*, ii. 245 f.

x. 30. Neither Tischendorf nor Swete observes that in addition to the readings διωγμῶν and διωγμόν the singular διωγμοῦ is exhibited by D. Has the mysterious reading εἰς που in Clem. Alex. (*Quis Dives*) anything to do with this? It is worth remarking that the Vienna Arabic manuscript (Lagarde: Storr) has a note after "post persecutionem" to the effect that this is the "Roman" reading.

xiv. 51. καὶ νεανίσκος τις, ℵ B C L; νεανίσκος δέ τις, D; καὶ εἷς τις νεανίσκος, A E etc. This last is rejected by Zahn on the ground that the text has evidently been accommodated to verse 47, under the false impression that another of the disciples is referred to. It is adopted, however, by Tischendorf^{8}, and supported by Brandt, *Die Evangelische Geschichte* etc., Leipzig, 1893, p. 23 ff.

[1] So given in Merx's edition, but not in Lewis.—*Tr.*

xiv. 65. ἔλαβον, ℵ A B and most authorities: ἐλάμβανον, D G, 1, 13, 69, 2^{pe}, al^{10}: ἔβαλλον, H. . . .: ἔβαλον, E M U etc. The simplest explanation of this variety of readings is that ἐλάμβανον was first, and that it was changed into the more common aorist ἔλαβον, which then became ἔβαλον or ἔβαλλον. The converse is not so likely, viz. that ἔβαλλον or ἔβαλον became first ἔλαβον and then ἐλάμβανον, or that ἔλαβον gave rise directly both to ἐλάμβανον and ἔβαλον or ἔβαλλον. On these and also on internal grounds the reading of D G is to be preferred: "they began to spit upon him, and continued to buffet him."

xv. 28. Syr^{sin} is now to be added to the authorities that omit the interpolation. On the interesting names, Zoatham and Chammatha, Dysmas and Gestas, Titus and Dumachus (*i.e.* Θεομάχος), see Berger in the notice of Wordsworth, and White's *Epilogus* mentioned above, and also J. R. Harris in the *Expositor*, March 1900, p. 162 ff., April, p. 304.

xv. 34. It is extraordinary that no reference is made in Swete's edition to the very singular reading of Codex D, ὠνίδισας instead of ἐγκατέλιπες. In addition to the testimony of the Old Latin manuscripts c (exprobrasti me), i (me in opprobrium dedisti), k* (maledixisti: see Burkitt in the *Journal of Theological Studies*, i. p. 278), this reading is attested in Greek by Macarius Magnes. No explanation of it has yet been given that is in all respects satisfactory. See *Expository Times*, August 1898, and February, March, and April 1900.

xvi. 9–20. The English Revisers had not the courage to omit the conclusion. They print it quite like the rest of the text, only they separate it from the foregoing by a somewhat wider space than usual, and give a note in the margin to the following effect—viz. "The two oldest Greek manuscripts and some other authorities omit from verse 9 to the end. Some other authorities have a different ending to the Gospel." The German Revised Version has no remark to offer, which is easily accounted for on the principles on which that version is made. The most careful discussion of the passage is now that of Swete, pp. xcvi–cv. See also Zahn, *Einl.*, ii. 227–235, 237, 240, and compare the Appendix in Chase's *Old Syriac Element*, pp. 150–157, "Note on Mark xvi. 9–20," and Arthur Wright, *The Gospel according to St. Luke*, p. xv.

The subscription of several minuscules bears that Mark's Gospel was written at Rome ten years after the Ascension, and delivered to the brethren there by Peter, the πρωτοκορυφαῖος of the Apostles. Others give Egypt as the place of origin. It is of more importance to observe that Λ 20, 262, 300 contain the note: ἀντεβλήθη ὁμοίως ἐκ τῶν ἐσπουδασμένων. This refers to the subscription to Matthew found in these manuscripts: ἐγράφη καὶ ἀντεβλήθη ἐκ τῶν ἐν Ἱεροσολύμοις παλαιῶν ἀντιγράφων τῶν ἐν τῷ ἁγίῳ ὄρει ἀποκειμένων. A similar subscription occurs in 2[pe], a minuscule of considerable importance for Mark (473 in Scrivener; see above, p. 151, n.).

Luke.

Apart altogether from the question how the numerous and decided peculiarities of Codex D are to be explained, we find a great many problems connected with the text of Luke's Gospel.

On the supposed title see Zahn, *Einl.*, ii. 383.

i. 26. In place of the definite indication of time, Blass follows certain Latin authorities, especially the Latin Irenæus, in giving: in ipso (or, eodem) autem tempore, ἐν αὐτῷ δὲ τῷ καιρῷ. Zahn points out (*Einl.*, ii. 354) that this is the customary formula for the beginning of a pericope in the Lectionaries, and that while no doubt in the later Greek system the pericope of the Annunciation began with verse 24, 26 is the more appropriate beginning. He adds that in any case the origin of this formula is evident, and that Cod. D, which here parts company with the Latin witnesses, gives other indications besides this of the influence of a pericope-system. See the Introduction to Scrivener's edition of the Codex, p. li.

i. 46. On the reading *Elisabeth*, see above, p. 238.

i. 63. The *β* text inserted the words ἐλύθη ἡ γλῶσσα

αὐτοῦ before καὶ ἐθαύμασαν πάντες, by way of explaining the astonishment of the people. Zahn thinks this an absurd misplacement, seeing that the mention of Zechariah's speaking does not come till the following verse, and the people could not know that his tongue was loosed till they heard him speak. Syr^{sin} accordingly corrects this by putting the mention of the astonishment after that of the speaking, in which it is followed by Blass.

ii. 4, 5. In the β text Blass adopts the reading αὐτοὺς, and transposes the clause διὰ τὸ εἶναι αὐτοὺς ἐξ οἴκου καὶ πατριᾶς Δαυείδ to the end of verse 5. This arrangement is also exhibited by D. Syr^{sin} reads "both." One Old Latin manuscript has *essent*, but as it exhibits the clause in the usual place, Zahn thinks that *essent* is manifestly a clerical error for *esset*. The Syriac, he points out, is derived from Tatian. See *Einl.*, ii. 355; *Forsch.*, i. 118; *GK.*, ii. 561; Vetter, *Der dritte Korintherbrief* (1894), 25.

ii. 7. One Latin manuscript (e) has *obvolverunt* and *collocaverunt*, which may be compared with *essent* in verse 4. Zahn thinks that the plural here is due to the reflection that the mother does not usually herself attend to a new-born infant.

ii. 14. How does the Christmas song of the angels run exactly? Is it ἐν ἀνθρώποις εὐδοκίας, or ἐν ἀνθ. εὐδοκία? The question belongs more to exegesis than textual criticism. The whole matter turns upon a single letter, but it divides Western Christendom in two parts. The Latin Church reads it as *in hominibus bonae voluntatis*, "among men of goodwill," or, as modern critics understand it, "among men of God's good pleasure." The second reading makes it "goodwill to men." Which should it be? The former reading, the genitive, is supported by ℵ* A B* D, the Latin, and the Gothic, whereas nearly all the other witnesses, including the Bohairic, the three Syriac, and A itself in the Hymns at the end of the Old Testament Psalter, have the nominative. One thing seems to me decisive in favour of the nominative. Scarcely any part of the New Testament is so steeped in the Hebrew spirit as the first two chapters of Luke's Gospel. As Field points out in the third part of his *Otium Norvicense*, the Greek ἄνθρωποι corresponds to the Hebrew expression "son of Adam," which cannot take another genitive after it—"sons of Adam of goodwill." On the other hand, the word *goodwill* in Hebrew is always followed by the preposition corresponding to the Greek ἐν. So that, till we have further testimony, I would retain the nominative and the tripartite division, notwithstanding the authority of Tischendorf, Westcott and Hort, Weizsäcker, Stage, and Blass, who, by the way, mentions no variants in the β text.

ii. 40. D here reads ἐν αὐτῷ in place of ἐπ' αὐτό. The difference is slight, but not unimportant from a theological point of view. It is not accidental, as is shown by the corresponding change of ἐπ' into εἰς in ch. iii. 22.

iii. 22. Zahn regards this as one of the passages wherein D and its associates have preserved the original reading. They exhibit here ἐγὼ σήμερον γεγέννηκά σε in place of ἐν σοὶ εὐδόκησα. He says, moreover, that "those who hold the former as original need not lament its disappearance from tradition subsequent to the year 300" (*Einl.*, ii. 240, 356). See Burkitt in Barnard's *Biblical Text of Clement*, pp. xiii. 38.

iii. 23 ff. May not the peculiar form of the genealogy in D be explaimed by the Diatessaron, which originally had no genealogy? The index of the Latin edition shows that there was none originally, but we find in the text one compiled from Matt. i. 1–16, Luke iii. 34–37, Matt. i. 17. The first-known manuscript of the Arabic Diatessaron had Matt. i. 1–17 in § 2, and Luke iii. 24–38 in § 9. The better manuscript, discovered later, has no genealogy in the text, but it contains one compiled from Matt. and Luke, inserted between the close of the work and the subscription by way of appendix. See Zahn, *GK.*, ii. 539; J. H. Hill, *Earliest Life of Christ* etc., p. 3 f.

iii. 27. The correct explanation of Ῥησά is that given by Plummer in his *Commentary* on Luke, and quoted by Bacon in Hastings' *Dictionary of the Bible*, ii. 140. "Rhesa, who appears in Luke, but neither in Matt. nor in 1 Chron., is probably not a name at all, but a title which some Jewish copyist mistook for a name. Zerubbabel Rhesa or Zerubbabel the Prince (רֵאשָׁא) has been made into 'Zerubbabel (begat) Rhesa.'" The interpretation of Rhesa as "prince" is, however, not new. See Pole's *Synopsis*: it was not safe to use the proper name Zerubbabel in Babylon, seeing that it meant "ventilatio Babelis," and the name Sheshbazzar was therefore substituted for it. Sic filii eius Meshullam et Hanania, quia vix ibi tuto aut proprie dici potuerunt Abiud, *i.e.* patris mei est gloria, et Rhesa princeps (Lightfoot, *Horae Hebraicae*). Reuchlin (*Rudimenta*, p. 18) gives the explanation רֵשָׁע (*sic*) qui cognominatur Mesollam. This interpretation, however, lends no real support to Sellin's theory.

iv. 34. The exclamation ἔα, which Zahn (*GK.*, i. 682) says is unknown in the New Testament, is omitted by D, eleven Old Latin manuscripts, and also by Marcion. It is supported by a considerable number of witnesses in Mark i. 24. According to Zahn, these witnesses took it from Luke, but of this I am by no means certain. Syr^{sin} omits it in both places. In Luke it is also omitted by four manuscripts of the Vulgate mentioned by Wordsworth and White.

iv. 34. Marcion invariably omits Ναζαρηνέ. There is, however, no other authority for its omission. See Zahn, *GK.*, i. 685; ii. 456.

iv. 44. Ἰουδαίας is the better attested reading, and on account of the improbability of its being invented, should be regarded as the original. See Zahn, *Einleitung*, ii. 373.

v. 5. Ἐπιστάτα in the New Testament is peculiar to Luke. In place of it D has διδάσκαλε here, and κύριε in viii. 24. It retains ἐπιστάτα, however, in viii. 45, ix. 33, ix. 49, and xvii. 13.

v. 14. The long interpolation at the end of the verse found

in D d is derived from Mark i. 45 and ii. 1, though there are slight differences. It is introduced here for harmonistic reasons. Was it taken from Tatian?

v. 27. After the name of Levi, D inserts τὸν τοῦ Ἀλφαίου, which, according to Zahn, is not original. See *Einl.*, ii. 263.

v. 39. Marcion agrees with D in the omission of this verse. Syr[sin] and Syr[cu] are, unfortunately, both defective here. To the authorities for its omission should be added r, which Weiss does not mention. On the reasons for the omission of the verse, see Zahn, *GK.*, i. 681.

vi. 5. Zahn is of opinion that the narrative of the man working on the Sabbath is taken from the same source as Mark xvi. 9 ff., and the pericope adulteræ, John vii. 53–viii. 11—viz. from Papias, and that it may be historically true. See his *Einleitung*, ii. 355. Westcott and Hort insert it among their "Noteworthy Rejected Readings," and Resch puts it among the "Logia Jesu." The Sinai-Syriac is defective here. For a long time it was thought that D and Stephen's β were different manuscripts, and they are here cited by Mill as "duo codices vetustissimi." This was shown to be a mistake by Bengel. Grotius also speaks of "nonnulli codices," and, according to Mill, thought the words were "adjecta ab aliquo Marcionita." The narrative seems to have remained quite unknown during the thousand years that elapsed between its relation by D and its publication by Stephen in 1550. According to Scrivener's edition of Codex Bezae, p. 435, none of the ten or twelve later hands that worked upon the manuscript down to the twelfth century and even later, seem to have touched the page on which this narrative stands (205*b*). It would seem, therefore, that no copy was ever made of this manuscript either. How much would have been lost had it also disappeared entirely?

vi. 10. Whether ὡς καὶ ἡ ἄλλη is genuine or not is of no material consequence so far as the exposition of the passage is concerned, but it is important in connection with the question of the relationship of Luke to the other Synoptics. The words are wanting in Mark iii. 5, but occur in Matt. xii. 13. See Zahn, *Einl.*, ii. 420.

vi. 31. Zahn is not sure if Marcion's text contained the Golden Rule in this passage in the negative form. *GK.*, i. 680; ii. 462.

vii. 27. Zahn thinks that ἔμπροσθέν σου should perhaps be omitted here (*Einl.*, ii. 316).

viii. 43. The words ἰατροῖς προσαναλώσασα ὅλον τὸν βίον are omitted in B D. Zahn holds it to be an "unworthy insinuation" to suppose that Luke, being himself a physician, toned down the expressions used by Mark as reflecting on the credit of his profession. The words are more likely to be a gloss from Mark. See *Einleitung*, ii. 437.

ix. 1. This verse is written three times over in codex Ξ. This cannot be a mistake. It might have been written twice by inadvertence, but not three times. The reason lies in the fact related—viz., the conferring of the power over evil spirits.

ix. 16. The reading εὐλόγησεν ἐπ' αὐτοὺς crept into the Vulgate manuscript called G by Wordsworth and White from the Old Latin. It is now attested also by Syr^{sin}. See Lewis, *Some Pages, in loco.* Zahn thinks it is deserving of special attention (*GK.*, i. 682). In this he is quite right.

ix. 18. Marcion here had τὸν υἱὸν τοῦ ἀνθρώπου. See Zahn, *GK.*, i. 686.

ix. 52–56. "It is impossible to suppose that the shorter form of the text is the original, and the longer due to a later interpolation, as this would imply what is incredible—viz., that one of Marcion's most antinomian readings found its way into a large number of Catholic manuscripts (D, the Peshitto, Harklean Syriac, most Latin witnesses, Chrysostom, etc.). The only probable explanation is that the Catholic writers objected to 54*b* and 55*b* on account of the use made of them by the Marcionites, and the apparently Marcionitic character of their contents. They were particularly offensive when taken together. Accordingly, some manuscripts like e and Syr^{cu} omitted only 54*b*, others, like A C, only 55*b*, while others again, like B L Syr^{sin}, boldly omitted both. . . . . The words were written by Luke and not invented by Marcion." Zahn, *GK.*, i. 681, ii. 468; *Einl.*, ii. 357.

x. 1. Instead of 70, B D, Tatian, the Syriac, and the Latin give 72. According to Zahn, the number has nothing to do with the Jewish enumeration of 70 Gentile nations, languages, or angels, nor the 70 members of the Sanhedrim, the 70 translators of the Old Testament, or with any other number 70. These 70 were not sent to the Gentiles, and Luke gives no hint of the allegorical significance of their number. Any such allegorizing was foreign both to himself and Theophilus, neither of whom was a Jew. See *Einl.*, ii. 392.

xi. 2. On βαττολογεῖν ὡς οἱ λοιποί in D, see my *Philologica Sacra*, pp. 27–36.

xi. 3. There is a certain amount of probability in Zahn's view that Marcion was led to insert σοῦ after ἄρτος ἐπιούσιος by thinking of John vi. 33 f., a passage which suggested itself to Origen also in this connection. See Zahn (*GK.*, i. 677, ii. 471), who thinks it probable that Marcion interpreted the words in a spiritual sense (=*supersubstantialis*).

xi. 53. The text of D here displays several marked variations, which, however, do not affect the sense of the passage. Zahn sees in them the arbitrary alterations of a later time; but Weiss thinks that in some particulars they may preserve the original.

xii. 1. Marcion, seemingly, and Jerome omit πρῶτον, which is attested by most of the Old Latin witnesses, with the exception of b. See Zahn, *GK.*, i. 692, ii. 474.

xii. 14. The words ἢ μεριστήν were omitted by Marcion (Zahn, *GK.*, i. 682). They are also wanting in the Sinai-Syriac (see Lewis, *Some Pages*).

xii. 38. The mention of the ἑσπερινὴ φυλακὴ by Marcion and other authorities is due, according to Zahn (*GK.*, ii. 683; *Einl.*, ii. 356), to the "magisterial consideration" that an orderly householder would not come home from the festivities after midnight or in the early hours of the morning, but at the latest in the first watch of the night, which was still called the evening. The reading is also found in Irenæus, but not in the Sinai-Syriac.

xii. 51. βαλεῖν (אַרְמָא) is found here in Syr[sin] in place of ποιῆσαι (D e Syr[cu]), mittere (b l), δοῦναι (usual text). This is interesting in view of Marcion. See Zahn, *GK.*, i. 604, ii. 476. Tertullian seems to have been mistaken in thinking that μάχαιραν was read in place of διαμερισμόν in this connection (machaeram quidem scriptum est. Sed Marcion emendat, quasi non et separatio opus sit machaerae).

xiii. 8. See above, p. 193 ff. Chase cites this passage as an indication of the laxity of transcription of which D was guilty in introducing what appears to be a common agricultural phrase. In Columella (*De Re Rustica*, xi. 3) we find "confecta bruma stercoratam terram inditam cophinis obserat." Chase also cites from the manuscript notes of Hort the reference to Plutarch, *Vita Pompeii*, 48, αὐτοῦ δέ τις κοπρίων κόφινον κατὰ κεφαλῆς τοῦ Βύβλου κατεσκέδασε. Better than any words of mine are those of Zahn, *Einleitung*, ii. 346:—No one with any perception of the difference between naïve originality and a regularity due to liturgical, dogmatic, and stylistic considerations can fail to assent to the following propositions—viz., (1) as regards contents and form of expression β (*i.e.* the text of D and its associates) has preserved much original matter, which from the very first was peculiarly liable to alteration, and which was set aside by the learned revisers from the end of the third century onwards (Lucian, Hesychius, Pamphilus), etc.

xvi. 12. While the common text with Syr[sin] reads ὑμέτερον, for which B L have ἡμέτερον, Marcion alone supports 157 e i l in reading ἐμόν. How is this to be explained? Compare above, p. 211, and Zahn, *GK.*, i. 682.

xvi. 19. Zahn denominates the introductory words found in D, εἶπεν δὲ καὶ ἑτέραν παραβολήν, "a liturgical gloss at the beginning of a pericope." Blass, too, omits them from the β text.

xvi. 22, 23. ℵ*, most Old Latin witnesses, and the Vulgate omit καί at the beginning of verse 23, and read ἐτάφη ἐν τῷ ᾅδῃ. This conjunction of the words is attested by Tatian and Marcion. The Sinai-Syriac presupposes the form "was buried. And being in Hades he lifted up his eyes." Attention may be drawn to the detailed notice of the different readings by Wordsworth and White. They say: Asyndeton in Johanne tolerabile, in Luca vix ferendum videtur. . . . Vix dubium est quin Lucas ipse scripserit καὶ ἐτάφη· καὶ ἐν τῷ ᾅδῃ, sed καί secundum in antiquissimis codicibus ut nunc in ℵ* casu omissum, ex conjectura tribus modis restitutum videtur, *sc.* καὶ ἐν τῷ ᾅδῃ, et ἐν δὲ τῷ ᾅδῃ et ἐν τῷ ᾅδῃ καὶ; quae lectiones omnes in codicibus Latinis referuntur, et tertiam ab Hieronymo ex traditione codicum suorum servatam magis quam ex ratione praelatam credimus. See Zahn, *GK.*, i. 682, ii. 480.

xvii. 11. "In all likelihood μέσον, without the preposition, as given by D, is the original form. This was variously replaced by ἀναμέσον (Ferrar Group), which is not amiss, by διὰ μέσου (A X, etc.), which is not so good, and by διὰ μέσον (ℵ B L), which is very bad." Zahn, *Einleitung*, ii. 391. Compare, also (for μέσον), Jülicher, *Gleichnisreden Jesu*, ii. 516.

xvii. 21. Marcion inserts ἰδοὺ before ἐκεῖ, which Zahn holds to be original. Syr^{sin} reads "here it is, or there it is," and therefore apparently omits the first ἰδοὺ as well. See Lewis, *Some Pages*. Wordsworth and White omit Tischendorf's $g^{1.2}$ from the authorities given by him in support of the omission of the second *ecce*.

xviii. 20. On the alterations made on the text here by the followers of Marcion, see Zahn, *GK.*, i. 616, ii. 484.

xviii. 25. The evidence in support of the readings τρήματος and βελόνης is very strong (ℵ B D L). The choice of the terms τρῆμα for τρύπημα or τρυμαλιά, and βελόνη for ῥαφίς, betrays the language of the physician. See *The Expositor's Greek Testament, Acts of the Apostles*, Introduction, pp. 9-11; Zahn, *Einleitung*, ii. 427 f., 435 f.

xx. 35. With reference to this verse, Tertullian makes the following charge against the Marcionites: Nacti enim scripturae textum ita in legendo decurrerunt: "quos autem dignatus est deus illius aevi"; "illius aevi" "deo" adjungunt .... cum sic legi oporteat, "quos autem dignatus est," ut facta hic distinctione post "deum" ad sequentia pertineat "illius aevi," etc. Zahn insists, as against Ritschl, Hilgenfeld, and Volkmar, that this requires not only the insertion of *ὑπὸ τοῦ Θεοῦ* after *καταξιωθέντες*, but also the active voice instead of the passive, as though the Marcionites had read *οὓς δὲ κατηξίωσεν ὁ θεὸς τοῦ αἰῶνος ἐκείνου, τυχεῖν καὶ τῆς ἀναστάσεως*. A similar change of construction occurs in Matt. xxv. 41, where it is quite certain that *τὸ ἡτοιμασμένον* is a correction of the stronger expression *ὃ ἡτοίμασεν ὁ πατήρ μου*, found in D, 1, 22, ten Old Latin manuscripts, and the earliest Fathers.

xxi. 30. The insertion of *τὸν καρπὸν αὐτῶν* may be but a trifling addition, intended to facilitate the sense (Zahn, *GK.*, i. 682), at the same time it is an interesting question how it comes to be in D, 157, 572 (see above, p. 211). Wordsworth and White say that D here is "ex Latinis forsan correctus." Syr[sin] agrees with Syr[cu] in inserting the words.

xxii. 16. For *πληρωθῇ* D reads *καινὸν βρωθῇ*. On this see my *Philologica Sacra*, p. 38, where it is suggested that these two readings are due to the confusion of כלה and אכל. This occurs several times in the Old Testament—*e.g.* 2 Chron. xxx. 22, where ויאכלו is represented in the LXX by *συνετέλεσαν*. But even apart from the question of a Hebrew foundation for the variant, I am inclined to regard *καινὸν βρωθῇ* as the original, and *πληρωθῇ* as the correction.

xxii. 16–21. The narrative of the Last Supper is extant in three forms. There is (1) the common text, (2) that exhibited by the two most important of the Old Latin witnesses (b, e), in which verse 16 is followed by 19*a*, after which come 17, 18, 21, so that 19*b* and 20 are wanting altogether. The text of Syr[sin] and Syr[cu] resembles this. There is further (3) the form exhibited by D and four Old Latins, which has the same order as (1), but omits verses 19*b*, 20. Zahn decides in favour of (2). See his *Einleitung*, ii. 357 ff. It is to be observed that the last discovered Syriac omits the nominatival clause τὸ ὑπὲρ ὑμῶν ἐκχυννόμενον after τῷ αἵματί μου, which is the only member that seems to be derived, not from 1 Cor. xi. 24 f., but from Matthew and Mark, and that does not agree in construction with the rest. This confirms the supposition that these two verses are not part of the original text. See Westcott and Hort, *Notes on Select Readings*, p. 63 f.; Plummer, *Commentary on St. Luke* in the International Series (T. & T. Clark). Compare also the article by the latter in Hastings' *Dictionary of the Bible* (Lord's Supper).

xxii. 36. On ἀράτω Basil the Great (d. 379) remarks: ἀράτω ἤτοι ἀρεῖ· οὕτω γὰρ καὶ τὰ πολλὰ τῶν ἀντιγράφων ἔχει . . . . ὡς μὴ εἶναι πρόσταγμα ἀλλὰ προφητείαν προλέγοντος τοῦ Κυρίου. At present D is quite alone in exhibiting the reading ἀρεῖ, which is worth noting in view of τὰ πολλὰ above.

xxii. 43, 44. These verses, with their mention of the Bloody Sweat and the Strengthening Angel, are omitted in A B R T, one Old Latin (f), the Bohairic, Sahidic, and Armenian versions, and the Sinai-Syriac. On the other hand, they are read by the Curetonian Syriac and the Peshitto, by the first and third hands of ℵ (the second hand enclosed them in brackets and cancelled them by means of dots), by D, as also by most of the Old Latin witnesses and the Vulgate. In the Greek Lectionaries they are omitted at the place where one would naturally expect them, but are found in the text of Matthew xxvi., together with portions of John xiii., in the Liturgy for Holy Thursday. This explains their insertion after Matt. xxvi. 39 in the Ferrar Group, at least in 13, 69, 124. The first of these, moreover, repeats the first two words of verse 43 (ὤφθη δὲ) in Luke, but no more. The necessary inference is that these verses are no part of the original text of Luke. They go back, however, to a time when extra-canonical traditions from the Life and Passion of Jesus were in circulation either orally or in writing. Zahn holds that D here has preserved what Luke wrote.

xxiii. 2. Zahn (*GK.*, i. 668) expressly points out that Marcion did not invent the additional words καὶ καταλύοντα τὸν νόμον καὶ τοὺς προφήτας, but found them in his exemplar. They occur in eight Old Latin and at least five Vulgate manuscripts, among which are four of the early codices collated by Wordsworth and White. One of them omits *et prophetas*, while some others have *nostram* after *legem*. Weiss takes no notice of this addition, nor of the further addition in verse 5 of the words ἀποστρέφοντα τὰς γυναῖκας καὶ τὰ τέκνα, supported by at least two Old Latin manuscripts, both of which add *non enim baptizantur sicut et nos*, while one of them exhibits the still further extension *nec se mundant*. If the addition were really made by Marcion, it would be all the more deserving of attention. The omission of the additional words in verse 2 is conceivably due to homoioteleuton, the eye of the scribe passing from καταλύοντα to κωλύοντα. In the case of verse 5, the mention of the women and children is quite consistent with what is said elsewhere in the narrative of the Passion, but the reference to baptism and purification is not so clear. Codex c has the singular *baptizatur*, but this is merely a clerical error.

xxiii. 34. The case of the First Word from the Cross is remarkable. This verse, containing the words, "Father, forgive them, for they know not what they do," is bracketed in א by an early corrector, and then restored; it is omitted by B without being replaced; it is inserted in D by a hand not earlier than the ninth century, and omitted by two Old Latin manuscripts, by two Bohairic codices, by the Sahidic version, and by the newly-discovered Sinai-Syriac. Is it possible to suppose that a Christian would have cancelled these words in a Bible manuscript like א, unless he had valid reasons for doing so in the tradition of the Gospel text? Zahn thinks they were omitted from D by mistake. On the Order of the Seven Words see my note in the *Expository Times* for June 1900, p. 423 f.

xxiii. 38. The notice of the three languages in which the Inscription on the Cross was written is taken from the text of John, and is read by all the Latin authorities with the single exception of codex Vercellensis (a). Syr[sin] is now to be added to the witnesses supporting the omission of the clause. Its use of the word בטקא reveals the ultimate affinity of this version with the Curetonian Syriac. The interpolation, as Zahn rightly asserts (*GK.*, i. 675), points to the estimation in which John's Gospel was held at an early date. Its insertion in Luke is undoubtedly erroneous.

xxiii. 43. The insertion of τῷ ἐπιπλήσσοντι in D, as well as the other variants found in this manuscript, viz. ἔλευσις, which is also read by D in Luke xxi. 7, and θάρσει, which is inserted by others in Luke viii. 48, is attributed by Zahn (*Einleitung*, ii. 356) to some preacher who sought in this way to contrast the penitent thief with his comrade. With the substantival expression ἔλευσις, compare δειπνοκλήτωρ exhibited by D in Matt. xx. 28. On the somewhat rare verb ἐπιπλήσσειν, compare the new edition of Origen, i. 5, 8; also Clement Alex. (ed. Dindorf), i. 186, 188.

xxiii. 53. After κείμενος U, with a few minuscules, reads καὶ προσεκύλισεν λίθον μέγαν ἐπὶ τὴν θύραν τοῦ μνημείου, while three Vulgate manuscripts have a similar addition *et inposito eo inposuit monumento lapidem magnum.* On the other hand D, with its Latin, reads καὶ θέντος (*leg.* τεθέντος) αὐτοῦ ἐπέθηκεν τῷ μνημείῳ λίθον ὃν μόγις εἴκοσι ἐκύλιον. The same thing is found in the Old Latin manuscript c, *et cum positus esset in monumento, posuerunt lapidem quem vix viginti volvebant.* The Sahidic and T[1] exhibit a similar expansion of the text. In this addition, which Scrivener thought was "conceived somewhat in the Homeric spirit," Harris detects a Latin hexameter which the scribe of Codex Bezae "deliberately incorporated into his text and then turned into Greek." See his *Study of Codex Bezae* in *Texts and Studies*, ii. 1, 47–52. Chase, on the other hand, adduces Josephus, *Bell. Jud.*, vi. 5, 3 (*Syro-Latin Text*, p. 62 ff.). Compare my *Philologica Sacra*, pp. 39, 58.

xxiv. 6. The reading *ὅσα* (D, c, Marcion, etc.) in place of *ὡς* is now attested also by the Sinai-Syriac.

xxiv. 32. In place of *καιομένη* (*α* text) and *κεκαλυμμένη* (D), Blass inserts *βεβαρημένη* in the *β* text on the authority of the old Syriac versions, the Armenian, and the Sahidic. But in the Syriac this last reading is due to a transcriptional error of יקיר for יקיד (see Blass himself, p. 120, and compare the variants מוקר and מוקד in Rahmani's *Testamentum D. N. Jesu Christi*, p. 112, 6); and as the Armenian is derived from the Syriac, the only question becomes whether the Sahidic reading is due to the same error. Κεκαλυμμένη in D, which has hitherto baffled explanation, is shown to be a purely clerical error by comparison with Heb. xii. 18, where also *κεκαυμένῳ* becomes *κεκαλυμμένῳ* in the Greek of D and in Pseudo-Athan. 57.

xxiv. 34. For *λέγοντας* D reads *λέγοντες*, which is simply a clerical error arising easily from the influence of the Latin, which would be the same in either case. For the conclusions drawn from this reading by Resch, see his *Aussercanonische Paralleltexte*, iii. 779 f. Other examples of the same mistake (—*ες* for, —*ας*) occur in Matt. xxii. 16; Acts vi. 11, xvi. 35; Rom. vi. 13. It is interesting to observe that Origen had *Σίμωνος καὶ* Κλεόπα (i. 184, ed. Koetschau).

xxiv. 37. Zahn (*GK.*, i. 681) rejects the supposition that the reading *φάντασμα* for *πνεῦμα* was coined by Marcion and taken from a Marcionite Bible into D. That he is right in doing so appears from Chase, who shows that *φάντασμα* here is the same as *δαιμόνιον ἀσώματον* in Ignatius (*Ad Smyrnaeos*, iii. 2). See my *Philologica Sacra*, p. 25. The Semitic equivalent of *φάντασμα* as well as of *δαιμόνιον* is שֵׁאד, שֵׁאדָא,[1] which is used in both the earlier Syriac versions,

[1] See also von Dobschütz, *Das Kerygma Petri*, p. 82, where he cites the passage of Origen relating to the *Doctrina Petri*, which is also quoted by Tischendorf on Luke xxiv. 39, and insists rightly that in the LXX. *δαιμόνιον* is never employed to represent רוּח. Conybeare's articles on "The Demonology of the New Testament" in the *Jewish Quarterly Review* (1896) I have unfortunately been unable to consult. Joh. Weiss never mentions *φάντασμα* in his article on *Dämonen und Dämonische* in the PRE³, iv.

the Curetonian and the Lewis, to represent φάντασμα in Matt. xiv. 26 and Mark vi. 49. I find that שארא is used for πνεῦμα in the translation of Eusebius (*Eccles. Hist.*, v. 16, ed. Wright-Maclean, p. 289).

xxiv. 39. All the authorities agree in saying that Marcion omitted the words ψηλαφήσατέ με καὶ ἴδετε, while Tertullian and Epiphanius state that he also omitted σάρκας καὶ. See Zahn, *GK.*, ii. 495, who adds that "the longer clause—*i.e.* ψηλαφήσατέ με καὶ ἴδετε—is also omitted by D, it (with the exception of Colbertinus), vg, but not Syr[cu], as Tischendorf wrongly states." This however is a misapprehension. The *om* in Tischendorf refers only to με after ψηλαφήσατε. This is omitted by Syr[cu] as well as by D and also by Syr[sin]. It would be more exact to say, however, that the καὶ before ἴδετε is also omitted by Syr[cu]. Moreover, Syr[sin] agrees with Syr[cu] in reading ὅτι ἐγώ εἰμι αὐτός after ἴδετε.

The subscription of certain minuscules states that Luke's Gospel was written fifteen years after the Ascension. Some say εἰς Ἀλεξάνδρειαν τὴν μεγάλην, others ἐν Ῥώμῃ, while one says very strangely, ἐν τῇ Ἀττικῇ τῆς Βοιωταίας, "for Theophilus, who became bishop after divine baptism." Λ, 262, 300 also contain here the notice of careful collation. The chapter enumeration in these manuscripts is not the same, being 342, 349, and 345 respectively.

John.

In this Gospel the attention of textual critics was long confined to the passage vii. 53–viii. 11. They failed to observe that in other places there are clauses and whole verses whose omission or interpolation has to be investigated in connection with vii. 53 ff., as, for example, iv. 9, v. 3, 4, and that interesting questions of textual criticism are raised in other parts of the book as well.

Chapter xxi., which the last two verses of the preceding chapter clearly show to be an Appendix, is equally well attested by all the authorities, while the omission of xx. 31 by the first hand of G is just one of those unaccountable phenomena which make their appearance so frequently in the domain of textual criticism. The same thing is probably to be said of the omission in א of the last verse of chapter xxi. Tischendorf was of opinion that this last verse in א, together with the concluding ornament and subscription, was not by the same hand (A) as had written the Gospel of John, but by another (D) who had acted as corrector, and had written part of the Apocrypha and six leaves of the New Testament. Tregelles, on the other hand, who examined the passage in Tischendorf's presence, thought the difference was due simply to the scribe having taken a fresh dip of the ink: that at all events the scribe who wrote the Gospel (A) did not intend it to conclude with verse 24, otherwise he would have added a concluding ornament and subscription as in the case of Matthew and Luke. The verse is found in all the other manuscripts and versions with which we are acquainted, and the question with regard to א is interesting only from the fact that a few manuscripts do contain a scholium to the effect that the verse is an addition (*προσθήκη*) inserted in the margin (*ἔξωθεν*) by one of the scholars (*τινὸς τῶν φιλοπόνων*),[1] and afterwards incorporated in the text by another without the knowledge of the former (*καταγέντος* (?) *δὲ ἔσωθεν ἀγνοίᾳ τυχὸν τοῦ πρώτου γραφέως ὑπό τινος τῶν παλαιῶν μέν, οὐκ ἀκριβῶν δέ, καὶ μέρος τῆς τοῦ εὐαγγελίου γραφῆς γενόμενον*). This entire note, however, is evidently no more than an inference drawn from the contents of the verse, as the Syriac Commentary of Theodore shows. See further, Zahn, *Einleitung*, ii. 495, and the reference to the Commentary of Ishodad in Sachau's *Verzeichnis der syrischen Handschriften in Berlin*, p. 307.

With respect to the pericope adulteræ, on the other hand, we may be quite certain that it did not originally stand in the

[1] This description is elsewhere understood as applying to Theodore of Mopsuestia.

position it now occupies (vii. 53–viii. 11), nor indeed in John's Gospel at all, although the decision of the Holy Office of the 13th February 1897, which was confirmed by the Pope two days later, obliges Catholic exegetes to hold it as genuine. It is omitted in a great many manuscripts and versions—*e.g.* in ℵ B L T. A and C are defective here, but the amount of space shows that they could not have contained it. It is omitted in the Syriac and Egyptian versions, in the Armenian and the Gothic, in some Old Latin codices, and in the earliest of the Greek and Latin Fathers. On the other hand it is found in all the manuscripts of Jerome and in Codex D, which is the only one of the earlier Greek manuscripts to contain it. In some minuscules and later Armenian manuscripts it stands at the end of the fourth Gospel, where now Westcott and Hort put it. In minuscule 225, written in the year 1192, it follows vii. 36; in the Georgian version it comes after vii. 44; while in the Ferrar Group—*i.e.* in minuscules 13, 69, 124, 346, 556—it is inserted after Luke xxi. 38. Its insertion after vii. 36 is probably the result of an accidental error. In the Greek Lectionaries the liturgy for Whitsunday begins at verse 37 and extends to verse 52, followed by viii. 12, so that the pericope was, by mistake, inserted before instead of after this lection. Its position in the Georgian version is the more remarkable, seeing that in the Old Latin Codex b, which contained the pericope by the first hand, the entire passage from vii. 44–viii. 12 has been *erased.* As a probable explanation of its position in the Ferrar Group after Luke xxi. 38, it has been suggested that the scribe inserted it there owing to the resemblance between Luke xxi. 37 and John viii. 1, and also between Luke xxi. 38 (*ὤρθριζε*) and John viii. 2 (*ὄρθρου*). Harris thinks that its proper place is in John between chapters v. and vi., because reference is made in v. 45, 46 to the Mosaic Law, which is also mentioned in viii. 5.

But the remarkable thing is that here again the text of D differs in a conspicuous manner from that of the other witnesses. In viii. 2 the words *καὶ καθίσας ἐδίδασκεν αὐτούς* are wanting: in verse 4 we meet the sentence *ἐκπειράζοντες αὐτὸν οἱ ἱερεῖς ἵνα ἔχωσιν κατηγορίαν αὐτοῦ*, which does not come till after verse 5 in the other text: for *μοιχείᾳ* D has *ἁμαρτίᾳ*: in verse 5 it reads, *Μωυσῆς δὲ ἐν τῷ νόμῳ ἐκέλευσεν τὰς τοιαύτας λιθάζειν*, for which the other text has *ἐν δὲ τῷ νόμῳ Μωσῆς ἐνετείλατο τὰς τοιαύτας λιθοβολεῖσθαι*: in verse 11, D has *ὕπαγε* where the other text has *πορεύου*. Now, if two persons got such an easy sentence as "Moses in the Law commanded to stone such" to translate from Latin, Hebrew, or any other language into Greek, one of them might quite well use *κελεύειν* and *λιθάζειν*, and the other *ἐντέλλεσθαι* and *λιθοβολεῖν*. And so the question is suggested whether the two forms in which the text exists were not derived from different sources, that of D, *e.g.*, from its Latin. But on closer examination the latter supposition is seen to be impossible. For the Latin corresponding to *ἔχωσιν κατηγορίαν αὐτοῦ* is "haberent accusare eum," showing that the Latin translator read *κατηγορεῖν* in his original,[1] and for *ὥστε πάντας ἐξελθεῖν* he has "uti omnes exire," where again the infinitive speaks for the priority of the Greek. On the other hand, it is to be observed that, according to Eusebius (*Eccles. Hist.*, iii. c. 39, *sub fin.*), Papias knew and recorded an incident *περὶ γυναικὸς ἐπὶ πολλαῖς ἁμαρτίαις διαβληθείσης ἐπὶ τοῦ Κυρίου, ἣν τὸ καθ' Ἑβραίους εὐαγγέλιον περιέχει*. So that the Gospel according to the Hebrews (*i.e.* the Palestinian Jewish Christians) contained a narrative similar to this, we may say quite confidently, contained this narrative. From that Gospel it was taken and inserted in some manuscripts after Luke xxi., in others after John vii. By the time of Augustine it was so widely propagated in the Latin that he thought it had been removed from certain manuscripts by people of weak faith, or rather by enemies of the true faith, "credo metuentes peccandi immunitatem dari mulieribus suis." The pericope is no part of John's Gospel, though it belongs to the oldest stock of evangelic tradition.

[1] The same variation occurs in Luke vi. 7, where ℵ* B S X read *κατηγορεῖν* (*κατηγορῆσαι* D), while ℵ[c] A E F have *κατηγορίαν*.

On the question whether it may not originally have stood between Mark xii. 17 and xii. 18, and so between Luke xx. 26 and xx. 27, see Holtzmann in the *ThLz.*, 1898, col. 536 f. *Vide supra*, p. 66.

i. 5. Zahn raises the question what word Ephraem found in his copy of the Diatessaron corresponding to κατέλαβε, seeing he gives *vicit.* In this connection I might (with the proviso that the reading may be more easily explained from the Armenian) point out that the Syriac word תשלט corresponds to καταλαβέτωσαν in Sirach xxiii. 6. This stands elsewhere for ἄρχω, δεσπόζω, ἐξουσιάζω, κατακυριεύω, κυριεύω, κρατῶ. כבש also frequently represents the Greek καταλαμβάνειν. The Sinai-Syriac for John i. 5 is unfortunately lost.

i. 13. The reading ὃς . . . . . ἐγεννήθη is, so far as is known at present, attested by Latin witnesses only, "qui natus est." But as Zahn is careful to point out (*Einl.*, ii. 518), it did not originate on Latin soil, for Justin presupposes it, and, moreover, Irenæus constantly applies the passage to the Incarnation, while the Valentinians, who had the usual text, were accused by Tertullian of falsification. And it is not proved that the two last-mentioned used anything but a Greek Bible.

i. 17. According to early testimony, this verse, so frequently quoted since the time of Ritschl, once ran: "The Law was given by Moses, but *its* truth came by Jesus." See Zahn, *Forsch.*, i. 121, 248.

i. 18. Zahn agrees with Hort in holding that the originality of the reading μονογενὴς θεὸς (without the article) is established. See Westcott and Hort, *Notes on Select Readings*; Zahn, *Einleitung*, ii. 544, 557; Westcott, *Commentary on John, in loco.* It may be mentioned here that Codex Monacensis of Origen's

Commentary on the Gospel of John has μονογενὴς θεός (with ὁ above μονογενὴς and υἱός above θεός) with ὁ and υἱός both written above the line in a later hand. This gave rise in the Codex Regius to the reading ὁ μονογενὴς υἱὸς θεός.

i. 28. Is it βηθαβαρά or βηθανίᾳ? The former is exhibited by the Sinai-Syriac, the Curetonian, and the margin of the Harklean, and the latter by the other three Syriac, and the Arabic Diatessaron. With regard to the former, is it the case, as is supposed by many, that it is due simply to a conjecture of Origen, and that Syr[cu] and Syr[sin] took it from him? According to Zahn (*GK.*, i. 406), Hilgenfeld pointed in this direction in the *ZfwTh.*, 1883, 119. See also Lagrange, *Origène, la critique textuelle et la tradition topographique* (*Revue Biblique*, iv., 1895, pp. 501–524). Origen explains *βηθανία* as *οἶκος ὑπακοῆς*, and the Syriac as "place of praise." Compare on this the much-discussed passage in the Gospel of Peter (*ὑπακοὴ ἠκούετο*, c. xi.). Βηθαβαρά, on the other hand, he interprets as *οἶκος κατασκευῆς*, so that he must either have spelt it Bethbara, בית ברא, as in Jud. vii. 24, or taken it as Beth-ha-bara. It is spelt *βηθααβαρά* in Lagarde's *Onomastica Sacra*, 240, 12, and Bethabara in 108, 6 (Bethbaara, Codex B). Jerome (see *Onomastica Sacra*) interpreted the name as "domus humilis (=?) vel vesperae" in Joshua xv. 6, as "domus multa vel gravis" in xv. 59, and as *ἀοίκητος* in xv. 61, following Symmachus. Luther had Betharaba, but in three impressions of the New Testament and in three of the Postils he had Bethabara (according to Bindseil-Niemeyer), and in the margin Bethbara, with a note in which reference is rightly made to Jud. vii. 24, "ut mysterium consonet." See my German or Greek-German New Testament. It may be asked if "Ainon" in John iii. 23 has any connection with Bethania. Compare בֵּית עֲנוֹת in Jos. xv. 59. For *ἐν Αἰνών* e has *in eremo* and f has *in deserto*. How is this to be explained? Compare Zahn, *Einleitung*, ii. 561.

i. 34. For *υἱὸς* ℵ*, Syr[cu], Syr[sin], and e read *ἐκλεκτός*. D is here defective. Zahn thinks the latter reading is original, and the former an example of an early and widely current alteration. Westcott and Hort insert *ἐκλεκτός* among their *Noteworthy Rejected Readings*. The two readings are combined in some manuscripts "electus filius Dei." See Zahn, *Einl.*, ii. 515, 544, 557.

i. 41. Zahn here decides for the nominative *πρῶτος*. Both the disciples of John who attached themselves to Jesus found their brother, but Andrew was the first to do so. See *Einleitung*, ii. 477 f.

ii. 2. In his Commentary on the Gospels, extant in the Armenian only, we find Ephraem saying, "Graecus scribit *recubuit et defecit vinum*" (§ 53), which shows that he had a Greek exemplar before him containing the itacism ἐκλίθη for ἐκλήθη. See Zahn, *Forsch.*, i. 62, 127, and compare Luke xiv. 8, where Antiochus, *Homil.*, iii., has κατακλιθῇς for κληθῇς.

ii. 3. Zahn is perhaps right when he says that no critic need doubt for a moment that the original reading is the longer, genuinely Semitic text exhibited by א*, the Harklean Syriac, and the best Latin manuscripts. D is defective, as also Syr^{cu} and Syr^{sin}.

iii. 5. βασιλείαν τῶν οὐρανῶν is attested only by א*, a few minuscules, by c m, and certain early Fathers, in place of βασιλείαν τοῦ θεοῦ, which has now the support of the Sinai-Syriac. Zahn thinks the former reading to be correct (*Einleitung*, ii. 294). If that is so, this will be the only place where the expression is found in the New Testament outside the Gospel according to Matthew, where it occurs some thirty-three or thirty-four times. See note on "The Kingdom of Heaven" in the *Expository Times* for February 1896, p. 236 ff.

iii. 24. Zahn (*Einl.*, ii. 515) thinks that the omission of the article before φυλακὴν shows that there was some uncertainty regarding the fact mentioned by John. This, however, is open to question. That the insertion or omission of the article may be of importance is shown by such examples as John v. 1; Matthew xxii. 23; Acts xvi. 6; James ii. 2.

iii. 34. Our knowledge of the text of the Sinai-Syriac here rests solely on the last reading of Mrs. Lewis: "Not according to his measure gave (or, gives) God the Father." This rendering, as well as the insertion of ὁ Θεός in many Greek texts, is due to the fact that πνεῦμα was not taken as the subject of the sentence.

iv. 1. For ὁ κύριος Tischendorf reads ὁ Ἰησοῦς, which is probably correct. Ὁ κύριος is elsewhere found only three times in John—viz., vi. 23, xi. 2, xx. 20. According to Zahn (*Einl.*, ii. 391) the first two passages are explanations outside the Gospel narrative interjected by the evangelist, while the words in the last passage are spoken from the point of view of the disciples.

iv. 9. The words *οὐ γὰρ συγχρῶνται Ἰουδαῖοι Σαμαρείταις* were retained by Lachmann and by Tischendorf in his seventh edition, because the only authorities known at that time for their omission were D a b e. But when the first hand of ℵ appeared in confirmation of the testimony of these witnesses, the words were dropped by Tischendorf and bracketed by Westcott and Hort. Syr[cu] and Syr[sin] insert them, and perhaps Tatian. Zahn is inclined to admit them. "The classic brevity of the interjected explanation speaks for its genuineness." See his *Einleitung*, ii. 549.

v. 1. *ἡ ἑορτή* is supported by ℵ C etc., and *ἑορτή* by A B D etc. On the chronology, see Zahn, *Einleitung*, ii. 516.

v. 3*b*, 4. After *ξηρῶν* D alone inserts *παραλυτικῶν*, and then adds, with A[2] C[3] I Γ Δ Λ Π (this last, however, with asterisks), the clause *ἐκδεχομένων τὴν τοῦ ὕδατος κίνησιν*. The shorter text is given by ℵ A* B C* L. The whole of the fourth verse is omitted by ℵ B C* D, 33, 157, 314. In this case D and A change sides. Within the limits of the verse there are a great many variations, which show that it is a very early addition. Some of the words are hapax legomena, like *δήποτε*, *ταραχή*, *νόσημα*. Zahn thinks the gloss may have been one of the "expositions" of Papias. According to the Commentary of Ishodad, Theodore of Mopsuestia did not consider this verse as part of the Gospel of John (Sachau, *Verzeichnis der syrischen Handschriften*, p. 308). See Zahn, *Einleitung*, ii. 557. Cyril says the incident occurred at Pentecost.

v. 36. Zahn (*Einl.*, ii. 557) calls *μείζων* a difficult reading, and one that could not have been invented: "I, as a Greater than John, have the witness of God."

vii. 8. *οὔπω* has taken the place of *οὐκ* in all the uncials except ℵ D K M P, a fact which reveals its antiquity. *Οὐκ* is retained also by Syr^{cu} and Syr^{sin}. The change was introduced to obviate the inconsistency between vii. 8 and vii. 10. Porphyry (apud Jerome, *Contra Pelagium*, ii. 17) on the ground of οὐκ, accused Jesus of "inconstantia et mutatio," and Schopenhauer (*Grundprobleme der Ethik*, 2nd edition, p. 225) cited this passage as justifying an occasional falsehood, saying that "Jesus Christ himself on one occasion uttered an intentional untruth." See Zahn, *Einleitung*, ii. 547.

vii. 15. See *Addenda*, p. xvi.

viii. 57. According to the authority cited in the *ThLz.*, 1899, p. 176, the first hand of Codex B is supposed to have written εορακεσε: "the final ε has been erased, and the ε preceding it changed into α." I have examined the photograph of B in the Stuttgart Library, and can find no trace of an ε ever having stood after σ. The blank space of the size of two letters is meant to divide the sentences. It is the case, however, though neither Tischendorf, Fàbiani, nor the pamphlet of 1881 mentions it, that the first hand wrote εορακες, which was then made into εωρακας by means of a stroke drawn through the ο. The matter is not insignificant in view of what is said in Westcott and Hort's *Notes on Orthography*, Appendix, p. 168. Burkitt supposes that εορακεσε was the reading of the ancestor of ℵ B (*Texts and Studies*, vol. v. 5. p. ix).[1]

[1] When examining Codex B I took occasion to look at certain other passages, and discovered some strange mistakes in Tischendorf's statements with regard to that manuscript, as I did previously in the case of Codex D. In 3 John 13 B has ἀλλὰ for ἀλλ', on which Tischendorf has no note. Westcott and Hort mention the passage in their *Notes on Orthography*, ii. p. 153, but say nothing about B. On Jude 5 we find Tischendorf saying in his Apparatus: ειδοτας sine υμας cum A B C^2 . . . . ς (Gb°°) add. υμας cum ℵ K L. But υμας stands quite plain in B. Had they known this, Tischendorf and Westcott and Hort would certainly have printed their text differently. How far back this false testimony with regard to B extends I am unable to certify. It is found in Tischendorf's seventh edition of 1859, and in Huther's Commentary of the same date. I repeat my Ceterum censeo, that two or three sharp eyes should really revise the statements current about B. This one is repeated from Tischendorf by Baljon, Weiss, and all our Commentators. At the same time, Weiss has quite properly inserted υμας in his text, on the ground that while there was no occasion for its interpolation, its omission is quite conceivable. He will, no doubt, be gratified to see his reasoning confirmed by this weighty testimony afforded by Codex B.

xii. 7. *τετήρηκεν*, without *ἵνα*, has the support of a comparatively large number of manuscripts. Peerlkamp and De Koe read *ἵνα τί . . . . τετήρηκεν*; Zahn (*Einl.*, ii. 518) has no doubt that the correct reading is *ἵνα . . . . τηρήσῃ*, and that it was replaced by *τετήρηκεν* (without *ἵνα*) on the ground that this Mary was not among the women who came to the sepulchre to anoint the body of Jesus. He says that the true text presupposes that Mary would like to use the remainder of the ointment to anoint the body of Jesus after his death, and that the words of Jesus were intended to prevent Mary and the disciples afterwards following the suggestion of Judas.

xiii. 2. The change of a single letter here is important from a harmonistic point of view. ℵ* B L read *δείπνου γινομένου*, *i.e.*, "during supper," but ℵ^c A D have *δείπνου γενομένου*, which means "after supper." Compare Zahn, *Einleitung*, ii. 520.

xiii. 34. On the form in which this saying was cited by the Marcionites, see Zahn, *GK.* i. 678.

xviii. 12 ff. The Sinai-Syriac, probably following Tatian, gives the following arrangement of the verses—viz., 12, 13, 24, 14, 15, 19–23, 16–18, 25–28. On this see Zahn, *Einl.*, ii. 521. Spitta would arrange the verses, 12, 13, 19–23, 24, 14, 15–18, 25*b*, 27, 28. See Zahn, *Einl.*, ii. 558. It does sometimes happen that a leaf of a manuscript is misplaced, but it is hard to account for such transpositions as these. Compare the *Journal of Theological Studies*, October 1900, p. 141 f.

xix. 5. Though not properly connected with the criticism of the text, the question may be asked here, by way of a contribution to a subject much discussed of late, whether the expression *ἰδοὺ ὁ ἄνθρωπος* may not be connected with בר נשא. Compare *ὁ ἄνθρωπος* and *ὁ υἱὸς τοῦ ἀνθρώπου* in Mark ii. 27, 28. In this passage of John, B omits the article before *ἄνθρωπος*, reading *ἰδοὺ ἄνθρωπος* simply. See the *Expository Times*, November 1899, p. 62 ff., "The Name Son of Man and the Messianic Consciousness of Jesus," where Schmiedel's article with the same title in the *Protestantische Monatshefte* is noticed.

xix. 37. The quotation, according to Zahn, is made from the Hebrew. The LXX has *ἐπιβλέψονται πρὸς μὲ ἀνθ' ὧν κατωρχήσαντο*. The later Greek versions all seem to have kept the first three words as in the LXX but to have variously corrected the second clause, for which Aquila gives *σὺν ᾧ ἐξεκέντησαν*, Theodotion *εἰς ὃν ἐξεκέντησαν*, Symmachus *ἔμπροσθεν ἐπεξεκέντησαν*. Compare with this Apoc. i. 7, *οἵτινες αὐτὸν ἐξεκέντησαν*; Barnabas vii. 9, *ὄψονται αὐτὸν . . . κατακεντήσαντες*; Justin, *Dial.* 32, *ἐπιγνώσεσθε εἰς ὃν ἐξεκεντήσατε*. It has accordingly been supposed that John in the Gospel and Apocalypse followed some unknown Greek version which exhibited the characteristic forms *ὄψονται* (found only in John and Barnabas) and *εἰς ὃν ἐξεκέντησαν* (given by John, Justin, Theodotion, and partly by Aquila). But this supposition is simply a proof of unwillingness to admit a palpable fact—viz., that in the Gospel and Apocalypse John gives an independent rendering of the original text of Zechariah xii. 10, and that Barnabas and Justin follow John. See Zahn, *Einleitung*, ii. 563.

The subscriptions state that the fourth Gospel was written thirty or thirty-two years after the Ascension, at Ephesus, in the reign of Nero, or, as some say, of Domitian. It is also said to have been published by Gaius, the host of the Apostles (*διὰ Γάϊον τὸν ξενοδόχον τῶν ἀποστόλων*). Others say that it was dictated to Papias of Hierapolis the disciple of the Apostle. On the alleged autograph (*ἰδιόχειρον*) preserved at Ephesus, see above, p. 30.

ACTS.

It would unduly enlarge the extent of this work were I to go on mentioning all the passages in the Acts that are more or less striking from the textual point of view. This book has already been more frequently referred to than the others. I would again refer the student to Zahn's *Introduction*. I agree with that writer in thinking it impossible in many cases to suppose that a scholiast manufactured the text we now find in Codex D with no other material before him save the usual text and his inkhorn. At the same time there is undoubtedly room for much diversity of opinion with respect to many matters of detail. I would instance such a simple narrative as that of Acts iii. 1–5, and ask what reasonable ground a copyist could have had for altering ὃς into *οὗτος*, *ἀτενίσας* into *ἐμβλέψας*, *βλέψον* into *ἀτένισον*, *ἐπεῖχεν* into *ἀτενίσας* or *vice versa*, or for omitting or inserting *ὑπάρχων* or *λαβεῖν*.[1] Such changes might, however, be introduced by an author who writes a passage twice over. Without himself being fully conscious of his reasons for doing so, he might substitute a final construction for a participle, introduce or remove an asyndeton, replace one word by its synonym, and make all the striking linguistic changes which a comparison of the two texts reveals.

Time will show whether I am right in my conjecture that *ἐβαρύνατε* in iii. 14 is due to an error in translation. In illustration of the interchange of *λαοῦ* and *κόσμου* in ii. 47, I have cited in *Philologica Sacra*, p. 39, a number of instances of the confusion of עם or עמא with עלם or עלמא, to which I would now add Daniel viii. 19, Sirach xlv. 7; xlvii. 4; Matt. i. 21 (in the Curetonian Syriac). Compare also Eusebius, *Eccles. Hist.*, iv. 15, 26; *History of Mary*, ix. 17; xiv. 11 (ed. Budge). Whether the change in the passage in question is really to be explained in this way, or by the supposition of an "anti-Judaic tendency," as Corssen prefers (*Göttinger gelehrte Anzeigen*, 1896, vi. 444), may be left an open question for the present. I would just point to one thing in favour of my view, and in answer to what Zahn says in his *Einleitung*, ii. 423. He says there: "Linguistic considerations are against the supposition that a pure Greek like Luke, the physician of Antioch, was

[1] Further instances of changes requiring investigation are:—*ερωταν* and *παρακαλειν*; *οραν* and *θεασθαι*; *αγειν* and *φερειν*; *ερχεσθαι* and *υπαγειν*; *υπαρχειν* and *ειμι*; *συν* and *μετα*; *εις* and *εν*; *εως*, *μεχρι* and *αχρι*; *ενωπιον* and *εμπροσθεν*; *ετερος* and *αλλος*; *οικος* and *οικια*; *παις* and *παιδιον*; *πολις* and *κωμη*; *λαος* and *οχλος*; *ναος* and *ιερον*; *φεγγος* and *φως*; active and middle voice, *αρχεσθαι*, etc.

able to read a Hebrew book. For a thousand Jews (Syrians and Copts) who were able at that time to read, write, and speak Greek, there would be at most a single Greek possessed of a corresponding knowledge of Hebrew or Aramaic. And I confess that I have hitherto sought in vain for this rara avis." Quite true, but how do we know that the physician of Antioch was a pure Greek? All the Prologues to the Gospels unanimously call him "natione Syrus." I have pointed out in my *Philologica Sacra*, p. 13, what is very generally admitted, that in the New Testament Ἕλληνες denotes simply the "heathen," whether they speak Greek or not.[1] The woman mentioned in Mark vii. 26 was a Ἑλληνὶς Συρο-Φοινίκισσα τὸ γένος, and in the same way Luke was a Ἕλλην of Antioch (Acts xi. 20), but Σύρος τὸ γένος. He is one of the thousand who could read, write, and speak Greek, though he was not above making such a mistake in translation when using a Hebrew or Aramaic book as I think he certainly does in Luke xi. 41, and as I am inclined to think he does in Acts iii. 14, till I find a better explanation of the reading ἐβαρύνατε than has yet been given.[2] I am glad to see from Zahn that more than seventy years ago, in his dissertation entitled *De Codice Cantabrigiensi* (1827), p. 16, Schultz suggested that the text of D may perhaps be

[1] See, however, Romans i. 14, and compare Zahn, *Einl.*, i. 263.—*Tr.*

[2] I have already (p. 37) referred to the frequency with which mistakes, often quite incredible mistakes, in translation occur. A few additional instances may be cited here.

There is, for example, that of Ephraem in John ii. 2, mentioned above, p. 287.

According to Aphraates 41, 16, Jesus promised to the mourners דלהין נתכשפון, *i.e.* that they should be *entreated*. The writer of the text, therefore, that Aphraates used, must have taken παρακαλεῖν here in the sense of "to entreat." See Zahn, *Forschungen*, i. 78.

The same writer (383, 16) renders the words in Luke xvi. 25 νῦν δὲ ὧδε παρακαλεῖται in the form יומנא דין בעית מנה, *i.e.* "but to-day thou *entreatest* of him", where παρακαλεῖν is again taken in the sense of "to entreat", though a different word is used for it. See Zahn, *ibid.*

Again, Aphraates (390, 4) renders παράκλησιν (αὐτῶν) in Luke vi. 24 בעותהין, "their *prayer*, their *request*." Zahn, *ibid.*

The last clause of John v. 14 is rendered "that thou mayest have need of nothing else," where χρεία must have been read instead of χεῖρον. Zahn, *Forschungen*, i. 161 f. Compare also the Syriac text of Apoc. ii. 13; viii. 13, etc.

derived from a Syriac version. According to what I have said above on Tatian, this view must certainly be admitted as possible, and I see that it has been revived by Chase.

A new solution of the textual problem in Acts has been suggested by Aug. Pott (*Der abendländische Text der Apostelgeschichte und die Wir-Quelle*, Leipzig, 1900). He thinks that the original narrative drawn up by Luke existed as a separate work for some time after it had been worked up into our canonical Acts, and that notes were taken from the former and inserted in the margin of the latter, and in this way came into the text of Codex D and its associates. Against this, however, there is the fact that similar problems emerge in the Gospel of Luke where this distinction cannot be made.

For the sake of brevity I append notes to a few passages only of Acts.

But at the outset I must express my surprise that Wendt, even in his eighth edition of 1899, repeats the statement that the title of the book in D is *πρᾶξις ἀποστόλων*. Even without the assurance given by Blass in his *Grammatik*, § iii. 1, 2, it should be borne in mind that "*δωσιν* stands equally for both *δῶσιν* and *δώσειν*," and that accordingly *πραξις* may be either *πράξεις* or *πρᾶξις*. In the case before us it is the former. As illustrations take the following from D in Acts:—*δυναμι*, iii. 12, iv. 7; *πιστι*, vi. 7; *ις*, iv. 30; *μηνας τρις*, vii. 20; and conversely *θλειψεις μεγαλη*, vii. 11; *μερεις*, viii. 21; *δυναμεσει* and *σημιοις* side by side in ii. 22. Compare also Mark vi. 2; vi. 14; xiii. 25; Luke xxi. 26; Acts viii. 13; (*δυναμις τοιαυται*; *αι δυναμις*; *δυναμις μεγαλας*). It is true that in every case in which the title is written out, which occurs only five times altogether, it is *πραξις*, but this is to be understood as plural, like *actus* in the Latin. It came afterwards to be used as singular in the Syriac (Zahn, *Einl.*, ii. 370, 383, 388), but that is nothing strange. We say "the Times *says*"; and we have an analogy in the use of the word *biblia* in the Middle Ages when the neuter plural *biblia bibliorum* became *biblia bibliae* (singular feminine).

i. 23. It is a matter of commentary rather than of textual criticism, but Wendt, in his eighth edition, asserts that nothing further is known of this Joseph surnamed Justus. Eusebius, on the authority of Papias, mentions παράδοξον περὶ Ἰοῦστον τὸν ἐπικληθέντα Βαρσαβᾶν γεγονός, ὡς δηλητήριον φάρμακον ἐμπίοντος καὶ μηδὲν ἀηδὲς διὰ τὴν τοῦ Κυρίου χάριν ὑπομείναντος (*Eccles. Hist.*, iii. 39). The name of Aristion is inserted in the margin of this passage in Rufinus's Latin translation of Eusebius. This marginal gloss acquires a peculiar importance from the fact that the name Ariston is inserted in the Etschmiadzin manuscript of the Gospels over Mark xvi. 9–20, apparently ascribing these verses or their main contents to him. Compare Zahn, *Einleitung*, ii. 231, and see Plate IX.

iv. 6. On the reading Ἰωνάθας in D for Ἰωάννης, see above, p. 243.

iv. 24. } See Harris, *Two Important Glosses in the Codex*
v. 39. } *Bezae*, *Expositor*, November 1900, pp. 394–400.

xi. 27, 28. In his treatise, "On the Original Text of Acts xi. 27, 28" (*Berliner Sitz.-Berichte*, Heft 17), Harnack comes to the conclusion that the Western text here cannot be the original.

xv. 20, 21. On Harnack's examination of the Apostolic Decree, see Selbie in the *Expository Times* for June 1899, p. 395. Harnack comes to the same results as Zahn, but draws the opposite conclusion from them. See above, p. 232 f.

xvi. 6. The article is omitted before Γαλατικὴν χώραν by ℵ A B C D minuscules. For this Blass, on the authority of p, which reads "Galatie regiones," substitutes τὰς Γαλατικὰς χώρας = "vicos Galatiae." On this see Zahn, *Einleitung*, i. 133. The omission of the article does not necessitate taking τὴν Φρυγίαν as an adjective (so Wendt[8]); it might still be rendered "through Phrygia and Galatian territory."

xvii. 27. In my *Philologica Sacra*, p. 42, I say that it was easier to change τὸ θεῖον (β) into τὸν θεόν (α) than *vice versa.* To this Wendt replies in his eighth edition, p. 294, by saying, "In all probability offence was taken at the representation of

God himself as an object of τὸ ψηλαφᾶν." Yes, there is a considerable difference between Hector alive and Hector dead, and of the latter it could be truly said (*Iliad*, xxii. 372 f.):

> Ὧδε δέ τις εἴπεσκεν ἰδὼν ἐς πλησίον ἄλλον·
> Ὢ πόποι ἦ μάλα δὴ μαλακώτερος ἀμφαφάασθαι.

But the θεῖον of which Paul speaks on the Areopagus is most assuredly no more and no less a *noli me tangere* than the θεός. Among the witnesses in support of τὸ θεῖον is Clement of Alexandria. I can only repeat what Zahn says: "Whoever is careful to bear in mind that our earliest manuscripts are some two hundred years later than Marcion, Tatian, and Irenæus, and has any sense of the difference between naïve originality and a regularity due to liturgical, dogmatic, and stylistic considerations," cannot but judge differently with respect to β.

xviii. 3. See my article, "The Handicraft of St. Paul," in the *American Journal of Biblical Literature*, xi. 2, 1892, on *lorarius* as the Syriac rendering of σκηνοποιός = ἱμαντοτόμος, σκυτοτόμος, leather-cutter, and the notes in the *Expository Times* for December 1896, and January and March 1897. Chrysostom calls Paul σκυτοτόμος, and in the *Inventio Sanctae Crucis*, it is said, "exercebat artem scaenographiam." This last word I have explained as a confusion with σκηνορραφίαν, as Professor Ramsay also does. In the *Compendious Syriac Dictionary* of J. Payne Smith (which must not be confounded with the *Thesaurus* of her father), *lorarius* is explained as "a maker of rough cloth for tents or horse-cloths." But there is nothing said about tents even by the Syriac scholiasts. The correct meaning will be found in Brockelmann. Celsus (Origen, *Contra Celsum*, vi. 33) speaks of ἐκεῖνος ἀπὸ κρημνοῦ ἐρριμμένος, ἢ εἰς βάραθρον ἐωσμένος, ἢ ἀγχόνῃ πεπνιγμένος, ἢ σκυτοτόμος, ἢ λιθοξόος, ἢ σιδηρεύς. Paul is evidently referred to after Judas Iscariot, but who are meant by λιθοξόος and σιδηρεύς?

xix. 6. I fail to understand how anyone can dismiss D here

with the remark, "On account of Paul's express declaration as to the desirability of the gift of tongues being supplemented by that of interpretation (1 Cor. xiv. 5, 13, 27), this addition seemed to be required in this case where Paul communicated the gifts of the Spirit" (Meyer-Wendt, eighth edition, p. 312).

xx. 4. For Δερβαῖος D* has Δουβεριος or Δουβριος, and g *doverius.* Moreover, D* has Βερυιαιος, not Βερυαιος, as Tischendorf has it. Valckenaer and Blass insert a comma after Γάϊος, and substitute δὲ for καὶ after Δερβαῖος, with the result that Gaius becomes a Thessalonian, and Timothy a Derbean. For this Zahn sees no necessity. See his *Einleitung*, i. 149.

xxviii. 16. On στρατοπεδάρχης (β) which Gigas renders *princeps peregrinorum*, see note on xxvii. 1, in Knowling's *Acts of the Apostles*, *Expositor's Greek Testament*, vol. ii. p. 516; article "Julius" in Hastings' *Bible Dictionary*; Ramsay in the *Expositor*, November 1900; Zahn, *Einleitung*, i. 389 f. Wendt (eighth edition, p. 420) omits the words in xxviii. 16, on the ground that their omission either by mistake or design is very unlikely, but their insertion, on the other hand, quite intelligible. This only shows how little reliance can be placed on subjective criticism.

We are not yet sufficiently well acquainted with the subscriptions of the minuscules, but it may be cited here that in one of them Luke is called συνέκδημος Παύλου, and in another θεηγόρος ὁ συγγράψας αὐτὰς ἐμπνεύσει θείᾳ.

Pauline Epistles.

In the arrangement of the books of the New Testament, it has become customary to follow the order adopted by Tischendorf and Westcott and Hort, who place the Catholic Epistles before the Pauline. In the Stuttgart edition of the New Testament, however, I have, in accordance with earlier usage, put the Pauline Epistles after the Gospels and Acts. Considering what is said by Hort himself in § 422 of his *Introduction*, and also what we find in No. 6 of Berger's List of the various arrangements of the books of the New Testament (*Histoire de la Vulgate*, p. 339 f.), it might have been more correct to have put Paul immediately after the Gospels, as in Codex Sinaiticus. But seeing that the Latin and German Bibles at present exhibit the order, Gospels, Acts, Pauline Epistles, Catholic Epistles, and that Meyer's Commentary is also arranged on this principle, I have retained this arrangement for the sake of uniformity.

Here again I must refer the student for matters of detail to larger works, especially to Zahn's *Einleitung*. A few of the more important passages will be considered in the sequel, but previously something may be said here of the origin and circulation of the collective writings of Paul.

1. Paul, accompanied by Silvanus and Timothy, came from Philippi to Thessalonica on his second missionary journey, somewhere about the year 54, though Harnack puts it as early as 49–50. There he gathered together a church in the short space of three or four weeks, if we may credit the account given in Acts xvii. 2 in this particular. At all events he was not long there. Disturbances similar to those in Philippi arose, which compelled him to leave the city. He came to Athens. In his anxiety over the internal and external circumstances of the newly-founded church at Thessalonica, he sent back Timothy from Athens to confirm those he had left behind. When his messenger returned he wrote to the Thessalonian Church, in all probability not from Athens but from Corinth, where he had gone in the interval of Timothy's absence. This letter we know as the First Epistle to the Thessalonians. It is uncertain whether the apostle, as in most other cases, dictated the epistle, writing only the salutation and concluding benediction with his own hand (compare 2 Thess. iii. 17: ὁ ἀσπασμὸς τῇ ἐμῇ χειρὶ Παύλου, ὅ ἐστιν σημεῖον ἐν πάσῃ ἐπιστολῇ· οὕτως γράφω),[1] or

[1] On the custom of dictating letters, see Norden, *Die antike Kunstprosa* (1898), p. 954 ff. On the autograph additions to the letters of the Emperor Julian, see Bidez and Cumont, *Recherches etc.*, p. 19 (see above, p. 174).

whether he wrote it all himself in large letters, as he did in the case of the Epistle to the Galatians which he wrote πηλίκοις γράμμασι (Gal. vi. 11), either on account of some affection of the eyes or because he was a craftsman and had little practice in writing. The epistle was intended for the entire church at Thessalonica, of which Aristarchus, Secundus, and perhaps also Gaius (see above, on Acts xx. 4), are known to us by name. It was probably addressed to the oldest, or most prominent, or most active member of the Christian community. At the close of the epistle, the writer expressly adjures them to see that it is read by all the brethren. It would, therefore, be read aloud at the next meeting of the congregation. There and then, some poor slave or aged woman would ask to have the letter for the purpose of copying it. What became of the original we do not know. In the very first copy that was made, mistakes and alterations would make their appearance, and these would be multiplied with every fresh copy.

2. At the close of the Epistle to the Colossians (iv. 16), Paul asks that when they have read it, they will see that it is also read in the Church of Laodicæans, and that they themselves read the epistle from Laodicæa (τὴν ἐκ Λαοδικείας). From this it has generally been supposed that an epistle of Paul to Laodicæa has been lost. An epistle with this title was restored at a very early date, in the second century. It is no longer extant in Greek, but many Latin manuscripts and editions of the Bible contain it, and it is also found in the pre-Lutheran German Bibles. But the epistle from Laodicæa referred to by the Apostle may perhaps have been the circular letter which we now know as the Epistle to the Ephesians, and which may have been intended to go, among other places, to Laodicæa, and from there to Colossae. However that may be, we see that at a very early date there were epistles of Paul to various places, and that copies of these might be made at each place, and still further distributed. A parallel case is that of the Koran, the different recensions

of which are distinguished according to the cities whence they originated. Even at that time, therefore, the beginnings of a collection of the Pauline Epistles might be made. By the time that the Second Epistle of Peter was written, it was known that "brother Paul, according to the wisdom given to him, had written many epistles, in which were some things hard to be understood" (2 Peter iii. 15).

3. When a great man dies, we have usually a collection of the letters he received in his lifetime, but not of those he himself wrote, and to collect these last is frequently a matter of considerable difficulty. We have therefore reason to congratulate ourselves that we have, within the covers of the New Testament, epistles of Paul addressed to the most diverse regions—to Macedonia (1 and 2 Thess., Philippians), to Achaia (1 and 2 Corinthians), to Asia Minor (Ephesians, Colossians, Galatians), and to Italy (Romans), not to speak of the so-called Pastoral or private Epistles—epistles, moreover, the dates of which extend over a period of at least eight years.[1] It is, of course, evident that the appearance of an epistle in this collection is not in itself a guarantee of Pauline authorship. But on the other hand, the collection must have been made at a very early date, because we find, almost without exception, not only the same number of Pauline epistles, but also the same order of their arrangement. There is scarcely any evidence of the circulation of a particular epistle by itself. True, the order now usually adopted, which has been the prevailing order from the fourth century onwards and which seems, for the most part, to arrange the epistles according to their length (Romans, 1 and 2 Corinthians, Galatians, Ephesians, and so on), is not the original. In the Muratorian Canon (so called from its discoverer), which is a very old catalogue of the books of the Bible, the Epistles to the Corinthians stand

[1] What an amount of perplexity would have been avoided had Paul been in the way of dating his letters exactly, or had the copyists preserved the dates, supposing they were there originally! One, but only one, of the epistles of Ignatius bears a date—viz. that to the Romans: ἔγραψα ὑμῖν ταῦτα τῇ πρὸ ἐννέα καλανδῶν Σεπτεμβρίων (x. 3).

at the head of the collection and that to the Romans at the end. Tertullian had the same arrangement, while Marcion, for dogmatic reasons apparently, put Galatians first, then 1 and 2 Corinthians, Romans. The present condition of our Epistle to the Romans is also supposed to point to its former position at the end of Paul's epistles to the churches. In that epistle the concluding doxology is found at different places, while many look upon chap. xvi. 1–23 as a separate document, originally intended for Ephesus, which was attached to the entire collection at the end. Among other varieties of arrangement it may be mentioned that Colossians frequently followed 2 Thessalonians. When and where the first collection took its rise, and by whom the second arrangement was introduced, can no longer be determined with certainty. Zahn thinks the first originated at Corinth about the year 85, his reason being that it seems to be presupposed in the Epistle to the Corinthians written by Clement of Rome about the year 95. The second he would date from Alexandria, between 220 and 260. If we might suppose that all our extant manuscripts are derived, not from separate copies of the Epistles, but from a copy of the earliest collection, it would serve to explain how it comes that certain corruptions have found their way into the text of all our manuscripts—*e.g.* in Colossians ii. 18. On the other hand, the variations at the end of Romans, *e.g.*, are of such a sort that their origin seems to be anterior to the formation of the collection.

It is not so difficult to understand how it is that the Epistle to the Hebrews, which, it is certain, was not written by Paul, varies so much with regard to its position in the collection. In the Syriac Bible, and in the majority of later Greek manuscripts, it comes after all the Pauline epistles, the reason being that the Syrian Church did not consider it to be really of the number of these. (See Westcott, *Bible in the Church*, p. 233 f.). In the earlier Greek manuscripts, however, it occupies the tenth place, standing between the epistles of Paul to the churches and the Pastoral Epistles. In the early Sahidic version, and in the Commentaries of Theodore of Mopsuestia, it is found between 2 Corinthians and Galatians; in the parent manuscript of Codex B it stood between Galatians and Ephesians. In his *Histoire de la Vulgate*, p. 539 f., Berger gives seventeen different ways in which the Pauline epistles are arranged in Latin Bibles—viz., Col., Thess., 1 Tim.; Thess., Col., 1 Tim.; Phil., Laod., Col.; Col., Laod., Thess.; Col., Thess., Laod.; Thess., Col., 1, 2 Tim., Tit., Laod.; Thess., Col., Laod.; Phil., Laod., Heb.; Heb., Laod.; Heb., 1, 2 Tim., Tit., Phil.; Apoc., Laod.; Ephes., Col.; Gal., Laod., Ephes.; Ephes., 1, 2, 3 Cor., Laod.; Phil., Thess., 1 Tim.; Apoc., 3 Cor.; Col., Phil.

Romans.

With regard to the very name and introduction of the Epistle to the Romans, it is worth observing, that while the words ἐν Ῥώμῃ are read in verses 7 and 15 by all our manuscripts, with the sole exception of G, their omission by Origen is attested by the critical work discovered by von der Goltz on Mount Athos (*vide supra*, pp. 90, 190), which says that Origen takes no notice of the words: *οὔτε ἐν τῇ ἐξηγήσει οὔτε ἐν τῷ ῥητῷ μνημονεύει.* The Latin commentary has them, and presupposes them in the exposition. Our editions of Origen have hitherto given them once in the Greek as well (iv. 287), but we must wait for the new edition before we can say with certainty that this is correct. The matter is not devoid of importance. If the omission is original, then it is possible to think that Romans, like Hebrews, was originally a circular letter; while on the other hand, if the words are an integral part of the epistle, we may suppose with von der Goltz that they were afterwards dropped when the epistle began to be read in church, so as to make it applicable to all Christians. See Jacques Simon, *Revue d'Histoire et de Littérature religeuses*, iv. 2 (1899), 177; Zahn, *Einleitung*, i. 278; *ThLbl.*, 1899, 179.

i. 3. On the Syriac reading "of the house of David," see Vetter, *Der apokryphe dritte Korintherbrief*, 1894, p. 25, and my

Note in the Lectionary published in *Studia Sinaitica*, vi. (see above, p. 106).

i. 13. For *οὐ θέλω* D* G Ambrosiaster read *οὐκ οἴομαι*, which Zahn thinks sounds more natural, and quite likely to be replaced by the other expression so common in Paul's epistles. *Einleitung*, i. 262.

i. 15. For *ὑμῖν* D* reads *ἐν ὑμῖν*, G *ἐπ' ὑμῖν*, g *in vobis*.

i. 16. Marcion was accused of having removed *πρῶτον* or *τε πρῶτον* from his text. This, however, is not so (see Zahn, *GK.*, i. 639; ii. 515). It is also omitted in B G, showing, as Zahn thinks, that it was regarded as obnoxious at an early date (*Einleitung*, i. 263). Marcion did, however, drop the quotation from Habakkuk in the next verse.

ii. 16. Marcion in all probability wrote *τὸ εὐαγγέλιον* without *μου*, which is now omitted only by 37 d*. In the time of Origen and in the centuries following, Marcion's disciples laid emphasis not on *μου*, but on the fact that *εὐαγγέλιον* is in the singular number. They charged the Church with having not one Gospel, but several. See Zahn, *Einleitung*, ii. 171.

v. 1. Tischendorf, Westcott and Hort, and Weymouth all follow the mass of the uncials in reading *ἔχωμεν*, and I was therefore obliged to give this as the text of my Stuttgart edition of the New Testament. For myself, however, I hold with Scrivener and Weiss that *ἔχομεν* is certainly the correct reading. The same mis-spelling occurs in several manuscripts in John xix. 7, *ἡμεῖς νόμον ἔχωμεν*. For the reason of it, see Schmiedel's *Winer*, § 19. According to Zahn, *ἔχωμεν* must be considered the right reading, and *καυχώμεθα* (verse 2) taken also as subjunctive. See his *Einleitung*, i. 264.

v. 21. The words *τοῦ κυρίου ἡμῶν* were omitted by Erasmus, and, therefore, also by Luther. This is not noticed by Tischendorf, nor by Baljon, who follows him.

xi. 13. *ὑμῖν δὲ* is read by א A B P, for which D G L have *ὑμῖν γὰρ*. Zahn thinks it difficult to say which is right, but that the sense is much the same in either case. *Einleitung*, i. 265 f.

xiii. 3. The conjecture *ἀγαθοεργῷ* is thought by Hort to

have a certain amount of probability (*Notes on Select Readings*, *in loco*). Schmiedel also thinks it deserving of consideration (*Winer*, § 19).

xiv. 5. On the omission of γὰρ (B D G), see Zahn, *Einleitung*, i. 266.

xiv. 23. **Conclusion of the Epistle.** The best discussion of the Conclusion of the epistle will now be found in Zahn's *Einleitung*, vol. i. § 22, pp. 267–298, *Die Integrität des Römerbriefs*. Compare also Riggenbach, *Kritische Studien über den Schluss des Römerbriefs*: two treatises published in the *Neue Jahrbücher für deutsche Theologie*, Erster Band, 1892. Bonn, 1892; *Die Adresse des 16. Kapitels des Römerbriefs*, pp. 498–525; *Die Textgeschichte der Doxologie, Röm. xvi. 25–27 im Zusammenhang mit den übrigen den Schluss des Römerbriefs betreffenden textkritischen Fragen erörtert.* Also, F. J. A. Hort, *Prolegomena to the Epistles to the Romans and the Ephesians*, 1895; Sanday and Headlam, *Commentary on Romans*.

In certain manuscripts prior to the time of Origen, the **Doxology** was found between xiv. 23 and xv. 1. It now stands after xiv. 23 in A L P and about 200 minuscules, while at the same time the epistle is certainly continued to xv. 13. Bengel alone has suggested a reason for this. He supposes that the solemn words in xiv. 23, πᾶν δὲ ὃ οὐκ ἐκ πίστεως ἁμαρτία ἐστὶν, were felt to form an unsatisfactory close to a church lection, and that the doxology was accordingly inserted here. Moreover, seeing that no part of xvi. 1–25 was included in any lection, this would be an additional reason for attaching the doxology to the end of chapter xiv., as otherwise this grand passage might not be read at all. It must be confessed, however, that this explanation is not altogether satisfactory.

It is further to be observed that the **Benediction** is found sometimes after xvi. 20, sometimes after xvi. 23, and sometimes in both places. In the last case it is found under three conditions: (1) before the doxology, (2) without it, (3) after it. With regard to the single Benediction, it is inserted after verse 20 in ℵ A B C, and after verse 23 in D G. An explanation of these variations has frequently been sought in the supposition that chapter xvi. is part of an epistle addressed to Ephesus, which has in some way been incorporated in the Epistle to the Romans. On this supposition the only question is whether the whole of chapter xvi. belongs to this Ephesian epistle or only the first twenty verses, while verses 21–23 belong to the original Epistle to the Romans. Improbable as this may appear at the first glance, it admits of an easy explanation. It may be due to the fact that Romans once stood at the end of the collection of Pauline epistles. Or we may suppose that the commendatory epistle for Phœbe addressed to Ephesus and the Epistle to the Romans were written at the same time, and that in sending them off, the sheet containing the former by some mistake slipped in before the last sheet of the Roman epistle. On this view, the first benediction in verse 20, ἡ χάρις . . . . μεθ' ὑμῶν, would belong to the Ephesian epistle, while the second, ἡ χάρις . . . . μετὰ πάντων ὑμῶν to the Roman. The uncial L would then be right in retaining both, while D E F G will have omitted the benediction the first time it occurred, and ℵ A B C the second time.

At the same time it cannot be disguised that there are difficulties in connection with the close of chapter xv. Minuscule 48 omits the last verse (33). In verse 32, B reads simply ἵνα ἐν χαρᾷ ἔλθω, while the other witnesses have ἐλθὼν, and vary between συναναπαύσωμαι ὑμῖν and ἀναψύξω μεθ' ὑμῶν.[1] Zahn thinks that the original position of the Doxology is after xiv. 23 and nowhere else. Now the authority for inserting the Doxology there only is L and many minuscules, A P and a few minuscules having it in both places. If Zahn is right, should not the testimony of L be accepted in other places as

[1] On these two verbs compare Exod. xxxi. 17. where the LXX has ἐπαύσατο and Aquila ἀνέψυξε; Isa. xxxiv. 14, LXX ἀναπαύσονται, Aquila ἀνέψυξε; Isa. xxviii. 12, Aquila ἀνάψυξις; compare also ἀνάπαυσις, Matt. xi. 29; καιροὶ ἀναψύξεως, Acts iii. 20. Weiss, in his Commentary, ignores the reading of B in Rom. xv. 32; in his discussion of the text he supposes that the text was mutilated by a translator, and that D E F G "sought to restore it in their own way."

well as this, or at least have more deference paid to it than seems now to be the case. The testimony for the omission of the Doxology there has recently been endorsed by that of the Palestinian Syriac Lectionary, published in *Studia Sinaitica*, vi.

xv., xvi. Zahn points out that we cannot consistently lay stress on the supposed entire absence of these chapters in Marcion, unless we are prepared to maintain at the same time that the other passages which he fails to mention, such as Gal. iii. 6–9, 15–25, iv. 27–30; Romans i. 19–ii. 1, iii. 31–iv. 25, ix. 1–33, x. 5–xi. 32; Coloss. i. 15*b*, 16, were unknown to him, and only smuggled into the text afterwards by falsifiers on the Catholic side. Zahn thinks it probable that Marcion struck out the numerous personal references in chapter xvi. as being useless and unedifying for the Church of his day.

xv. 23, 24. Zahn holds that the later Antiochean reading ἐλεύσομαι πρὸς ὑμᾶς (א^c L Euthal., etc.) is undoubtedly spurious, and the γὰρ as certainly genuine (*Einleitung*, i. 267).

xvi. 27. Zahn (*Einleitung*, i. 286) is inclined to regard ᾧ as the correct reading here for two reasons: (1) because the incompleteness of the sentence made it liable to correction, and (2) because the correction is effected in very different ways. In some manuscripts ᾧ is changed into αὐτῷ (P, Copt., 31, 54), in others it is omitted altogether (B F-lat. Syr.), while in others again εἴη takes the place of ᾧ ἡ (55, 43-scholion).

Subscription: πρὸς Ῥωμαίους simply, א A B C D; others, ἐγράφη ἀπὸ Κορίνθου διὰ Φοίβης τῆς διακόνου, to which some add τῆς ἐν Κεγχρεαῖς ἐκκλησίας; others, ἐγράφη διὰ Τερτίου ἐπέμφθη δὲ διὰ Φοίβης ἀπὸ Κορινθίων.

1 Corinthians.

All the manuscripts in which the number of the epistle is indicated by a word and not by a numeral (ά) call it πρώτη, never προτέρα. Origen, however, says ἐν τῇ προτέρᾳ πρὸς Κορινθίους ὁ Παῦλος (ii. 347).

i. 2. The words ἡγιασμένοις ἐν Χριστῷ Ἰησοῦ are read immediately after θεοῦ by B D* G. This arrangement is adopted by Weiss, and supported by Zahn as undoubtedly genuine (*Einleitung*, i. 210). Heinrici is inclined to regard it as a transcriptional error which was very apt to occur in copying stichometric manuscripts. But were there stichometric manuscripts antecedent to the time of Codex B?

iii. 22. Marcion seems to have dropped the name of Apollos here. Indeed, there is no trace in Marcion of any of the passages where Paul mentions his name. "What was Apollos to the Church of the second century?" (Zahn, *GK.* i. 649.)

v. 2. For ἐπενθήσατε Naber suggests ἐπενοήσατε. This is not noticed by Baljon, who is elsewhere careful to mention the conjectural emendations proposed by his countrymen.

vi. 20. It was doubtless owing to a transcriptional error that Marcion read ἄρατε between δοξάσατε and τὸν θεόν. But how it originated, whether from ἄρα δὲ = ἄρα δὴ or by dittography, it is hard to say.

x. 9. In place of τὸν κύριον we find τὸν Χριστὸν read by D G K L, Marcion, Irenæus (iv. 27, 3), Clement (*Ecl. Proph.*, 49), and the early versions. See above, p. 152, and compare Zahn on the reading Ἰησοῦς for κύριος in Jude 5 (*Einleitung*, ii. 88 f.).

xiv. 19. For νοΐ μου Marcion read "per legem" διὰ τὸν νόμον, which was arrived at partly by a transcriptional error and partly by conscious alteration. This could not have occurred, however, unless the original reading was διὰ τοῦ νοός μου, which is still found in a good many manuscripts, and not τῷ νοΐ μου, the reading preferred by most of our editors. The latter is perhaps the result of an assimilation to the construction of γλώσσῃ.

xiv. 31–34. These verses are variously punctuated by recent editors, the main difference being with regard to the arrangement of the clause ὡς ἐν πάσαις ταῖς ἐκκλησίαις τῶν ἁγίων. This clause is referred to verse 31 by Westcott and Hort, who place a comma after παρακαλῶνται and bracket the intervening words (32, 33*a*) as a parenthesis. Tischendorf and Weiss place a period after εἰρήνης, and link the ὡς clause to what follows. This arrangement Westcott and Hort indicate in their margin. For details and reasoning, see the Commentaries.

xiv. 34, 35. These two verses follow verse 40 in D E F G 93, Ambrosiaster, and Sedulius. In Codex Fuldensis, verses 36–40 are found in the margin after verse 33, where they were inserted by Victor of Capua (see p. 122), who did not, however, remove them from their place further down. He must therefore have had before him a manuscript exhibiting this arrangement. We must suppose either that all these manuscripts are ultimately derived from one and the same exemplar, in which this arrangement of the verses occurred, or, as Heinrici suggests, that the original document itself gave occasion to this variety by having these verses written in its margin. Our modern editors are unanimous in following the usual order.

xv. 38. Zahn has shown that in all likelihood the substitution of πνεῦμα for the first σῶμα was due to certain followers of Marcion. See his *GK.* i. 615; also *Zeitschrift für Kirchengeschichte*, ix. 198 ff.

xv. 47. On Marcion's reading, ὁ δεύτερος κύριος ἐξ οὐρανοῦ, see Zahn, *GK.* i. 638, who suggests that this may have been an early gloss that Marcion made use of, seeing that it is in the highest degree improbable that the heretic and some of his most violent opponents should alter the original text in exactly the same way.

xv. 55. Tertullian found νεῖκος in Marcion, and he therefore leaves it an open question whether the word signifies *victoria tua* or *contentio tua* (v. 10, p. 306). See Zahn, *GK.* i. 51.

xvi. 22. On "Maranatha," see Zahn (*Einleitung*, i. 215 ff.), who, while admitting that no objection on the ground of language or grammar can be made to reading the word as מרן אתא = ὁ κύριος ἡμῶν ἦλθεν (not ἔρχεται or ἐλεύσεται), prefers with Halévy, Bickell, and Nöldeke, to take it as מרנא תא = κύριε ἔρχου, which corresponds to the Peshitto rendering of

Apoc. xxii. 20, תא מריא ישוע (ἔρχου κύριε Ἰησοῦ). See note by Schmiedel in the *Hand-Commentar* on 1 Cor. xvi. 22, and the article by Thayer in Hastings' *Dictionary of the Bible*, *sub voce*. Luther has "Maharam Motha," but whence he derived this I do not know.

Subscription: ἐγράφη ἀπὸ Φιλίππων (τῆς Μακεδονίας) διὰ Στεφανᾶ καὶ Φορτουνάτου καὶ Ἀχαϊκοῦ (Κουάρτου) καὶ Τιμοθέου; *al.* ὑπὸ Παύλου καὶ Σωσθένους; *al.* ἀπὸ Ἐφέσου τῆς Ἀσίας.

2 Corinthians.

i. 12. Recent editors adopt the reading ἁγιότητι on the authority of א* A B C K M P etc. Zahn, however (*Einleitung*, i. 243), prefers ἁπλότητι as given by א^{c} D E G etc. Meyer thinks that ἁπλότητι was substituted for ἁγιότητι as being the more usual expression. Tischendorf is wrong in saying: de suo add. syr^{sch} *et cum puritate*. The Syriac has בפשיטותא ובדכיותא ובטיבותא דאלהא—*i.e.* ἐν ἁπλότητι καὶ ἐν εἰλικρινείᾳ[1] καὶ ἐν χάριτι [τοῦ] θεοῦ ἀνεστράφημεν ἐν τῷ κόσμῳ καὶ οὐκ ἐν. . . .

vii. 2. Zahn (*GK.* i. 650; ii. 515) thinks perhaps the whole section vii. 2–xi. 1 was omitted by Marcion: "Let us cleanse ourselves from defilement of the flesh and blood . . . . for I espoused you as a pure virgin to one husband, (even) Christ."

Subscription: ἐγράφη ἀπὸ Φιλίππων (+ τῆς Μακεδονίας) + διὰ Τίτου (+ Βαρνάβα) καὶ Λουκᾶ.

Galatians.

i. 8. As illustrating how far the sharpest critic may be led astray by his fondness for conjectural emendation, it may be mentioned here that Hitzig (*Das Buch Hiob*, 1874, p. 199), suggested that Η ΑΧΣ formerly occupied the place of ἡμεῖς in this verse, and that this means ἡ ἀρχιερεύς!

[1] See 1 Cor. v. 8, where the Syriac has קדישותא—*i.e.* ἁγιότητος—for ἀληθείας.

i. 18. For Κηφᾶν, as given in our critical editions, Zahn (*Einleitung*, ii. 14) would read Πέτρον. He accounts for the remarkable transition from the name Πέτρος in ii. 7, 8 to Κηφᾶς in ii. 9, 11, 14 very well by saying that Paul in the latter verses is echoing the language used by the Judaizers from Palestine, just as he does in speaking of the Three as στῦλοι. Seeing that Paul persistently employs the name Κηφᾶς in 1 Corinthians, a scribe might have introduced this name, with which he had become familiar, into Galatians i. 18 also, just as Ἰσκαριώτης was carried over from the Synoptics into most manuscripts of John's Gospel, displacing the title ἀπὸ Καρυώτου. The following table will show the distribution of the Greek manuscripts in support of the readings Κηφᾶς and Πέτρος in Galatians :—

	Κηφᾶς.	Πέτρος.
Gal. i. 18,	א* A B 17, 67**, 71.	א^c D E F G K L P.
ii. 7,	———	omnes.
ii. 8,	———	omnes.
ii. 9,	א B C K L P etc.	D E F G (A omits).
ii. 11,	א A B C H P.	D E F G K L.
ii. 14,	א A B C 10, 17, 67**, 137.	D E F G K L P.

It will be observed that in ii. 9 K L P take the side of א (A) B, while in verse 11 P alone does so, and that D E F G are the only witnesses that are consistent.

ii. 5. *οἷς οὐδὲ* is omitted by D*, by Tertullian, who ascribes the negative to Marcion (*Adv. Marcionem*, v. 3), by certain manuscripts known to Victorinus Afer, who says "in plurimis codicibus et latinis et graecis ista sententia est *Ad horam cessimus subjectioni*," and by the Latin translator of Irenæus (*Adv. Haereses*, iii. 13, 3). Ambrosiaster calls attention to the discrepancy between the Greek and Latin manuscripts: "Graeci e contra dicunt *Nec ad horam cessimus*," and similarly Sedulius. Bengel remarked on the proneness of scribes to insert or omit a negative: "Omnino apud Latinos lubrica sub calamo est *non* particula. . . . . Saepe etiam in graecis aliisque οὐκ omissum." See Haussleiter, *Forschungen*, iv. 31 ff., who says that the subject is one deserving of special treatment. Bengel refers to the exhaustive discussion "de negationibus quae Pandectis Florentinis recte male additae vel detractae sunt," but there might be a good deal said on these theological *Sic et Non* also.

A single letter or little word more or less, and the sense of a passage is completely changed. Did Paul say that in his contention with the Apostles he gave place "for an hour," or "*not* for an hour," οἷς πρὸς ὥραν, or οἷς οὐδὲ πρὸς ὥραν, or πρὸς ὥραν simply? In Gal. v 8 is it ἡ πεισμονὴ ἐκ τοῦ καλοῦντος ὑμᾶς, or οὐκ ἐκ? In I Cor. v. 6 is it "your glorying is good" or "*not* good," καλὸν or οὐ καλὸν? In Rom. iv. 19, κατενόησεν or οὐ κατένοησεν? In 2 Peter iii. 10, εὑρεθήσεται or οὐχ εὑρεθήσεται, or are both these wrong? Compare, for example, the reading μακράν in Matt. viii. 30, where almost all the Latin witnesses, and Jerome too, read "*non* longe"; and John vi. 64, where we have οἱ μὴ πιστεύοντες, and also οἱ πιστεύοντες (ℵ G). In this latter passage the reading "credentes" was adopted in the Sixtine edition of the Vulgate, but "*non* credentes" in the Clementine; Wordsworth and White decide for the latter against the Sixtine text. In John vii. 8, ℵ D R etc., read οὐκ, for which B and the majority of the witnesses have οὔπω, but this is manifestly a correction. In John ix. 27 we have οὐκ ἠκούσατε, where a solitary Greek manuscript (22), which, however, has the support of the Vulgate and half the Old Latin witnesses, reads ἠκούσατε: audistis. In Romans v. 14 we find both τοὺς μὴ ἁμαρτάνοντας and τοὺς ἁμαρτάνοντας. In I Cor. iii. 7 A reads ὥστε ὁ φυτεύων ἐστίν τι, omitting the negative; in ix. 8 we have both ταῦτα λέγει and ταῦτα οὐ λέγει; while in xiii. 5 B and Clement of Alexandria actually assert that "love seeketh what is *not* her own, τὸ μὴ ἑαυτῆς"! Again, in I Cor. xv. 51 the position of the negative fluctuates between the first and second member of the sentence, so that we have πάντες μὲν οὐ and οὐ πάντες. Similarly, in Col. ii. 18 we find ἃ ἑόρακεν and ἃ μὴ ἑόρακεν;

and in Apoc. iv. 11 ἦσαν καὶ ἐκτίσθησαν and οὐκ ἦσαν καὶ ἐκτίσθησαν—*i.e.* "they were called out of nothingness into existence."

In Codex D seven cases of this variation occur in Acts alone—viz. iv. 20, v. 26, 28, vii. 25, xix. 40, xx. 20, 27. Compare, further, Matt. xii. 32, where in place of ἀφεθήσεται B* reads οὐκ ἀφεθήσεται. In Matt. xvii. 25 one Latin manuscript makes Peter say "utique non" in answer to the question, "Doth not your master pay tribute?" We have in Matt. xxi. 16, ἀκούεις and οὐκ ἀκούεις; xxi. 32, μετεμελήθητε and οὐ μετεμελήθητε; xxiv. 2, οὐ βλέπετε and βλέπετε. In Mark viii. 14, οὐκ εἶχον and εἶχον; xiii. 19, καὶ οὐ μή, οὐδὲ μή and οὐδ' οὐ. Luke xi. 48, συνευδοκεῖτε: μὴ συνευδοκεῖτε; xxi. 21, ἐκχωρείτωσαν: μὴ ἐκχωρείτωσαν. John ii. 12, οὐ πολλάς: πολλάς; xv. 19, οὐκ ἐστὲ: ἦτε; xx. 8, ἐπίστευσεν: οὐκ ἐπίστευσεν. Acts xxv. 6, πλείους: οὐ πλείους. Rom. iv. 5, μὴ ἐργαζομένῳ: ἐργαζομένῳ (*Studia Sinaitica*, vi. p. lxvi); x. 3, οὐχ ὑπετάγησαν: ὑπετάγησαν (*ibid.*). 1 Cor i. 19, συνετῶν : ἀσυνέτων; iv. 6, ἵνα μή: ἵνα; iv. 19, οὐ τὸν λόγον: τὸν λόγον; vi. 5, οὐδεὶς σοφός: σοφός; vi. 9, οὐ κληρονομήσουσιν: κληρονομήσουσιν (B* 93) and *vice versa* in verse 10. 2 Cor. v. 1, ἀχειροποίητος: οὐκ ἀχειροποίητος (*non manufactam*). Gal. iv. 14, οὐκ ἐξουθενήσατε: ἐξουθενήσατε (א*). Heb. x. 2, οὐκ ἄν: ἄν: κἄν. 2 Pet. i. 12, μελλήσω: οὐκ ἀμελήσω: οὐ μελλήσω. 1 John v. 17, οὐ πρὸς θάνατον: πρὸς θάνατον. Apoc. iii. 8, μικράν: οὐ μικράν.[1]

ii. 20. Tischendorf fails to mention that Marcion read ἀγοράσαντος (redemit) in place of ἀγαπήσαντος. The variant is of sufficient importance to justify a reference to Zahn, *GK*.

[1] To these examples, gathered quite incidentally, one might add as many from the Old Testament and other books if one paid any attention to them in reading. Take, for example, Herodotus i. 24. Was the votive offering that Arion set up at Taenarum μέγα or οὐ μέγα? In the *Germania* xv. 1 did Tacitus say of the Germans "*non multum* venationibus, plus per otium transigunt," or "*multum* venationibus, etc."? In the new edition of Origen (i. 87, 16) Koetschau reads ἀχρήσιμα where the manuscript and the earlier editions have χρήσιμα, and he lets an οὐκ stand which others omit, etc.

ii. 499. I cannot at this moment recall any instance of a confusion between *ἀγοράσας* and *ἀγαπήσας*, though it is not an unlikely mistake to make. In Leviticus xxvii. 19, the first hand of B by mistake wrote *ἀγοράσας* for *ἁγιάσας*.

v. 9. Epiphanius accused Marcion of having altered *ζυμοῖ* to *δολοῖ*. See Zahn, *GK.* i. 639; ii. 503. *Cf.* above, p. 76.

Ephesians.

Tertullian says (*Adv. Marcionem*, v. 17): Ecclesiae quidem veritate epistulam istam ad Ephesios habemus emissam, non ad Laodicenos, sed Marcion ei titulum aliquando interpolare gestiit, quasi et in isto diligentissimus explorator. Nihil autem de titulis interest, cum ad omnes apostolus scripserit, dum ad quosdam.

iv. 19. For *ἀπηλγηκότες* D here reads *ἀπηλπικότες*. A glance at ΑΠΗΛΓΗΚΟΤΕC and ΑΠΗΛΠΙΚΟΤΕC will show how easy it was to make such a mistake in the days of uncial script.

v. 14. The reading *ἐπιψαύσεις τοῦ Χριστοῦ* is attested by D*, some Latin manuscripts, and Theodore of Mopsuestia. See above, p. 254.

Subscription: *ἐγράφη ἀπὸ Ῥώμης*: + *διὰ Τυχίκου*.

Philippians.

i. 3. *εὐχαριστῶ τῷ θεῷ μου* is read by ℵ A B D^c E^2 K L P; and *ἐγὼ μὲν εὐχαριστῶ τῷ κυρίῳ ἡμῶν* by D* E* F G. Zahn defends the latter in the *Zeitschrift für kirchliche Wissenschaft*, 1885, p. 184, and in his *Einleitung*, i. 376 calls it the "genuine text." Haupt says (Meyer[7], 1897, p. 3): The reading *ἐγὼ μὲν εὐχαριστῶ*, which is commonly ignored, is, it appears to me, rightly recommended by Zahn and Wohlenberg. But Haupt himself ignores the second half of the reading *τῷ κυρίῳ ἡμῶν* (for *τῷ θεῷ μου*), which is far more important from a theological point of view, and is content merely to explain at length why Paul should thank *his* God. Weiss, in his *Text-*

kritik der paulinischen Briefe (pp. 6, 7), mentions ἐγὼ, but says nothing about μὲν, or the change from κυρίῳ ἡμῶν to θεῷ μου. But you cannot run with the hare and hunt with the hounds. If you accept ἐγὼ μὲν εὐχαριστῶ you cannot reject τῷ κυρίῳ ἡμῶν. Haupt, moreover, thinks it is far-fetched to suppose with Zahn that ἐγὼ μὲν contains an allusion to something the Philippians had said. But that is by no means the case, as we may learn from what Deissmann and Harris tell us of the epistolary style of those days (see *A Study in Letter Writing*, Expositor, September 1898, p. 161 ff.). But if the Western group preserves the correct text at the very outset of the epistle, what about it further down?

i. 7. For χάριτος Ambrosiaster has "gaudii," so that he must have read χαρᾶς. J. Weiss proposes to read χρείας (*ThLz.*, 1899, col. 263). χάρις and χαρά are frequently interchanged—*e.g.* in Tobit vii. 18; Sirach xxx. 16. Χόρον is found for χαράν in Ps. xxix. (xxx.) 11. The scribes felt a difficulty with χρεία in Rom. xii. 13, and still more so in Ephes. iv. 29. Ephraem found χρεία in place of χεῖρον in John v. 14 (see above, p. 293, note 2).

i. 14. Zahn and Haupt omit τοῦ θεοῦ with D K etc. So does J. Weiss, who takes occasion to make certain important observations on the attempts hitherto made to restore the text. See *ThLz.*, 1899, col. 263.

iii. 14. Till lately Tertullian was our only authority for the reading "palmam incriminationis" in place of τὸ βραβεῖον τῆς ἄνω κλήσεως (*De resurrectione carnis*, 23). It was accordingly supposed that he had read ἀνεγκλήσεως instead of ἄνω κλήσεως. We learn now from the Athos manuscript, discovered by von der Goltz, that Origen also cited the reading ἀνεγκλησίας in his commentary as being ἀνεγνωσμένον ἔν τισιν ἀντιγράφοις. Even supposing that τινα ἀντίγραφα turned out to be no more than a single copy, or even Tertullian's quotation which Origen had become acquainted with in some way, his mention of this reading is in the highest degree interesting.

Subscription: ἐγράφη ἀπὸ Ῥώμης: + δι' Ἐπαφροδίτου: + διὰ Τιμοθέου καὶ Ἐπαφροδίτου.

Colossians.

ii. 16. On the reading κιρνάτω suggested by the rendering of the Peshitto, and the Latin version of Ephraem's Commentary on the Pauline Epistles, see above, p. 168 f. It was advocated by Lagarde in his *Prophetae Chaldaice*, p. li. Zahn rejects it on the ground that it would require περὶ βρώσεως in place of ἐν βρώσει, and also that κρίνειν agrees better with καταβραβεύειν in verse 18.

ii. 18. On this difficult passage see above, p. 168. Zahn thinks it quite certain that μὴ is a later insertion even in the Syriac, seeing that Ephraem knows nothing of it. Of the various conjectural emendations, he regards that of C. Taylor as the most probable—viz. ἀέρα κενεμβατεύων. This is also the view of Westcott and Hort. See their *Introduction*, "Notes on Select Readings," *in loco*; Zahn, *Einleitung*, i. 339.

iv. 14. The words ὁ ἰατρὸς ὁ ἀγαπητὸς were omitted by Marcion. See Zahn, *GK.* i. 647; ii. 528. Two minuscules omit the words ὁ ἀγαπητὸς.

Subscription: ἐγράφη ἀπὸ Ῥώμης διὰ Τυχίκου (+ καὶ Τιμοθέου) καὶ Ὀνησίμου.

1 Thessalonians.

ii. 7. One can easily see how doubt should arise as to the correct reading here when we observe the form of the words in the uncial script, ΕΓΕΝΗΘΗΜΕΝΝΗΠΙΟΙ. Moreover, we must remember that N at the end of a line was very frequently indicated merely by a stroke above the preceding letter, thus: ΕΓΕΝΗΘΗΜΕ̄. The same alternative readings are presented in Hebrews v. 13, and in Clement of Alexandria, i. 140, 7, where Codex F exhibits ἤπιοι, and M, which is the most important manuscript, has νήπιοι in the text and ἤπιοι in the margin.

ii. 15. Zahn (*GK.* ii. 521; *cf.* also i. 644) restores Marcion's text here in the form τῶν καὶ τὸν κύριον ['Ιησοῦν] ἀποκτεινάντων καὶ τοὺς προφήτας αὐτῶν. Marcion founds throughout upon a Western text, and the fact of his agreement in this instance with the Antiochean Recension (D_2 E_2 K_2 L_2) is declared by Zahn to be a mere coincidence, more especially as the latter here reads τοὺς ἰδίους προφήτας. "Had Marcion," he says, "really written ἰδίους, Tertullian would have translated the passage differently, and would scarcely have applied the term *adjectio* to a qualifying expression inserted *before* προφήτας." What Tertullian says is, "dicendo *et prophetas suos* licet *suos* adjectio sit haeretici." The term ἴδιος is employed so frequently to represent the pronoun when no particular emphasis is intended to be conveyed, that there seems to me no necessity for Tertullian translating τοὺς ἰδίους προφήτας *suos prophetas*, or rendering the words in any other way than *prophetas suos*. Compare above, p. 211.

iii. 3. Lachmann here reads μηδὲν ἀσαίνεσθαι with Reiske and Venema. Beza and Bentley suggested σαλεύεσθαι, Holwerda ἀναίνεσθαι, Peerlkamp σινιάζεσθαι. Zahn has no hesitation in adopting μηδένα σαίνεσθαι, which he understands in the original (metaphorical) sense of to flatter, to talk over or cajole. See *Einleitung*, i. 158.

1 Timothy.

i. 4. Οἰκοδομίαν, or οἰκοδομήν, which is attested by Irenæus and a good many Latin witnesses, and received into his text by Erasmus, is nothing but an early transcriptional error for οἰκονομίαν.

iii. 1. "The reading ἀνθρώπινος ὁ λόγος is attested in Greek only by D*, but it was the prevailing reading in the West till the time of Jerome. When I consider the improbability of its being invented, and its liability to alteration in conformity with 1 Tim. i. 15, iv. 9; 2 Tim. ii. 11; Tit. iii. 8, I am compelled, in spite of the one-sided nature of the testimony, to conclude that it is original. It is a proverbial expression of general application and profane origin" (Zahn, *Einleitung*, i. 482). This reading is usually ignored by our editors and commentators, and yet the passage is one that plays an important part in the ordination of the clergy, and therefore one on the correct interpretation of which a good deal might depend. Westcott and Hort merely mention it in their *Notes on Select Readings* and insert it in their *Appendix*. It is not cited by von Gebhardt in his edition. For my own part I am not quite convinced of its originality. At the same time it is hard to understand how ΠΙΣΤΟΣ by any clerical error could be transformed into $\overline{\text{ANINO}}\Sigma$, and so become ΑΝΘΡΩΠΙΝΟΣ.

iii. 16. In his *Forschungen*, vol. iii., Beilage iv. p. 277, "Zum Text von I Tim. iii. 16," Zahn published two or three lines from some parchment fragments in the Egyptian Museum of the Louvre, which, he thinks, belong to the IV–VI century. The last three lines run—*ευσεβειας μυστηρ . . . . | ω εφανερωθη ε . . . . | και εδ . . . .* He says, "The *ω* in the second last line is undoubtedly meant for ὃ. This adds another to the Greek witnesses supporting this reading, which has till now been attested only by the Latin manuscripts, by other ambiguous or doubtful witnesses, and probably by the first Greek hand of Codex Claromontanus. The *και* in the last line is, so far as I am aware, supported by no other evidence." The reading *θεος*, which was formerly so much discussed, seems to be simply an early transcriptional error, OC being read as $\overline{\Theta C}$—*i.e.* *θεος* with the usual mark of abbreviation. The old dispute over the reading of the earliest manuscripts (most of them exhibit a correction at the place), whether the middle stroke of the Θ in the oldest codices A C is by the first or second hand, or whether in the case of A it may not be simply the tongue of an E shining through from the other side of the parchment, cannot seemingly be decided now in the present state of the manuscripts.[1] Codex A was examined by

[1] In his *Lucian* Lagarde gives examples of his being deceived by certain letters shining through from the opposite side—*e.g.* Esther v. 22 and 27. This

Scrivener both with and without the aid of a magnifying glass perhaps twenty times in as many years. Dean Burgon devotes seventy-seven pages of his *Revision Revised* to a discussion of the reading. The facility with which a variant of this sort may arise is shown by the perfectly analogous passage, Joshua ii. 11. Here B and F read *κυριος ο θεος υμων* OC *εν ουρανω ανω*, while on the other hand A in place of OC has ΘC, which in this instance is correct. In 1 Tim. iii. 16 the other witnesses—viz. the versions and the Fathers—throw their weight into the opposite scale.

iv. 3. Isidore asks whether *κωλυόντων . . . . ἀπέχεσθαι βρωμάτων* may not be a *σφάλμα* of the scribes for *ἀντέχεσθαι*, to which Oecumenius replies that it is no *σφάλμα καλλιγραφικόν* but good Attic Greek for *κωλύειν ἀπὸ τῆς βρώσεως*. The explanation of Theophylact, however, is nearer the mark, that *συμβουλεύειν* is to be supplied from *κωλύειν*. Bentley, Toup, Bakhuyzen, and Bois would supply *κελευόντων* before *ἀπέχεσθαι*, while Hort suggests the substitution of *ἢ ἅπτεσθαι* or *καὶ γεύεσθαι* in place of *ἀπέχεσθαι*. There seems to be no need of such expedients.

Subscription: *ἐγράφη ἀπὸ Λαοδικείας + ἥτις ἐστὶν μητρόπολις Φρυγίας τῆς Καπατιάνης* (*Πακατιάνης*): *al. ἀπὸ Νικοπόλεως*: *al. ἀπὸ Ἀθηνῶν*: *al. ἀπὸ Ῥώμης + διὰ Τίτου.*

2 Timothy.

iv. 19. After *Ἀκύλαν* two minuscules (46 and 109) insert *Λέκτραν τὴν γυναῖκα αὐτοῦ καὶ Σιμαίαν* (*Σημαιαν* 109) *καὶ Ζήνωνα τοὺς υἱοὺς αὐτοῦ*. The interpolation is derived from the *Acta Pauli*, and is to be connected not with Aquila, but with the "house of Onesiphorus." See Zahn, *Einleitung*, i. 411.

Subscription: *ἐγράφη ἀπὸ Λαοδικείας*: *al. ἀπὸ Ῥώμης + ὅτε ἐκ δευτέρου παρέστη Παῦλος τῷ καίσαρι Νέρωνι.*

latter is a most interesting case. The following verse begins with *μη*, and Lagarde thought that the first scribe had added another *μη* by mistake and afterwards erased it, whereas it turned out that what he took to be MH was nothing else than HN shining through from the other side.

Titus.

i. 9, 11. Considerable additions are made to the text after both these verses by Codex 109. This manuscript is numbered 11 in the Library of St. Mark at Venice, and described by Gregory as "haud malae notae." It contains both a Latin and an Arabic version, and dates from the thirteenth or fourteenth, or, as some suppose, the eleventh, century. After verse 9 we read: *μὴ χειροτονεῖν διγάμους μηδὲ διακόνους αὐτοὺς ποιεῖν, μηδὲ γυναῖκας ἔχειν ἐκ διγαμίας· μηδὲ προσερχέσθωσαν ἐν τῷ θυσιαστηρίῳ λειτουργεῖν τὸ θεῖον· τοὺς ἄρχοντας τοὺς αδικοκριτὰς καὶ ἅρπαγας καὶ ψεύστας καὶ ἀνελεήμονας ἔλεγχε ὡς θεοῦ διάκονος.* After verse 11 we find *τὰ τέκνα τοὺς ἰδίους γονεῖς ὑβρίζοντας ἢ τύπτοντας ἐπιστόμιζε καὶ ἔλεγχε καὶ νουθέτει ὡς πατὴρ τέκνα.*

Subscription: *πρὸς Τίτον (+τῆς Κρητῶν ἐκκλησίας πρῶτον ἐπίσκοπον χειροτονηθέντα) ἐγράφη ἀπὸ Νικοπόλεως τῆς Μακεδονίας* (missa per Arteman: *al.* per Zenam et Apollo).

Hebrews.

i. 3. Instead of *φέρων*, the first hand of B wrote *φανερῶν*, which a second hand altered to *φέρων*, while a third restored *φανερῶν*, and wrote in the margin *ἀμαθέστατε καὶ κακέ, ἄφες τὸν* [? *τὸ*] *παλαιόν, μὴ μεταποίει.* A great deal of material might be collected from the margin of old manuscripts, not only for the history of Prayer, as von Dobschütz recently observed, but for other interesting departments of the history of civilisation.

ii. 9. The reading *χωρὶς θεοῦ* instead of *χάριτι θεοῦ* is now found only in M and in the second hand of 67. Origen, however, was aware of the various reading: *χωρὶς θεοῦ ἢ ὅπερ ἔν τισι ἀντιγράφοις χάριτι θεοῦ.* It seems to be a primitive transcriptional error.

x. 34. We have here to choose between *δεσμοῖς* and *δεσμίοις*. The latter is manifestly the correct reading. It is attested by A D* and certain minuscules, among which are 37**, 67**. This last is a Vienna manuscript (Vindob. gr. theol. 302), whose marginal readings exhibit a text closely resembling that of the uncials B M, which are defective in Hebrews x. Δεσμοῖς μου is supported by ℵ D^c H K L P, Clem. Alex., Origen (i. 41, where, however, μου is omitted by M* P, according to Koetschau's new edition), and by d e (*vinculis eorum*). Zahn (*Einleitung*, ii. 122) thinks that the connection of the reading δεσμοῖς μου with the tradition of the Pauline authorship of the epistle is suspicious. We find the reading adopted in those regions where the tradition was accepted. It may, however, have been the means of confirming and spreading the tradition, seeing that Clement of Alexandria is actually aware of it. Pseudo-Euthalius, *e.g.*, employs the reading in support of the Pauline authorship (Zacagni 670).

In this same verse ℵ A H have preserved the proper reading ἑαυτούς. Ἑαυτοῖς, as given by D E K L, is a would-be correction.

xi. 23. In certain manuscripts (D and three Vulgate codices) an entire verse is inserted after verse 23: Πίστει μέγας γενόμενος Μωϋσῆς ἀνεῖλεν τὸν Αἰγύπτιον κατανοῶν τὴν ταπείνωσιν τῶν ἀδελφῶν αὐτοῦ. Its position shows it to be an interpolation.

xiii. 9. The present tense περιπατοῦντες is exhibited only by ℵ* A D*, all the other witnesses having περιπατήσαντες. The minority are in the right here. A correction is not always an improvement.

xiii. 18. Zahn accepts the καὶ before περὶ ἡμῶν. It is found only in D d and Chrysostom. This combination of witnesses is very rare.

Subscription: ἐγράφη (+ἑβραϊστὶ 31) ἀπὸ τῆς Ἰταλίας διὰ Τιμοθέου: *al.* ἀπὸ Ἀθηνῶν: *al.* ἀπὸ Ῥώμης.

Catholic Epistles.

The variety in the order of the Catholic Epistles is even more significant than that of the Pauline. When the Syrian

Church of Edessa obtained the New Testament, it consisted only of the Gospels, the Pauline Epistles, and the Acts. It contained neither the Apocalypse nor the Catholic Epistles. This is proved among other things by the fact that not a single quotation from these writings is found in the Homilies of Aphraates, the date of which falls between 336 and 345. At a later date the Syrian Church accepted the Epistle of James, 1 Peter, and 1 John, but the four so-called Antilegomena—viz. 2 Peter, 2 and 3 John, and Jude—are to this day excluded from their Canon of the New Testament. Even in the West, James was not reckoned among the books of the New Testament previous to the fourth century. There is no mention made of it in Africa about the year 300, although it was cited at Rome and Carthage at an earlier date. At Alexandria, however, all the seven Catholic Epistles were counted in the New Testament as early as the time of Clement,[1] and their place in the Canon becomes more and more firmly assured from the time of Eusebius onwards.[2] At the same time, the order of their arrangement varies very considerably. Indeed, every possible variety occurs, except that Jude seems never to have been placed first, nor 2 Peter last. Thus we find James, 2 Peter, 3 John, Jude; James, Jude, 2 Peter, 3 John; 2 Peter, James, Jude, 3 John; 2 Peter, 3 John, James, Jude; 2 Peter, 3 John, Jude, James, etc.[3] It follows that in the case of this group of New Testament writings, as well as in that of the preceding, it is necessary and possible to distinguish the three longer from the four shorter epistles in tracing the history of the text. And we see at the same time what justification Luther had in drawing a line between these epistles and the principal books of the New Testament as having been held in quite a different estimation in early times.

[1] *Cf.* Westcott, *Canon*, Part II. ch. ii. § 1, p. 354 ff.; *Bible in the Church*, p. 125 f.

[2] *Cf.* Westcott, *Bible in the Church*, p. 153 ff.

[3] See Article on *The Catholic Epistles*, by Salmond, in Hastings' *Dictionary of the Bible*, i. p. 359 f.

1 Peter.

iii. 22. After θεοῦ the Vulgate inserts *deglutiens mortem ut vitae aeternae haeredes efficeremur*, "apparently from a Greek original which had the aorist participle καταπιών; *cf.* 1 Cor. xv. 54" (W-H, *Notes, in loco*). See Vetter, *Der dritte Korintherbrief.*

2 Peter.

i. 1. Zahn considers ἐν δικαιοσύνῃ the original reading, and εἰς δικαιοσύνην a later correction due to taking πίστιν ἐν δικαιοσύνῃ together as "faith in righteousness." The last two words are to be taken with λαχοῦσιν. *Einleitung*, ii. 59.

i. 2. Zahn agrees with Lachmann and Spitta in holding that ἐν ἐπιγνώσει τοῦ κυρίου ἡμῶν is the correct text here—that is to say, he omits τοῦ θεοῦ καὶ Ἰησοῦ. Tischendorf's Apparatus is very diffuse on this verse, and Baljon's note, which is extracted from it, is accordingly not quite satisfactory.[1] Like all the other editors, he gives ἐν ἐπιγνώσει τοῦ θεοῦ καὶ Ἰησοῦ τοῦ κυρίου ἡμῶν in the text, but the only variants he mentions are the insertion of Χριστοῦ after Ἰησοῦ, and the omission of ἡμῶν. There is no notice of the omission of the words τοῦ θεοῦ καὶ Ἰησοῦ by any of the witnesses. They are not found in P, the best manuscripts of the Vulgate (am fu dem harl), Philoxenian and Harklean Syriac, nor in minuscules 69, 137, 163. These last, however, the Syriac and the minuscules with m, insert Ἰησοῦ Χριστοῦ after ἡμῶν. Kühl believes that the shorter form is probably due to the fact that in the epistle Christ is everywhere regarded as the object of ἐπίγνωσις. But this is really very improbable. For the scribe could not have been aware of this when he began

[1] It is certainly difficult to construct an Apparatus which shall be concise and yet clear. In Jude 22 Baljon adopts ἐλεᾶτε in the text, and yet he leaves the apparatus arranged in such a way as to suggest that he intended to read ἐλέγχετε with Tischendorf.

to write the epistle, so that he must have turned back and deleted the words καὶ θεοῦ καὶ Ἰησοῦ afterwards. At the same time it is a fundamental principle of textual criticism that the *lectio brevior* is to be preferred. Reference may be made to the *Epilogus* of Wordsworth and White, ch. vi., *De regulis a nobis in textu constituendo adhibitis*, where the very title of section 4 implies this principle: "Cum brevior lectio probabilior sit, codices A F H* M Y plerumque praeferendi sunt," and where the most conspicuous examples of this rule are said to be "Additamenta nominum propriorum, et praecipue sanctorum—*e.g.* Jesus, Christus, Dominus, Deus." It is true that in the passage before us we have not simply a case of the insertion of a word or words understood; at the same time, here if anywhere the text is more likely to have been extended than abbreviated. It remains to be seen whether P exhibits a good text in other passages of the Catholic Epistles as well as this, but so far as the minuscules 69 and 137 are concerned, they justly bear a good reputation. Hort calls 69 one of the better cursives, and 137 has a text so closely resembling that of Codices D E as to be of material assistance when these are defective. The minuscules are too often regarded as mere ciphers; as if a cipher more or less behind a number did not make a vast difference. In the very next verse we find 137 supporting ℵ A in reading τὰ πάντα, which is accepted by Tischendorf and Weiss, and preferred also by Kühl. In this instance it contradicts P, which omits τὰ with B C K L.

i. 12. Here μελλήσω is given by ℵ A B C P, οὐ μελλήσω by 8 f tol (*non differam*), and οὐκ ἀμελήσω by K L etc. ("the Antiochean recension and the Syriac versions," Zahn). "Μελλήσω, with the present infinitive, can hardly be simply a periphrastic future. The idea is rather that the writer will be prepared in the future, as well as in the past and in the present, to remind them of the truths they know, whenever the necessity arises. As they had no evidence of the fulfilment of this promise, the copyists and translators found a difficulty with this expression, and hence the variants." Zahn, *Einleitung*, ii. 53 f.

i. 15. The reading σπουδάζω, found in ℵ 31, and the Armenian, is also attested by the Philoxenian Syriac, a fact which Zahn regards as important. "On transcriptional grounds the reading σπουδάσω, preferred by our editors, would appear to be confirmed by the reading σπουδάσατε, exhibited by the Harklean Syriac and a few minuscules. But in reality both these latter readings merely serve to show that a difficulty was felt again in admitting a promise on the part of Peter which he seemed never to have fulfilled." *Einleitung*, ii. 54. Compare on μελλήσω above.

i. 21. It is probable that Theophilus of Antioch (*Ad Autolycum*, ii. 9) read (οἱ) ἅγιοι (τοῦ) θεοῦ ἄνθρωποι, the form exhibited by ℵ and A ("the chief representatives of the Antiochean family"), and also by several Latin witnesses. See Zahn, *GK.* i. 313; Chase on 2 Peter in Hastings' *Dictionary of the Bible*, vol. iii. p. 801.

ii. 13. On this passage Zahn remarks (*Einleitung*, ii. 53): "The similarity of 2 Peter to the Epistle of Jude was doubtless a source of textual corruption. But it may also aid us in correcting the text. Because, whichever of the two we regard as the original, in any case the one is our earliest witness to the text of the other. If we accept the reading ἀγάπαις in Jude 12, it follows either (1) that Jude read ἀγάπαις in 2 Peter, and that this is the original reading there, or (2) that Peter, supposing he wrote second, altered Jude's ἀγάπαις to ἀπάταις, which it is hard to conceive, the former being so unmistakable, and the latter much less suitable to the context. In either case, therefore, ἀγάπαις would seem to be the correct reading in 2 Peter ii. 13." No doubt the alteration of ἀγάπαις to ἀπάταις is "hard to conceive," but it is not inconceivable. As illustrating how a piece of writing may be misread, it is sufficient to point to Justin's mistake with regard to "Semoni Sanco Deo Fidio."[1] As regards the par-

[1] The inscription on a column at Rome dedicated to a Sabine god which Justin

ticular words before us, I may be allowed to cite my *Philologica Sacra*, p. 47, where I have referred to the frequent confusion of ἀγαπάω and ἀπατάω, ἀγάπη and ἀπάτη in manuscripts of the Old Testament. In Ps. lxxviii. 36, for example, out of more than one hundred manuscripts that have been collated, not one has preserved the correct reading ἠπάτησαν; all have ἠγάπησαν. In 2 Chron. xviii. 2 again only one has the correct text ἠπάτα. From a psychological point of view, therefore, it would seem more natural to suppose that ἀπάταις is the original reading in the passage under consideration, and ἀγάπαις the transcriptional error. The authorities for each are distributed as follows :—

	ἀγάπαις.	ἀπάταις.
2 Peter ii. 13,	A[c] B m vg, Syr[phil], Syr[hark. mg], Sahid.	ℵ A* C K L P . . . . Syr[hark], Copt., Arm.
Jude 12,	ℵ B K L vg, Sahid., Copt., Syr[phil], Syr[hark], Arm.	A C 44, 56.

In the first edition of this work I said it was strange, considering the frequent confusion of ἀγάπη and ἀπάτη, that Tischendorf goes by the majority of his witnesses in the case of 2 Peter ii. 13 (Westcott and Hort in their text, Weiss, Weymouth, and Baljon all do the same), "whereas the same word should be read in both cases, and that ἀγάπαις. Otherwise it would be necessary to suppose that the text was already corrupt when the one writer used the epistle of the other, no matter whether Peter or Jude: quod variat, verum esse non potest." I cannot understand an argument like that of Kühl (Meyer[6], on 2 Peter ii. 13, p. 428): "ἀπάταις is presumably original in one of the passages, most likely in 2 Peter, as ἀγάπαις goes better with ὑμῶν in Jude 12 than with αὐτῶν here. B has ἀγάπαις in both places, and C in the same way ἀπάταις, which is explainable on the supposition

read as "Simoni Sancto Deo," and understood as referring to Simon Magus. See Kurtz, *Church History* (Macpherson), i. p. 97 ; Neander, *Church History* (Bohn), ii. p. 123, note.

that originally the one word stood in the one passage and the other in the other. Nearly all recent expositors favour the reading ἀπάταις in 2 Peter." I am glad now to have the powerful support of Zahn in my dissent from that view. Reference may be made to the excellent article on Jude by F. H. Chase in Hastings' *Dictionary of the Bible*, ii. 799–805. His first paragraph is on the "Transmission of the Text," and the article is a model of what such things should be.[1] On the Philoxenian Syriac see the work of Merx mentioned above, p. 106 (5). On the rest of the verse, see Zahn, *Einleitung*, ii. 71. He points out that Tischendorf's apparatus is misleading here, as it fails to notice the omission of ὑμῖν by the Philoxenian Syriac, the Sahidic version, the Speculum of Pseudo-Augustine (m), and by Pseudo-Cyprian. In his opinion it is an interpolation due to the συν— of συνευωχούμενοι. These pronouns are very liable to be interpolated, as is pointed out by Wordsworth and White in their *Epilogus*, p. 729, where these "additamenta" come next after "Proper Names"; see above, p. 238.

ii. 15. On Βοσόρ, see p. 243 f.

ii. 22*b*. In Hippolytus, *Refutatio*, ix. 7, we find: μετ' οὐ πολὺ δὲ ἐπὶ τὸν αὐτὸν βόρβορον ἀνεκυλίοντο. On the connection of this with 2 Peter ii. 22, see Zahn, *GK*. i. 316. Wendland tried to make out that it is a saying of Heraclitus. Compare also Clement, Λόγος Προτρεπτικός, x. 96: ὕες γάρ, φασίν, ἥδονται βορβόρῳ μᾶλλον ἢ καθαρῷ ὕδατι, καὶ ἐπὶ φορυτῷ μαργαίνουσιν κατὰ Δημόκριτον.

iii. 6. The conjectural reading δι' ὃν for δι' ὧν Schmiedel thinks well worthy of consideration. See his *Winer*, § 19.

iii. 10. None of the variants here appears to be the correct reading (κατακαήσεται in various forms: ἀφανισθήσονται: εὑρεθήσεται). What is required is a passive form of ῥέω, or one of its compounds (? διαρρυήσεται).

iii. 16. The article is inserted before ἐπιστολαῖς by א and K L P ("the Antiochean recension"), but omitted by A B C.

[1] Compare also the articles on 1 and 2 Peter by the same writer in vol. iii.

Zahn, who would omit it, points out that ἐν πάσαις ταῖς ἐπιστολαῖς would imply a complete collection of Paul's Epistles, and would include all the constituents without exception, whereas without the article the phrase contrasts one epistle known to the readers with those of all kinds that he had written. See *Einleitung*, ii. 108. Tischendorf admitted the reading now favoured by critics in his seventh edition, but rejected it in the eighth. This same thing occurs not infrequently. See the article on 2 Peter by Chase in Hastings' *Dictionary of the Bible*, vol. iii. p. 810.

1 John.

iv. 3. Von der Goltz has shown conclusively what was long a matter of conjecture, that Origen not only knew the reading ὁ λύει τὸν Ἰησοῦν, but seemingly preferred it; and that Clement also cites the text in this form in his work on the Passover, which is all but entirely lost. He has also established anew the reliable nature of the Latin version of Irenæus in the matter of Biblical quotations. See Zahn in the *ThLbl.*, 1899, col. 180; *Einleitung*, ii. 574.

v. 7. The "comma Johanneum" needs no further discussion in an Introduction to the *Greek* Testament, but its history on Latin soil is all the more interesting. The fact that it is still defended even from the Protestant side is interesting only from a pathological point of view. On the decision of the Holy Office, confirmed by the Pope on the 15th January 1897, see Hetzenauer's edition of the New Testament, and the notice of it by Dobschütz in the *ThLz.*, 1899, No. 10. On the literature, compare also Kölling (Breslau, 1893); W. Orme's *Memoir of the Controversy respecting the Three Heavenly Witnesses, 1 John v. 7* (London, 1830), New Edition, with Notes and Appendix by Ezra Abbot (New York, 1866); C. Forster, *A New Plea for the Authenticity of the Text of the Three Heavenly Witnesses* (Cambridge, 1867); H. T. Armfield, *The Three Witnesses: The disputed Text in St. John* (London, 1893).

James.

An Arabic scholion, attributed to Hippolytus, cites this epistle under the name of Jude. See Zahn, *GK.* i. 320, 2; 323, 3. In two minuscules cited by Tischendorf, Ἰακώβου is followed by τοῦ ἀδελφοῦ θεοῦ or ἀδελφοθεοῦ, and in one of the subscriptions by τοῦ ἀδελφοθεοῦ. The subscription in ff reads "explicit epistola Jacobi filii Zaebedei (*sic*)." See Zahn's *Einleitung*, i. 75.

ii. 2. συναγωγὴν appears without the article in ℵ* B C and one of Scrivener's minuscules. This reading is accepted by Zahn, who sees in it an indication that those to whom the epistle is addressed were in possession of several synagogues, that is supposing the word to mean *meeting-place*, and not simply assembly, as he himself is inclined to believe. See *Einleitung*, i. 60, 66.

Jude.

5. This verse exhibits an uncommonly large number of variants. Thus εἰδότας occurs with or without ὑμᾶς after it; for πάντα we find both πάντας and τοῦτο; while the position of ἅπαξ varies, the word being found before πάντα, ὅτι, and λαὸν. But even that is not all. Most recent editors read ὅτι Κύριος, but we find also ὅτι Ἰησοῦς: ὅτι ὁ θεὸς: and ὅτι ὁ Κύριος (*textus receptus*). Tischendorf's apparatus might lead one to suppose that the witnesses for Ἰησοῦς and ὁ θεὸς omit ὅτι altogether, but that is not so. The ambiguity is due to the loose way in which the note is given. Westcott and Hort think it probable that the original text was OTIO, and that this was read as OTIIC̅, and perhaps as OTIKC̅. Kühl thinks that the easiest explanation of the variants is to suppose that κύριος was the original reading, and that Ἰησοῦς and θεὸς were derived from it. But it seems to me that Zahn has better reason on his side when he argues for ὅτι Ἰησοῦς as the original reading.

He first of all eliminates ὁ θεὸς as having no great attestation, and as being found alongside of κύριος in Clement (*dominus deus*). The choice, therefore, lies between κύριος and Ἰησοῦς. The latter has by far the stronger external attestation, it is the *lectio ardua*, and is, on internal grounds, also to be preferred. See *Einleitung*, ii. 88.

22, 23. Zahn has a strong impression that this passage lies at the foundation of *Didache*, ii. 7: οὐ μισήσεις πάντα ἄνθρωπον, ἀλλὰ οὓς μὲν ἐλέγξεις, περὶ δὲ ὧν προσεύξῃ, οὓς δὲ ἀγαπήσεις ὑπὲρ τὴν ψυχήν σου. If this is really so, we have here a piece of very early testimony, not certainly to the actual words, but to the thought conveyed. See *Einleitung*, ii. 86.

Subscription: At the end of the Armenian Bible of 1698 we find a note to the effect that "this epistle was written in the year 64 by Judas Jacobi, who is also called Lebbaeus and Thaddaeus, and who preached the Gospel to the Armenians and the Persians."

APOCALYPSE.

Apart from particular passages, the last book of the Bible cannot be unreservedly recommended to the devout laity for special study, but it is peculiarly well adapted as an introduction to the method of textual criticism, and that for two reasons. First of all, because the number of available witnesses to the text is comparatively small, and, secondly, because these are more easily grouped here than in the other divisions of the New Testament. Reference may be made in this connection to the first part of Bousset's critical studies on the text of the Apocalypse, where the distinction drawn by Bengel between the Andreas and Arethas groups of manuscripts is correctly emphasized. At the same time Bousset himself comes to the rather unsatisfactory conclusion that an eclectic mode of procedure is all that is possible at present. An attempt has been made above (p. 157) with the conclusion of the Apocalypse. We shall now try a few further examples.

In order to ascertain the relationship of the manuscripts we must select passages that exhibit a considerable divergence of meaning with a small variation of form. Such a passage occurs in the last chapter. In Apoc. xxii. 14, after the words "blessed are they," we read, in the one class of witnesses, "that wash their robes," in the other, "that do his commandments." That is to say, we have in the one case ΟΙΠΛΥΝΟΝΤЄϹΤΑϹϹΤΟΛΑϹΑΥΤΩΝ and in the other ΟΙΠΟΙΟΥΝΤЄϹΤΑϹЄ̄ΤΟΛΑϹΑΥΤΟΥ. The difference is exceedingly small, especially when we consider that in early times ΟΙ was frequently written Υ, and ЄΝ at the end of a line Є̄. I have no doubt that "wash their robes" is the original reading here and that "do his commandments" is the later alteration, though, of course, others will hold the opposite view. For the former we have the authority of ℵ A, for the latter that of Q (*i.e.*, B[apoc]; see above, p. 80) with its associates. The question now becomes: Are there any passages where ℵ and A part company, and which are decisive in favour of ℵ? It is impossible to say offhand whether ℵ or A has preserved the correct text. ℵ contains corrections that A does not, and *vice versa*. Take another example.

The author of the Apocalypse follows the Hebrew idiom, according to which the word or phrase in apposition to an oblique case is put in the nominative.[1] Thus we have:

ii. 20. τὴν γυναῖκα Ἰεζαβὲλ ἡ λέγουσα. Q makes this ἣ λέγει, and the corrector of ℵ τὴν λέγουσαν. Similarly, iii. 12, τῆς καινῆς Ἱερουσαλὴμ ἡ καταβαίνουσα, where again Q has ἣ καταβαίνει, and ℵ[c] τῆς καταβαινούσης. But it is not only the later corrector of ℵ that does this: the first scribe of that manuscript does it himself. For example:

xiv. 12. ℵ has τῶν τηρούντων instead of οἱ τηροῦντες; in verse 14 ἔχοντα instead of ἔχων; in xx. 2, τὸν ὄφιν instead of

[1] See Blass, *Grammar of N. T. Greek*, § 31, 6, Eng. Tr., p. 80 f. Compare the similar German idiom used in the titles of books, "von X. Y. ordentlicher Professor." How naturally this comes to a Hebrew is shown by the fact that Sal. Bär, in his translation of the Massoretic note at the end of the books of Samuel (Leipzig, Tauchnitz, 1892, p. 158), among other lovely things has "ad mortem Davidis *rex* Israelis."

ὁ ὄφις, etc. In other places A, in this last A *alone*, it appears, has preserved the correct text.

There are other places, again, where the correct reading is preserved, perhaps, only in a later manuscript, or in none at all. We may compare with the idiom in the Apocalypse what we find at the beginning of the book in the passage about the seven spirits before the throne of God.

i. 4. ἀπὸ τῶν ἑπτὰ πνευμάτων . . . . ἐνώπιον τοῦ θρόνου αὐτοῦ. In the space indicated by the dots Erasmus has ἅ ἐστιν, Codex 36 has ἅ εἰσιν, Q and C have ἃ, which is adopted by Tischendorf and Westcott and Hort, ℵ and A have τῶν, which is adopted by Lachmann, Tregelles, and by Westcott and Hort in their margin, while Codex 80 has nothing at all. All these variants are explainable on the supposition that the original reading was τὰ. Exception being taken to this construction, one copyist made it τῶν, the other ἃ, the third supplied the copula, and the fourth dropped the offending word altogether. Similarly, in chap. v. 13, ℵ alone has preserved the correct reading τὸ, for which the others have ὃ or ὅ ἐστιν. Another case is ii. 13, where the writer wished to say, "in the days of Antipas, my faithful witness, who was slain." According to the idiom mentioned above, while Ἀντίπα was in the genitive, ὁ μάρτυς would be in the nominative of apposition. But owing to the influence of this nominative, Ἀντίπα was made nominative so as to agree with it, and the sentence then ran, ἐν ταῖς ἡμέραις Ἀντίπας ὁ μάρτυς μου . . . . ὃς . . . . which could not be construed. The consequence was corrections of all sorts. The boldest expedient was simply to drop the ὃς, but other means were adopted to relieve the construction. After ἡμέραις some inserted αἷς or ἐν αἷς, Erasmus read ἐμαῖς, ℵ has ἐν ταῖς, and some Latin witnesses *illis*. But read Ἀντίπα in the genitive and all is in order.[1]

[1] In this (independent) suggestion I am glad to find myself in agreement with Lachmann (*Studien und Kritiken*, 1830, p. 839), and Westcott and Hort (ii., App., 137). I see that Baljon and Zahn too follow it. But Bousset still writes ἡμέραις αἷς.

The Apocalypse presents quite a number of passages enabling us to distinguish the manuscripts. There is very little difference in form between λύσαντι and λούσαντι (i. 5), ἀετοῦ and ἀγγέλου (viii. 13), λίθον and λίνον (xv. 6), but it makes a great difference whether we read "who redeemed us" or "who washed us," an "eagle flying" or "an angel flying," "wearing pure linen" or "wearing pure stone." These variations are the result of *accidental* errors in transcription. But we meet an instance of *intentional* alteration in xiii. 18, where the number of the beast is variously given as 666 and 616.

Grouping the witnesses for the former variants we have—

i. 5.	λύσαντι,	א A C, Syriac,[1] Armenian.
	λούσαντι,	Q P, Vulgate, Coptic, Ethiopic.
viii. 13.	ἀετοῦ,	א A Q, Vulgate, Syriac,[1] Coptic, Ethiopic.
	ἀγγέλου,	P, Armenian.

The two readings are combined not only by certain commentators, but in some manuscripts, ἀγγέλου ὡς ἀετοῦ.

xv. 6.	λίθον καθαρόν,	A C, am fu demid tol.
	λίνον καθαρόν,	P, Syriac,[1] Armenian, Clementine-Vulgate.

λινοῦν καθαρόν is read by Q, and καθαροὺς λίνους by א.

Tregelles and Westcott alone accept the reading λίθον; all the other editors regard it as an early transcriptional error. Holtzmann refers to the parallel passages i. 13, iv. 4, vii. 9, 13, xvii. 4, xviii. 16, xix. 8, 14, in support of λίνον, but they point rather the other way. For "fine linen" Apocalypse has βύσσινος five times, but never once λίνος, which means only the material, and not the garment made of it. Moreover, we find a parallel in the Old Testament, though in another connection, in Ezekiel xxviii. 13, where we read πάντα λίθον χρηστὸν ἐνδέδεσαι, so that λίθον here must not be so confidently rejected. Λίθον was more liable to be changed to

[1] Including Gwynn's Syriac manuscript; see above, p. 102.

λίνον than *vice versa*, as the Vulgate shows, in which the authorised printed edition has *linteo* where the manuscripts read *lapidem*. At the same time one cannot but admit that primitive transcriptional errors do occur. The reading ἀγγέλου in viii. 13, to which certain manuscripts prefix ἑνὸς, seems to me to be corroborated by ἄλλον ἄγγελον πετόμενον in xiv. 6. Or are we to read ἀετόν there in the face of all the witnesses?

v. 1. The correct text here is that adopted by Zahn: γεγραμμένον ἔσωθεν καὶ ὄπισθεν κατεσφραγισμένον. Grotius, though mistaken as to the true text, was the first to give the right interpretation of the words by taking ἔσω (ἔσωθεν) with γεγραμμένον, and ἔξωθεν (ὄπισθεν) with κατεσφραγισμένον. "Locus sic distinguendus γεγραμμένον ἔσω, καὶ ἔξωθεν κατεσφραγισμένον." This combination of the words ("haec nova distinctio") was combated for the reason among others that it deprived them of all their force and rendered them superfluous, for who ever saw a roll that was written on the outside and sealed on the inside. See Pole's *Synopsis*, where it is said of Grotius, "tam infelix interpres Apocalypseos est magnus ille Hugo in rebus minusculis." Zahn (*Einleitung*, ii. 596) improves the text of Grotius, but retains his connection of the words. He holds that ἔσωθεν and ὄπισθεν are not correlative terms, and that the idea of a papyrus roll written on both sides (ὀπισθόγραφον) must be abandoned; compare above, p. 43, n. 2. The book was, in fact, not a roll but a codex. Two things point to this. There is, first, the fact that is said to be ἐπὶ τὴν δεξιάν. Had it been a roll it would have been ἐν τῇ δεξιᾷ. Moreover, the word used for opening the book is ἀνοῖξαι, and not, as in the case of rolls, ἀνελίσσειν, ἀνειλεῖν, or ἀναπτύσσειν. That it was not written on the outside is also shown by the fact that it was sealed with seven seals, the purpose of which was to make the reading of the book impossible. Not till the seventh seal is broken is the book open and its contents displayed. This βιβλίον is quite different from the βιβλαρίδιον mentioned in chapter x. 2, 9. See also

E. Huschke, *Das Buch mit 7 Siegeln* (1860), to which Zahn refers (*lib. cit.* 597).

ix. 17. For ὑακινθίνους Primasius has *spineas* (=ἀκανθίνους), a reading which neither Bousset nor Baljon, strange to say, think worth recording. Bousset rightly observes that in the following verse πῦρ corresponds to πύρινος, and θεῖον to θειώδης, so that καπνός lets us see what the writer understood as the colour of hyacinth—viz. the colour of smoke. But the ideas of "thorns" (*spineae*) and "smoke" are even more closely related.

xiii. 18. Irenæus found 616 given as the number of the beast in some manuscripts, which he could only explain as a transcriptional error: "hoc autem arbitror scriptorum peccatum fuisse ut solet fieri quoniam et per literas numeri ponuntur, facile literam Graecam quae sexaginta enuntiat numerum in *iota* Graecorum literam expansam." In reality, however, the change from ξ to ι would be a contraction rather than an expansion, and the alteration would seem to be intentional, seeing that 666 in Hebrew characters gives the Greek form Neron Kesar, and 616 the Latin Nero Kesar. Irenæus himself, however, appeals to the fact that the number 666 was found ἐν πᾶσι τοῖς σπουδαίοις καὶ ἀρχαίοις ἀντιγράφοις, μαρτυρούντων αὐτῶν ἐκείνων τῶν κατ' ὄψιν τὸν Ἰωάννην ἑωρακότων (v. 30, 1–3). The opening words in the Latin translation run, "in omnibus antiquis et probatissimis et veteribus scripturis." The subscription which he himself appended to his own principal work (see above, p. 149) shows how scrupulously exact he was with respect to ἀντίγραφα, so that we may give him credit for having consulted old and reliable manuscripts of the Apocalypse. The erroneous reading (616) is now found only in C and two minuscules (5 and 11).

xxii. 11. The only authorities cited by Tischendorf in support of the reading δικαιωθήτω (in place of δικαιοσύνην ποιησάτω) are the two minuscules 38 and 79 and the Clementine Vulgate. But we find the passage alluded to in the epistle which the Church of Lyons wrote giving an account of the Martyrdom of the year 177: ἵνα πληρωθῇ ἡ γραφή· ὁ ἄνομος ἀνομησάτω ἔτι, καὶ ὁ δίκαιος δικαιωθήτω ἔτι (apud Euseb., *Eccles. Hist.*, v. 1, 58). This lends such support to the reading δικαιωθήτω in Apoc. xxii. 11, that Zahn not unnaturally speaks of it as "certainly the original text" (*GK.* i. 201). E. A. Abbott places the date of the Epistle of the Church of Lyons as early as 155 (see *Expositor*, 1896, i. 111–126). Another aspect would be given to the question if the Greek form of the Epistle were derived from a Latin, or if, as Resch supposed, the words were a quotation of a saying of Jesus (*Agrapha*, § 133, p. 263 ff.).

I take the opportunity of appending to Resch's work the fine saying which Zahn cites from Augustine's *Contra Adversarium Legis et Prophetarum* (ed. Bassan. x. 659 ff.) as an otherwise unknown Apocryphum. The disciples asked Jesus "de Judaeorum prophetis, quid sentire deberet, qui de adventu eius aliquid cecinisse in praeteritum putantur." And He, "commotus talia eos etiam nunc sentire, respondit: Dimisistis vivum qui ante vos est et de mortuis fabulamini." A similar saying from the *Acta Petri Vercell.* 10 is cited by Harnack in connection with the third of the Oxyrhynchus Logia: "Qui mecum sunt, non me intellexerunt."

APPENDIX I.

THE following is a list of writers most frequently cited in critical editions of the New Testament. They are arranged chronologically, but it must be remembered that the dates are more or less uncertain, and that in the case of many writers the period of activity lies in two centuries :—

FIRST CENTURY.

GREEK.		LATIN.	
Clement of Rome,	fl. 95		
Ignatius,	d. 107?		
Barnabas,	?		

SECOND CENTURY.

GREEK.		LATIN.	
Didache,	?		
Hermas,	140?		
Marcion (in Epiphanius and Tertullian),	fl. 145		
Aristides,	139		
Polycarp,	d. 155		
Justin Martyr,	d. 165		
Clementine Homilies and Recognitions,	ca. 190		
Papias,	fl. 140		
Gospel of Peter,	ca. 170		
Tatian,	fl. 170		
Athenagoras,	fl. 177		
Theophilus of Antioch,	d. 182		
Celsus (in Origen),	ca. 180		
Hegesippus,	fl. 180		
Irenæus (see Latin),	d. 202	Tertullian,	fl. 200
Clement of Alexandria,	fl. 194	Irenæi Interpres (according to Tischendorf and Gregory, but see below).	

Third Century.

Greek.		Latin.	
Hippolytus, . . .	fl. 220		
Julius Africanus, . .	fl. 220		
Gregory Thaumaturgus,	d. 265		
Origen, ...	d. 248	Cyprian, ...	d. 258
Dionysius of Alexandria,	d. 265	Novatian, . . .	fl. 251
Porphyry, . . .	d. 304	Lactantius, . . .	fl. 306
Pamphilus, . . .	d. 308	Arnobius, . . .	d. 306
Methodius, . . .	d. 310	Victorinus of Pettau, .	d. 303
Didascalia, . . .	?		
Apostolic Constitutions (and fourth century, etc.).			

Fourth Century.

Arius, ...	fl. 325		
Jacobus Nisibenus (Syrian),	d. 338	Juvencus, . . .	fl. 330
Eusebius of Cæsarea, .	d. 340	Irenæi Interpres (according to Westcott and Hort).	
Aphraates (Syrian), .	fl. 340		
Eustathius, Bishop of Antioch, . . .	fl. 350	Hilary of Poictiers, .	d. 368
Zeno, ...	fl. 350	Victorinus of Rome, .	fl. 360
Athanasius, . . .	d. 373	Damasus, Pope, . .	fl. 366
Ephraem (Syrian), .	d. 373	Lucifer, ...	d. 371
Basil the Great, . .	d. 379	Pacianus, . . .	fl. 370
Evagrius of Pontus, .	d. 380	Optatus, ...	fl. 371
Cyril of Jerusalem, .	d. 386	Philastrius, . . .	fl. 380
Amphilochius, . .	fl. 370	Gaudentius, . . .	fl. 387
Macarius Magnes, .	fl. 373	Rufinus, ...	fl. 397
Gregory Nazianzen, .	d. 390	Ambrose, ...	d. 397
Gregory of Nyssa, .	d. 394	Ambrosiaster, . .	fl. 390
Diodorus of Tarsus, .	d. 394	Chromatius, . . .	fl. 390
Didymus of Alexandria,	d. 394	Tyconius, . . .	fl. 390
Theophilus of Alexandria,	fl. 388	Jerome, ...	d. 420
Epiphanius, . . .	d. 403	Priscillian, . . .	ca. fin.
Chrysostom, . .	fl. 407	Auctor libri *De Rebaptismate*.	
Isidore of Pelusium, .	fl. 412		

Fifth Century.

Greek.		Latin.	
Nonnus, ...	fl. 400	Faustus, ...	fl. 400
Theodore of Mopsuestia,	d. 429	Hilary of Arles, . . .	d. 429
Victor of Antioch, .	d. 430	Augustine, ...	d. 430
Cyril of Alexandria, .	d. 444	Prosper of Aquitania, .	fl. 431
Theodotus of Ancyra, .	fl. 431	Sedulius, ...	fl. 431
Basil of Seleucia, . .	fl. 440	Leo the Great, . .	fl. 440
Socrates, ...	fl. 440	Petrus Chrysologus, . .	d. 455
Theodoret, Bishop of Cyrus, ...	d. 457	Gennadius, ...	fl. 459
		Vigilius, ...	fl. 484
Euthalius, ...	d. 458	Auctor libri *De Promissionibus*.	
Sozomen, ...	fl. 440		

Sixth Century.

Candidus Isaurus, .	fl. 500	Fulgentius, Bishop of Ruspe, . . .	d. 533
Severus of Antioch, .	fl. 512	Justinian, ...	fl. 530
Theodorus Lector, .	fl. 525	Cæsarius of Arles, .	d. 543
Andreas, Bishop of Cæsarea, . . .	ca. fin.	Primasius, ...	fl. 550
Maxentius, ...	?	Victor, Bishop of Tunis,	d. 565
Cosmas Indicopleustes,	fl. 535	Cassiodorus, . .	d. 575
Eutychius, ...	fl. 553	Gregory the Great, .	d. 604
Chronicon Paschale.			

Seventh Century.

Antiochus the Monk, .	fl. 614	Peter the Deacon, .	?
Andreas of Crete, .	fl. 635 ?		
Maximus Confessor, .	d. 662		
Modestus of Jerusalem,	?		

Eighth Century.

Damascenus, Johannes,	fl. 730	Bede, ...	d. 735
Nicephorus, . . .	fl. 787		
Petrus Siculus, . .	?		

Ninth Century.

Greek.		Latin.
Photius of Constantinople,	d. 891	

Tenth Century.

Greek.		Latin.
Arethas,	?	
Symeon,	?	
Œcumenius,	ca. 950?	
Suidas the Lexicographer,	ca. 980	

Eleventh Century

Greek.		Latin.
Theophylact, Bishop of Bulgaria,	fl. 1077	

Twelfth Century.

Greek.		Latin.
Euthymius Zigabenus,	fl. 1116	
Nicetas of Byzantium,	d. 1206	

APPENDIX II.

Ἀντίγραφα.

I HAD intended to give in full those passages of the Fathers known to me in which mention is made of manuscripts prepared by themselves or others. In this way I hoped to make a start towards supplying the desideratum spoken of on p. 154 above. But I feel that in order to be anything like complete, this would occupy too much space for the present work. Even the passages in which Origen speaks of ἀντίγραφα, though not "innumerable," as Zahn says with a touch of exaggeration, are yet too numerous to be included here. A considerable number of such passages are already given in full in Tischendorf's Editio Octava. I have contented myself with giving here an alphabetic list of these, in order to facilitate a geographical and chronological survey of the relevant matter. Where only one passage is given, it will be found in full in Tischendorf. Passages in which the word ἀντίγραφον itself or its synonyms (codex, exemplar, etc.) does not occur, but where express mention is yet made of readings found in manuscripts, are given in brackets.

Some surprising facts are brought to light by such quotations. Witness the remark made by Basil the Great (ob. 379) on Luke xxii. 36, who tells us that in Cappadocia in his time many manuscripts, indeed, if the text is correct the majority of manuscripts (τὰ πολλὰ τῶν ἀντιγράφων), exhibited a reading now found in only one single manuscript, and that the main representative of the "Western" text; I refer to Codex Bezae. See above on Luke xxii. 36. I may mention here that a certain "Basilius diaconus" was the possessor of a magnificent Bible, the cover of the first part of which was used for Codex Syrohexaplaris Ambrosianus. The inscription ran: † ΒΙΒΛΟΣ Ᾱ ΤΩΝ ΘΕΙΩΝ | ΓΡΑΦΩΝ ΠΑΛΑΙΑΣ ΚΑΙ || ΝΕΑΣ ΔΙΑΘΗΚΗΣ ΔΙΑΦΕΡ | ΕΙ | ΔΕ ΒΑΣΙΛΕΙΩ ΔΙΑΚΟΝΩ † |. See the facsimile and description in Ceriani's edition, *Monumenta Sacra et Profana*, vol. vii., folio.

Adamantius (*i.e.* Origen), see Hieronymus.
Ambrosiaster, Rom. v. 14; the quotation should be corrected in accordance with Haussleiter, *Forschungen*, iv. 32; (Rom. xii. 13); 1 Cor. v. 3; Gal. ii. 5.
Ambrose, Luke vii. 35; Gal. iv. 8.
Anastasius, Matt. xxvii. 18.
Andreas, Apoc. iii. 7.
Apollinarius, possibly mentioned in the scholia in Codex Marchalianus (see Swete's *Septuagint*, iii. p. viii), John vii. 53.
——, see Macedonius.
Apollonides, Eusebius, *Eccles. Hist.*, v. 28.
Arethas, Apoc. i. 2, iii. 7.
Asclepiades, Eusebius, *Eccles. Hist.*, v. 28.
Athanasius (also Pseudo-Athanasius), Matt. v. 22; 2 Thess. ii. 9; for his mention of the πυκτία made for the Emperor Constans, see above, p. 181, note, and p. 184; Zahn's *Forschungen*, iii. 100, *GK.* i. 73.
Augustine, Matt. xxvii. 9; Luke iii. 22; Rom. v. 14; (Rom. xiii. 14); 1 Cor. xv. 5; Phil. iii. 3.
Basil (the Great), Luke xxii. 36; Ephes. i. 1; Zahn, *Einleitung*, i. 345.
Bede, Acts, *passim.*
Chronicon Paschale, John xix. 14 (see above, p. 30).
Chrysostom, John i. 28.
Didymus, 2 Cor. i. 1.
Epiphanius, Matt. i. 8, ii. 11 (τὰς πήρας ἑαυτῶν, ἢ τοὺς θησαυρούς, ὡς ἔχει ἔνια τῶν ἀντιγράφων, i. 430, 1085). See Westcott and Hort, "Notes," *in loco*; Matt. viii. 28; Luke viii. 26, xix. 41, (xxii. 43 f.); John i. 28; Ephes. i. 1.
Eusebius, Matt. xiii. 35, xxvii. 9; Mark i. 2, xvi. 3, 9 ff.; John xix. 14.
Euthalius, Jude 25.
Euthymius, (Mark xvi. 9); John vii. 53.
Gregory of Nyssa (Pseudo-), Mark xvi. 2, 9.
Hermophilus, Eusebius, *Eccles. Hist.*, v. 28.
Hesychius, Mark xvi. 2, 9.
Hieronymus (Jerome), Matt. xiii. 35, xxi. 31, xxiv. 17; Mark iii. 17,

xvi. 9; Luke ii. 33, (xviii. 30), xxii. 43 f.; John vii. 53; Acts xv. 29; 1 Cor. ix. 5; Gal. ii. 5, iii. 1; Ephes. iii. 14; 1 Tim. v. 19; Heb. ii. 10.

Irenæus, Apoc. xiii. 18 (see above, *in loco*).

Isidore, Heb. ix. 17.

Macedonius (see Draeseke, *ThStKr.*, 1890, 12), Rom. viii. 11.

Marcion, see Epiphanius, Ephes. i. 1.

Maximinus, 1 Cor. xv. 47.

Œcumenius, Acts xiv. 26.

Origen, Matt. ii. 18, viii. 28, xvi. 20, xviii. 1, (xix. 19), (xxi. 15), (xxvii. 9), xxvii. 16 ff. (see above, *in loco*); Mark ii. 14; Luke i. 46; John i. 28; Rom. iv. 3, xvi. 23 (see Zahn, *Einleitung*, i. 276, 285); Col. ii. 15.

Pierius, see Hieronymus.

Severus, Mark xvi. 9.

Socrates, 1 John iv. 3.

Theodoret, Rom. xvi. 3.

Theodore of Mopsuestia, Heb. ii. 10.

Theodotus, Eusebius, *Eccles. Hist.*, v. 28.

Theophylact, 2 Thess. iii. 14; Heb. ii. 10, x. 1.

Victor, Mark xvi. 9.

Mention is made of ἀντίγραφα in anonymous scholia on Matt. ii. 18, xx. 28, (xxii. 12); Mark xi. 13; Luke xvi. 19 (giving the name of the Rich Man as Ninive, *i.e.*, Phinees; see Rendel Harris in the *Expositor*, March 1900); Luke xxii. 43 f., xxiv. 13; John i. 29, vii. 53, xxi. 25; Rom. viii. 24.

INDEX I.

INDEX II.

Passages of the New Testament referred to.

NOTE.—*Passages treated in the Critical Notes are not entered here.*

ΘΕΩ ΔΟΞΑ.

PLATE I.

ΑΥΤΟΥΔΙΑΙ̅Υ̅Χ̅Υ̅ΩΗ
ΔΟΞΑΕΙΣΤΟΥΣΑΙΩ
ΝΑΣΤΩΝΑΙΩΝΩ̅
ΑΜΗΝ·
ΠΑΡΑΚΑΛΩΔΕΥΜΑΣ
ΑΔΕΛΦΟΙΑΝΕΧΕ
ΣΘΕΤΟΥΛΟΓΟΥΤΗΣ
ΠΑΡΑΚΛΗΣΕΩΣΚΑΙΓΑΡ
ΔΙΑΒΡΑΧΕΩΝΕΠΕ
ΣΤΙΛΑΥΜΙΝ
ΓΕΙΝΩΣΚΕΤΕΤΟΝ
ΑΔΕΛΦΟΝΗΜΩΝ
ΤΙΜΟΘΕΟΝΑΠΟΛΕ
ΛΥΜΕΝΟΝΜΕΘΟΥ
ΕΑΝΤΑΧΙΟΝΕΡΧΗΤΑΙ
ΣΘΕΟΨΟΜΑΙΥΜΑΣ
ΑΣΠΑΣΑΣΘΑΙΠΑΝ
ΤΑΣΤΟΥΣΗΓΟΥΜΕ
ΝΟΥΣΥΜΩΝΚΑΙ
ΠΑΝΤΑΣΤΟΥΣΑΓΙΟΥΣ·
ΑΣΠΑΖΟΝΤΑΙΥΜΑΣ
ΟΙΑΠΟΤΗΣΙΤΑΛΙΑΣ
ΗΧΑΡΙΣΜΕΤΑΠΑΝ
ΤΩΝΥΜΩΝΑΜΗΝ

ΠΡΟΣ ΕΒΡΑΙΟΥΣ

ΣΤΙΧΟΙ

(1) א. Codex Sinaiticus.
Last column of Hebrews (xiii. 21–25).

ΠΡΟΣΕΧΕΤΕΕΑΥΤΟΙΣΚΑΙΠΑΝΤΙΤΩ
ΠΟΙΜΝΙΩΕΝΩΥΜΑΣΤΟΠΝ̅Α̅ΤΟ
ΑΓΙΟΝΕΘΕΤΟΕΠΙΣΚΟΠΟΥΣ·
ΠΟΙΜΑΙΝΕΙΝΤΗΝΕΚΚΛΗΣΙΑΝ
ΤΟΥΚ̅Υ̅ΗΝΠΕΡΙΕΠΟΙΗΣΑΤΟΔΙΑ
ΤΟΥΑΙΜΑΤΟΣΤΟΥΙΔΙΟΥ·

(2) A. Codex Alexandrinus.

Acts xx. 28, showing the reading *κυρίου* in line 5.

PLATE II.

ΚΑΤ. ΙΩΑΝ.

CΗΜΕΝΩΝΠΟΙΩΘΑΝΑΤΩΔΟΞΑCΕΙΤΟΝΘΝ
ΚΑΙΤΟΥΤΟΕΙΠΩΝΛΕΓΕΙΑΥΤΩΑΚΟΛΟΥΘΕΙΜΟΙ
ΕΠΙCΤΡΑΦΕΙCΔΕΟΠΕΤΡΟCΒΛΕΠΕΙΤΟΝΜΑΘΗΤΗΝ
ΟΝΗΓΑΠΑ ΙΗC ΑΚΟΛΟΥΘΟΥΝΤΑ
ΟCΚΑΙΑΝΕΠΕCΕΝΕΝΤΩΔΕΙΠΝΩ
ΕΠΙΤΟCΤΗΘΟCΑΥΤΟΥ ΚΑΙΕΙΠΕΝΑΥΤΩ
ΚΕ ΤΙCΕCΤΙΝΟΠΑΡΑΔΙΔΩΝCΕ
ΤΟΥΤΟΝΟΥΝΕΙΔΩΝΟΠΕΤΡΟCΛΕΓΕΙΑΥΤΩ ΙΗΥ·
ΚΕ ΟΥΤΟCΔΕΤΙ· ΛΕΓΕΙΑΥΤΩΟΙΗC
ΕΑΝΑΥΤΟΝΘΕΛΩΜΕΝΕΙΝΟΥΤΩC
ΕΩCΕΡΧΟΜΑΙΤΙΠΡΟCCΕ CΥΜΟΙΑΚΟΛΟΥΘΕΙ
ΕΞΗΛΘΕΝΟΥΝΟΥΤΟCΟΛΟΓΟCΕΙCΤΟΥC

(1) D. CODEX BEZAE CANTABRIGIENSIS.
John xxi. 19–23.

ΟΥΚΑCΧΗΜΟΝΕΙ
ΟΥΖΗΤΕΙΤΑΕΑΥΤΗC
ΟΥΠΑΡΟΞΥΝΕΤΑΙ
ΟΥΛΟΓΙΖΕΤΑΙΤΟΚΑΚΟΝ
ΟΥΧΑΙΡΕΙΕΠΙΤΗΑΔΙΚΙΑ
CΥΝΧΑΙΡΕΙΔΕΤΗΑΛΗΘΕΙΑ
ΠΑΝΤΑCΤΕΓΕΙ
ΠΑΝΤΑΠΙCΤΕΥΕΙ
ΠΑΝΤΑΕΛΠΙΖΕΙ
ΠΑΝΤΑ ΥΠΟΜΕΝΕΙ
Η ΑΓΑΠΗ
ΟΥΔΕΠΟΤΕΕΚΠΙΠΤΕΙ +

(2) D^{paul}. CODEX CLAROMONTANUS.
1 Corinthians xiii. 5–8.

PLATE III.

SEC IOHAN

SIGNIFICANSQUAMORTEHONORIFICABITDM̄
ETHOCCUMDIXISSETDICITILLISEQUEREME
CONUERSUSAUTEMPETRUSUIDETDISCIPULUM
QUEMDILIGEBATIHS SEQUENTEM
QUIETRECUBUITINCENA
SUPERPECTUSEIUS ETDIXITILLI
DME QUISESTQUITRADIDITTE
HUNCERGOUIDENSPETRUSDICITADIHM
DMEHICAUTEMQUID· DICITILLIIHS
SIEUMUOLOSICMANERE
USQUEDUMUENIOQUIDADTETUMESEQUERE
EXIUITERGOHICUERBUS. APUTFRATRES

(1) d CODEX BEZAE CANTABRIGIENSIS
John xxi. 19-23.

NONAMBITIOSAEST
NONQUAERITQUAESUASUNT
NONINRITATUR
NONCOGITATMALUM
NONGAUDETSUPERINIQUITATEM
CONGAUDETAUTEMUERITATI
OMNIASUFFERIT
OMNIACREDIT
OMNIASPERAT
OMNIASUSTENET
CARITAS
NUMQUAMEXCIDET

(2) d^{paul}. CODEX CLAROMONTANUS.
1 Corinthians xiii. 5-8.

PLATE IV.

ΜΙΝΤΟΝΛΙΘΟΝΕΚΤΗϹ
ΘΥΡΑϹΤΟΥΜΝΗΜΕΙΟΥ
ΚΑΙΑΝΑΒΛΕΨΑϹΑΙΘΕΩ
ΡΟΥϹΙΝΟΤΙΑΝΑΚΕΚΥ
ΛΙϹΤΑΙΟΛΙΘΟϹΗΝΓΑΡ
ΜΕΓΑϹϹΦΟΔΡΑΚΑΙΕΛ
ΘΟΥϹΑΙΕΙϹΤΟΜΝΗΜΕΙ
ΟΝΕΙΔΟΝΝΕΑΝΙϹΚΟΝ
ΚΑΘΗΜΕΝΟΝΕΝΤΟΙϹ
ΔΕΞΙΟΙϹΠΕΡΙΒΕΒΛΗΜΕ
ΝΟΝϹΤΟΛΗΝΛΕΥΚΗΝ
ΚΑΙΕΞΕΘΑΜΒΗΘΗϹΑΝ
ΟΔΕΛΕΓΕΙΑΥΤΑΙϹΜΗ
ΕΚΘΑΜΒΕΙϹΘΕΙΝΖΗΤΕΙ
ΤΕΤΟΝΝΑΖΑΡΗΝΟΝΤΟ
ΕϹΤΑΥΡΩΜΕΝΟΝΗΓΕΡ
ΘΗΟΥΚΕϹΤΙΝΩΔΕΙΔΕ
ΟΤΟΠΟϹΟΠΟΥΕΘΗΚΑ
ΑΥΤΟΝΑΛΛΑΥΠΑΓΕΤΕ
ΕΙΠΑΤΕΤΟΙϹΜΑΘΗΤΑΙϹ
ΑΥΤΟΥΚΑΙΤΩΠΕΤΡΩ
ΟΤΙΠΡΟΑΓΕΙΥΜΑϹΕΙϹ
ΤΗΝΓΑΛΙΛΑΙΑΝΕΚΕΙΑΥ
ΤΟΝΟΨΕϹΘΕΚΑΘΩϹΕΙ
ΠΕΝΥΜΙΝΚΑΙΕΞΕΛΘΟΥ
ϹΑΙΕΦΥΓΟΝΑΠΟΤΟΥ
ΜΝΗΜΕΙΟΥΕΙΧΕΝΓΑΡ
ΑΥΤΑϹΤΡΟΜΟϹΚΑΙΕΚ
8 ϹΤΑϹΙϹΚΑΙΟΥΔΕΝΙΟΥ
ΔΕΝΕΙΠΟΝΕΦΟΒΟΥΝ
ΤΟΓΑΡ:

ΚΑΤΑ
ΜΑΡΚΟΝ

B. CODEX VATICANUS.
Last column of Mark (xvi. 3–8), showing the absence of vv. 9–20.

PLATE V.

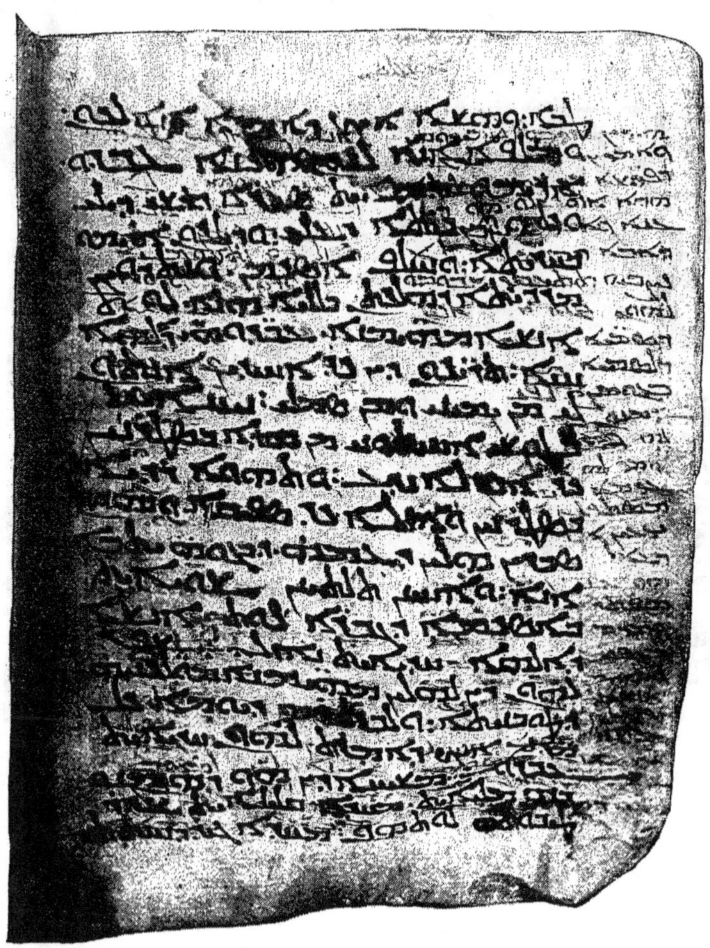

SINAITIC SYRIAC PALIMPSEST (Lewis).
Matthew xv. 12–27.

PLATE VI.

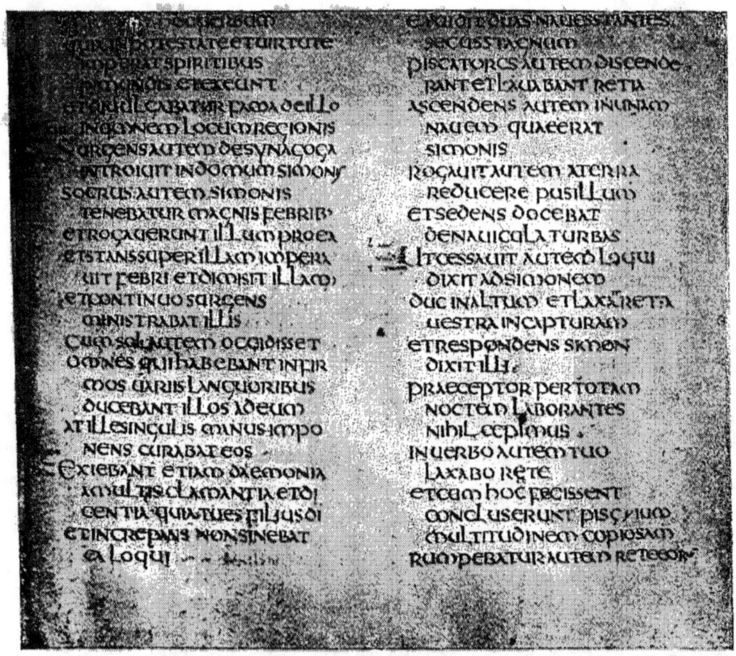

am. CODEX AMIATINUS, circa 700 A.D.
Luke iv. 36–41 ; v. 2–6.
(reduced.)

PLATE VII.

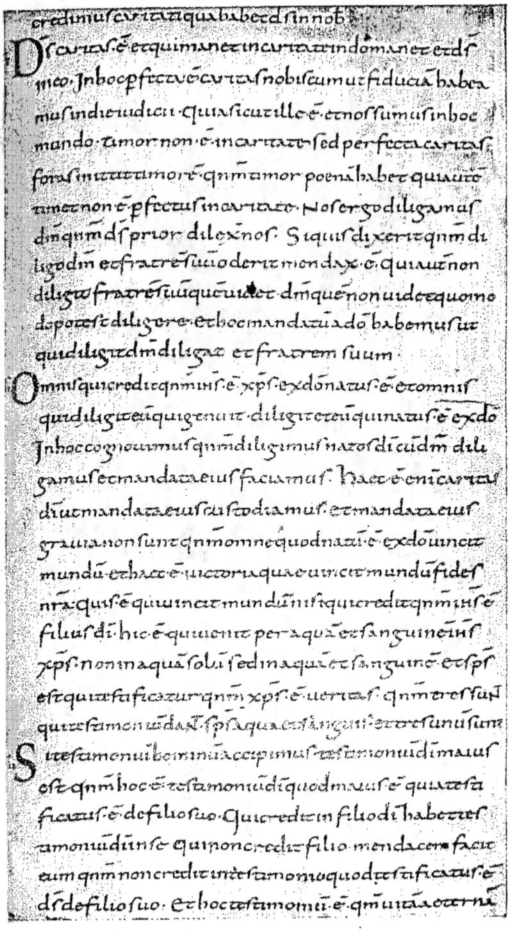

"CHARLEMAGNE'S BIBLE," or BIBLE OF GRANDVAL, of the ninth century, in the British Museum (reduced).

I John iv. 16—v. 10, showing the omission of the "comma Johanneum," v. 7.

PLATE VIII.

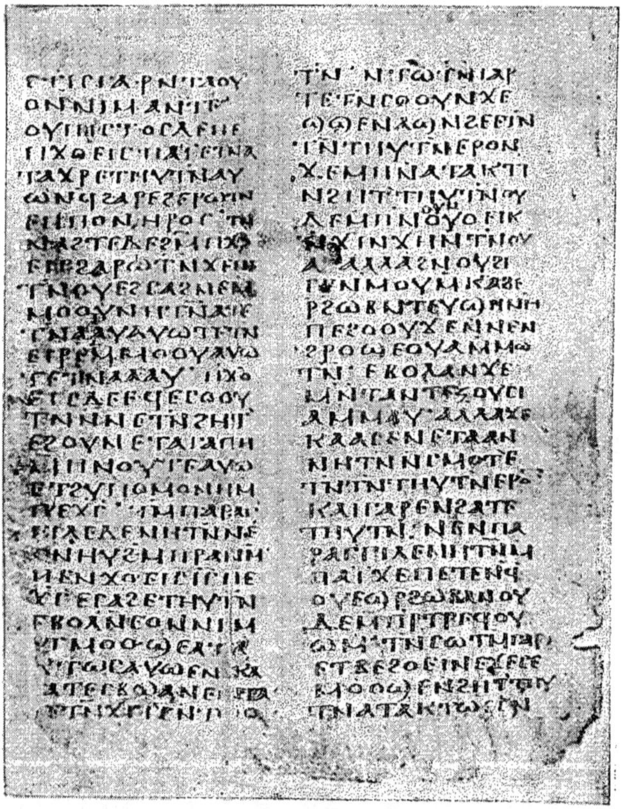

SAHIDIC MANUSCRIPT, probably of the fifth century, in the British Museum.
2 Thessalonians iii. 2–11.

PLATE IX.

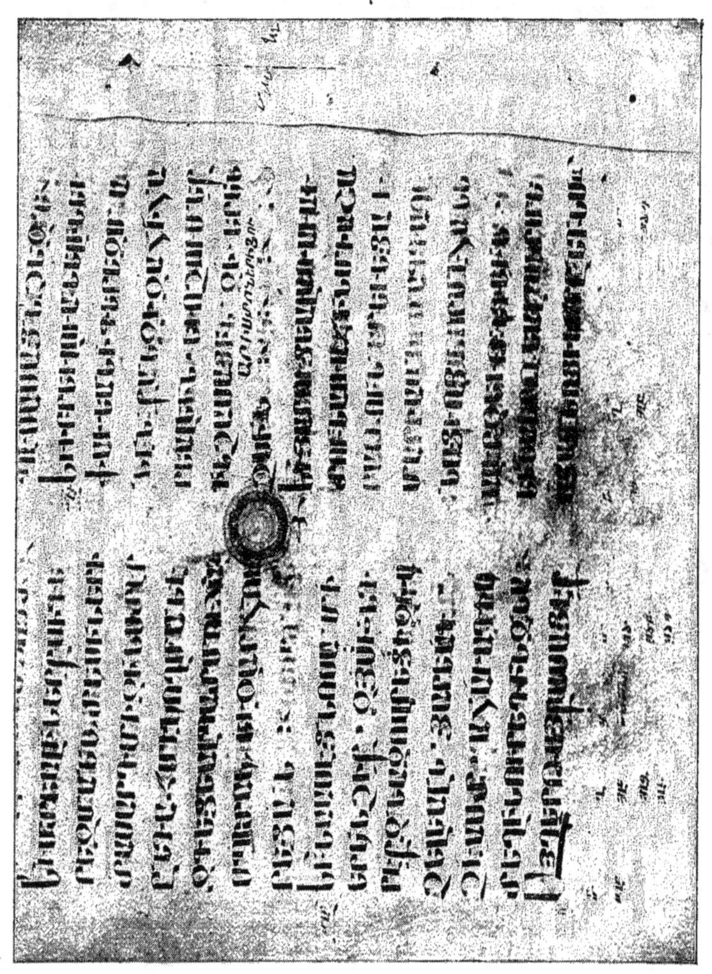

Armenian Manuscript of Etschmiadzin, A.D. 986.

End of Mark, showing the note "of Ariston the Presbyter," after c. xvi. 8 in column 2, line 7.

PLATE X.

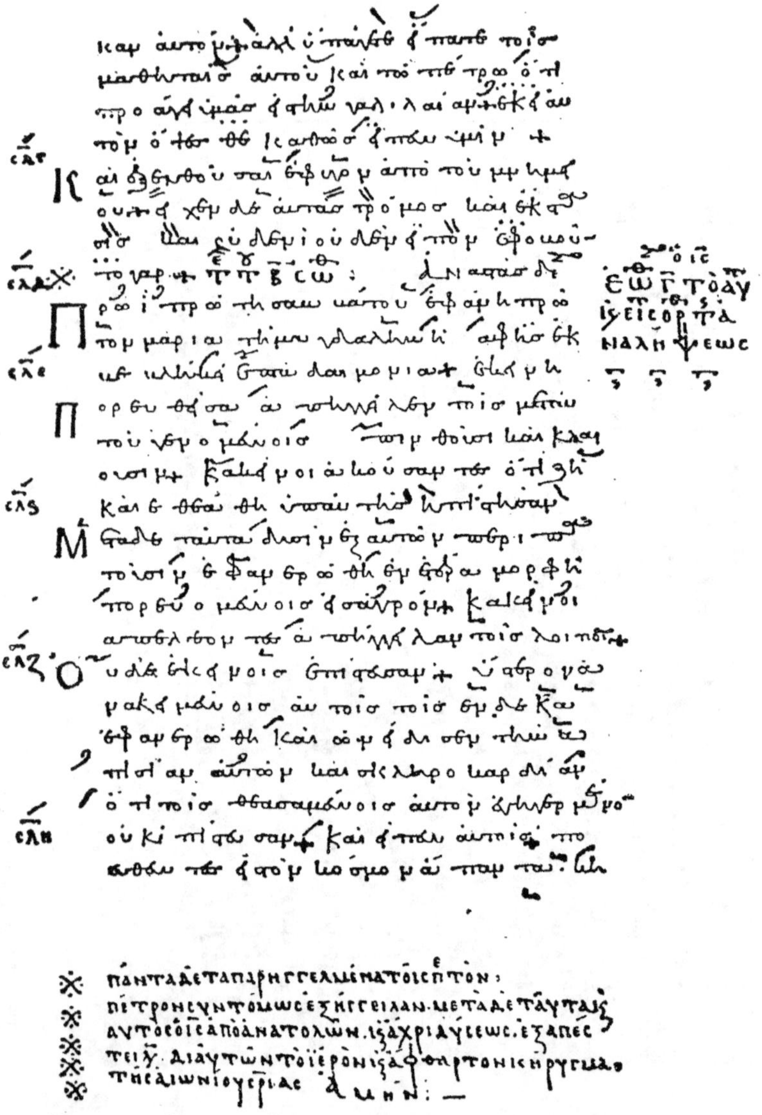

MINUSCULE EVV. 274 (Par. Nat. Suppl. Gr. 79) of the tenth century.
Mark xvi. 6–15, exhibiting the shorter conclusion in the lower margin.

www.ingramcontent.com/pod-product-compliance
Lightning Source LLC
Chambersburg PA
CBHW052339230426
43664CB00041B/2214

* 9 7 8 1 5 7 9 1 0 7 6 9 7 *